*H*ow the EU Institutions Work

and...

*H*ow to Work with the EU Institutions

2nd Edition

Edited by

Alan Hardacre and Erik Akse

How the EU Institutions Work *and...* **How to Work with the EU Institutions**
2nd Edition

Published by John Harper Publishing
27 Palace Gates Road
London N22 7BW, United Kingdom
www.johnharperpublishing.co.uk

ISBN: 978-0-9929748-8-6

© John Harper Publishing Ltd 2015. All rights reserved. Reproduction or quotation of short extracts is permitted, provided the source is fully acknowledged.

The publisher has no responsibility for the persistence or accuracy of the addresses of any external or third party websites referenced in this book, and does not guarantee that the content on these websites is, or will remain, accurate or appropriate.

Printed and Bound in the EU at the Gutenberg Press, Malta.

Table of contents

About the authors — IX
Acknowledgements — XIII

Introduction — 1

Section 1: How the EU Institutions Work — 9

1. **The European Commission** — 11
    1.1 Roles of the European Commission — 12
    1.2 Internal structure of the European Commission: Outline — 16
    1.3 Internal structure of the European Commission: The College of Commissioners — 17
    1.4 Internal structure of the European Commission: Directorates-General and Services — 21
    1.5 How the European Commission works: Strategic Planning and Programming — 22
    1.6 How the European Commission works: Preparation of a dossier — 27
    1.7 How the European Commission works: Administrative decision-preparation — 36
    1.8 How the European Commission works: Political decision-taking — 40
    1.9 Key stages and key actors - European Commission — 44

2. **The Council of the EU and the European Council** — 49
    2.1 The European Council — 50
    2.2 The Council — 53
    2.3 The roles of the Council — 54
    2.4 Internal structure of the Council — 59
    2.5 Internal structure of the Council: The Council as a meeting of Ministers — 60
    2.6 Internal structure of the Council: The Presidency — 63
    2.7 Internal structure of the Council: COREPER 1 & 2 — 66
    2.8 Internal structure of the Council Committees and Working Parties — 69
    2.9 Internal structure of the Council: General Secretariat of the Council — 72
    2.10 How the Council works: Setting the agenda — 73
    2.11 How the Council works: The Working Party — 75
    2.12 How the Council works: From Working Party to COREPER — 77
    2.13 How the Council works: From COREPER to Council — 79
    2.14 Key stages and key actors - The Council — 82

3. The European Parliament — **85**
　3.1　Roles of the Parliament — 86
　3.2　Internal structure of the Parliament: Outline — 88
　3.3　Internal structure of the Parliament: Political Groups — 92
　3.4　Internal structure of the Parliament: Committees, Delegations and Intergroups — 98
　3.5　How the Parliament works: From the European Commission into a Committee — 101
　3.6　How the European Parliament works: Preparation in Committee — 105
　3.7　How the European Parliament works: Vote in Committee — 108
　3.8　How the European Parliament works: From Committee to Plenary vote — 111
　3.9　Key stages and key actors - European Parliament — 119

4. Other EU Institutions and Bodies — **123**
　4.1　The Court of Justice of the European Union — 124
　4.2　The European Economic and Social Committee — 126
　4.3　Committee of the Regions — 130
　4.4　Key stages and key actors - EESC and CoR — 133
　4.5　EU Agencies — 135

Section 2: How EU Decision-Making Works — **143**

5. The Ordinary Legislative Procedure — **145**
　5.1　EU Decision-Making: The Basics — 145
　5.2　The rise of Codecision — 149
　5.3　Ordinary Legislative Procedure: First reading — 152
　5.4　First reading agreements - Informal trilogues — 157
　5.5　Ordinary Legislative Procedure: Second reading — 165
　5.6　Ordinary Legislative Procedure: Third reading/Conciliation — 169
　5.7　Key stages and key actors - Ordinary Legislative Procedure — 172

6. Delegated and Implementing Acts: 'New Comitology' — **175**
　6.1　Why do the legislators delegate implementing powers to the Commission? — 180
　6.2　The rise and spread of Comitology — 182
　6.3　The Treaty of Lisbon and the 'new Comitology' — 186
　6.4　The 'new' procedures: Implementing Acts — 187
　6.5　The 'new' procedures: Delegated Acts — 194
　6.6　Delegated and Implementing Acts - The new worlds of delegated powers — 197
　6.7　Case Law Developments — 198
　6.8　Key stages and key actors - Delegated and Implementing Acts — 198

Section 3: How to Work with the EU Institutions & Decision-Making   **201**

7. Ethics and Transparency in the EU   **203**
   7.1   The Register of Interest Representatives   205
   7.2   The European Commission's Code of Conduct   209
   7.3   Registration in the European Parliament   210
   7.4   Review of the Commission Register   211
   7.5   The Establishment of a Joint Transparency Register   212
   7.6   Review of the Transparency Register   216
   7.7   Access to documents   220
   7.8   Rules in place for European Commission officials and Commissioners   222
   7.9   Rules in place for Parliament officials and Members of Parliament   224
   7.10 The outlook for transparency and ethics in the EU   225
   7.11 Key practical conclusions on Ethics and Transparency   227

8. Practical Guide to Working with the EU Institutions   **229**
   8.1   Working with the EU institutions: The fundamentals   230
   8.2   Working with the European Commission   235
   8.3   Working with the Council of Ministers   242
   8.4   Working with the European Parliament   255

9. Practical Guide to Working with EU Decision-Making   **269**
   9.1   Working with EU Decision-Making: The fundamentals   269
   9.2   Working with OLP: First reading   271
   9.3   Working with OLP: Second reading   277
   9.4   Working with OLP: Third reading   279
   9.5   Working with Delegated and Implementing Acts: New Comitology   281
   9.6   Identifying Delegated and Implementing Acts   283
   9.7   Working with Implementing Acts   286
   9.8   Working with Delegated Acts: The Commission   291
   9.9   Working with Delegated Acts: Parliament   293
   9.10 Working with Delegated Acts: Council   297

10. Conclusion: Designing a Successful EU Lobbying Campaign   **301**
   10.1 Phase 1: Selecting and monitoring your interests   303
   10.2 Step 1.1: Identifying European issues   303
   10.3 Step 1.2: Monitoring key EU issues   304
   10.4 Step 1.3: Defining your EU identity   310
   10.5 Step 1.4: Prioritisation of issues - defining your investment   312
   10.6 Phase 2: Building your argumentation   314
   10.7 Step 2.1: Assessment of the issues   314
   10.8 Step 2.2: Drafting arguments   318
   10.9 Step 2.3: Identifying and building up a network   323

10.10	Phase 3: Arena management - stakeholder mapping	324
10.11	Step 3.1: Identifying balance of powers, cleavages and common interests	325
10.12	Step 3.2: Identifying priority targets	326
10.13	Step 3.3: Classifying actors	329
10.14	Phase 4: Lobbying actions	329
10.15	Step 4.1: Key skills for lobbying	330
10.16	Step 4.2: Defining your lobbying approach	332
10.17	Step 4.3: The lobbying plan - How to structure and evaluate the work	338

Appendix: Suggested Reading and Social Media — **345**
Index — **357**

About the authors

Erik Akse
Erik Akse is both an author and co-editor of this book. Erik has been working with the European Union for many years. He works currently as a trainer, coach and author on EU decision-making in particular and policy development in general. In his work, Erik focuses on the practical aspects of decision-making by administrations. He trains and advises EU officials, EU Member States and stakeholders on working with EU decision-making, in particular in the area of Impact Assessment (IA) and Legislative Evaluation. He advises countries within and outside the EU on how policy development practices can be improved based on IA. Erik previously worked as a National Expert at the European Commission and as a civil servant for the Dutch administration. Erik's book *Influencing the Preparation of EU Legislation: A Practical Guide to Working with Impact Assessments* was published in 2013.

Alan Hardacre
Alan Hardacre is both an author and co-editor of this book. Alan has worked in varying capacities with the EU institutions and EU decision-making for over a decade. He currently works in the private sector as a lobbyist in Brussels having previously worked for the European Institute for Public Administration (EIPA) in Maastricht. Alan has also previously worked as a lobbyist in Brussels for the Confederation of British Industry as well as consulting for Brazilian, Thai and African business groups, and UN bodies, on advocacy and communication strategies in the EU. Alan teaches modules and runs simulations on lobbying at the University of Maastricht, the University of Chulalongkorn in Bangkok and for a joint HEC-St Gallen Executive Masters programme. Alan holds a BA (Hons) in Modern European Studies from Loughborough University in the UK and a DEA de Science Politique from the Institut d'Études Politiques de Lyon in France. In 2008 he was awarded his PhD in International Economic and Political Relations from Loughborough University.

Nadia Andrien
Nadia Andrien obtained her Masters in European Studies at the University of Liège, Belgium. Having a particular interest in European decision-making and advocacy, she carried out several internships in the private and public sectors to develop her knowledge and gain first-hand

experience in these fields. During her work placements Nadia was mainly involved in researching EU-related topics and developing public affairs strategies. Working at the European Institute for Public Administration (EIPA) in Maastricht for a year, she among other things assisted in setting up a seminar on lobbying in the EU. During her employment as EU Public Affairs Adviser at Strauss & Partners, Nadia worked closely with the European institutions and advised a variety of stakeholders on their EU public affairs strategies. In recent years, she worked as Business Developer at IncubatorEurope, a young company that supports its clients in identifying and reaching their EU policy and funding objectives in an innovative manner.

Natacha Clarac

Natacha Clarac is a senior consultant and partner at ATHENORA Consulting, with expertise in environment, health, network utilities and consumer affairs. A lobbyist in Brussels for over a decade, she has conducted numerous lobbying campaigns, advising companies and federations on their public affairs strategies and activities. She has developed broad expertise in the lobbying tools that can be used in Brussels, including specific tools for coalition building to create consensus between stakeholders and decision-makers and to resolve conflicts and complex situations. Natacha graduated from Sciences-Po in Aix-en-Provence, and then did a Masters in European Politics at the Institute of European Studies in Brussels. Natacha also set up in 2003 the association 'Eyes on Europe' which aims to promote a European public space through the organisation of meetings and the publishing of a bilingual magazine. She was its first chairwoman for over four years. Natacha is a lecturer at Sciences-Po Aix-en-Provence and she also gives lectures on lobbying at ESSEC, EIPA and ENA. In 2012 she published *The golden rules of lobbying* with Stéphane Desselas.

Stéphane Desselas

Stéphane Desselas is the founder and Chairman of ATHENORA Consulting. He is a European public affairs specialist and has been active in Brussels since 1994 as a legal advisor and consultant for many big businesses and as Secretary General of a European Federation. He was also a partner in a British lobbying firm before creating ATHENORA. Over the years, Stéphane has advised a large number of companies, European federations and national organisations on their public affairs strategies and on pan-European regulatory and policy issues. He created and currently manages professional alliances and interest groups, such as the Group of New Lobbyists. He was formerly on the Board of EPACA (European PA professionals) in Brussels and the PRGN (an international network with more than 30 agencies). Stéphane is a lecturer at Sciences-Po Paris and contributes to courses at ESSEC, EIPA and ENA. In 2007, he published *Open Professional Lobbying*, explaining how EU interests are represented in Brussels, and in 2012 co-authored *The golden rules of lobbying* with Natacha Clarac. He has also published several articles on EU lobbying.

Michael Kaeding

Michael Kaeding is Professor for European Integration and European Union Politics at the Department of Political Science of the University of Duisburg-Essen, Germany and holds an ad personam Jean Monnet Chair in 'Understanding EU Decision Making and Member States' Compliance with EU Policies'. He graduated from the University of Konstanz and Leiden University, where he received his PhD ('Transposition of EU transport directives in EU Member States') and conducted postdoctoral studies on alternative forms of EU policy-making. Meanwhile, he has been a consultant for the EU institutions and various national ministries. Michael is part of the editorial team of the *Journal of European Integration* and has written articles and books on the EU institutions, Comitology, EU Agencies, European social dialogue, and the transposition of EU legislation across Member States. Since 2007 he has provided training for European and national civil servants. He is a Visiting Fellow with the European Institute of Public Administration (EIPA) and teaches the course on "The Reform of National Public Administrations and the Role of the European Union" at the College of Europe, Bruges. Michael is a Fulbright alumnus.

Sabina Kajnč Lange

Sabina Kajnč Lange is Lecturer in the 'European Decision-Making' Unit at the European Institute of Public Administration (EIPA) in Maastricht and Research Fellow at the Centre for International Relations of the University of Ljubljana. As an EIPA trainer she focuses on decision-making processes in the EU institutions and in particular on Presidency preparations. She is a Fellow of the University of Maastricht, where she coordinates the multidisciplinary Master in European Public Affairs (EPA). Her research focuses on leadership in the Council of Ministers and on managing inter-institutional relations in the EU. She has published articles, think-tank pieces and book chapters on the role of the Presidency of the Council, the effect of the Trio Presidency, and the positions of the Commission and the High Representative in the EU's leadership architecture after the 2014 European elections. She is also the author of several expert and academic papers as well as book chapters on Slovenia's Foreign and European policy. Sabina is an alumna of the European Foreign and Security Policies Studies (EFSPS programme), through which she gained experience working on foreign policy at the Centre for European Policy Studies (CEPS) and at the University Institute for European Studies of the Universidad Autónoma of Barcelona. In 2014, she worked as Associate Analyst at the European Institute for International Security Studies in Paris.

Robert Mack

Robert Mack has been active in government relations and public affairs in Europe, Eurasia and Africa since 1991. He currently works as a government relations director for a multinational company. During a consultancy career in Brussels spanning more than 20 years, Robert has advised many leading companies, helping them to develop strategies and implement campaigns to engage successfully on challenging issues. From January 2011 until the end of 2013 he served as Chairman of the EMEA Public Affairs Practice of Burson-Marsteller. Before that, he was CEO of Burson-Marsteller Brussels, the leading EU public affairs consultancy. Robert served as Vice-Chairman of the European Public Affairs Consultancies' Association from 2008 to 2013 and has been very active in the discussions in Brussels on lobbying transparency. He has presented to government ministers, parliamentarians, companies, multilateral organisations and NGOs across Europe on the topic of lobbying transparency and ethics.

Joost Mulder
Starting his Brussels career in 2004 as an assistant to a Member of the European Parliament, Joost joined a consultancy in the financial services field in 2007 to advise and lobby the European Union on behalf of the financial services industry. His major clients included investment banks, hedge funds and rating agencies - organisations that were all caught in the middle of the post-crisis regulatory rollercoaster. In 2011 Joost went through the revolving door again to set up the advocacy work of Finance Watch, a newly created non-partisan public interest lobby group that has the aim to 'make finance serve society'. Joost is a strong advocate of transparency in those EU procedures that take place behind closed doors, such as trilogues. In his current role as Head of Public Affairs at Finance Watch he spends a fair amount of time on scrutinising the Level 2 process of Delegated and Implementing Acts, where supposedly technical but often highly political calibrations determine whether the political agreements reached to re-regulate the financial industry actually make the impact they ought to.

The views expressed in this publication are those of the authors and are not in any way intended to reflect those of their respective employers, nor any of the institutions they describe, analyse and comment on.

Acknowledgements

Writing, and editing, a second edition is in many ways more challenging than a first edition and in this case it simply would not have been possible without a co-editor. Erik Akse, himself an author in the John Harper stable, provided the drive, enthusiasm and gentle reminders to enable this book to see the light of day. That there is a second edition at all is very much thanks to Erik.

Just as important for this second edition was the fact that all the original authors were happy and willing to update their respective chapters - which has made the process much smoother than might otherwise have been the case. Even though some authors had changed jobs, countries and professions they were more than happy to continue the work they started some 5 years ago. In addition one new contributor, Joost Mulder, joined the team, writing about the European Parliament, to further enrich the content. A big thank you to all the authors for their continuing partnership in this project.

In the first edition I thanked the many people who actually gave me the idea to write the book - that was the officials and students from 2008 and 2009 who repeatedly asked me which book they could use to find out 'how the EU institutions really work'. For this second edition thanks must go to all the people who have bought the first edition and passed on comments and suggestions - assuming as they did that a second edition would see the light of day. Hopefully this updated and improved version will be as helpful as the first edition, if not more so.

Once again I would also like to extend my appreciation to John Harper, the Publisher, for his continued support on this book. Always a source of ideas, contacts and suggestions it has been a real pleasure to continue working with John.

Finally I can once again only hope that this book answers your questions and helps you navigate through the maze of EU institutions and decision-making procedures - and how to work with them.

Alan Hardacre

Introduction

By Alan Hardacre

The European Union (EU) is a multinational organisation of policy-making and law which encompasses 28 Member States, with just over 500 million inhabitants. It is a complex system of governance that supersedes the national level, operating in 24 official languages with institutions and bodies based in a number of European cities, but centred in Brussels. This supranational and intergovernmental system of governance is the largest political and economic entity in Europe, boasting a single market, a customs union, a common currency and a nascent diplomatic service amongst other achievements. Any stakeholder trying to pursue public policy goals in the EU, or that involve the EU, is obliged to engage with Brussels in some way, shape or form. The EU is responsible for a significant percentage of the legislation its Member States implement, legislation that impacts not only the Member States themselves but also the rest of the world. There is now virtually no policy area that is not directly, or indirectly, impacted by decisions taken collectively in Brussels. A direct consequence of this is that there is effectively no civil society stakeholder (social, environmental, consumer or business) or third country, who can avoid having to work with the EU institutions and decision-making in some capacity - irrespective of where they are based in the world, or what their specific issue is.

The rise of Brussels as an important centre of decision-making has had the direct result that it has also become a world centre of lobbying and influence, in almost direct proportion to the rise in powers attributed to the EU over time. The fact that almost all policy areas, all civil society stakeholders and all countries around the world are, to some degree, impacted, has been a strong recipe for the growth of a vibrant and diverse lobbying industry in Brussels. This is also evidenced in the way lobbying itself has evolved in Brussels, from a very informal activity to a professional and increasingly regulated profession. Two of the reasons why there is such a dynamic, and increasingly professional, lobbying industry are worth briefly exploring. Firstly the EU, like all democratic systems of government, is built on the principles of political legitimacy including accountability, information for citizens, and open participation in the political process. Lobbying is invaluable for generating dialogue and providing evidence and facts between stakeholders and EU officials to enhance the quality of the legislation, and decisions, taken at the EU level - and to improve implementation and compliance later down the line. More than at the national level, EU institutions need information and evidence from different stakeholders across the 28 Member States that they cover with their legislation, and from other countries and companies around the world who are also impacted. In this sense the input of various stakeholders to officials across the institutions is an important means of creating democratic decision-making in the EU. In essence the EU institutions need to derive legitimacy from their legislative output. Secondly, the reason why so many stakeholders engage in lobbying is that the costs and benefits of EU legislation are rarely shared equally, and they can have very important localised consequences. This situation generates intense activity as stakeholders try to defend their positions and create new opportunities, by working with the EU institutions and decision-making. Rarely is an issue one-sided - and at its most complex one single issue can motivate a huge spectrum of stakeholders such as the discussions of the Transatlantic Trade and Investment Partnership.

Fundamental to any attempt to work with the EU is a solid understanding of the idiosyncratic institutional and decision-making architecture. The importance of understanding this EU system, and how to interact with the institutions, is increasingly important as the EU adds new powers to its extensive existing competences. To succeed in defending, or promoting, an interest or position in the EU depends entirely on understanding the institutions and how they individually and collectively take decisions. The Treaty of Lisbon[1] brought about a number of modifications to this system. The Treaty addressed the issue of participatory democracy (Article 11 TEU) in which it states that interested parties are to be consulted and that 'the institutions shall maintain an open, transparent and regular dialogue with representative associations and civil society'. This book is intended to contribute to this objective of better participatory democracy in the EU by offering a practical guide for all stakeholders on how the EU institutions and decision-making work, and on how to work with them. It fills a gap by offering practical assistance to those coming to Brussels, those currently working in, or with, Brussels and for students and other interested stakeholders on how things really work and what they need to know and do to fulfil their objectives.

> **Why this book is different**
>
> It is increasingly important to understand how the EU institutions and EU decision-making work, and how to work with them, if you are pursuing any public policy objective in the EU.
>
> Whilst there is no secret formula for working with the institutions and decision-making there are a number of fundamentals that any successful work must be built on.
>
> **This book provides a practical step-by-step guide for anyone wanting to understand, study, or work with the EU institutions and decision-making.**

To achieve this objective of enabling stakeholders to work effectively with the EU institutions, this book seeks to equip readers with the ability to identify the right people at the right stages of the internal and inter-institutional decision-making procedures - and to know what these people need

---

[1] This book refers to the Treaty of Lisbon. The Treaty of Lisbon is composed of the Treaty on European Union (TEU) and the Treaty on the Functioning of the European Union (TFEU). The Treaty of Lisbon modified the Treaty establishing the European Community (TEC).

to make their jobs easier and more effective. The book aims to make the EU institutions, and decision-making, understandable for stakeholders so that they can identify the right person to speak to, at the right time, with the right information. The difference that this book offers is that it is not reciting the theory of the institutions but rather the actual daily practice. While knowing this practice is alone no guarantee of success, it is an essential prerequisite for any successful engagement. In contrast, a failure to understand the process, the timelines, who takes decisions, what your interlocutor needs, or how the system works, will almost certainly lead to failure. Enabling all stakeholders to get the right message to the right person at the right time is an objective that will simultaneously allow officials across the institutions to get the best available information to make their choices and take their decisions. It is only if they get accurate, timely, comprehensive and tailored information and evidence from a variety of stakeholders that they can make informed choices in their public policy interventions.

The book is directly concerned with how the EU institutions take decisions individually and collectively, with a clear focus on how they deal with legislative files as this is the main area of their activity. In this sense the book will not deal with, although it will at times mention, some major areas of EU work and decision-making, notably budgetary decision-making, Common Foreign and Security Policy (CFSP) and international agreements and negotiations.

How to work with the EU institutions and decision-making: A practical guide

Working with the EU institutions has been the subject of increasing scrutiny and study in recent years, culminating in a small number of specific publications and guides on lobbying and interest representation. In addition there are already a number of books on the EU institutions themselves, notably in the John Harper collection, detailing their history and general workings. This book will sit alongside all of these publications as a practical guide to how the EU institutions and decision-making work, and how to work with them. By covering all the main EU institutions, bodies and agencies and the two main decision-making procedures in one book, with a focus on how decisions are taken, the book serves as a practical reference guide to how to work with EU policy-making.

It is important to quickly clarify what this book understands by 'working with'. At its most basic this is any attempt to engage with, or influence, the EU institutions, or decision-making. In Brussels we could simply term this lobbying although the activity itself goes under many different names. Lobbying is now an integral, and accepted, part of the democratic process where different interests interact. At its simplest it is any activity undertaken with the objective of trying to influence decisions taken by the EU institutions. In a broader sense lobbying can also be described as being about understanding politics, decision-making, government infrastructures and policy-making and how best to work with this knowledge to advance your interests. While these are rather short and simplistic outlines of the understanding of lobbying they are nonetheless essential in framing the context of this book, and also in understanding lobbying as a positive communication activity and not as a negative activity to be shunned. The three key dimensions of lobbying can be seen in Figure 1 on the next page.

Figure 1: The three key dimensions of lobbying

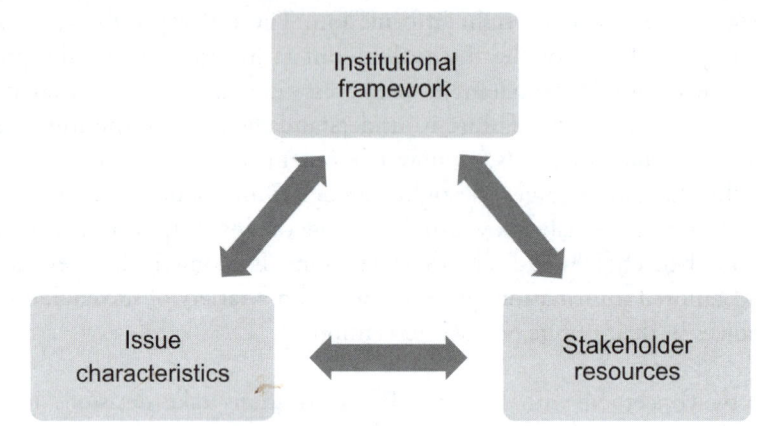

Source: Adapted from Mahoney, C. (2008) Brussels versus the Beltway: Advocacy in the United States and the European Union, Georgetown University Press, Georgetown

The three main dimensions of lobbying:

1. **Institutional framework:** This refers to democratic accountability, the decision-making processes and the institutions that are involved in these decisions, as well as media coverage. This dimension frames any lobbying work as it is horizontal, i.e. it is applicable for all stakeholders and all issues. This book will be focused on this dimension because it underpins any attempt to work with the EU institutions and decision-making.

2. **Issue characteristics:** This refers to the key characteristics of any particular issue such as its scope, salience, level of stakeholder conflict, its history and whether there was an event that focused public awareness. This dimension frames the lobbying context of a specific issue and is thus not horizontal: it is case by case. For this reason this dimension will not be dealt with by this book, although examples will be used to highlight important points. The objective of this book is to deal with the institutional framework of the EU so as to be able to understand how to work with individual cases and issues thereafter.

3. **Stakeholder resources:** The financial and human resources of a stakeholder are vitally important for lobbying. This is linked to things like memberships, organisational structures, and ultimately their knowledge of the institutions and issues they are working with and on. Again this will not be dealt with by this book because it is individual and case specific.

It is the interaction of these three fundamental dimensions that will determine the presence and subsequently the success of lobbying in any political system. These three dimensions are clearly interlinked and successful lobbying will depend on a combination of all of them, but the need to understand the institutional framework is fundamental to any attempt to situate an issue or deploy stakeholder resources. If you know your issue inside-out and have extremely good resources, but do not grasp the institutional framework, then you risk wasting your knowledge and resources. Having a solid understanding of how the EU institutions take decisions, individually and collectively in the evolving environment of inter-institutional relations, will better equip stakeholders to situate their issue and deploy resources.

Objectives and structure of the book

The chapters in this book all have the double objective of presenting the most relevant information and of rendering it usable: that is, equipping the reader with the knowledge and the tools to use it. The book provides readers with all the basic institutional and decision-making knowledge, details on where to find the right information, and a practical guide on how to build an effective lobbying strategy. This approach will equip readers to deal with their day to day, or occasional, work with the EU institutions with more confidence and insight. The five key objectives of this book are highlighted in the table below.

Table 1: Five key objectives of the book

1. Understanding how the main EU institutions, bodies and Agencies work - through a detailed analysis of their internal decision-making processes.
2. Identifying who the key actors within each institution are, at every stage of the internal decision-making process, and identifying what information they need.
3. Understanding where to find the right information in the myriad of sources that exist.
4. Outlining practical, and targeted, guidance on how to work with each institution and decision-making procedure, and analysing the transparency and ethical framework of this engagement.
5. Presenting how to structure a professional EU lobbying campaign - by analysing all the steps and possible tools involved.

To achieve these objectives the book has to cover a number of institutions, bodies and procedures in the EU policy cycle. The different key actors and the EU policy cycle are highlighted below in Figure 2.

Figure 2: The EU policy cycle

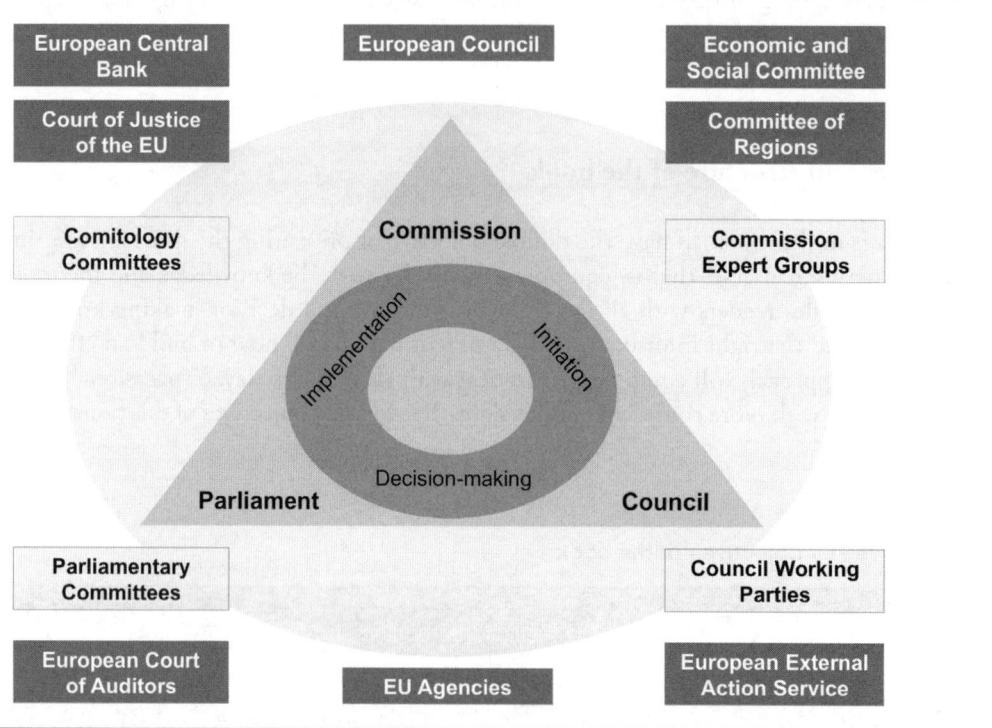

Figure 2 highlights the complexity of the EU policy cycle and of the institutions and bodies that all play a role. From this the difficulty of approaching the right person with the right information, at the right time in the internal and inter-institutional decision-making procedures becomes more apparent. Figure 2 introduces the key institutions and policy-making phases that this book deals with:

1. The three main phases of EU policy-making: initiation, decision-making and implementation.
2. The three main EU institutions: the European Commission, the Council of the EU and the European Parliament.
3. The four other EU institutions and EU Agencies and bodies.
4. Four of the most important Committees in the EU policy cycle: Expert Groups, Council Working Parties, Parliamentary Committees and Comitology Committees.

This book will address how each of these phases, institutions, bodies, Committees and decision-making procedures work such that at the end the reader is able to understand the cycle and, more importantly, how, when, with whom and with what they can engage to maximise their, and their interlocutor's, interests.

1. **Section one** of the book deals with the institutions and how their internal decision-making procedures work. The three core EU institutions, the European Commission, the Council of the EU and the European Parliament, are addressed in detail in Chapters 1-3. These chapters have the explicit objective of detailing the internal decision-making processes in a practical way so that readers can understand exactly when and where they would need (and would be able) to intervene, and also of highlighting all the key actors who play a role within these internal processes. In addition to the three main EU institutions, the first section has a short chapter (Chapter 4) on the European Economic and Social Committee (EESC), the Committee of the Regions (CoR), the Court of Justice of the European Union and EU Agencies. These institutions and bodies all play a role in the EU policy cycle and need to be discussed briefly to give the reader a full picture of the EU policy-making environment.

2. The **second section** of the book applies this individual institutional knowledge to the question of how to work with the two main policy decision-making procedures in the EU - the Ordinary Legislative Procedure (OLP) and the new Comitology procedures. The section starts with OLP or Codecision (Chapter 5) because this is the principal legislative procedure used in the EU and the one that stakeholders most commonly have to work with. Chapter 6 details the workings of the less well-known, but equally important, Delegated and Implementing Acts - the new Comitology. It is increasingly important to work with Delegated and Implementing Acts, and any holistic lobbying strategy needs to include them. This section of the book focuses on helping readers understand how these procedures work, and how to work effectively with them by putting the institutional chapters into an inter-institutional context. These two chapters explain in a clear step-by-step manner the workings of the two main decision-making procedures, detailing formal and informal practices and the key inter-institutional dynamics.

3. The **third section** is much more practically orientated as it deals directly with the issue of how to work with the institutions and decision-making procedures. It has chapters on transparency and ethics when working in Brussels, practical guidance on working with the individual institutions and both decision-making procedures, and finally a chapter on how to structure a professional EU lobbying campaign. The first chapter of this final section (Chapter 7) is devoted to transparency and ethics in the EU and when working with the EU institutions. This chapter explains how to engage with the EU institutions in a transparent and ethical manner - something that has become very important in Brussels in recent years. Since the first edition of the book this is perhaps the area that has changed the most. The second and third chapters in this section are devoted to specific practical guidance on how to engage with the individual institutions (Chapter 8) and decision-making procedures (Chapter 9). These chapters do not claim to be exhaustive, or definitive, but they give readers solid practical guidance that represents the basis

of any interaction they wish to undertake with the EU institutions. The final chapter (Chapter 10) rounds up all the information presented in the book by outlining how to design and structure it all into a successful EU lobbying campaign. This chapter sets out the different stages of lobbying, the tools that can be used to help and where to find information and help when putting this together. The chapter is written in such a way that the reader can apply this knowledge to their own cases and situations because it presents a clear structure for strategic thinking with lobbying tools which readers can use themselves.

Whilst the authors recognise that there is no magic formula for successfully working with the EU institutions, they set out in this book a number of fundamentals upon which successful work can be built. It must finally be stressed that working with the EU institutions is an ever-evolving process, because the institutions and the people in them change, the mixture of stakeholders working on issues changes, the public affairs industry is getting more sophisticated and professional and because lobbying can change due to business and political needs. Even taking all of this into account, this book will help Brussels newcomers and old-hands from all policy sectors, third country officials, Member State officials, civil society stakeholders, regional representatives and students in their understanding of how the EU actually works - and how to work with it.

Section 1

How the EU Institutions Work

1. The European Commission

By Alan Hardacre and Erik Akse

The European Commission (the 'Commission' or 'EC') is the largest institution of the EU, in terms of human resources, and equally the focal point of the EU system - the executive body of the European system of governance. With the various formal and informal roles that it plays, the Commission is crucial to the pace of European integration, especially as it is the EU institution that is charged with thinking, acting and delivering European solutions to cross-national policy problems. Whilst the Commission is important for the big picture of European integration, it is equally, if not more, important for the minutiae and details of legislation. The Commission does not really allow for any form of national comparison given its idiosyncratic powers and nature - it really is a hybrid institution at the core of the EU project. This chapter will outline the roles, structure and functioning of the Commission whilst simultaneously identifying the key officials at each and every stage of the process. Key facts about the Commission can be found below in Table 1.1.

Table 1.1: European Commission - Key facts

Role:	EU Executive
Established:	1958
President:	Jean-Claude Juncker
VP & High Representative:	Federica Mogherini
First Vice-President:	Frans Timmermans
Other Vice-Presidents:	Kristalina Georgieva, Andrus Ansip, Maroš Šefčovič, Valdis Dombrovskis, Jyrki Katainen
Term:	5 years (currently 2014-2019)
Decision-taking body:	College of 28 Commissioners (simple majority)
Internal structure:	42 Directorates-General and Services
Staff:	33,197 (2015 figure)
Procedural languages:	English, French, German
Location:	Brussels (Belgium) and Luxembourg

The Commission has been in place for over 50 years as the EU executive body. It has grown at both the political level, with subsequent enlargements bringing new Commissioners, and at the technical level as the EU project has widened and deepened, and its own powers have increased with treaty revisions. In 2015 the Commission is headed by the 28-strong College of Commissioners as the ultimate decision-taking body, served by a staff of 33,197 officials based mostly in Brussels (65.4%), but also in Luxembourg (11.7%), in EU Member States (11.3%) - which includes agencies and Commission representations - and in EU Delegations around the world (11.5%).

1.1 Roles of the European Commission

The Commission has four traditional roles that it derives directly from the Treaties (Article 17 TEU). These four roles are presented in Figure 1.1 below.

Figure 1.1: The main roles of the European Commission

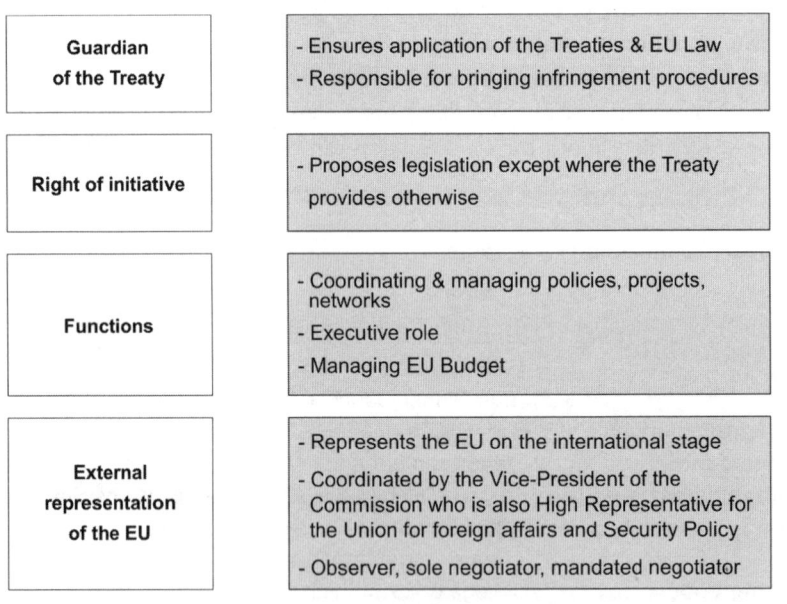

1. **Guarding the Treaty:** The first, and most important, Commission role is that of guardian of the Treaty because it covers all aspects of the Commission's activities, including the three others listed in Figure 1.1.

   The European Commission promotes the European general interest. This role underpins all the tasks that the Commission undertakes: thinking European and delivering European solutions and value-added.

The main aspect of this guardianship comes through the Commission having the responsibility, and authority, to ensure that Treaty provisions are applied correctly (with the Court of Justice of the EU as the final arbiter). Through these Treaty provisions the Commission is empowered to monitor the implementation and application of Union law by Member States. If necessary the Commission is able to open **infringement proceedings**, of which there were 1300 cases open by the end of 2013. These are 1300 cases where the Commission investigates whether the Member States have breached EU law in respect to their obligations to implement and apply what they agreed at the European level. In the last five years the number of infringement cases brought by the Commission, according to its own Annual Reports on National Implementation of EU Law (available on the Secretariat-General website), were: 2009 - 2,900, 2010 - 2,100, 2011 - 1,775, 2012 - 1,343, 2013 - 1,300. By the volume of infringement cases, and despite their steadily decreasing number, one understands the workload that guarding the Treaty requires of the Commission Services. Interestingly enough, a significant number of infringement cases stem from individual complaints which, as long as they are made in writing, can be submitted by anyone.

2. **Initiating legislation:** As a link with the second role, that of the right of initiative, one could mention a quasi-formal role of the Commission here - that of 'promoter of the general European interest' which is perhaps the most understated role that the Commission actually has. This is a horizontal function that is derived from a number of Treaty-based provisions, notably those making the Commission the guardian of the Treaty and through the so-called Community method in which the Commission is the initiator of legislation. This second role, initiating legislation, is a sacrosanct right of the Commission, one that it guards jealously.

> Technically the Commission now has the **quasi-exclusive right of initiative** - not the sole right as known before. The Treaty of Lisbon changed the provisions on Police and Judicial Cooperation in Criminal Matters, whereby in specific areas the Commission shares the right of initiative with the Council of the European Union.

The right of initiative has some very important implications, not least that **the Commission must prepare, draft and present every legislative proposal**; a situation that gives the Commission a significant amount of influence over legislative outcomes. The ability to draft the initial text in the EU system of compromise and consensus means that a very high portion of what the Commission originally includes in a proposal remains at the end of the process. This is even more significant when one considers that over 90% of what the Commission proposes eventually becomes law, albeit after modifications by the legislators. This is, for example, almost the exact opposite of the United States legislative system where, in the 113th Congress (2013-2015), only 296 out of 9,184 proposed bills (3%) became law (https://www.govtrack.us/congress/bills/statistics). Having the sole right to draft the first text therefore gives the Commission a considerable power in legislative and non-legislative procedures.

The right of initiative can lead stakeholders to the rather misleading conclusion that the Commission is only involved, and important, at the drafting stages of legislation. This could not be further from the truth because, as will be seen throughout this book, the Commission is omnipresent in the entire process of decision-making, operating influentially in both the European Parliament (the 'Parliament' or 'EP') and the Council of the EU (the 'Council').

Some final points with regard to the right of initiative are important, the first of which relates to the limits on the Commission's ability to propose legislation, which are three-fold. The first two are legal constraints, namely that the Commission needs to have a legal basis in the Treaty for the proposal and that secondly the proposal must respect the principle of subsidiarity whereby in areas outside of its exclusive competence (see the box above) the EU can only take action in so far as the objectives of the proposed action cannot be sufficiently achieved in the Member States making the EU level the most appropriate level for action. In addition, the Commission must respect the principle of proportionality, whereby any action it proposes must be proportionate to the issues it is dealing with. If these legal constraints are met then the Commission must consider a third, political, consideration, notably as to whether there is sufficient political will and appetite for the proposal in the Council and the Parliament, as well as from civil society stakeholders. Assuming that these conditions are fulfilled, the Commission will exercise its right of initiative and present the legislators with a text for them to base their negotiations on.

> **Five exclusive competences of the EU**
>
> "When the Treaties confer on the Union exclusive competence in a specific area, only the Union may legislate and adopt legally binding acts, the Member States being able to do so themselves only if so empowered by the Union or for the implementation of Union acts." (Article 2 TFEU).
>
> The exclusive competences are (Article 3 TFEU):
> 1. Competition Rules for the Internal Market;
> 2. Customs Union;
> 3. Common Commercial Policy;
> 4. The Euro (Monetary Policy);
> 5. Conservation of Marine Biological Resources in the Common Fisheries Policy.

> **European Citizens' Initiative** (Articles 11 TEU and 24 TFEU)
>
> The European Citizens' Initiative (ECI) enables more than one million EU citizens from at least seven Member States to directly request the Commission to bring forward a legislative initiative of interest to them in an area of EU competence.
>
> 'Right2Water' was the first ECI to have met the requirements set out in the Regulation on the Citizens' Initiative. On 20 December 2013 it was presented to the Commission to formally request a legislative proposal implementing the human right to water and sanitation, as recognised by the United Nations, and promoting the provision of water and sanitation as essential public services for all.

Having outlined that this right of initiative is so important for the Commission it must be noted that it is something strongly coveted by the two legislators – the Parliament and the Council. The Commission right of initiative can be pre-empted by things such as Council Conclusions that request action from the Commission, or from international commitments, both of which are important influences on the Commission right of initiative. The Parliament also frequently requests action from the Commission in a variety of different ways from own-initiative reports to Oral and Written Questions.

3. **Managing and implementing EU policies and the budget:** This is a huge task that requires a significant proportion of the Commission's human resources to undertake. In addition to this, the Commission also has to implement the execution powers given to it by the legislators – the much talked about implementing (with so-called comitology procedures) and delegated acts (see Chapter 6).

4. **Representing the EU in external relations:** The final major treaty-based role of the Commission is that of representing the EU on the international stage. The Commission does this for all areas, except for the Common Foreign and Security Policy (CFSP), in a variety of different capacities. For example, it can act as a simple observer or member, in international organisations, or it could be the sole negotiator for the EU such as in the area of climate change. The most common form of representation, as understood by the outside world, is in the sense of trade negotiations in which the Commission negotiates on behalf of the Council with a strict mandate - as it does in trade negotiations such as the World Trade Organisation (WTO). The Commission also represents the EU through its staff sitting in the 139 EU Delegations around the world as well as interacting on a daily basis with the approximately 162 non-Member State missions accredited to the EU and approximately 38 international organisations and other representations to the Commission – all based in Brussels. Whilst much of this representation role has now been incorporated into the new European External Action Service (EEAS) after the Treaty of Lisbon, the Commission still has its staff on the ground across the world and has to deal with third country missions in Brussels.

In addition to these four treaty-based formal roles, one needs to add a number of less formal, but by no means less important, roles. Firstly, the Commission plays a very important role as mediator and deal broker between the legislative institutions (loosely based on Article 294 TFEU). This role will be touched on later in this chapter, and again in a number of other chapters such is the importance of the Commission's role as 'honest broker' . A further informal role is that of information gatherer/disseminator and network organiser, because the Commission is at the centre of a huge network of experts, Member State officials and civil society representatives. Through these informal roles the Commission is usually extremely well-informed, connected and updated on all developments related to its dossiers.

> **Official Journal of the EU (OJ)**
>
> The OJ is the official gazette of the EU and only legal acts published in the OJ are binding. It is available online at: http://eur-lex.europa.eu/JOIndex.do?ihmlang=en.

1.2 Internal structure of the European Commission: Outline

To go about all of these important tasks, the Commission has structured its 33,197 staff into some 42 **Directorates-General (DGs) and Services** and a number of **Executive Agencies**, reflecting the different roles and policy areas that it has to cover. Whilst the number of staff the Commission has might appear high to some eyes, it is in fact low relative to the tasks that the Commission has to carry out, which has important consequences. Compared to national administrations, in the EU Member States or internationally, the Commission has significantly less staff. An example highlights the case in point: the US Food and Drug Administration (FDA) employs just over 14,000 people to focus on its specific areas of competence. The main reason for this comparative under-resourcing, as advocated by the Member States, is that the Commission does not implement EU legislation on the ground, hence does not need the same levels of human resources. The single biggest implication of this is that the Commission is constantly in need of information, notably about how things work on the ground - as it does not necessarily have its own adequate sources of information and expertise (see Chapter 4.5 that deals with EU Agencies for more on this issue). It is for this reason that the Commission uses a variety of different means to get information - all of which will be considered in detail in this chapter.

The Commission was originally structured along the lines of the national administrations of its founding members, notably the French administration, but it rapidly evolved to meet the new challenges that treaty revisions and enlargements have created. Whilst there are a sizeable number of DGs and Services, a corollary objective has been to increase internal coordination and cohesion, based notably on IT systems and internal procedures, to avoid 'silo' effects (when DGs work alone and in isolation from their colleagues across the Commission). The internal organisation of the Commission is underpinned by a series of internal rules, the most important of which are the **Commission's Rules of Procedure (RoP)**, which are published in the Official Journal of the EU (OJ), and hence publicly available. The Commission RoP have their own implementing rules to flesh out the details and give a precise guide as to how things happen in the Commission - this document is not officially made public but can be requested from the Commission. On an equal footing with the RoP, is the Communication from the President **'The Working Methods of the European Commission 2014-2019' (C2014, 9400)**. Most of the details in this chapter have been taken from these documents and hence they will not be systematically referenced, other than in cases of importance where it is necessary to highlight the source of the information.

The internal structure of the Commission is presented on the next page.

Figure 1.2: The internal structure of the European Commission

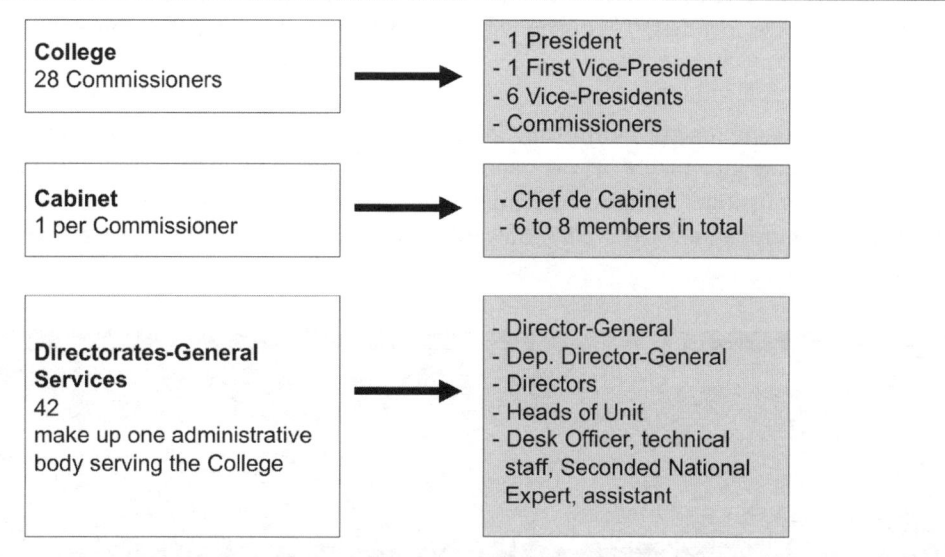

1.3 Internal structure of the European Commission: The College of Commissioners

At the top of the Commission's structure is the College of Commissioners, led by the President. The College represents the highest political level of the Commission. The Commissioners swear an oath to be completely independent when carrying out their functions which is as shown in the box below.

The Commissioner's oath

"Having been appointed as a Member of the European Commission by the European Council, following the vote of consent by the European Parliament, I solemnly undertake:
- To respect the Treaties and the Charter of Fundamental Rights of the European Union in the fulfilment of all my duties.
- To be completely independent in carrying out my responsibilities, in the general interest of the Union.
- In the performance of my tasks, neither to seek nor to take instructions from any Government or from any other institution, body, office or entity.
- To refrain from any action incompatible with my duties or the performance of my tasks.

I formally note the undertaking of each Member State to respect this principle and not to seek to influence Members of the Commission in the performance of their tasks. I further undertake to respect, both during and after my term of office, the obligation arising there from, and in particular the duty to behave with integrity and discretion as regards the acceptance, after I have ceased to hold office, of certain appointments or benefits."

Source: http://europa.eu/rapid/press-release_IP-10-487_en.htm

Despite swearing this oath, many Commissioners retain strong links to their home Member State, a fact that manifests itself in various ways, from their interventions in College meetings to the places in which they give speeches. This issue will be revisited in Chapter 8.2 on how to engage with the Commission.

The Commissioners together form the College and it is the College that formally takes decisions, gives political guidance to the Services and DGs and leads the Commission. The College is made up of one Commissioner from each Member State. The Treaty of Lisbon foresaw a reduction in the number of Commissioners from 2014 onwards to two-thirds the number of Member States (Article 17 TEU).

IN - Investiture (Article 17(7) TEU)

Step 1: The European Council proposes a candidate for President (taking into account the elections of the Parliament) to the Parliament, who must then vote to elect or reject the candidate by absolute majority of its members.
- President Juncker was approved by the Parliament in July 2014 by 422 votes in favour, 250 against and 47 abstentions.

Step 2: The General Affairs Council, along with the President-designate, adopts a list of intended Commissioners on the basis of suggestions by Member States.

Step 3: Each individual Commissioner-designate is required by the Parliament to go for a hearing, where they will be questioned on issues of competence, and since the Treaty of Lisbon, on their 'European Commitment'.
- In 2004, 2010 and 2014 the EP requested that one Commissioner-designate be replaced - which was on each occasion respected.

Step 4: The Parliament votes its 'consent' to the full College in a single ballot.
- In 2014 the Juncker College was voted in by 423 votes to 209 with 67 abstentions.

Step 5: The European Council appoints the Commission by qualified majority voting (QMV).

OUT - Censure of the College (Article 17(8) TEU)

Step 1: If the Parliament deems necessary it can bring a resolution for a motion of censure. This vote requires an absolute majority in which case the College must resign as a body.
- There have been nine motions of censure tabled in total, the last in November 2014 following the 'Luxleaks' plenary debate with Commission President Juncker.
  All motions have failed, but they have received varying levels of support.

> **Accountability of an Individual Commissioner**
>
> **Step 1:** Each Commissioner goes before the relevant Committee of the Parliament on a regular basis to give updates on their work and answer questions.
>
> **Step 2:** In the Framework Agreement on Relations between the Parliament and Commission, voted by the Parliament in October of 2010, it states that the Parliament can request the removal of an individual Commissioner - which the President of the Commission must either accept, or explain his reasoning to the next Parliament Plenary session.

Source: Article 17 TEU & Framework Agreement on Relations between the European Parliament and Commission

However the Member States had already agreed at the December 2008 European Council meeting to maintain the one Commissioner per Member State rule beyond 2014 (European Council Conclusions, 11-12 December 2008, point 2, page 2). All the DGs and Services of the Commission work to serve the College and assist the Commissioners in their decision-taking capacity. The College is the focal point of the work of the Commission. It is worth briefly outlining how the Commissioners come into office and how they can be removed from office - and hence the mechanisms that exist to scrutinise their activities and hold them to account.

The key political figure in the Commission is the **President** who has to find a balance between effective chairmanship of the Commission, maintenance of collegiate consensus and leadership of the policy orientation of the Commission. The President of the Commission has increasingly become a pivotal and powerful voice in the EU - a solid advocate of European solutions. President Juncker is affiliated to the Group of the European People's Party (EPP) in the EP and is a former Prime Minister of Luxembourg. He occupies one of, if not the, most powerful political positions in Brussels.

The President of the Commission has a Service answerable directly to him - the **Secretariat-General (SG)**. This Service has about 600 staff who ensure that all the Commission departments work together effectively to meet the identified political priorities. In this vein, the SG coordinates, advises and arbitrates to ensure that coherence, quality and delivery of policy, legislation and operations occurs smoothly and in accordance with the rules and the prescribed procedures.

> **The Commission President**
>
> - is head of the European Commission;
> - allocates portfolios;
> - chairs the College meetings;
> - establishes College meeting agendas;
> - is a non-voting member of the European Council;
> - is the representative of the Union on internal policies;
> - is a crucial political actor in Brussels.
>
> **Some past Presidents:**
>
> 2010-2014: Jose Manuel Barroso
> 2004-2009: Jose Manuel Barroso
> 1999-2004: Romano Prodi
> 1995-1999: Jacques Santer
> 1985-1995: Jacques Delors

Commission President Juncker, in 2014, decided to organise the work of the Commissioners very differently compared to his predecessors. He entrusted priority projects outlined in his political guidelines to seven **Vice-Presidents (VPs)**, each in charge of coordinating and steering the delivery of the priority projects. The Vice-Presidents lead project-teams of Commissioners. Individual Commissioners need to cooperate closely with their Vice-President as well as with the other Commissioners in their respective project-teams. This new working arrangement was a radical departure from previous practice with regards to both the focus on delivery against specific objectives and in terms of having a rather formal hierarchy amongst Commissioners.

Commissioners seeking to prepare, develop and table proposals to the College of Commissioners require prior approval by the responsible Vice-President. In addition, Vice-President Timmermans, in charge of Better Regulation, Inter-institutional Relations, the Rule of Law and the Charter of Fundamental Rights, has been assigned a newly established role of First Vice-President. Besides the policies in his portfolio, the **First Vice-President** acts as a gatekeeper for policy initiatives that have to be entered on the Commission Work Programme and the College agenda.

> **Commission Vice-Presidents**
>
> - 1st VP Better Regulation, Inter-institutional Relations, the Rule of Law and the Charter of Fundamental Rights (Frans Timmermans, NL)
> - High Representative of the Union for Foreign Affairs and Security Policy / Commission Vice-President (Frederica Mogherini, IT)
> - VP Budget and Human Resources (Kristalina Georgieva, BG)
> - VP Digital Single Market (Andrus Ansip, EE)
> - VP Energy Union (Maroš Šefčovič, SK)
> - VP Euro and Social Dialogue (Valdis Dombrovskis, LV)
> - VP Jobs, Growth, Investment and Competitiveness (Jyrki Katainen, FI)

> **A Commissioner's Cabinet**
>
> - composed of the personal team and advisers of the Commissioner;
> - provides a combination of private office secretariat, political advice and additional policy input;
> - acts as political antenna for Commissioners by keeping them aware of politically sensitive or difficult issues;
> - helps to coordinate policy and mediate among competing interests both within the Commission and from the outside;
> - reflects the personality and working style both of the Commissioner and the Chef de Cabinet.
>
> A Commissioner's reputation depends largely on their Cabinet's efficiency in providing sound advice and guidance.

At the level of Commissioners, each is aided by their own private office (**Cabinet**) which is headed by the **Chef de Cabinet**. This post is a vital appointment and is one that the Commissioner handpicks due to its importance: Chef de Cabinet is one of the most influential positions in the Commission as he or she has access to significant information and has a high level of discretion to take decisions. Under the Chef de Cabinet there are usually between six and eight people in the Cabinet, at least three positions of which are reserved for Commission officials, meaning each Commissioner can bring in a number of advisors from outside the Commission. The Cabinet must also respect gender, nationality and geographical constraints. The main role of the Cabinet is to give political guidance and support to the Commissioner, which requires liaison and interaction with the Commissioner's DG(s). In this way the Cabinet filters the issues and the information for the Commissioner to ensure they are updated on everything they need to be updated on - be it political or technical issues. The Cabinets are rather unique in the technical and political overview that they have of dossiers - and also regarding the fact that they will have a more holistic institutional picture within the Commission.

It is important to remember that all issues, files, questions and dossiers discussed later in this chapter cross the desks of the Cabinet - and the Cabinets can have an important say in all of them. The Cabinet has to look over all texts to see what issues the DG has raised on a technical level. It then has to think about the Commissioner's political priorities, any promises they have made to either the Parliament or Member States, and any personal issues the Commissioner might wish to see addressed. This is a very difficult balance to strike and leads to Cabinet members being heavily solicited internally and externally, resulting in a considerable workload. Most Cabinet members will get anything upwards of 40-60 e-mails per day from external stakeholders with information, reports, questions, meetings requests, etc. This is in addition to the internal Commission work that a Cabinet member will have to cover.

All Commissioners' Cabinets can be found on the Commission website, with very useful information on the composition of each Cabinet, their responsibilities and their contact details. Each Cabinet member has a portfolio that will include both sectorial and horizontal issues, and it is always important to identify the right person in the Cabinet. Whilst Commissioners' Cabinets work in different ways they all have an extremely good overview of the politics, detail and mechanics of a proposal - and crucially they have the influence to get involved in almost all procedures and proposals and can make changes. This role of the Cabinet will become clear in the sections that follow.

1.4 Internal structure of the European Commission: Directorates-General and Services

Below the political level of Commissioner and Cabinet, comes the administrative level. The basic operational building block in the Commission is the Unit, managed by a **Head of Unit (HoU)**, which varies in size and composition depending on its role. Within the Unit you will find a number of Desk Officers and administrative support staff, as well as Seconded National Experts. Several Units form a **Directorate** which is overseen by a **Director**. These Directorates are sub-divisions of a **Directorate-General** which is managed by a **Director-General**, who is usually supported by a Deputy Director-General, special advisers and a dedicated administrative staff. A final important point about the internal staffing of the Commission is that there is an active mobility policy in place, which means that officials often move internally. For the sensitive positions this rotation can be every four years. This has a number of important consequences for the Commission itself, and also for engaging with the Commission (as will be seen in Chapter 8.2).

The Commission has two broad principles that guide its functioning and operations, principles that are rigorously pursued by the SG on a daily basis:

1. **Collegiality:** The College of Commissioners takes over 10,000 decisions a year, decisions that are taken collectively - and hence are the responsibility of all College members. This is a principle that is taken very seriously within the Commission and one that manifests itself in the working processes of the organisation. As every Commissioner is co-responsible for every decision in every policy area they are all accorded the opportunity to participate in the formulation and approval of all decisions.

2. **Administrative coherence:** All the Services and DGs of the Commission make up one administrative body to serve the College. This translates into a core area of work for the SG, ensuring coherence in Commission actions, especially when communicating with other institutions. So while it might sometimes appear that an individual DG operates as if it were a self-standing administration – the so-called 'silo' effect that used to dominate in the Commission – the DGs are now more tightly bound to the centre than ever before. The broad political objectives of the Commission filter down into the work of every DG, notably through the Strategic Planning and Programming cycle (SPP), as we shall now see.

1.5 How the European Commission works: Strategic Planning and Programming

The internal decision-making procedures of the Commission can be split into a series of different phases. Before looking at these in more detail the broader context needs to be established.

The SPP cycle is the macro-planning framework within which the Commission operates. What is shown in Figure 1.3 is an example for the year 2013. Changes to the cycle occurred as a result of the new incoming Commission in 2014 but these changes had not yet been finalised at the time of writing. We therefore present the example for the year 2013 and indicate the main changes foreseen for 2015 - but this is something the reader is encouraged to investigate further.

The SPP system is born out of the desire of the Commission to define and deliver clear objectives and priorities and to allocate resources effectively in light of political priorities. The SPP system was a direct result of the 1999 Santer Commission crisis when all 20 members of the then College resigned. A resulting Committee of Independent Experts reported back to the new Prodi Commission with suggestions to avoid the errors of the past. A major part of the response by President Prodi was the SPP cycle, a cycle that has been evolving ever since at the heart of the Commission. Following this cycle is essential for solid upstream information and planning on behalf of an external stakeholder.

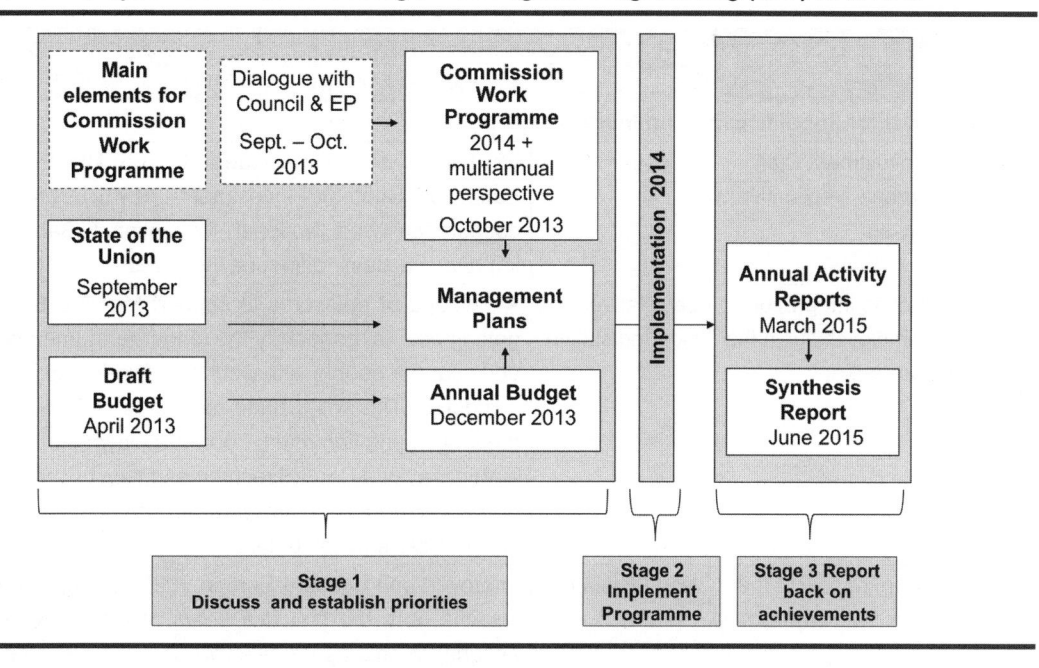

Figure 1.3: European Commission Strategic Planning and Programming (SPP) 2012-2013

As Figure 1.3 shows, the SPP cycle is multi-annual, although there are three clear processes that we can identify and elaborate on:

1. **Discuss and establish priorities:** In this phase the emphasis is on the Commission elaborating what it considers to be the policy and regulatory priorities, and discussing these with stakeholders before narrowing down to a more focused work programme detailing exactly what it intends to do. The Political Guidelines for the Next Commission, a 12-page document issued by President Juncker in July 2014 set out the broad strategic guidelines and objectives of the five-year Commission term.

2010 saw the first ever 'State of the Union' speech delivered by President Barroso to the EP Plenary in Strasbourg, a speech which is scheduled to take place every September as part of the process of discussing the major political priorities for the Union in the coming year. This speech is therefore part of the broader discussions with stakeholders that the Commission then translates into concrete actions in the Commission Work Programme (CWP) by the end of October. The CWP gives a detailed list of forthcoming concrete actions that the Commission intends to undertake - generating transparency and predictability for stakeholders and facilitating cooperation with the legislators. The core 11-page document for 2015 is a description of how the 'political guidelines' are being translated into action. Of more interest are its annexes which outline, in list format, the new initiatives that the Commission will take forward, the modifications or withdrawals of pending proposals, the simplification or evaluation initiatives foreseen and finally the adopted measures that will become applicable during the next year. This can be seen in the examples of new initiatives for 2015 in Table 1.2 on the next page.

Table 1.2 New Commission Initiatives for 2015

No.	Title	Type of initiative	Description of scope and objectives
A New Boost for Jobs, Growth and Investment			
1	The Investment Plan for Europe: Legislative Follow-up	Legislative	The follow-up actions include setting up of the European Fund for Strategic Investments (EFSI), promoting cooperation with National Promotional Banks and improving access to finance for SMEs.
2	Promoting integration and employability in the labour market	Legislative/ Non-legislative	A package of measures to support Member States in getting people, especially the longer term unemployed and younger people, into work and developing a skilled workforce. This will include measures to follow up on the implementation of the Youth Employment Initiative, a proposal for a Council recommendation on integration of the long-term unemployed, as well as measures to promote skills development.
3	Mid-term review of the Europe 2020 strategy	Non-legislative	Improved and updated Europe 2020 strategy, drawing lessons from the first four years of the strategy and ensuring it acts as an effective post-crisis strategy for growth and jobs in Europe. Follows up on the recent public consultation.
A Connected Digital Single Market			
4	Digital Single Market (DSM) Package	Legislative/ Non-legislative	The aim is to ensure that consumers enjoy cross-border access to digital services, create a level-playing field for companies and create the conditions for a vibrant digital economy and society. The package will include, among other legislative proposals, the modernisation of copyright.

Source: Annex 1 to Commission Work Programme 2015, COM (2014) 910 final, page 2

The CWP is a very important political, technical and practical document. Politically the Commission sets itself the target of delivering what it says it will do - hence it will be focused internally on delivering what it has stated in this document, and it will only delay, or not deliver, in light of strong mitigating circumstances. The actions that the Commission will focus on are the new initiatives - the major political priorities. From a technical and practical perspective the document gives a very transparent forward looking overview of the main actions to come from the Commission in the next few years - very useful for forward planning and anticipation.

The Commission updates the CWP on a monthly and annual basis. The Commission sends monthly updates on the CWP, with revisions, to the other EU institutions, simultaneously publishing these on the SG website. These updates give an extremely good picture of fluid and changing timelines to actions and priorities and allow stakeholders to keep up with progress and deadlines. The second way in which the CWP is updated is through the annual update - whereby the Commission adopts a new multiannual CWP for the next years. A parallel document of interest is the **Roadmap** document which, for every single DG, offers a picture of the work that will be carried out by the DGs in preparation of the delivery of CWP items.

> When an **Impact Assessment** (IA - see below) is made, there will always be a Roadmap (also known as Inception Impact Assessment). But a Roadmap can also state that there will be no IA.

In parallel to this legislative planning through the CWP, the Commission also issues a **Draft Budget (DB)** in April of every year to launch the budgetary procedure. This 1000+ page document is drawn up on the basis of the activities that the Commission, and the other institutions, is undertaking and foresees, in the context of the CWP, and aims to ensure that resources are allocated according to priorities. Although the **Annual Budget (AB)** operates in a multiannual framework – **the multiannual financial framework (MFF)** which sets a 7-year spending framework– there is still room for manoeuvre on an annual basis, which is why there are such arduous negotiations taking place every October/November to finalise the budget before December of any given year. In this way, the Commission has set the priorities, outlined the concrete actions it will take forward and also received a budget to enact all of this.

The final documents are the **Management Plans (MP)**, documents with an internal focus, which are prepared by each DG to translate the Commission's priority objectives into general and specific objectives at the level of the DG. These plans are issued every year and they contain details of all initiatives in each DG and how they relate to the broad goals of the Commission. In addition these MPs have also moved towards a multiannual approach to take account of the multiannual nature of both the budget and the CWP. Each MP contains specific objectives and targets for every single activity, as well as all the resources that are being used on each activity. In this way the Commission, and also the legislators who receive this document, are able to monitor and evaluate its progress in an objective manner. The MPs are also published on the Commission website (http://ec.europa.eu/atwork/synthesis/amp/index_en.htm) and are very useful documents to understand not only the initiatives within a DG, but the objectives and indicators of their work; this is helpful information if you are interacting with the DG.

With these three documents, the CWP, the DB (and ultimately the adopted budget) and the MP, the Commission has set its priorities, discussed them with stakeholders, crafted an Annual Budget to help it deliver its priorities (and other actions) and converted this into detailed internal documents stating the objectives and indicators that every DG has to strive towards in the coming year(s).

2. **Implement programme:** The second stage is where the Commission endeavours to deliver everything it laid out in the CWP, to execute the budget and to achieve the indicators it set itself in the MPs. The Commission sends monthly reports to the other institutions on the execution of the CWP and an overview of planned Commission initiatives until the end of each year. The Commission will politically drive forward the strategic priorities, the SG acting as the President's lookout to make sure the DGs deliver on the Commission's most important promises. Every year there will be mitigating circumstances for a small number of initiatives, strategic and other items that were foreseen for the year in question - but for the vast majority the Commission will successfully deliver what it set out to deliver.

> **Evaluation - The start, not the end**
>
> The 2010 Smart Regulation agenda put ex-post evaluation as the key priority area for investment in the Commission. All policies are subject to an evaluation - which has extremely important consequences for any future action. This evaluation is the starting point for anything new.
>
> For legislation specifically, the Commission's Regulatory Fitness and Performance Programme (REFIT) identifies opportunities for simplifying existing legislation and reducing administrative burdens.

3. **Report back on achievements**: The final stage of the SPP process concerns the **Annual Activity Report (AAR)** which is a report compiled for the Commissioners by each Director-General and Head of Service. These reports assess the results of their department against the objectives and indicators set in the MPs. These documents are also accompanied by a **declaration of assurance** on the proper use of resources and on the quality of financial management which is signed by the Director-General or Head of Service. These AARs are important evaluation documents that the Commission should then use in preparing future initiatives.

The outcome of the SPP cycle is the **Synthesis Report (SR)** that is published in June of every year. The SR reports on achievements by the Commission as a whole, but is more important as the moment when the College of Commissioners takes political responsibility for the management and work of its Directors-General and Heads of Service. This brings to a close the SPP cycle, although at any given point in time the Commission Services will be dealing with implementing their actions for the given year, preparing actions and priorities for the next year and simultaneously reporting back on (and learning from) what they did in the previous year. The SPP cycle places a heavy workload on those involved within the Commission, but from an external perspective it allows for a transparent and accessible process in which all stakeholders are able to identify their issues at an early stage. It is from this broad framework of prioritisation and resource allocation that individual files are taken forward within the Commission - as the next section describes in detail.

1.6 How the European Commission works: Preparation of a dossier

If a legislative dossier is under preparation in the Commission it will have already been flagged in the CWP, and if it is a legislative proposal (therefore requiring an Impact Assessment as we will see later) it would also have been flagged in the Roadmaps. This section will follow the process from the macro-level of Commission planning into the detail of the preparation of an individual dossier in the Commission Services. Here the emphasis will shift away from the President of the Commission and high-level political discussions to the basic organisational block of the Commission: the Unit. A proposal will be taken forward within the most relevant Unit of the most relevant DG, the so-called lead Unit in the so-called lead DG. This Unit will take responsibility for a dossier and thus coordinate the preparation of the proposal and all supporting documentation. The Unit will draft the documents, proposals and IA, and consult all other DGs and external stakeholders, before tabling the resulting documents for final adoption by the College. It is these stages that will be addressed in the next sections. The initiation of work in the Commission is represented in Figure 1.4.

> **EU legal acts**
>
> When the Commission is preparing its legal acts for adoption by the College it can use one of three legal acts:
>
> **Regulation** - shall have general application and be binding in its entirety and directly applicable in all Member States.
>
> **Directive** - binding, as to the result to be achieved and shall leave to the national authorities the choice of form and method.
>
> **Decision** - binding in its entirety. A decision which specifies those to whom it is addressed shall be binding only on them.
>
> **Recommendation & Opinion** - encourages those to whom they are addressed to act in a particular way - without being binding on them. This allows the Commission to issue non-binding rules.
>
> The choice of legal act is very important and has significant consequences for MS.

The flowchart in Figure 1.4 shows the start of an individual dossier's journey. The dossier will be included in the CWP once it is advanced enough that the Commission can confidently announce to the outside world that it will be delivered within the period of the CWP. Otherwise the earliest the outside world will officially know about the dossier is through it being flagged in the Roadmaps.

Figure 1.4: Proposal - From European Commission Work Programme (CWP) to Regulatory Scrutiny Body (RSB)

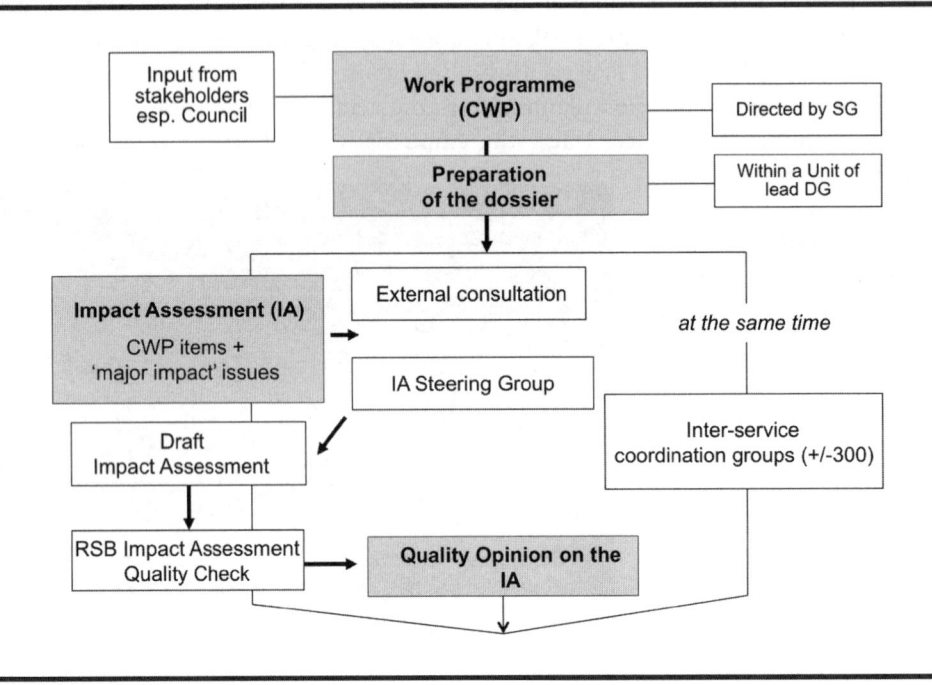

```
Input from                  Work Programme
stakeholders  ───────────      (CWP)           ─────────  Directed by SG
esp. Council
                                │
                          Preparation                     Within a Unit of
                         of the dossier       ─────────       lead DG
                                │
        ┌───────────────────────┼──────────────────────────┐
        │                       ▼
  Impact Assessment (IA)   External consultation          at the same time
  CWP items +
  'major impact' issues    IA Steering Group
        │                                              Inter-service
        ▼                                         coordination groups (+/-300)
     Draft
  Impact Assessment
        │
        ▼
  RSB Impact Assessment  ──▶  Quality Opinion on the
    Quality Check                     IA
```

Within the Unit that has been designated as the lead on a specific issue, one or two Desk Officers will take a lead on the specific file. At this stage the first major undertaking, for a legislative proposal, is the IA which we will come to shortly. There are two major aspects of the Unit's work that need to be addressed in relation to its drafting of an IA and a proposal. This is the dual obligation for the Unit to consult internally and externally. At the very earliest stage the Unit has to associate other DGs to its preparatory work, which is done in two possible ways.

The first is through **Inter-Service Coordination Groups (ISCGs)**, which are permanent internal groups with a clear mandate to discuss a series of issues. There were about 300 such groups in the Commission in 2014 and they all have the objective of increasing cooperation and coherence between DGs. They are informal groups for discussion where the lead DG can canvass the opinions of interested DGs, and where interested DGs can raise their thoughts, concerns and objections. Discussion in an Inter-Service Coordination Group does not lead to any binding outcomes - but the discussions will be reported back to Cabinets across the Commission if problems arise. It is also in these Groups that positions for the **formal Inter-Service Consultation (ISC** - also known by its French acronym **CIS**), that we will see shortly, are formed. Through this group the responsible Unit will hope to generate internal agreement on its proposals and work, and associated DGs will hope to influence the proposal to take into account their specific points and interests.

The second internal mechanism is the **IA Steering Group (also referred to as Interservice (Steering) Group)**, which is solely focused on assisting the Unit with the IA process. The Unit, before starting an IA, must circulate details of the proposed IA to all other DGs who can then respond by taking a place in the IA Steering Group if they feel their DG's interests are touched on in some way. The Unit will keep close contact with the Steering Group throughout the IA process - again with the objectives of internal cohesion and consistency. We see therefore that whilst a Unit drafts everything there are a significant number of other associated officials closely involved in the process.

The other side of the coin is **external consultation**, where the Commission has a variety of tools at its disposal - any of which can be used, in varying combinations, from the very inception of the drafting process in the Commission. The main forms of Commission consultation are presented below.

1. **Commission Work Programme (CWP)**
   http://ec.europa.eu/atwork/key-documents/index_en.htm
   As described above, a rolling multi-annual programme that outlines the main Commission proposals to be adopted in the future - with the most detail concentrated on the next 12 months. The CWP is constantly open to consultation, internally and externally as new priorities and issues arise.

2. **Impact Assessment (IA)**
   http://ec.europa.eu/smart-regulation/impact/index_en.htm
   A major component of an IA is consultation of the stakeholders in the area being investigated. In this sense stakeholders will likely be formally consulted, via the Roadmap, hearings or questionnaires etc, to attain their opinion. If an IA is ongoing, interested stakeholders should make their opinions known to the lead Unit running the IA, as well as any other impacted/interested DGs likely to support their position. This will be taken up in more detail in the section on IAs.

3. **Open hearings** (check individual DG websites to keep informed)
   The Commission organises a number of open hearings to gather interested stakeholders and exchange views and gather information. As a forum for consultation they are limited because they will usually bring together 50-250 people listening to presentations by the Commission and/or key interested stakeholders. Whilst limited in the sense of information exchange they are extremely useful events for visibility with the Commission and other stakeholders. These events are very good networking opportunities.

4. **Green Papers**
   http://ec.europa.eu/green-papers/index_en.htm or
   http://ec.europa.eu/yourvoice/index_en.htm
   A Green Paper is one of the old-school formal consultation techniques used by the Commission, whereby it presents a paper (not actually green) outlining the options that it is considering on a certain question. This document must be no longer than 30 pages and is translated into all official languages. There are minimum standards of consultation that apply, meaning that everything, including responses and the Commission's summary, has to be published on the website of the

DG concerned and that stakeholders get a minimum of twelve weeks to reply. A Green Paper is an excellent opportunity to bring your concerns to the attention of the Unit and Desk Officer that will eventually draft the proposal - because at this stage the ideas are still general.

5. **White Paper**
   http://ec.europa.eu/white-papers/index_en.htm or
   http://ec.europa.eu/yourvoice/index_en.htm
   A White Paper is, like the Green Paper, one of the formal consultation techniques used by the Commission. It is a document in which the Commission outlines which legislative option(s) it favours, seeking any additional comments and ideas. This document must be no longer than 15 pages and it is translated into all official languages. The same minimum standards of consultation as explained above apply. A White Paper is an excellent opportunity to bring your concerns to the attention of the Unit and Desk Officer that will eventually draft the proposal - but, compared to the Green Paper, at this stage the ideas are more concrete and established.

6. **Small and Medium-sized Enterprises Test (SME Test)**
   http://ec.europa.eu/enterprise/policies/sme/small-business-act/sme-test/index_en.htm
   The SME Test is the application of the 'Think Small First' principle and is an integral part of the Commission's regulatory Impact Assessment. The aim is to take into account the impact of regulation on SMEs as soon as possible during the policy-making process. The SME Test is aimed at avoiding legislation which could put a disproportionate burden on small and medium-sized enterprises. It entails a separate analysis that comes under four main steps:
   - Consultation with SME representatives (via focus groups, business test panel, questionnaires and interviews among others).
   - Preliminary assessment of businesses likely to be affected (based on the previous consultation step to determine whether SMEs are affected and the extent of impact).
   - Measurement of impacts on SMEs (quantitative analysis of cost and benefits of the policy options to SME operations, performance and administrative compliance).
   - Assessment of alternative options and mitigating measures (full/partial exemption, transition period, financial aid and general simplification initiatives benefiting SMEs). The Commission obliges itself to focus on the findings of the SME test in one part of the Impact Assessment report and provide as much detail as possible for each of the different steps.

7. **Online questionnaires and open forum on the Internet**
   http://ec.europa.eu/yourvoice/index_en.htm
   The Commission almost systematically consults via the Internet these days - with different types of questionnaires. This is mostly done via the 'Your Voice in Europe' website. See the box for all the details.

> **Your Voice in Europe** is the single portal on which the Commission posts all consultations. In addition it has discussion forums and tools to help you find and address your local MEP, Economic and Social Committee representative and Committee of the Regions representative.
>
> It is here that you can find the Commission summary and all responses to closed consultations - an invaluable source of information for mapping the position of stakeholders and getting a good overview of the issues at stake. http://ec.europa.eu/yourvoice

8. **Expert Groups** (see below)
    http://ec.europa.eu/transparency/regexpert

9. **Informal meetings, events, gatherings, etc.** (see below)
    The Commission will use differing combinations of the consultation tools identified above according to its needs. It is often obliged to use several during the preparation of an initiative as it seeks to find all the relevant stakeholders and information.

It is essential, from an external perspective, to engage in all forms of consultation - firstly to monitor the progress of a dossier, but also to keep the Commission informed of your opinions and ideas. The lead Unit will keep a record and know whether you have responded to their consultations. It is important to be identifiable from an early stage as an interested stakeholder. Consultations are a formal part of lobbying and should best be followed up with direct meetings. Respondents to consultations should also bear in mind what the Commission needs most of all - facts, figures and evidence. In addition, responses should always be constructive and positive in tone.

There are a series of minimum requirements that surround these consultation tools. For example, when undertaking a public consultation there should be adequate time to respond - usually taken to be 12 weeks. If the Commission is organising a meeting or a hearing it should allow at least 20 working days' notice; consult representatively; make sure stakeholders know exactly what they are being consulted on; report back on the consultation, and report back, with justifications, on what it intends to do as a result. A key aspect of all of these forms of consultation is the requirement that the Commission post detailed feedback on the Internet so that external parties can see how the Commission has analysed and evaluated the information that was submitted.

The two most important sources of information for the Commission, above and beyond open consultations, are without doubt (in order) Expert Groups and informal meetings and gatherings. Expert Groups are possibly the single largest source of information for the Commission, because they give the organisation access to information that it would otherwise have difficulty attaining. The Commission, in late 2014, had around 800 Expert Groups registered on its Expert Group Register (http://ec.europa.eu/transparency/regexpert/index.cfm). As and when a Unit in the Commission considers that it needs expert input the most convenient, and substance rich, way of doing this is to create an Expert Group. This used to be done

Expert Groups

- approx. 800;
- 95% created informally by the Commission (Unit level choice);
- 5% created formally by legislators or political decision of College;
- Hand-selected membership (by Commission Unit);
- Chaired by Commission;
- Objectives set by Commission;
- Meet (usually) in Brussels as and when needed;
- 70% of Expert Groups composed of national MS officials.

Vital source of information for the Commission

by the Commission most frequently to assist it with legislative proposals, but Expert Groups are now used more regularly to assist the Commission with Implementing and Delegated Acts as well (see Chapters 6 and 9 for more information). The Unit in question is free to invite who it wants to participate in its Expert Group, depending on its needs. The Commission calls the meetings, sets the agenda and the objectives (discussion, draft a report, etc.), chairs the meetings and drives discussions according to its needs. Members of these groups are entitled to claim travel and accommodation costs if needed. Expert Groups are extremely important sources of information for the Commission, notably on how things work in Member States, and through this importance they represent a direct channel of influence on the Commission. For this reason there has been persistent pressure on the Commission to be more transparent about what the Groups do and who sits on them, resulting in a more accessible and detailed register. On this register you find information on all the existing Expert Groups and their composition, with names for those sitting in an individual capacity and affiliations for those representing an association or Member State. In addition to all of this the register also identifies the Unit responsible in the Commission, and is thus overall a useful source of information.

Expert Groups will be constantly feeding into the drafting process within the Commission, alongside the internal support from the ISCG and the IA Steering Groups. This creates an early crucial network of about 40-50 people with strategic input on a Commission draft text. The crux of this process is without doubt the IA, the process of which is outlined in Figure 1.5.

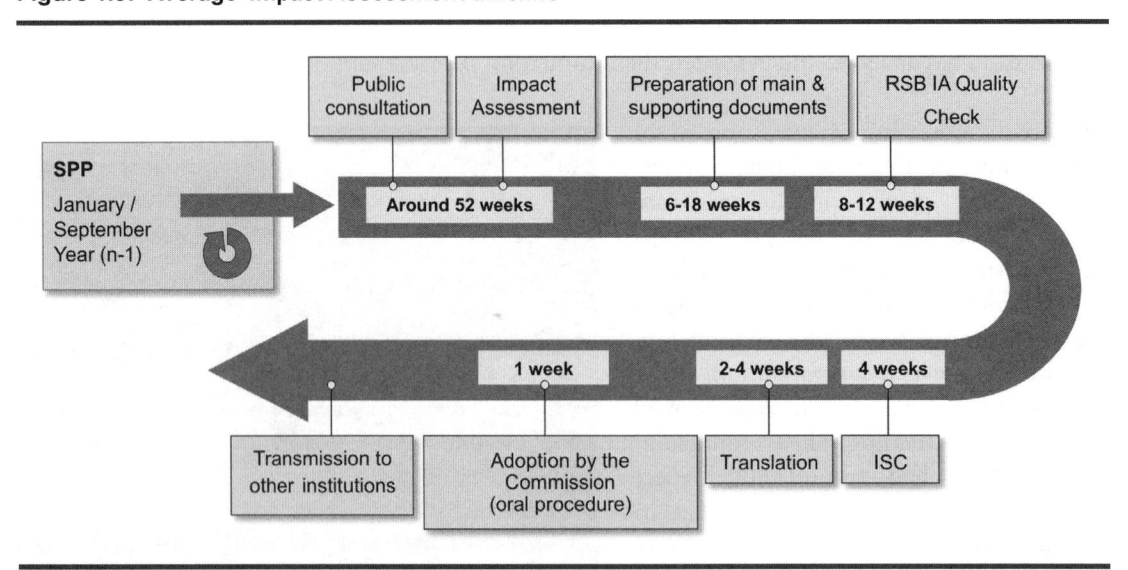

Figure 1.5: 'Average' Impact Assessment timeline

Source: Impact Assessment Guidelines, page 8: available at: http://ec.europa.eu/governance/impact/commission _guidelines/docs/iag_2009_en.pdf (updated)

The IA is a process that prepares evidence for the College, as political decision-makers, on the advantages and disadvantages of possible policy options by assessing their potential impacts. It ensures that when the Commission brings forward a proposal it does so in a transparent, comprehensive and balanced way based on a solid bank of evidence. In this way an IA is a tool for the College and not a formal treaty-based legal obligation. That said, the Commission has committed to undertake IAs as stated in the **Inter-institutional Agreement on Better Lawmaking** of 2003. The Commission has been doing IAs since 2003, when it had to start with one of the most difficult IAs it has had to do - REACH (European Union Regulation, of over 800 pages, concerning the Registration, Evaluation, Authorisation & Restriction of Chemicals. It came into force on 1 June 2007). Since then the Commission has completed about 700 IAs.

> **Impact Assessment: Key facts**
>
> - All major policy initiatives, legislative proposals + proposals with significant impacts.
> - Three pillar approach: economic, social and environmental.
> - IA Guidelines to guide desk officer.
> - Assisted by IA Steering Group.
> - Is a technical aid to the political decision of the College.
>
> **Final documents:**
> IA report
> RSB Opinion
> Executive summary of IA (24 languages)

The timeline in Figure 1.5 highlights all the important stages in the drafting of an IA and the average time attributed to each stage of the process. Seeing all of these stages and the time involved allows an appreciation of the investment and workload on behalf of the Commission in this stage of policy development - the single biggest investment of the Commission in its Better Regulation package.

An IA is required for all major policy initiatives and legislative proposals on the CWP and other proposals with potential significant impacts. The first category is quite clear-cut and can be seen transparently in the CWP and the Roadmaps, but the second category is one of increasing importance. More and more Implementing and Delegated Acts proposals are being deemed to have significant impacts and thus require an IA. The Commission has now put a screening mechanism in place so that a Unit in a DG or the SG can request, or suggest, an IA on a non-CWP measure that is on the Commission's agenda. Once it has been established that the proposal requires an IA the Unit sets up the IA Steering Group and starts to consult (if required) with the Inter-Service Group. The first port of call of the Desk Officer(s) responsible for drafting the IA will be the **Better Regulation Guidelines** prepared by the SG (available at: http://ec.europa.eu/smart-regulation/guidelines/toc_guide_en.htm). The Unit responsible will in most cases do the research and consultation itself, with some Units choosing to outsource data collection to external companies. This is the most important and time-consuming part of the IA process, which along with the initial drafting of the IA can take around one year. To give a clearer picture of what an IA seeks to address a list of fundamental IA questions are in the box on the next page.

1. What is the nature and scale of the problem, how is it evolving, and who is most affected by it?
2. What are the views of the stakeholders concerned?
3. Should the Union be involved?
4. If so, what objectives should it set to address the problem?
5. What are the main policy options for reaching these objectives?
6. What are the likely economic, social and environmental impacts of those options?
7. How do the main options compare in terms of effectiveness, efficiency and coherence in solving the problems?
8. How could future monitoring and evaluation be organised?

Once the Unit has drafted the IA report and both the Steering Group and Inter-Service Group are satisfied (this is not a procedural obligation, but an internal political constraint), the Unit will submit the draft IA report to the **Regulatory Scrutiny Board (RSB)**. The RSB was established in 2015 as a central quality control and support function and replaced the Impact Assessment Board (IAB).

Reform of the Impact Assessment Board

The Impact Assessment Board was established in November 2006 by a note of the then Commission President Barroso. Its role was to oversee Impact Assessment quality within the Commission. The Board operated under the direct authority of the President and consisted of high-level Commission officials.

These were:
1. Deputy Secretary General for Smart Regulation - Chair of IAB
2. Directors from:
    - DG Economic and Financial Affairs;
    - DG Taxation and Customs Union;
    - DG Home Affairs;
    - DG Climate Action;
    - DG Employment, Social Affairs and Inclusion;
    - DG Enterprise and Industry;
    - DG Enlargement.

The Juncker Commission decided in December 2014 to strengthen the Commission's approach to Better Regulation and to further increase the quality of its Impact Assessment system. The IAB would be remodeled as the **Regulatory Scrutiny Board**. The RSB consists of four Commission officials and three external members that work full-time. This is in contrast to the part-time nature of the position of the members of the IAB.

2015 is a transition year in which both the IAB and the RSB will be active. The IAB will be formally abolished only when the RSB is fully operational and can take over the tasks related to IA scrutiny and quality control from the IAB.

The role of the RSB is to scrutinise the quality of all Commission IAs. In essence the RSB is the internal quality control mechanism to guarantee horizontal standards and provide solutions to common issues and problems. The RSB issues an opinion on each and every IA and is a formal procedural requirement in the Commission decision-making procedure. Without an RSB opinion, a proposal cannot be submitted to the College.

Once the author DG has submitted its IA to the RSB, the RSB sends back detailed comments. The author DG then responds to these comments, either in writing or orally during an RSB meeting. From this the RSB will proceed to issue an opinion - these opinions are also made public and are posted, along with the IA, on the website at: http://ec.europa.eu/governance/impact/index_en.htm.

Once the RSB has delivered its opinion and the modifications have been made by the lead DG, the IA is ready to accompany the proposal into the formal internal procedures that follow, on its way to adoption by the College. After the IA has been finalised, the Unit will also have to draft its legislative (or non-legislative such as a Delegated Act) proposal, based on the IA findings. The proposal and the IA are intimately connected and should be complementary.

> **The 'evaluate first' principle**
>
> In 2015 the European Commission published updated guidelines on the implementation of the so-called Better Regulation principles. The Commission declared that its most favoured approach to developing new legislative and policy proposals was to first evaluate the actual effects that the existing EU acquis had brought about. Such evaluations are meant to provide insight into the costs and benefits of EU legislation. They also should provide evidence if there are (regulatory) shortcomings and thus be the basis of an Impact Assessment for a new proposal.
>
> The Commission's new approach for developing its proposals according to this 'evaluate first' principle will, at the earliest, deliver concrete proposals in 2017. The years 2018 and after should see a continuous rise in proposals that are supported by both an evaluation and an Impact Assessment.

It is important to stress the significance of the IA for all EU-related actors. The Commission IA is the basis for discussions and negotiations within the Commission as to what options it should present to the legislators. The Council and the Parliament use the IA in their discussions and internal negotiations, before coming together for their inter-institutional negotiations on a Commission proposal. The importance of following and engaging in the IA process for all involved actors is now taken for granted.

> For more information on how to work with the Impact Assessment process, see also: E. Akse, *"Influencing the Preparation of EU Legislation: A Practical Guide to Working with Impact Assessments"*, John Harper Publishing, London, 2013.

1.7 How the European Commission works: Administrative decision-preparation

Once the IA has been completed it is possible to proceed internally with a dossier. This phase is represented in Figure 1.6.

Figure 1.6: Proposal: From Regulatory Scrutiny Body (RSB) to College adoption

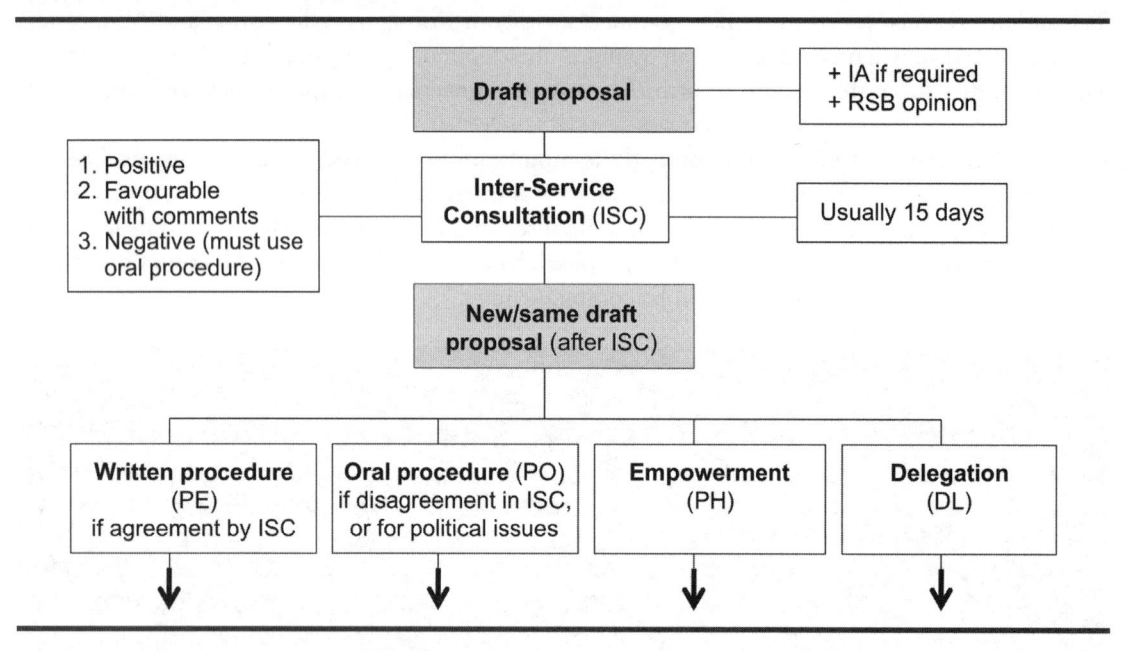

```
                              ┌──────────────┐      + IA if required
                              │Draft proposal│      + RSB opinion
                              └──────┬───────┘
┌─────────────────────┐       ┌──────┴───────┐
│1. Positive          │       │Inter-Service │
│2. Favourable        ├───────┤Consultation  ├──── Usually 15 days
│   with comments     │       │   (ISC)      │
│3. Negative (must use│       └──────┬───────┘
│   oral procedure)   │              │
└─────────────────────┘       ┌──────┴───────┐
                              │New/same draft│
                              │proposal (after ISC)│
                              └──────┬───────┘
        ┌──────────────┬─────────────┼─────────────┬──────────────┐
┌───────┴──────┐┌──────┴──────┐┌─────┴─────┐┌──────┴──────┐
│Written procedure││Oral procedure (PO)││Empowerment││Delegation │
│    (PE)      ││if disagreement in ISC,││   (PH)    ││   (DL)    │
│if agreement by ISC││or for political issues│         │           │
└──────┬───────┘└──────┬──────┘└─────┬─────┘└──────┬──────┘
       ▼               ▼              ▼             ▼
```

In this flowchart we see the progress of a dossier from its draft form into the final decision-making procedures. At this stage the draft proposal will have been crafted by the Unit responsible with internal and external input through the various groups and tools we have identified thus far. Much of this consultation and cooperation will have been of an informal nature - there has, as yet, not been a technical blocking point for a proposal. The closest to this was the possibility of a negative opinion of the RSB and the obligation to rework an IA to concur with the quality control issues that were raised - to which the lead DG would have re-submitted a revised version of the IA for a second RSB opinion.

Once the Unit has obtained a satisfactory RSB opinion, and has prepared its draft proposal and all supporting documents, it will check with the DG hierarchy and the Commissioner's Cabinet to seek political approval to launch the procedure in ISC. This is the formalised procedure to seek input from all other Commission DGs and Services and is done via a dedicated IT tool called **CIS-Net**. The ISC, and the use of CIS-Net, have been compulsory in the Commission since 2001 and about 40-60 ISCs are launched in the Commission every day. ISC is launched by the lead DG once the file is sufficiently advanced and needs formal adoption by the College. The DGs and Services consulted via ISC will often be similar to those who have already worked with the

Unit via ISCGs and IA Steering Groups - although there will now be additional compulsory consulted DGs and Services according to certain issues: for example, the SG will be consulted on any CWP item as it will be interested in the political ramifications and any institutional matters (such as Subsidiarity, Implementing and Delegated Acts, etc.); the Legal Service will be consulted on any draft legal acts (including Implementing and Delegated Acts) as well as any document with legal implications; DG Human Resources will be consulted on any proposal with personnel implications; DG Budget on any proposal with financial implications; OLAF on any proposal with the possibility for fraud; and finally DG Communication on any proposal with a possible impact on Commission communication policy.

When the Unit receives the green light from its Cabinet and where necessary from the relevant Commission Vice-President and the First Vice-President, it will get in touch with its **DG CIS-Net coordinator**, an official who coordinates all CIS-Net entries for the DG as a whole. The CIS-Net coordinators within the DGs organise specific access to CIS-Net for the DGs and see that procedures are followed. The draft proposal, and accompanying documentation, is entered into CIS-Net and the consultation is launched. All consulted parties receive the documentation and the deadline for responses - the minimum deadlines for answering are either 10 or 15 working days, depending on the size of the documents submitted to ISC.

Submission of texts to ISC is the point at which there is the most document leakage in the Commission. It is here that many stakeholders get hold of Commission proposals and are able to exert some influence over the ISC process. In this time consulted DGs and Services are expected to deliver one of three possible answers:

1. **Agreement:** The consulted DG, or Service, is in agreement with the documents circulated and has no comments to make.

2. **Favourable opinion subject to taking comments into account:** The consulted DG is in general agreement with the documents circulated, but has one, or a series, of comments that it would like the lead DG to take into account.

3. **Negative opinion:** The consulted DG has one, or several, objections to the content of the consulted documents.

There is one further possibility in the ISC, and that is that the consulted DG does not actually respond within the deadline. In this case automatic agreement is assumed in the form of a tacit accord after the deadline passes. In almost all cases consulted DGs will be prepared for ISC because they have already worked with the lead DG in the ISCG and they have already formed their positions. In the three cases above we need to elaborate on two of them. If a DG gives a '**favourable subject to comments**' opinion the lead DG is not obliged to take these comments into account - but it must justify to the DG concerned why it did not do so. If the lead DG receives negative opinions it is also not obliged to take them into account, so from a technical perspective it could continue with its proposal. From an internal political perspective this is, however, unlikely to happen because a

DG, and ultimately the Commissioner, will not want to leave these unresolved issues behind them. The lead DG and the DG(s) and/or Service(s) that placed the negative opinion(s) may have a bilateral meeting to try and iron out their differences and agree on a final ISC text.

The resulting ISC text will likely be a modified version of the original document submitted for consultation, the first of a series of modifications that are likely to take place to the text before final adoption by the College. Seeing the modifications, and where they came from, is a useful source of information on where, and with whom, stakeholders might want to work within the Commission. Working with consulted DGs in ISC is a very fruitful exercise if mapped and executed correctly. The philosophy behind the ISC boils down to the fact that one DG cannot go ahead on its own because it has to respect the principle of collegiality. Final Commission texts are therefore always the result of compromises between different internal perspectives and represent the Commission position.

Once the ISC is closed, the Unit, with the authorisation of the Director-General and the Commissioner's Cabinet, can submit the dossier for final approval of the College. As Figure 1.6 above highlighted there are four formal decision-making procedures in the Commission, and the lead DG has to follow one of these to get its file adopted.

Commission decision-making procedures

Oral Procedure (PO) (approx. 200 a year)
What: The College decides during its weekly meeting on issues that are sensitive, political or otherwise in need of the attention of the College. The President decides the agenda.
Documents: Major political or financial implications, CWP strategic priorities, no agreement among DGs and Services at ISC, need for discussion of College.

Written Procedure (PE) (approx. 3,000 a year)
What: The proposed decision is submitted to all members of the Commission (at Cabinet level) and is deemed adopted if there are no reservations stated within the deadline (Five days for a normal PE). Urgent PEs are possible and have a shortened deadline (usually three days).
Documents: Issues where all DGs and Services agree that a discussion by the full College is not needed, no negative opinions in ISC.

Empowerment (PH) (approx. 2,500 a year)
What: A mandate is given by the College in its meeting, or there is a standing mandate, to one or more College members to take measures in its name, under its responsibility within strict limits and conditions. Empowerment does not have to be exercised, but if it is the Commissioner, he/she must notify the next College meeting.
Documents: Management or administrative measures.

Delegation (DL) (approx. 4,000 a year)
What: The principle is exactly the same as the Empowerment Procedure but a Delegation can be given to a Director-General or Head of Service.
Documents: Management or administrative decisions with a more limited margin for discretion and manoeuvre.

The box above highlights the low number of Oral procedures (known internally by its French acronym PO - Procédure Orale) that are used each year, but this is a reflection of the fact that only the most important files are left for discussion and adoption by the College. It is also important to stress that all the decision-making procedures detailed in the box are the ultimate responsibility of the College.

Once the lead DG has chosen which procedure to submit their dossier under, their Unit will have to submit the full dossier into E-Greffe, the IT tool that manages this stage of the internal decision-making procedure. The dossier is not simply a single draft proposal, but an important collection of documents.

Table 1.3 Documents in the dossier submitted to E-Greffe

Obligatory documents submitted for approval by College
Act (in up to 24 languages) + Annexes. This is the only document to be 'adopted'.
Fiche de Renseignements - identity card of the file. Drafted by official in charge.
+ Supporting documents when necessary
Impact Assessment - the full version as drafted by the Unit.
Executive Summary of Impact Assessment - (in 24 languages) a short description of the main elements of the IA.
RSB opinion on the Impact Assessment
Financial information - if there is going to be financial incidence.
Results of Inter-Service Consultation
Committee voting results - If act is an Implementing Act that required a Committee vote.
Technical support documents, memos and info notes, Staff Working Papers, etc.

The course of the dossier depends, thus, on the decision-making procedure chosen, or imposed, within the Commission. It is important to consider the Written and Oral procedures in more detail because this is where the politically and financially important decisions are made.

1.8 How the European Commission works: Political decision-taking

Figure 1.7: Preparation of a dossier - Written and Oral adoption procedures

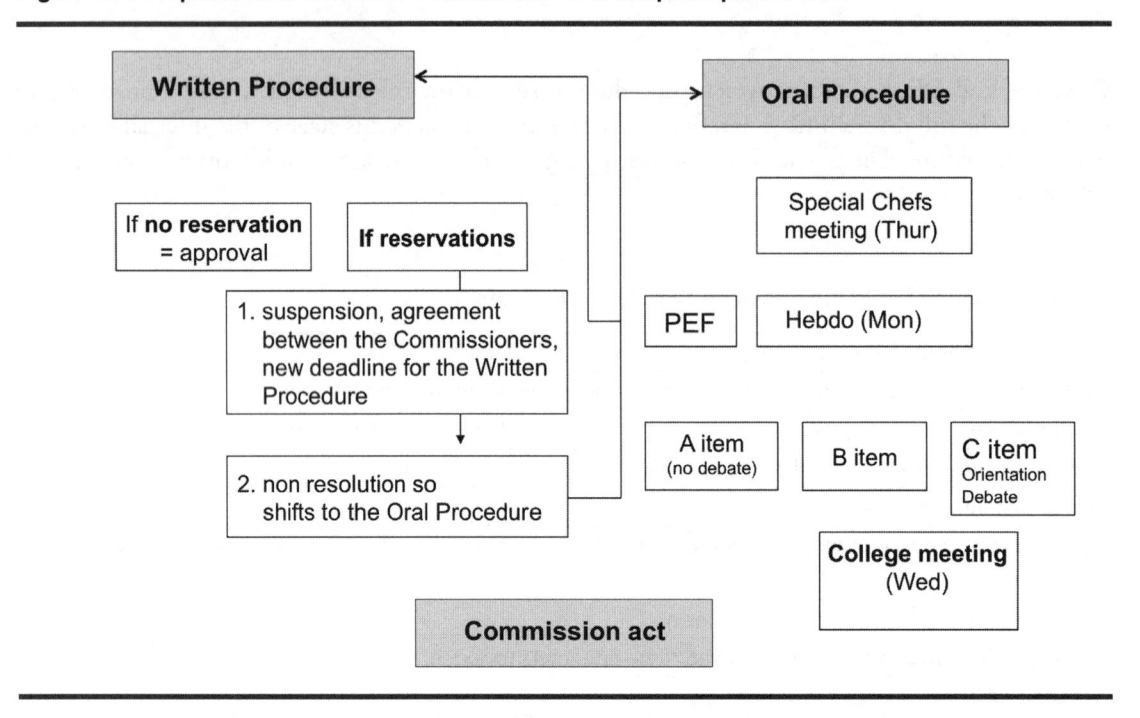

```
Written Procedure ←----------→ Oral Procedure

If no reservation    If reservations           Special Chefs
   = approval                                  meeting (Thur)

                  1. suspension, agreement
                     between the Commissioners,    PEF    Hebdo (Mon)
                     new deadline for the Written
                     Procedure
                                                 A item              C item
                                                (no debate)  B item  Orientation
                  2. non resolution so                                Debate
                     shifts to the Oral Procedure
                                                   College meeting
                                                       (Wed)
                  Commission act
```

The flowchart in Figure 1.7 details the processes of the **Written and Oral procedures**. The most widely used of the two is the Written procedure (known internally by its French acronym **PE - Procédure Écrite**). In this case the dossier that has been through ISC and needs College approval will be submitted, via the E-Greffe system, to every Cabinet. The Cabinets, acting on behalf of their Commissioner, have five working days to respond. Most cases will lead to no reservations being made, and the decision is therefore deemed to be adopted. This decision is taken on behalf of the College. When the deadline passes, the Registry, Directorate A of the SG, will ensure that all of the post decision-making formalities are respected, something we will come to a little later. If reservations are placed by one or more Cabinets then the Cabinet of the lead DG and the Cabinet(s) with reservations will have bilateral discussions to try and find common ground with a view to jointly opening a new Written procedure with a new deadline. If such an agreement proves impossible the dossier that was foreseen as Written procedure is switched to an Oral procedure item and it drops into the weekly Oral procedure cycle.

Table 1.4: The Oral procedure weekly cycle

Week	Day	Events
W-2	Thursday	**Delivery of files 48 hours before Special Chefs**
	Friday	
W-1	Monday	
	Tuesday	**Special Chefs**
	Wednesday	
	Thursday	**Special Chefs** Delivery of files
	Friday	
W	Monday	**HEBDO 11h00**
	Tuesday	Special Chefs
	Wednesday	**College Meeting 9h00**
	Thursday	Special Chefs Delivery of files
	Friday	
W+1	Monday	HEBDO 11h00
	Tuesday	
	Wednesday	College Meeting 9h00

The Oral procedure effectively operates over a two-week cycle, as outlined in Table 1.4. The objective of this system is the efficient preparation of the College meetings that take place, in general, every Wednesday on the thirteenth floor of the Berlaymont from 9h00, or on Tuesdays in Strasbourg when the Parliament has its Plenary weeks. The cycle starts on Thursday of week W-2, when the dossiers that are being placed in Oral procedure for College discussion and decision are uploaded into E-Greffe for transmission to all Cabinets. From this point we can address each stage in the process individually:

1. **The Special Chefs meetings** (Tuesdays and Thursdays): The initial discussions are those that take place in the Special Chefs configuration. These meetings are chaired by a member of the President's Cabinet and are composed of a member from each Commissioner's Cabinet, a Legal Service representative

   > **'Special' Special Chefs**
   >
   > If an issue needs in-depth discussion, a special meeting of the Special Chefs will be convened i.e. outside of the standing Tuesday and Thursday meetings.

   and the SG as the organiser of the meeting. In addition, the Cabinet member from the lead DG of a proposal under discussion can invite officials from their DG to accompany them on their specific files. In this sense this is the last involvement of the technical officials from DGs before the political decision-making takes over. The agenda for the meeting is done by drawing the dossiers that are ready for, or need, a decision or discussion from the Commission internal rolling four- to six-weekly agenda of all items on the Commission's immediate radar (known by its French acronym of **LPP** for **Liste des Points Prévus**). The objective of these meetings is to start preparing the next meeting of the College by holding in-depth discussions on the dossiers on the initial draft **Ordre du Jour (OJ)** - the meeting agenda for the College. The outcome of the discussions in the Special Chefs meeting is a more concrete OJ that is then sent to the Hebdo meeting of the Chefs de Cabinet, the next step in the process for approval and completion. The objective of the Special Chefs meeting is to find agreement where possible and highlight sensitivities for the Chefs de Cabinet, and if needed the College, to deal with. The Special Chefs meetings work from the text that came out of ISC, likely to be version II of a proposal. The Special Chefs can also make modifications during their meetings which can lead to them sending a version III to the next step in the process.

2. **The Hebdo meetings:** The Hebdo meeting is the weekly meeting of the Chefs de Cabinet that takes place in the Berlaymont every Monday. The Hebdo meeting is chaired by the Secretary-General and is composed of the Heads of all the Commissioners' Cabinets, the Director-General of the Legal Service and the Director-General of the Spokesperson's Service. This Monday meeting has the objective of finalising the agenda for the College meeting by splitting the decisions that need to be taken into:

> **Finalisation Written Procedure**
>
> This procedure was introduced in 2007 by President Barroso. A dossier is submitted into E-Greffe as an Oral Procedure and hence goes into the weekly cycle, ending with the Chefs de Cabinet on a Monday morning. At this meeting they can decide to switch the dossier to a Written Procedure, and simultaneously decide when the Written Procedure will expire. This switch has a double objective:
>
> - Better timing of press conferences because there is more control of when to announce news - not everything 'big' is decided on a Wednesday.
> - College will discuss only the key issues.

- **A item:** Hebdo has found agreement, therefore to be adopted without discussion.
- **B item:** Hebdo has not found agreement, therefore College discussion is needed before decision. There are also a number of so-called 'false B' items, where there is agreement but also a need for visibility, thus College discussion.
- **C Item:** Orientation debates: Where the College needs to hold a broader discussion around an issue, or current event. At the end of the Hebdo meeting, an agenda will be in place for the next College meeting, which usually has four to ten 'B' items and a series of 'A' items for adoption. It is also at the Hebdo that a fifth decision-making procedure is possible - the **Finalisation Written procedure** (see box). The minutes of the Hebdo meeting are called the **Compte Rendu (CR)** and they are sent to the College meeting with the agenda and documents (they are not made public).

3. **The College meetings:** As mentioned earlier, the College meets once a week in Brussels or Strasbourg. The President can also call special meetings on his own initiative or at the request of one or more Commissioners. The President chairs the meeting and presents the agenda items

in order. 'A' items will therefore be adopted at the meeting without any discussion, and 'B' items will be subject to discussion and adoption or deferral. If a 'B' item is deferred it will fall back into the weekly cycle for further discussion, or be sent back to the DG responsible for further work and modifications. Formally the Commission Rules of Procedure foresee that the College can vote by simple majority but in practice the College tends to decide by consensus - despite some very difficult and controversial dossiers passing through the College.

The College meeting minutes, called the **Procès-Verbal (PV)**, are drawn up by the SG after the meeting. These are drawn up in two parts. The first part is general information on the matters discussed and the decisions that will be made public. These minutes are duly posted on the website of the SG. The second part of the minutes is the restricted section which contains other decisions, any votes held and any declarations specific Commissioners wanted entered in the minutes. (You can find all these PVs at http://ec.europa.eu/transparency/regdoc/index.cfm?fuseaction=list&coteId=10061). In general, the best source of information on what happened in a College meeting is the press, which is usually a better source of information than the press conference that takes place in the Berlaymont after the College meeting. They will report, on Thursdays, in some detail the discussions of the previous day's meeting.

The College meeting represents the culmination of the work of the Commission whereby the final political choices are made on the basis of all the technical and supporting material that has been provided by the DGs and Services. The final aspect of the Commission internal procedure, concerns the transmission of the draft proposal, outlined in Figure 1.8 below.

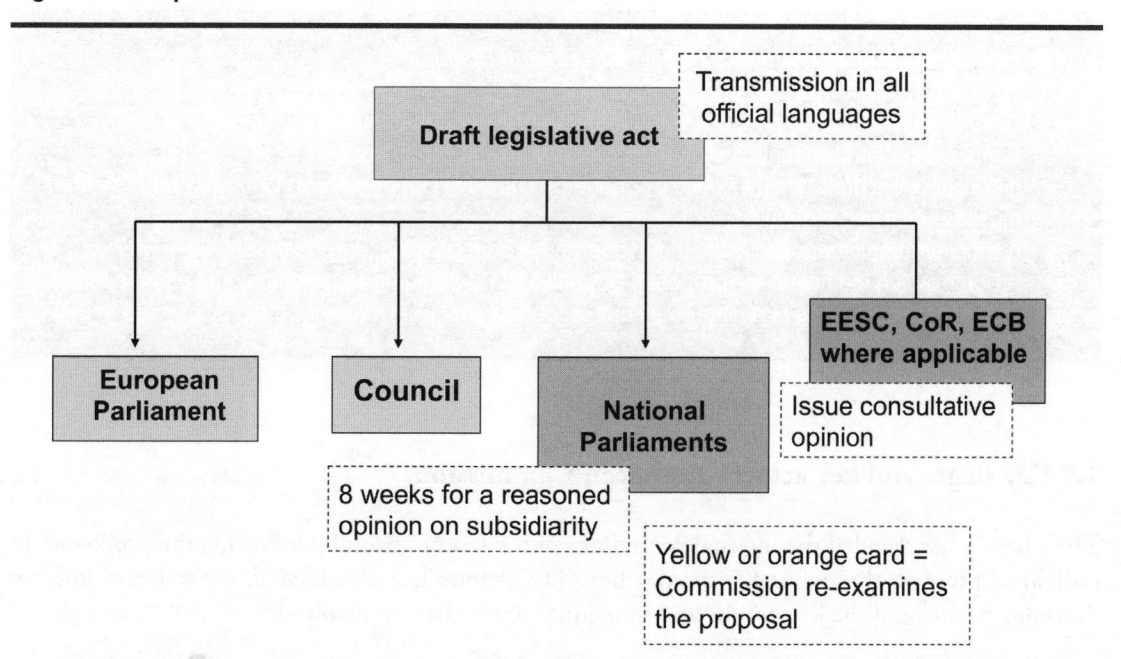

Figure 1.8: Preparation of a dossier - Transmission

The SG within the Commission is responsible for the transmission of draft legislative acts to the other institutions, for the notification to external addressees (certified documents) and also for the publication in the Official Journal of decisions taken by the Commission. Of most interest in the context of this book is the transmission of documents to the other institutions, as illustrated by Figure 1.8. The SG is responsible for making sure that the Commission proposal is correctly transmitted along with the key accompanying documents (such as the IA). Only the most important legislative proposals are adopted by the College on a Wednesday and here the Registry is tasked with sending all the relevant documents, in all the relevant languages (if legislative, 23 or 24), within 48 hours to the institutions that require these documents. The majority of legislative proposals are adopted by Written procedure and are thus not necessarily finalised on a Wednesday, in which case their transmission can take place on any day of the week.

First and foremost the documents need to be sent to the co-legislators, the Parliament and the Council, for the formal start of their decision-making procedure. The legislators will not formally start their clock until they receive all language versions. In addition, the Commission is also legally obliged, in a series of determined cases, to send the proposal to the European Economic and Social Committee (EESC) and the Committee of the Regions (CoR). All of these institutions and bodies will be dealt with in later chapters of this book. The starting point of all of these chapters, on the internal decision-making of the institutions, is the transmission of the draft legislative act from the Commission as seen above. The final obligatory recipients of Commission legislative proposals, following the entry into force of the Treaty of Lisbon, are the national parliaments, who are required to have the documents to enact their eight-week subsidiarity check. It is also now common practice for the Commission to send national parliaments all other official documents (outside their legal obligations) that they send to the European Parliament.

The role of National Parliaments *(Article 12 TEU and Protocol 1)*

- Each Member State accorded 2 votes (may be one per chamber if applicable).
- Eight weeks for a reasoned opinion on subsidiarity and proportionality.
- If 1/3 oppose a draft (1/4 for Police Cooperation / Judicial Cooperation in Criminal Matters), draft must be reviewed (so-called 'yellow card').
- If simple majority opposes draft, it must be reviewed (so-called 'orange card').
- If Commission maintains the proposal, Council and Parliament may take account of the position of national parliaments and either may halt procedure (55% of Council or majority of votes in EP).

1.9 Key stages and key actors - European Commission

This chapter has detailed the internal procedures of the Commission by following the process of an individual proposal through the entire pipeline. The chapter has identified all the stages of internal decision-making and the key groups and individual actors that are involved.

The first division that needs to be stressed in the work of the Commission is that between the technical and political. The work of the Commission is all under the collegiate responsibility of the College at the very highest political level. It is the weekly meeting of the College that takes the decisions and then assumes the political responsibility for them. Below the College, yet still political, is the level of the Commissioner's Cabinet where the objective is to ensure that the interests of the Commissioner and DG are adequately represented and defended across the Commission. It is at this level that conflict is resolved and outstanding technical details are finalised for College approval. The Chefs de Cabinet provide the essential link between ultimate political decision-making and the technical details of all proposals and dossiers. It is the Chefs de Cabinet who agree on the College agenda, with the ability to designate 'A' items and switch Oral procedures to Finalisation Written procedures. The interface between technical and political is the Special Chefs meetings, where members of the Cabinet discuss detailed proposals with lead DG technical officials for the last time.

At the technical level, the lead DG is obviously the most important actor driving a proposal through all the various stages of Commission decision-making. The principal powers of the Unit in the lead DG are the fact that it has done all the research and consultation and it has all the facts and information at its disposal, and also the fact that it drafts the original proposal. Knowing the members of the Unit is a pre-requisite to engaging with them on any issue, and this should be done through meetings and e-mail exchanges (not lunches and dinners) - in a structured manner and not via a one-off meeting. (One thing worth noting, that we will come back to in later chapters, is that officials in all the institutions talk to each other – so what you say in one setting can often migrate to another one.) Whilst these powers are important, they need to be put into context because the lead DG must, at all times, collaborate closely with other interested DGs through the IA Steering Group and the ISCG and then finally through the formal and obligatory ISC and final decision-making procedures for the College. Through these interactions, draft proposals presented by the lead DG are often altered in small, but important, ways for the sake of collegiality.

From this analysis the main actors (in chronological order) in the elaboration of a Commission proposal are as follows:

Table 1.5: Key stages and key actors: The European Commission

Key stage	Comment	Key actors
Political Guidelines State of the Union	The overarching political guidelines have, over time, become increasingly Presidential documents. **Key** for political direction and major political issues.	The President Secretariat-General President's Cabinet
Commission Work Programme	The CWP is the technical translation of the political priorities. The annex is an outline of what to expect in the next 12-24 months - a key planning document. **Key** for individual issues and 12-24 month planning.	First Vice-President Secretariat-General DGs

Key stage	Comment	Key actors
Impact Assessment	The IA is the most important part of the drafting process as it will have a direct bearing on the text of the proposal. The lead DG must form an IA Steering Group to assist its work. **Key** for detail of a proposal - will underpin legislative proposal.	Unit within lead DG Secretariat-General IA Steering Group members RSB
External consultation	The lead DG can choose to use an Expert Group, open consultations, hold hearings as well as have informal contacts. Interested Units in other DGs will also use their informal contacts for their specific interests. **Key** for the detail of a proposal - the Unit will need to find (and justify) a compromise position.	Unit within lead DG Units within associated DGs Expert Groups
Inter-Service Consultation	Once the IA is sufficiently advanced, the Unit in the lead DG will turn to drafting a legislative proposal and this it will do accompanied by an ISCG. Once the lead DG Unit is ready to submit the file for formal ISC it will seek Cabinet approval. **Key** internal process for finding Inter-service positions. Important, and detailed, changes can be made.	*Informal:* Inter-Service Coordination Group *Formal:* CIS-net Inter-Service Consultation Units in other DGs Lead DG Cabinet Cabinet of responsible Vice-President Other DG Cabinets in case of problems
Special Chefs	The Special Chef meeting is an important interaction with technical Services as they try to put together a draft College meeting agenda. **Key** meeting to finalise agreement, iron out technical differences and highlight potential political problems.	President's Cabinet Members of Cabinets Lead DG Unit officials Legal Service
Hebdo	The weekly Chefs de Cabinet meeting is tasked with finalising the College agenda. It also has a considerable discretionary power to take decisions. **Key** meeting that can take important decisions and make important changes.	Chefs de Cabinets Secretary-General

Key stage	Comment	Key actors
College meeting	The decision-taking body of the Commission meets once a week to take final decisions, give political impetus and take responsibility for the actions of the Commission as a whole. **Key** political decision-taking body.	President Commissioners Members of Cabinets

Every proposal that needs to be adopted by the College will go through the stages outlined in Table 1.5, and all of the people identified will play a role (which will be different on a case by case basis). The exact role will, of course, depend on the issue at stake and also to an extent in how external stakeholders engage in the processes detailed here. The volumes of procedures, documents and decisions also highlights that the officials identified here are involved in a significant number of dossiers at any given time. It is important, however, to be able to clearly identify and map all the different internal stages and actors so as to be able to interact with the most relevant people at the most opportune moments. Practical guidance on how to work with the Commission, individually, and as part of a wider engagement strategy, will be taken up in Section 3 of the book (notably in Chapter 8.2).

2. The Council of the EU and the European Council

By Sabina Kajnč Lange[1]

The **Council of the European Union** (most commonly referred to as the **Council of Ministers**, and **in short form simply as the Council**) lies at the heart of EU decision-making. It brings together the 28 EU Member States at the level of Ministers. It is first and foremost an EU legislative body, sharing its legislative powers in an ever increasing number of areas with the Parliament. Although there is only one Council, it takes decisions in various configurations, depending on the policy field, with foreign policy-making forming a world of its own. Its work is prepared in numerous preparatory bodies of a diverse nature, meeting in the Council's Justus Lipsius building in Brussels, under the watchful eyes of the rotating Presidency (see below) and with the support of the **General Secretariat of the Council (GSC)** - while the work in the capitals of the Member States also feeds into the work of the Council.

The **European Council** brings together Heads of State or Government of the Member States, together with its President and the President of the Commission, and is charged with giving momentum and direction in the development of the EU. The European Council was established as a body in 1974, after a series of 'Summit meetings' at the highest political level in the Member States in the 1960s and was finally turned into a fully-fledged institution of the EU with the Lisbon Treaty. The Council of the European Union and the European Council are together often portrayed as obstacles to European integration, downsizing the pro-European initiatives of the Commission in attempts to safeguard national interests.

> **Which Council?**
>
> **The Council**, also referred to as the Council of Ministers or the Council of the European Union, is one of the three key EU institutions, together with the Parliament and the Commission.
>
> **The European Council** became an EU institution with the entry into force of the Treaty of Lisbon. It provides the Union with the necessary impetus for its development and defines the general political directions and priorities.
>
> **The Council of Europe** is not part of the EU but a separate pan-European organisation based in Strasbourg, whose primary aim is to promote human rights.

---

[1] The author would like to express special thanks to Daniela Cuciureanu for background research and for her valuable comments on earlier stages of the chapter.

Quite often confused with the Council and the European Council is the **Council of Europe**, whose seat is in Strasbourg. This is *not* an institution of the European Union. The Council of Europe was established by the 1949 Treaty of London and therefore pre-dates the creation of what is now the EU by the Rome Treaties of 1957. It is an intergovernmental organisation comprising both EU and non-EU European states which operates primarily through the adoption of conventions, the first and most important of which is the 1950 European Convention for the Protection of Human Rights and Fundamental Freedoms. The European Court of Human Rights, sitting in Strasbourg, exists to hear cases involving the Convention. It is unrelated to the Court of Justice of the European Union, which sits in Luxembourg.

This chapter will focus mainly on the Council of Ministers, in view of its legislative role, but in the following section we will first outline the main characteristics and roles of the European Council.

2.1 The European Council

There are a number of characteristics which make the Council and European Council easy to differentiate. Firstly, their composition: while the Council of Ministers (as the name suggests) is composed of Ministers from Member State governments, the European Council is composed of Heads of State or Government (thus Presidents or Prime Ministers, depending on the constitutional order of the Member State), together with the President of the European Commission. The Lisbon Treaty created a new position of semi-permanent **President of the European Council**. This post was first held by former Belgian Prime Minister Herman van Rompuy, who was succeeded in December 2014 by Donald Tusk, who stepped down as Polish Prime Minister. The High Representative of the Union for Foreign Affairs and Security Policy (the 'High Representative') also takes part in its work. In contrast, the **Presidency of the Council of Ministers** rotates on a six-monthly basis among the Member States.

A second distinguishing characteristic is the nature of the decisions taken: the Council is mainly a legislative and executive body (it also has other functions which will be explained in detail later). The European Council does not have legislative functions, but it is the highest body for setting the strategic goals and direction for the Union, as well as being the last instance in striking compromises in negotiations. A third important difference derives directly from the previous one - the way in which decisions are taken. While the Council is characterised by complex decision-making rules and a weighted voting system (in place since the European Communities were set up, but being phased out with the Lisbon Treaty), the European Council largely operates by consensus.

The key facts on the European Council are found in Table 2.1.

Table 2.1: European Council - Key facts

Roles:	General political direction
	Priorities of the Union
	High-level political discussions
Established:	1974 (as a political body), 2009 (as an EU institution)
President:	Donald Tusk (as of 1 December 2014)
Term:	2.5 years - renewable once
Location:	Brussels

Though European Council meetings originated in summits held in the 1960s and were brought within the realm of the European Communities' Treaties with the Single European Act in 1986, it was given the formal status of an EU institution only with the Lisbon Treaty in December 2009. The European Council is often portrayed as a defender of intergovernmentalism and national interests in the EU, but its composition, which includes the President of the Commission and now also a full-time President who does not hold a national mandate, as well as the participation of the High Representative in its work, makes such claims more relative. The European Council is the highest level political body in the Union, charged with giving political guidance and defining the priorities. It also nominates the President of the Commission, the High Representative, and the Commission as a whole (after the approval by the EP), as well as choosing its own President.

The European Council meets at least four times a year. It has become customary for the European Council to concentrate on the economic situation in the Union at its spring meeting and to look at monetary policy and enlargement at its autumn meeting. The other two meetings traditionally take place before the end of the six-month term in office of the rotating Presidency of the Council of Ministers (such terms running from January - June and from July - December). Additional meetings can be convened by the President if the situation so requires. Such additional meetings were a feature of the Presidency of Herman van Rompuy as European leaders sought to tackle the financial crisis and its consequences. Occasional thematic one day meetings have also become customary. Since the second half of 2003, the European Council meetings take place in Brussels and no longer in the country of the Council Presidency. Meetings of the European Council are often accompanied by many demonstrations, protests and road blocks in Brussels making travel around Rond-Point Schuman very difficult on these days (important to be aware of if one is planning a meeting in the area).

A meeting of the European Council can last one day or be spread over two days, starting on the afternoon of the first day and finishing at lunch time of the following day, not rarely with negotiations stretching long into the evening hours and compromise papers appearing in the early morning hours. Delegations, whose size is limited to 20 official staff (excluding technical staff), usually arrive on the previous afternoon to participate in numerous bilateral and multilateral meetings. It is customary for the leadership of the Political Groups from the Parliament to meet on the evening before the European

Council with the Heads of State or Government belonging to their Political Group. Several bilateral meetings also take place over breakfast on the morning of the day of the meeting itself, with the President of the European Council also meeting Heads of Delegations bilaterally or in smaller groups to facilitate later negotiations. The President of the European Parliament addresses the European Council (but does not participate in its meetings).

> It is always important to keep an eye on **European Council Conclusions** as they indicate priorities for the Commission and the legislators and set a particular direction for the Commission's policy choices. They can request the European Commission to prepare legislative proposals, reports or other forms of action.

Prior to the Lisbon Treaty's entry into force, European Council meetings were the highlight of the rotating Council Presidency's activity. With the creation of the post of full-time President of the European Council, the Treaties charge him or her with the preparation of European Council meetings (and also the follow-up to them), proposing the agenda of the meetings and the preparation of the conclusions of meetings, building on the work of the General Affairs Council (GAC, see section 2.5) and in close cooperation with the country holding the rotating Presidency. At the end of the six-month Council Presidency term the Head of State or Government of the country holding the rotating Presidency reports to the European Council, in consultation with the President of the European Council, on progress achieved in the Council.

The President of the European Council also chairs the meeting. He is no longer 'first among equals', but is entirely dedicated to serving the European Council, although without a vote. There have been many characterisations of this new role, but Van Rompuy as the first holder of the office defined it as that of 'facilitator', preparing the ground and brokering compromises among Member States.

With 28 Member States involved, European Council meetings are a far cry from the original intention of small intimate gatherings of national government leaders. With successive rounds of enlargement those participating in meetings became so numerous that the Lisbon Treaty made a significant change - Foreign Ministers no longer have an automatic seat at the table, though the Heads of State or Government may be joined by a Minister with responsibility for the subject under discussion. A representative of the GSC orally briefs the group of senior officials from all the Member States seated in a neighbouring room (the Antici, see later in chapter) who then inform their respective Delegations.

The outcome of European Council meetings is **European Council Conclusions** which can touch on a variety of subjects with annexed strategic documents and declarations which provide guidance for the future work of the Council of Ministers. A press conference is held after the meeting, jointly by the President of the European Council and the President of the Commission. Press briefings during and after the European Council are also given by staff members from all Delegations. Shortly afterwards the President of the European Council presents the achievements of the meeting to the Plenary session of the Parliament.

The European Council is the tip of the iceberg of EU politics. The President of the European Council and his Cabinet, and the support provided by the GSC, give the European Council a solid presence in Brussels and ensure that it is well-integrated into the EU structures. Van Rompuy and European Commission President Barroso institutionalised their joint 'Monday breakfasts', and the Cabinet of the President of the European Council works closely with the rotating Council Presidency to ensure continuity in the work of the Council and the European Council. The prominence and visibility of the European Council were increased by its involvement in the handling of the economic and financial crises, especially between 2010 and 2012.

2.2 The Council

The key facts of the Council can be found below in Table 2.2.

Table 2.2: Council - Key facts

Names:	The Council of the EU, the Council of Ministers, the Council
Role:	EU (co-)legislative and (co-)executive body
Established:	1952, 1958 (separate for the three Communities), 1967 (a single Council)
Presidency:	rotating, among Member States (six months term)
Decision-taking body:	Council (10 configurations)
Internal structure:	Working Parties/Groups (approx. 160)
	Committees
	COREPER, parts 1 and 2
	Council of Ministers
	General Secretariat of the Council
Working languages:	24 official and working languages
Location:	Brussels, Luxembourg

As the key facts in Table 2.2 show, the Council is not only complex with regard to its roles and structures, but also because of its rotating Presidency, with a different Member State taking the steering wheel of the Council's machinery every six months (with the exception of the Foreign Affairs Council). In this sense the Council is the most intangible of the EU institutions due to its nature of being a body of national decision-makers, which stretches it (and its legitimacy base) right back to the Member State capitals. In addition, the Council also uses all EU official languages. Though in practice only a handful of meetings take place in full interpretation regime (all 24 official languages), and more and more meetings are taking place in a lesser number of languages or without interpretation altogether, the fact that all documentation for Council meetings needs to be translated into all the official languages is an onerous burden on the work of the Council Secretariat. In addition to these linguistic challenges there are a number of separate working language regimes within the Council structures which further affects the workings of the Council, and attempts to work with it.

The Council's headquarters are in Brussels in the Justus Lipsius building on the opposite side of the street from the Commission's Berlaymont building on the rue de la Loi. The Ministers meet here, all the preparatory meetings take place in its meeting rooms and the GSC is based in the building (though it also has other premises in buildings nearby). While each Member State has its delegation room in the building, Member State representatives coming to the preparatory (and Council) meetings are either based at the Permanent Representations scattered around the 'European district' in Brussels or in the Member State capitals. In the months of April, June and October the Council, as a decision-taking body (i.e. the Ministers), meets in Luxembourg. In comparison to the monthly move of the Parliament to Strasbourg, the Council's move is on a much lower scale, meaning that not all the GSC's services are present in Luxembourg.

The rotating system of the Presidency had long been a source of confusion and even frustration to those trying to deal with the EU; every six months a new Head of State or Government would lead the European Council, a new country represented the EU externally and a new set of priorities seemed to have been developed for the work of the Council. However, the system remained virtually unchanged until it was reformed by the Lisbon Treaty in 2009, with the aim of achieving more continuity and a stable leadership in the EU. By introducing the post of the permanent President of the European Council, and with the Foreign Affairs Council Presidency being taken over by the new High Representative, the rotating Presidency has been curtailed and the role of President of the European Council decoupled from it. Nevertheless, the rotating Presidency still remains in place and still holds the Presidency of nine (out of ten) Council formations. The General Secretariat of the Council serves both institutions and thus provides a link at the service level, supporting coherence and continuity in the work of both institutions.

2.3 The roles of the Council

The Council brings together representatives of the Member States who are able to make decisions on behalf of their respective governments. First and foremost the Council's role is to safeguard national interests while acting on the basis of the Treaties. The Treaties not only define the scope of the action, but also the competences of the Union, which affect the powers of the Council as well as the way in which it takes decisions.

The Treaty (Article 16.1 TEU) clearly defines the **legislative and budgetary powers** of the Council (both exercised jointly with the Parliament) and extends its powers to carrying out policy-making and coordinating functions. The more the legislative and budgetary powers came to be shared with the Parliament, the more the **policy-making and coordinating powers** grew in scope and importance. Although the Commission is the primary executive body in the EU, the Council exercises **executive powers** in some specific cases as well.

The **primary role**, and the primary activity, of the Council is the exercise of its legislative powers. No legislative decision in the EU is taken without the Council's involvement and approval. The way in which it decides, the procedure (and with it the involvement of other actors) and the nature of the act adopted, despite it having been simplified to an extent, still varies. The first key element of how the Council works relates to the way it votes.

Figure 2.1: Voting in the Council

	Pop. (2014)	Votes
Germany	80.5	29
France	65.6	29
UK	63.7	29
Italy	59.7	29
Spain	46.7	27
Poland	38.5	27
Romania	20.1	14
Netherlands	16.8	13
Greece	11.2	12
Belgium	11.1	12
Portugal	10.5	12
Czech Rep.	10.5	12
Hungary	9.9	12
Sweden	9.6	10
Austria	8.5	10
Bulgaria	7.3	10
Denmark	5.6	7
Slovakia	5.4	7
Finland	5.4	7
Ireland	4.6	7
Croatia	4.3	7
Lithuania	3.0	7
Latvia	2.1	4
Slovenia	2.0	4
Estonia	1.3	4
Cyprus	0.9	4
Luxembourg	0.5	4
Malta	0.4	3
EU 28	**505.6**	**352**

QMV until 30 October 2014 and if requested by 31 March 2017

⬇

The votes must be cast by a majority of Member States *(2/3 of Member States if not on Commission proposal)*

Qualified majority of votes is 260 *(= 73.9% of votes)*
Blocking minority is 93

A Member State may request verification that the qualified majority of votes represents 62% of population

QMV since 1 November 2014

⬇

55% Members States
65% EU population
Blocking minority must comprise at least 4 MS

The Lisbon Treaty introduced a break with the **weighted voting system** which had been in place since the European Coal and Steel Community was established. The new, much-simplified system of a dual majority of Member States and population, only came into effect in November 2014. In order for a decision to be adopted a **qualified majority** of at least 55% of Member States, which comprise 65% of the Union's population, needs to vote in favour of a decision.

An additional rule states that at least four countries are needed to block a decision. Theoretically there could be as few as three countries representing more than 35% of the EU's population, thus forming a so-called 'blocking minority' - the minority which prevents the Council from reaching a qualified majority to adopt a decision.

> **Passerelle Clauses**
>
> These are clauses within the Treaty of Lisbon that allow the European Council to unanimously decide on:
> - changes in voting in the Council;
> - change from SLP to OLP;
> - specific policy areas or issues to be subject to QMV or OLP.

The old system of majorities with the distribution of votes as shown in Figure 2.1 can be used on the request of at least one Member State until the end of March 2017. Qualified majority is a general rule, unless the Treaties provide otherwise. The first alternative is **simple majority** which is mainly used for procedural issues, but also in cases where Council requests the Commission to undertake any study it considers desirable for the attainment of the common objectives and to submit to it any appropriate proposals (Article 241 TFEU). The second alternative is **unanimity** which is needed mostly for (non-implementing) decisions in the areas of Common Foreign and Security Policy (CFSP) and Common Security and Defence Policy (CSDP) (which are non-legislative in nature), in some policies in the area of freedom, justice and security, as well as in Passerelle Clauses (entrusted to the European Council, see box above) and for establishing Enhanced Cooperation. These also characterise most decisions taken by Special Legislative Procedures (SLP), requiring the consent or consultation of the Parliament. Unanimity is also needed in the Ordinary Legislative Procedure (OLP) in cases where the Council wants to adopt changes to the Commission's proposal without the Commission's agreement to these changes (see Chapter 5 for more detail).

Though qualified majority is the rule, it is, however, important to understand that a highly consensual tradition and practice have become cemented in the functioning of the Council. Being aware of the long-term nature of EU integration, the Council strives to accommodate as many national interests as possible and, at the same time and with increasing difficulty, reach an agreement with the European Parliament under the OLP. An estimated 85% of all decisions which could have been taken by a qualified majority are in fact taken by **consensus**. This has wider implications for the nature of negotiations (it is a long-term relationship, which does not end after the adoption of one act and decisions often come in packages) and often for the character of adopted measures (compromises with transition periods, exemptions, differentiations, etc.). Given the importance of the population factor and the vast differences in size of population among the Member States, it might easily be assumed that the big Member States are more influential and dominate proceedings in Council. While this partly holds true, one should never neglect the influence and expertise of smaller Member States, especially on specific issues and dossiers. It is often the case that certain smaller Member States can steer the direction of the debate with convincing arguments - and they are often the source of compromises. Therefore due attention should always be given to all Member States in the Council.

Since the Lisbon Treaty the OLP is, as the name suggests, the ordinary way of taking legislative decisions. The procedure is described in detail in Chapter 5. Worth pointing out here are the agenda-setting practices in the Council with regard to the files in OLP. While the deadlines are fixed once the Council has adopted its position in the first reading (if it is not in total agreement with the Parliament's position), the first reading is itself completely free of time pressure, and it is usually up to the Presidency to decide whether or not to put the file on the Council's agenda. Since most legislative files are now concluded with first reading agreements, the negotiations with the EP take place at this stage. The Presidency will be in close touch with the rapporteur in the Parliament in order to find possible compromises between the two institutions. The Presidency thus has a key role in finding and steering compromises through the Council. One should always keep track of the discussions taking place between the two legislative institutions and the compromise proposals coming from the Presidency. The role of the Presidency at this stage can prove to be quite instrumental.

The Presidency is of course not entirely free to choose which files to put on the agenda and which not, even in the first reading. The **Trio 18-month Presidency programme** which outlines the activities of the three successive Presidencies (the 18-month programme was introduced in 2007 in order to tackle the problems of discontinuity and varying priorities every six months) provides guidance. The programme itself is prepared by the three Presidencies (heavily assisted by the GSC) in close cooperation with the Commission, and since the entry into force of the Lisbon Treaty, also the President of the European Council and the High Representative for the **Foreign Affairs Council (FAC)**. This means that decisions on what to put on the agenda are already, to a certain extent, taken when setting up the 18-month programme, thus giving a rough sense of orientation on what the Council intends to deal with in the coming 18 months. The actual operational programme under the term of each Presidency is fine-tuned in the last month before the beginning of each Presidency, taking into consideration progress under the previous Presidency, the Commission's Work Programme, and also when the incoming Presidency tries to find agreements with the Parliament on cooperation in terms of agenda-setting for files in OLP. It is thus only in this period that it becomes a lot clearer which files are going to be prioritised and put on the agenda of the Council, and for the OLP files by definition also of the Parliament, in the coming six month period.

Though the OLP is the most common procedure, the **Special Legislative Procedures (SLP)** are characterised by the greater role of the Council. There is more than one type of SLP and they vary in terms of the majority needed in the Council (usually unanimity, but qualified majority in the case of specific R&D programmes) and by the nature of the involvement of the Parliament. In some cases the latter is only consulted (among them tax harmonisation, approximation of laws, measures in energy policy with a fiscal character, sensitive areas of social policy, family law with cross-border implications, operational police cooperation and system of own resources); in other cases the consent of the Parliament is required (e.g. in actions to combat discrimination, strengthening citizens' rights, the establishment of a European Public Prosecutor's Office, implementing measures for system of own resources). Furthermore, there are still areas of decision-making with no involvement of the Parliament (such as measures on fixing prices, levies, aid and quantitative limitations on the fixing and allocation of fishing opportunities, approving state aid in exceptional circumstances, implementing measures to freeze assets). The procedure for the adoption of the Annual Budget is also a special legislative procedure. Before approaching any institution it is important to clarify under which procedure, with what majorities, and with what involvement of the Parliament and the Commission the issue in question is to be adopted.

The Council's role as **budgetary authority** is of course extremely important and hardly a year passes without intense and difficult negotiations with the EP in an effort to settle the budget appropriations for the coming year. After a series of budgetary crises in the 1980s a multiannual financial perspective, also known as the **Multiannual Financial Framework (MFF)**, was introduced in order to set the broader lines for the period across several years (the most recent perspectives have covered seven years), which would make the Annual Budgets less vulnerable to the negotiating powers of the institutions. With the Lisbon Treaty the budgetary procedure has been simplified, reducing the number of readings to one, after which there is a Conciliation meeting should there be no agreement in the first reading. Between 2010 and 2014 all Annual Budgets for the Union were adopted in time, though the Conciliation meeting was convened each year and the Commission submitted new budget proposals for 2011, 2013 and 2015 after the failure of the two budgetary authorities to agree in Conciliation.

It is important to understand that since the Lisbon Treaty (and for the first time in 2010) the Parliament and the Council have an equal say over the entire budget. The MFF, however, is according to the Treaty adopted by the Council unanimously, after obtaining the consent of the Parliament. Given that the MFF needs to be observed in adopting the Annual Budget, we could, on a strict reading of the Treaty, claim that by setting the contours via the MFF, the Council limits the action of the Parliament. This is legally speaking true, and, the Parliament is aware of that, which is why it also strives to assert its role in the process of the adoption of the MFF.

The **policy-making function of the Council** is widely understood to be prevalent in the areas which do not fall under the exclusive or shared competences of the Union, but are subject to coordinating and supporting or supplementing competences of the Union. The Council adopts non-binding measures primarily in order to coordinate economic and employment policy. The Europe 2020 Strategy, which has succeeded the Lisbon Strategy, and the European Semester, which brings together coordination of Member States' fiscal, macroeconomic and structural policies, provide the framework for coordination in these policies. Other areas in which the Council coordinates are industrial policy, research and technological development, space and most aspects of public health policy. In exercising its coordinating function the Council usually adopts guidelines in the form of **Council Conclusions** or Council recommendations. The most obvious policy-making in the Council, with the aim of coordinating Member State policies, is in the area of foreign policy, more specifically CFSP, including the CSDP. However, Member States exercise their policy-making function across all areas where the Council acts as a legislator. In the initiation phase of the EU policy cycle, the representatives of the Member States take part in the expert and consultative bodies. In the decision-making phase, Member States (as the Council) scrutinise and amend the Commission's proposal. In the implementation phase, Member States provide an opinion on the Commission's draft Implementing Acts and in the Council they can object to Delegated Acts (see Chapter 6). This means that the Member States, both individually and acting collectively in Council, are a crucial actor all through the EU policy-making process even if the interventions of the Member States, and their room for manoeuvre, can change from file to file and during the policy cycle stages.

A distinction can be made between representatives of the Member States who take part in the decision-making processes of the Council because they represent the position of their Member State, usually via an explicit mandate, and those officials from Member States who sit in Committees scrutinizing proposed Implementing Acts and/or Expert Groups. These national officials are only very rarely based in Brussels and come from the Member State capitals only for the purposes of the meetings. In these cases the officials often have a greater margin of influence over their positions, notably because they are usually the technical experts in the domain. This distinction is important if you are trying to approach a national official - because knowing their room for manoeuvre and possibilities will condition how you can work with them. It is therefore important to clearly establish in what capacity and in what relationship to the decision-making authorities, representatives from the Member States take part in these meetings – something that will be discussed in more detail in Chapter 8.3.

Lastly, there are some **executive powers** that the Council shares with the Commission. There are three aspects to this. One is the implementation of EU legislation and (coordinated) policies at the national level, which gives Member States (and not the Council) the executive powers. The other is the involvement of the Council in the implementing stage of EU policies via Implementing and Delegated Acts (dealt with in detail in Chapter 6). And, thirdly, there are a limited number of areas in which the Council acts as the body in charge of exercising implementing powers itself. The area of CFSP is partially subject to this (e.g. the missions in the framework of the CSDP) as well as monitoring economic developments in the Member States and the EU.

Having reviewed the functions of the Council, we will now turn to the internal structures which enable it to carry out these roles.

2.4 Internal structure of the Council

This section explains the main elements of the Council architecture - with the objective of detailing the key actors and structures. Figure 2.2 outlines the broad picture of the internal structure of the Council. We will address each hierarchical level in turn, highlighting the basic organisational features of the Council, COREPER, Special Committees and Working Parties (also referred to as Working Groups - the two terms are used synonymously in this book). At the end the GSC is presented in detail. The next section thus starts to explain how these levels all work together in order to produce the legislative and policy-making activities of the Council - starting at the top with the Council of Ministers.

Figure 2.2: The internal structure of the Council

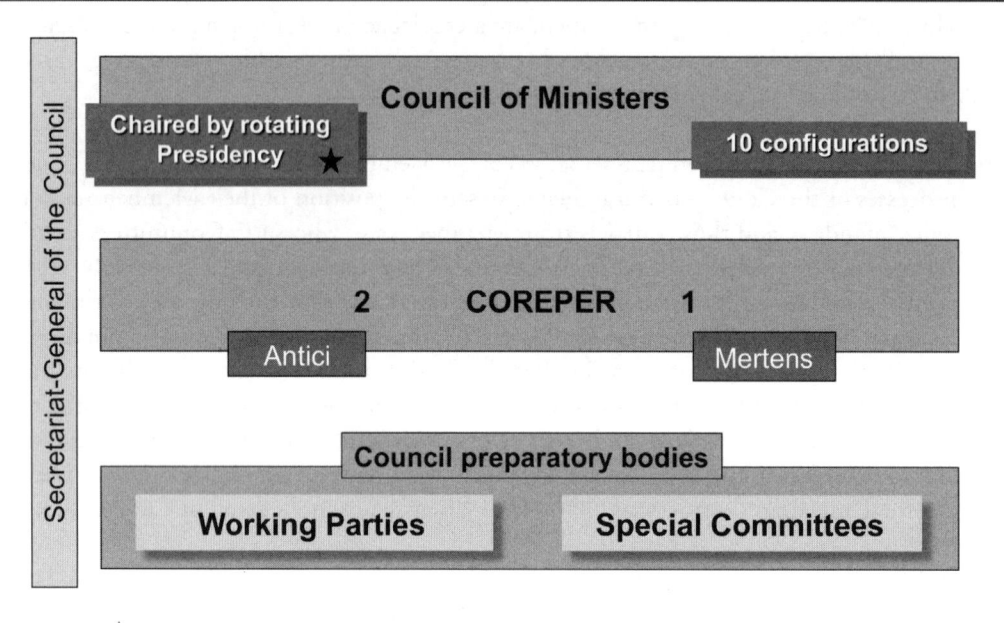

- Secretariat-General of the Council
- **Council of Ministers** — Chaired by rotating Presidency ★ — 10 configurations
- **COREPER** 2 (Antici) / 1 (Mertens)
- **Council preparatory bodies**: Working Parties, Special Committees

★ With the exception of the Foreign Affairs Council and some of its preparatory bodies. Some specialised committees also have elected chairs.

2.5 Internal structure of the Council: The Council as a meeting of Ministers

The Council as a meeting of Ministers constitutes the final stage of the work of the entire Council machinery composed of the preparatory bodies and the GSC. The Treaty states that the Council consists of a representative of each Member State at Ministerial level, who may commit the government of the Member State in question and cast its vote. The attendance lists of the various Council meetings point to differing practices of the Member States with regard to the seniority of their representatives. Though Ministers' attendance is a rule, junior Ministers, State Secretaries, even Directors-General or Permanent Representatives to the EU might represent their Member States at a particular meeting. The decision on attendance can be based on competences, domestic priorities, or other reasons for unavailability of the Minister. With regard to the membership it also needs to be mentioned that in some instances involving federal or largely decentralised Member States, representatives of a sub-federal level might take part, either in a capacity to take decisions (Belgium, Germany) or to coordinate sub-state units (Spain) in Council formations (or policy fields) for which in that particular Member State a sub-federal level has a legislative competence. Some Council meetings also cover areas which are the responsibility of more than one national Ministry and are therefore attended by several representatives. It is always necessary to establish at what level and under which competence of which Minister, and in what capacity, a Member State will take part in a Council meeting.

Though there is only one Council, it meets in several **configurations** to discuss different policy areas. It is worth noting, however, that any Council configuration can adopt (legislative) acts in any policy field. Following the changes introduced by the Lisbon Treaty, there are now ten Council configurations, as indicated in Figure 2.3.

Figure 2.3: Council configurations

- General Affairs
- Foreign Affairs (including European Security and Defence Policy, Trade and Development Cooperation)
- Economic and Financial Affairs (including Budget)
- Justice and Home Affairs (including Civil Protection)

⟫ **COREPER 2**

- Employment, Social Policy, Health and Consumer Affairs
- Competitiveness (Internal Market, Industry, Research and Space)
- Transport, Telecommunications and Energy
- Agriculture and Fisheries ★
- Environment
- Education, Youth, Culture and Sport (including Audiovisual)

⟫ **COREPER 1**

★ Dossiers based on Common Agriculture Policy are studied by the Special Committee on Agriculture, instead of COREPER 1, before going to Ministerial level

There used to be many more configurations, but with the reforms undertaken in the late 1990s and early 2000s (the Conclusions of the 1999 Helsinki European Council and 2002 Seville European Council), their number had fallen even pre-Lisbon Treaty from over 20, first to 16 and finally to 9, resulting in many Council meetings being so-called **composite Councils**, covering issues which spread across several Ministries in Member States. The Lisbon Treaty has finished the process, started already at Seville, of enhancing the role of the GAC, by splitting the General Affairs and External Relations Council (GAERC) into the GAC and FAC. These two Council formations are the only ones with a Treaty base; the rest of the Council configurations are determined by the European Council.

The **General Affairs Council** is charged with ensuring the consistency of the work of the Council (in all its configurations), preparing the work of the European Council and ensuring the follow-up of its meetings. The GAC is thus placed in a somewhat awkward position between a *primus inter pares* and a coordinator. In the Council's Rules of Procedure (RoP) this role is further elaborated, charging the GAC with responsibilities for overall coordination of policies, institutional and administrative questions, and horizontal dossiers which affect several of the EU's policies, such as the MFF in regard to operating rules for the Economic and Monetary Union (EMU). The awkwardness of the GAC's position is more understandable once you see this detailed list. By dealing with enlargement it crosses the thin line between enlargement and foreign policy, which is the subject of the FAC. On the other hand, its coordinating function, and especially the part to do with the EMU, places it in competition with the Economic and Financial Council (ECOFIN). One question that arises from these vast areas of policies is: who is the most appropriate Minister to take part in the GAC meetings? By looking at the attendance at GAC meetings in the years following its separation from the Foreign Affairs Council, we observe four broad types of representatives of the Member States in the GAC: Foreign Affairs Ministers, European Affairs Ministers, State Secretaries from the Foreign Affairs Ministries and State Secretaries from the Prime Minister's cabinet. The choice depends largely on the tradition and current system of coordination of EU affairs in each Member State.

Delegation sizes to the Council meetings vary by Member State. In the Council meeting room itself the Minister is accompanied by the Permanent Representative (or the Deputy Permanent Representative) seated next to the Minister (except in the case of the ECOFIN Council where Ministers sit alone at the inner table) and a small number of advisors are seated behind in the second row. The Presidency is given more seats and it usually uses its Member State seat for the highest civil servant in the administration covering the given policy area. The Commission is present with a Delegation composed of a Commissioner, Director-General and a small number of staff, including staff from the Secretariat-General of the Commission (SG). The representatives of the GSC are also in the room. The relevant Director-General is seated on the left of the Presidency to assist it and further officials as well as a representative from the Legal Service are seated behind. For the meetings of the FAC the European External Action Service (EEAS) is also present. With around 100 people in the room, the Council meetings are far from intimate, though the Council formations meeting on a regular basis tend to have a more intimate atmosphere. Legislative parts of Council deliberations can be accessed via the Internet (see box).

> **Council live on the Internet**
>
> You can follow the Council on the Internet for:
> 1. Council deliberations under the OLP.
> 2. The Council's first deliberations on legislative acts other than those adopted under the OLP.
> 3. The Council regularly holds public debates on important issues.
> 4. The Council regularly holds policy debates on Council programmes.

There are around 70-75 Council meetings a year. Some configurations meet monthly (GAC, FAC, ECOFIN, Agriculture and Fisheries) and others once or twice per Presidency term. Usually a Council meeting lasts one working day, but some are scheduled over two days, starting after lunch on the first day and finishing with lunch on the second day. Besides the official agenda, the draft version of which is distributed by the GSC two weeks prior to the Council meeting, the attending Delegations and Ministers can engage in a number of other meetings. Bilateral meetings in the morning or on the margins of the Council are a routine part of the cooperation among Ministers. Sometimes there is also an informal dinner among the Ministers on a preceding evening. We can also find Ministers holding meetings in different groupings, usually in the evening before the meeting. The custom of Prime Ministers meeting the leadership of a particular European Political Group in the Parliament before European Council meetings has been replicated in some cases before Council meetings. However, more often the so-called 'like-minded' countries meet to discuss and possibly align their views before important decisions are to be taken. Such groupings include the Visegrad four (Poland, Czech Republic, Slovakia and Hungary), the Franco-German couple or the Baltic and Nordic states.

Ministers also meet in **informal Council meetings** hosted by, and held in, the country of the Presidency. Though the 1999 Helsinki European Council agreed to limit the number of informal Council Meetings to five per Presidency, in practice almost every Council formation holds an informal meeting during each Presidency. These meetings are informal in the sense that they do not adopt any decisions and they do not follow the RoP of the Council. They are intended to advance the work of the Council on specific issues, to promote a certain issue by the Presidency or to discuss long-term policy developments. Discussions at informal Councils, which are usually only followed by a statement of the Presidency, may be formalised at a subsequent formal Council meeting. Informal Council meetings are attended by the Minister and usually up to two assistants. The Commission as well as the GSC are also present. It has become customary to invite a prominent expert to speak on the subject matter under discussion. Often a Presidency underpins discussions on its prioritised subjects by background studies it orders or requests (e.g. from the Commission), and by its own 'non-papers' as well as those contributed by other delegations. (A non-paper is a position paper that is supposed to trigger a discussion but does not bind the organisation that issues it. They do not have an official status.) It is important to watch out for the informal Council's agenda and discussions as major breakthroughs might happen on legislative or non-legislative files and issues. It holds true for the informal Council meetings just as for the formal meetings, however, that they are not an occasion at which Ministers are available for a meeting or susceptible to persuasive arguments. These need to be channelled through the Council hierarchy.

2.6 Internal structure of the Council: The Presidency

The top of the Council hierarchy, as first among equals and changing every six months, is the Presidency of the Council. Already in setting up the European Coal and Steel Community, the founding governments opted for a rotating Presidency to manage the Council's work and represent it internally as well as externally. The tasks of the Presidency came to extend far beyond management (which also become an extraneous task itself with the widening and deepening of the Union) to include tasks such as political initiator and broker. This relatively stable system of a single Council Presidency resisted any major change until its reform with the Lisbon Treaty in 2009.

Following the entry into force of the Lisbon Treaty, the rotating Presidency has been somewhat curtailed, with the view of ensuring more continuity, especially with regard to the European Council, and coherence with regard to external action and external representation of the Union. The European Council, as explained in detail above, is thus no longer chaired by the rotating Presidency, but by its full-time President. The FAC is chaired by the High Representative (except when trade is on the agenda, in which case the rotating Presidency remains in the chair) and some of the Working Parties which feed into the FAC (including the Political and Security Committee, PSC), but not all, are chaired by permanent chairs from the European External Action Service (EEAS). With these two chairing arrangements (of the European Council and the FAC) also the most visible role of the Presidency - that of external representative of the Union - has now been entrusted to the Chairs of these two bodies. There are two possible exceptions to this: a Foreign Minister of a country of the Trio-Presidency (see below) can be asked to act as a deputy to the High Representative in matters of CFSP; and in a case where the EEAS lacks representation in a third country, a rotating Presidency (via its embassy) still represents the Union in that country. Aside from this representational role for the rotating Presidency in the area of CFSP, representation of the EU in external affairs is no longer in the hands of the Presidency. For any other issue, e.g. environmental issues, it is the Commission which is entrusted with representing the Union externally, although this issue is occasionally contentious, also due to the lack of full-member status of the European Union in a number of international organisations. Therefore the Presidency may still be seen, along with the Commission, representing the EU at certain international gatherings.

> **Forthcoming Presidencies**
>
> The order in which the office of President of the Council shall be held was decided through a Council decision in 2007 and covers the period up to and including 2020. The next order will be decided by the European Council by qualified majority.
>
> The last list was adopted on 1 January 2007 (2007/ EC, Euratom).

For all the other nine Council configurations, however, the tasks of the Presidency have not changed. The issues of continuity and coherence have been addressed with regard to regular Council work (in addition to the above mentioned strengthened coordinating roles for the GAC) via the establishment of a system of pre-established **Trio-Presidencies**, whereby three consecutive Member States holding the Presidency work towards the execution of the joint programme. Each Presidency still draws up its own individual programme, prioritising issues it feels strongly about as well as making available to the Member States the list of all forthcoming Council agendas, indicating the dossiers that will be discussed as well as the objectives of the deliberations. This list should be sent at the latest one week prior to taking up the Presidency. The calendar and the agenda of the Council's work for the Presidency's term, subject to modifications as required, are thus available within the last weeks of the previous Presidency's term. It is worth keeping this in mind for planning purposes, especially longer-term planning. With these agendas you have a good idea when your particular issue is going to reach COREPER or Council levels. These calendars and agendas are also important if you are trying to set up meetings with the representatives of the Presidency - because the days around any meeting of the Council are extremely busy for the Presidency. In addition, in order to plan the Presidency, the respective Member State will know in advance when a certain new legislative proposal will be issued by the Commission. Even though this information will not be included in the calendars and agendas made available, the Presidency is an additional source of information when trying to establish more precisely when the Commission will issue a specific proposal.

The Presidency convenes the meetings, drafts the agendas and chairs the meetings at all levels of the Council machinery (with the aforementioned exceptions in the foreign affairs area and with exceptions to some Committees and Working Parties, outlined below). It aims at driving the Council's work forward by trying to bring the discussions to the adoption of decisions. The norm of having an **'impartial Presidency'** has become deeply rooted in the Council's culture, though each Presidency can exercise its tasks with different objectives in mind. These may be promoted consciously by the government or adopted individually by its Presidency teams, especially the chairs of Working Parties, Committees and COREPER, and eventually by the Ministers. An outline of 'ideal' styles by the Presidency as identified often in the literature is presented in Table 2.3.

Table 2.3: Different styles of the Presidency

Organiser (task-oriented)	Broker (group-oriented)	Political leader (transformational)
• Plans meetings (with GSC) • Drafts agendas (with GSC) • Makes sure that the machinery is running smoothly (with GSC)	• Listens to the Member States positions • Creates a good atmosphere • Identifies the midway position, bargains and trade-offs • Formulates compromises • Serves the group process	• Puts current discussions in a long-term perspective of EU challenges • Steers the debate in specific directions • Convinces delegations to abandon short-term interests
Focus on **effectiveness**	Focus on **fairness**	Focus on **long-term objectives**

Source: adapted from Schout, J.A. and Vanhoonacker, S. (2005) 'Nice and the French Presidency'. In Laursen, F. (ed.) The Treaty of Nice: Actor Preferences, Bargaining and Institutional Choice (Dordrecht: Martinus Nijhoff)

The Presidency has three advantages which allow it to exercise its brokerage role. The first one is control over procedures. The Presidency arranges the meetings and sets the agendas, not in a vacuum, but it does have a certain margin of manoeuvre (via the frequency of the meetings, shaping of their agendas, proposing the introduction of a new (ad hoc) WP, deciding over its composition, forming a Friends of Presidency group, etc.) for prioritisation on all levels, from Working Party to the Council of Ministers: bringing attention to new issues, reviving issues, speeding up (or slowing down) dossiers. The Council RoP set the framework for the businesslike conduct of Council meetings, aimed at efficiency (Article 20 and Annex IV). The Presidency also enjoys an informational advantage. Presidencies start preparing for their term of office a couple of years in advance; they pay attention to the process and the dossiers they will tackle; they consult their counterparts in other Member State capitals; and during the Presidency they enjoy privileged access to information. This is why it is important to take into consideration the Member States that will hold the rotating Presidency in the future and engage with them in good time. In the run-up to taking over the Presidency, the Member

State, and its Permanent Representation, are very busy with planning the next six months and it is very challenging to be able to secure a meeting with the relevant persons at that time.

Furthermore, the GSC fully supports the Presidency in its tasks by providing advice on procedures, positions, strategies and tactics, as well as suggestions on compromise proposals. In order to promote issues and policies the Presidency wants to prioritise, it organises numerous events, in Brussels, in its own capital as well as by its embassies in other Member State capitals. These are also occasions to establish contact with the most relevant attachés, advisors to the (Deputy) Permanent Representatives, or the person in charge of your particular issue, if you have not done so previously. All these actors can be instrumental when trying to find out the progress reached on a certain dossier during Council workings. During the Presidency all its representatives in Brussels are under enormous time pressure, filling in the time between meetings with bilateral talks and testing the water for compromise proposals in order to achieve the objectives the Presidency set itself and those it announced in the draft agendas of the Council submitted prior to its Presidency. Therefore, approaching the Presidency is much easier in the period before, when it is still reshuffling its priorities and when it is becoming clearer what issues it will have to deal with and is seeking information on.

2.7 Internal structure of the Council: COREPER 1 & 2

The **Committee of Permanent Representatives** (**COREPER**, after the French acronym) of the governments of the Member States is charged with the preparation of the work of the Council and with carrying out the tasks assigned to it by the Council. Hiding behind this very modest, and rather general, job description is a body with the highest level of political awareness and insight. It is also the only horizontal body in the Council architecture. With two exceptions explained below, every single dossier passes through the discussions of the COREPER meetings prior to being placed on the agenda of the Ministers' meeting.

As the name suggests, COREPER is a body composed of Permanent Representatives of the Member States in Brussels. They head Permanent Representations of the Member States to the EU. Already in 1962 COREPER split into two, with **COREPER 2 composed of the Permanent Representatives (PR)** ('ambassadors') and **COREPER 1 composed of Deputy Permanent Representatives (DPR)**. COREPER 2 ambassadors are usually very senior diplomats from the national Foreign Ministries. COREPER 1 representatives may be slightly junior to their COREPER 2 colleagues, and they may also come from outside the Foreign Ministries (e.g. from bodies coordinating EU policies in the Member States). Both carry out tasks which are very time-consuming and also very different from the work done by their diplomatic colleagues in embassies around the world. As Figure 2.3 shows, the split refers to the Council meetings they prepare. In COREPER 2 the more senior 'ambassadors' deal with horizontal, institutional, financial, justice and home affairs and foreign affairs. COREPER 1 is seen as more technical as it prepares for the other six internal market orientated Council configurations.

Figure 2.4: Composition of COREPER

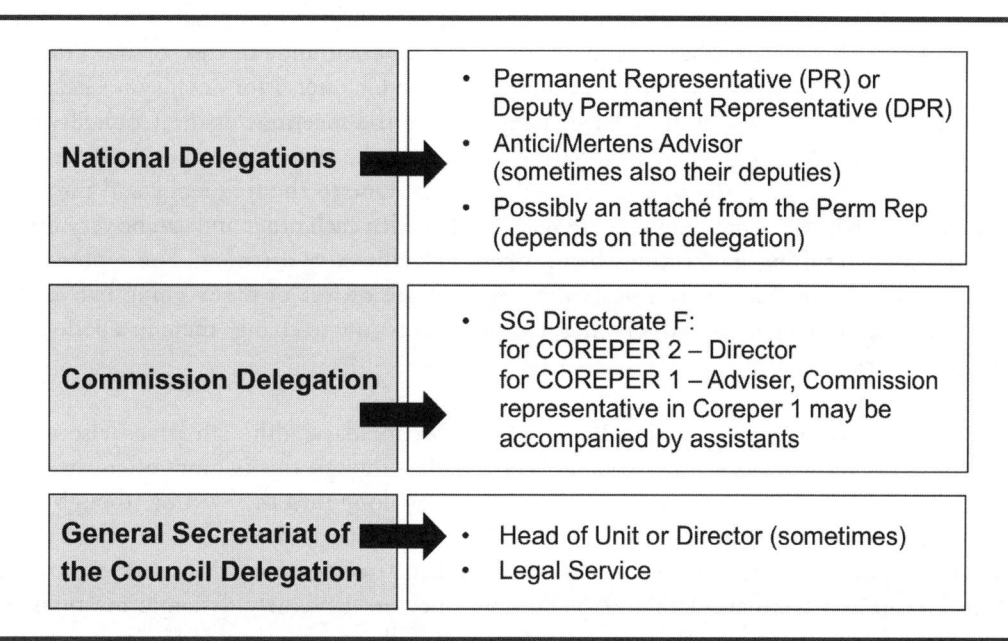

National Delegations	• Permanent Representative (PR) or Deputy Permanent Representative (DPR) • Antici/Mertens Advisor (sometimes also their deputies) • Possibly an attaché from the Perm Rep (depends on the delegation)
Commission Delegation	• SG Directorate F: for COREPER 2 – Director for COREPER 1 – Adviser, Commission representative in Coreper 1 may be accompanied by assistants
General Secretariat of the Council Delegation	• Head of Unit or Director (sometimes) • Legal Service

It is worth briefly outlining the main roles and functions of a Permanent Representation in Brussels because they are such important actors in the Council architecture. Table 2.4 highlights below the main elements of the role of a Permanent Representation.

Table 2.4: Roles and functioning of a Permanent Representation

Information gatherer	Monitor the proposals being generated by the Commission and, where appropriate, work for changes.
Information conductor	Links EU institutions and national governments. Assist national organisations to contact the Commission, Parliament or other EU institutions for lobbying purposes.
Information provider	Brief ministers who attend meetings of the Council, with particular attention to negotiating tactics and the politics of the files.
Policy formulation	Assist in putting together national policy towards EU issues and proposals (takes place in national capitals, although to differing degrees depending on the Member State).
Negotiator	The staff negotiates at official level in line with instructions given by national governments. This can be done either through informal contacts or the formal process.

COREPER 2 and COREPER 1 representatives are highly knowledgeable and experienced. They are unique in public administrations in the sense that they are diplomats with an in-depth knowledge about the policies they negotiate on in the Council and, in case of the Presidency, with the European Parliament for the files under OLP (see Chapter 5 for details on Codecision). They are also unique in the task they have. They prepare the meetings of the Council with the objective of facilitating progress in negotiations, while at the same time they have their own national mandates and need to observe national interests. Due to the frequency and intensity of the meetings, COREPER representatives are very familiar with each other and can be very informal in their dealings, resulting in meetings being open and efficiency-oriented. The representatives are usually rotated after four or five years precisely because of fear of them 'going native'. Some countries, though, prolong their term of office, usually in order not to change them in a period before assuming the Presidency.

COREPER meets weekly (both 1 and 2), usually on Wednesdays, although it can also meet on Fridays to continue discussions from Wednesday's agenda - though this is more often the case for COREPER 1. Meetings begin at about 10h30 and can last long into the evening, though a lot of effort has been made in recent years to avoid COREPER meetings lasting beyond usual working hours. The precise arrangements vary from one Presidency to the other. Meetings are trilingual (English, French and German, with interpretation). They are extremely dynamic meetings, with people rushing in and out as the dossiers under discussion follow each other. As Figure 2.4 shows, in addition to the PRs or DPRs, there are also senior officials (Antici and Mertens) assisting them and the relevant attachés on the dossiers under discussion on the Council side. Similarly the Commission is present with senior officials from its SG and a shifting representation of experts from the relevant DGs. A small delegation from the GSC assists the Presidency, takes notes, advises on separate files and officials from its Legal Service may be asked to clarify any legal questions.

The senior officials assisting the (D)PR form special groups, who meet a day prior to the COREPER meeting to go through the agenda, clarify positions and signal points of contention that could arise during negotiations.

In the case of COREPER 2 this preparatory group is called the **Antici group** and in each Permanent Representation there is an Antici attaché. Similarly the **Mertens group** meets to go through the agenda of COREPER 1 and Mertens attachés assist the DPR. The Antici attachés are usually more senior, often coming from the Foreign Ministries. Their discussions can also go beyond technical and procedural issues and they can indeed undertake limited political negotiations themselves. More often this is the case for institutional issues such as the implementation of the Treaty provisions (although the Mertens group was tasked with some elements of Lisbon Treaty implementation as well). The Antici attachés also have a special role with regard to the meetings of the European Council. There they act as **sherpas**, or information carriers, for their delegations on the proceedings in the European Council meeting. Mertens attachés on the other hand, due to the number of Council configurations that are prepared by COREPER 1, also act as a point of contact for a number of attachés and experts and have a coordinating role in the Permanent Representation, as well as a reporting role to the capital (however, this may vary between Permanent Representations). The Presidency's Antici and Mertens attachés are also important actors with regard to negotiations with the Parliament. They are another channel for the Presidency to brief other Member States and also to check on their positions with regard to the continuation of the process.

Considering all of the above it is important to stress the importance of Mertens and Antici attachés as they can be crucial contacts to have in the Permanent Representations. They have access to in-depth and updated information on an extensive number of dossiers, and they are also updated regularly on other Member State positions and compromise solutions once negotiations are at COREPER level.

2.8 Internal structure of the Council Committees and Working Parties

The work of COREPER and the Council is assisted and prepared by a number of Committees and Working Parties (WPs). **Committees** have a higher standing in the Council hierarchy and can be of a very diverse nature with regard to their status (Treaty-based or based on Council decision), tasks (delivering opinions, giving recommendations, contributing to policy developments), composition (especially with regard to chairmanship), relations to the Council (direct or via COREPER) and frequency of the meetings (from several meetings in a single week in the case of the Political and Security Committee to only twice yearly in some other cases).

The Special Committee on Agriculture (SCA) is a unique case in the sense that it is an equal counterpart to COREPER 1 in preparing the work of the Agriculture and Fisheries Council. It covers issues of a technical nature in the agricultural markets and rural development, while COREPER 1 deals with fisheries, food safety and budgetary issues. The Political and Security Committee (PSC, or COPS) is a Treaty-based Committee (Article 38 TFEU), charged with monitoring the international situation in the area of CFSP, contributing to the definition of policies by issuing opinions, and also monitoring the implementation of the agreed policies. Its members usually also hold the rank of ambassador and might be referred to as PSC (or COPS, after the French acronym) ambassadors or even CFSP ambassadors. Like the COREPER they have a senior-level official group called the Nicolaidis group, which prepares their work. They usually meet on Tuesdays and Thursdays, but can also meet on a daily basis if an international situation so requires. Though they do not enjoy a position of a parallel counterpart to COREPER, like the SCA to COREPER 2, issues considered by the PSC are rarely re-opened by COREPER 2. Following the implementation of the Lisbon Treaty, the PSC is no longer chaired by the ambassador from the Presidency, but by a representative of the High Representative, who took up post in January 2011. The Economic Policy Committee (EPC) provides analyses, opinions and draft recommendations on structural policies and its chair (together with the chair of the Economic and Financial Committee – EFC) assists the meeting of the ECOFIN Council. Other Committees are tasked with reporting and giving opinions. They are usually composed of high-level experts coming from the capitals, joined by the attachés from the Permanent Representations.

The PSC is not the only Committee not to be chaired by the Presidency. The EFC has an elected chair for two and a half years (and as an exception a Secretariat provided for by the Commission and not the GSC), the Employment Committee, the Social Protection Committee and the Economic Policy Committee have an elected chair for two years, the EU Military Committee has an appointed chair for three years and the Security Committee (dealing with security issues related to Council proceedings) is chaired by the representative of the GSC.

Other important Committees with a specific position in their respective policies include the Trade Policy Committee (TPC), Committee on Internal Security (COSI), Article 36 Committee (CATS) and Strategic Committee for Immigration, Frontiers and Asylum (all chaired by the Presidency) and Committee for Civilian Aspects of Crisis Management (chaired by the representative from EEAS). Committees' websites (others than those pertaining to the CFSP) are available on the Europa portal under respective policies.

The bulk of preparation work in the Council is done in its 160 or so **Working Parties (WPs) (also called Working Groups, WGs)**, of which about 15-20 hold meetings every day in the Justus Lipsius building. They are tasked with examining all the relevant files and dossiers in their area and reducing the number of open issues to be dealt with by COREPER and eventually by the Ministers. This means they tackle general questions as well as technical issues related to any file. They meet with a varying frequency, with some scheduled to meet several times a week, others with fortnightly sessions and others again on a much less frequent basis. Also some have a fairly stable and well-established schedule of meetings while others might be more ad hoc or irregular. This all depends on the different 'traditions' that the WPs have developed over time. They also vary with respect to the breadth of issues they might cover, with some being highly specialised (e.g. WPs under the Agriculture and Fisheries Council) and others covering policy more broadly (e.g. Environment Council is mainly - but not exclusively - served by one Environment WP, with an International Environment WP addressing specifically the international dimension of environment policy). It is important to know that unless urgency requires differently, a WP will not discuss the same issue with less than two weeks passing from one meeting to another due to logistic constraints related to translation and document production (i.e. if they do meet more often, they will discuss other items from the agenda). WPs are composed of national representatives, based at the Permanent Representations in Brussels and/or flying in from the national capitals, along with a representative from the Commission. Just like higher in the Council's hierarchy, representatives from the GSC are charged with providing assistance to the Presidency and drawing up notes. Figure 2.5 depicts the delegations in the WP meetings.

Member States may be represented in a WP by up to four people, drawn from the PRs or coming from the national capitals. They may be attachés or experts in the area and they work based on instructions given to them by the national capital. The breadth of their mandates, as well as their involvement in coming up with the mandate and their level of autonomous action, vary enormously not only between Member States and among issue-areas, but also depending on their personalities, expertise and experience. It is vital to understand that Council WPs work on the basis of consensus and according to some estimates they resolve around 70% - 75% of all the

Figure 2.5: Working Party composition

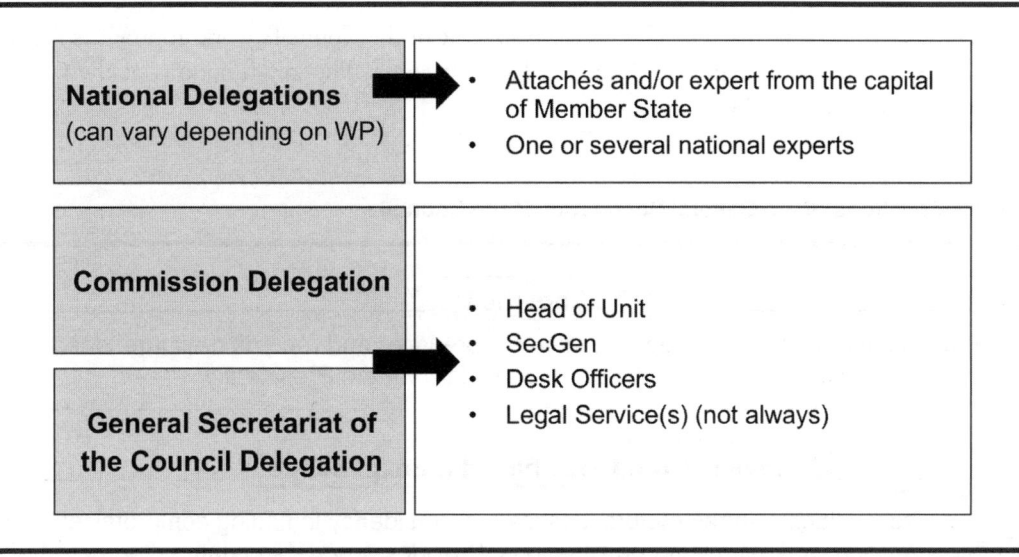

| National Delegations (can vary depending on WP) | → | • Attachés and/or expert from the capital of Member State
• One or several national experts |

| Commission Delegation | | |
| General Secretariat of the Council Delegation | → | • Head of Unit
• SecGen
• Desk Officers
• Legal Service(s) (not always) |

issues, with the rest being left for the COREPER and the Ministers. WPs, especially those which meet regularly and are frequented by staff from the Permanent Representations, can develop a very informal atmosphere, with friendly relations among its members whose contacts go beyond just WP meetings. The line between what is political and what is technical is hard to draw. WPs aim at agreeing on as many issues as possible and only pass them on for consideration by COREPER where further instructions are needed, or for placement on the Ministers' agenda when the Presidency believes that all possibilities for finding a compromise have been exhausted. Though it is left to Member States as to how they organise their representation at the WP meetings, efficiency and economic considerations suggest whether the representatives are permanently based in Brussels or fly in for the meetings from the capital. Usually, for those WPs which meet more regularly the representatives come from the Permanent Representations, while the not so regular groups are attended by both an attaché from the Permanent Representation and an expert from the capital. It is first and foremost the attachés, due to their permanent status in Brussels, deep knowledge of procedures and understanding of broader processes beyond the file under consideration, who can give you the information you need regarding a certain dossier and who have a better overview of the negotiations.

Before we go on to look at how this machinery works, in the opposite hierarchical order, we need to look at the mostly invisible helping hand provided by the relatively small number of officials in the GSC.

2.9 Internal structure of the Council: General Secretariat of the Council

As already indicated several times the GSC is the backbone of the Council's work. It provides logistical services, gives advice and guidance and delivers legal opinions. The key functions of the GSC are highlighted below in Figure 2.6.

Figure 2.6: Functions of the General Secretariat of the Council

1. Logistics
Prepares meetings, drafts reports, minutes, prepares and records draft agendas.
Hugely important function, especially for the Presidency.

2. Advice & guidance based on experience
Provides intellectual infrastructure, assists the Presidency in finding compromises, coordinating work, summing up situations. Provides reports and data on ad-hoc basis. Gives advice also on the process – timeframes, language issues.

3. Legal Opinion on form, substance, procedure
The Legal Service gives opinions to the Council and its committees.
Its opinion is very important – it is difficult for Member States to go against it.
It is a politically aware body that can provide strategic advice.

It is a fairly small secretariat, headed by a Secretary-General (who by tradition enjoys a long term of office), with about 300 administrators. It is divided into the private office of the Secretary-General, policy DGs, a Legal Service and a Press Office. In the period following the entry into force of the Amsterdam Treaty in 1999, and until the entry into force of the Lisbon Treaty, the Secretary-General of the GSC was also the High Representative. Since the introduction of the post of full-time President of the European Council, the GSC also supports him and his cabinet. In the course of the years the GSC has earned itself a reputation of being not only an impartial, but also highly competent and highly dedicated, service. Its officials are almost invisible and its services, such as document production (and ensuring the quality of drafting of Council's documents), interpretation and translation, are taken for granted by the delegations. For the Presidency, however, the GSC provides crucial support. Not all Presidencies make use of it to the same extent. Bigger Member States, which can rely on their vast domestic administration, are less likely to use the GSC's full potential, while smaller Member States tend to rely heavily on it. Officials of the GSC also help the Presidency in its preparation stage, by providing it with information from the screening of files and helping in setting up the 18-month agenda. During the Presidency the officials help it by arranging the meetings and structuring the agendas, briefing it before and supporting it with any advice needed during the meetings. Representatives of the GSC also sit next to the chair during all meetings, at all levels. They advise the Presidency on how to achieve its objectives and they help draft compromise proposals, but they do not decide.

Approaching the GSC staff can be very useful when engaging with the Council, especially when it comes to Treaty provisions, trilogue discussions or general decision-making procedures. They know the issues in detail as they need to be able to offer advice and expertise to the chair at any time during the negotiations. Also, due to their extensive experience, the GSC is often aware of the direction that a dossier is likely to take inside the Council. At the same time, however, the GSC's officials work under a strong code of conduct, with the principles of professionalism and confidentiality observed in any contacts with the delegations and other actors.

2.10 How the Council works: Setting the agenda

The internal decision-making procedures of the Council can be split into a series of different phases, which will be elaborated one by one in the following pages. At the outset it needs to be said that in comparison with decision-making in the Parliament and in the Commission, decision-making in the Council can be considered much more straightforward and simpler to understand at the level of outline and actors. It is, on the other hand, when it comes to the level of an individual file much more elusive and less transparent - making it more difficult to work with. Furthermore, with the Presidency changing every six months, practices can change as well, to better suit the goals and the style of the Presidency.

Given the variety of the Council's roles, the output of the Council is highly differentiated. The box on the right presents a variety of types of decisions the Council can adopt.

As explained above, the bulk of decisions that the Council takes is of a legislative and policy-making nature. In principle, the

A variety of activities undertaken by the Council:

1. adoption of legislative acts;
2. signing international agreements;
3. signing accession treaties;
4. adopting Council conclusions;
5. adopting decisions on the seat of the EU agencies;
6. concluding inter-institutional agreements;
7. adoption of decisions in foreign policy area;
8. monitoring military and civilian operations.

Council works in the same way irrespective of the nature of the decision to be adopted. Differences in proceedings, however, arise among some policy areas, due to the difficulty of the issues being decided, the urgency of a matter, and also depending on the Presidency style (see Table 2.3). The procedures of the Council are laid out in its RoP.

Before we look at how the Council works, we first need to establish how the Council plans its work. It has already been mentioned that the Trio-Presidencies prepare and present their 18-month programme. The programme is prepared with the High Representative for the activities of the FAC and in close cooperation with the Commission and the President of the European Council. Since the Trio programmes were established for the first Trio beginning in 2007 we have seen that the practice of the cooperation in preparation of the programme has varied among them and across the sectors, predominantly with regard to the importance attributed to the programme and with regard to the approach (top-down or bottom-up). The Trio programme is composed of two parts: a strategic framework and an operational programme. Practice differs, but the necessary components are:

1. Screening of the dossiers to understand the state of play and legal and procedural issues to be tackled (i.e. on-going negotiations, mid-term reviews, reports, health checks and observing deadlines in the Codecision procedure).
2. Double-checking with the Commission's Work Programme.
3. Checking the obligations stemming from European Council's conclusions.

From this point onwards, the three countries can add or prioritise issues they feel strongly about and discussions follow in order to finalise and produce a coherent text. The final programme is presented at the GAC at least a month before the first of the Trio members takes office. In some sectors, the three countries may prepare separate programmes. Each Presidency is then obliged, on the basis of this programme and after consultation, to prepare draft agendas for Council meetings for the entire time of its Presidency, showing the legislative work and operational decisions envisaged. The box to the right lists the types of work and decisions that the Council takes.

Operational objectives for the Council agenda items:

1. information and presentation;
2. policy debate and exchange of views;
3. orientation debate;
4. progress report;
5. general approach;
7. political agreement;
8. position;
9. adoption;
10. adoption of Council conclusions.

Though this is not required, Presidencies usually prepare and publish their own programme and their own priorities, which can be found, alongside many other useful documents, on the Presidency's website.

Based on this programming, and taking into consideration the cooperation with the Parliament, the Presidency arranges the work of the Council. A simplified version of the work of the Council follows the pattern presented below. This process is elaborated in more detail in the subsequent sections.

1. The Commission submits the proposal.
2. The proposal is assigned to a specific WP.
3. The WP discusses it and when it reaches an agreement, or exhausts its discussions, it passes it on to COREPER.
4. If discussions are still needed, it is first screened by the Antici or Mertens group.
5. COREPER then, if needed, further negotiates the proposal and decides whether it is ripe for discussion by the Ministers or sends it back to the WP for further discussions there.
6. The Ministers adopt a decision on the file or instruct COREPER on further proceedings.

2.11 How the Council works: The Working Party

The process in the Council starts at the WP level, as represented in Figure 2.7 below.

The Presidency announces the assignment of a file to a WP. At the last session of the WP under an out-going Presidency (also at any other hierarchical level in the Council) or at the first session under the incoming Presidency, the chairperson briefly outlines the Presidency programme and objectives for the coming six months. The WP schedule is also drafted in advance for the entire Presidency term of office, although it is obviously subject to changes and only indicative. Often a Presidency will only plan the exact WP meetings a month ahead. In cooperation with the chairperson, the GSC sends out the invitations, the agendas and relevant documentation to the delegates coming to the WP (the same holds true for other levels in the Council hierarchy as well). A Presidency generally aims at discussing a dossier at no more than three WP meetings, with the first meeting dedicated to the more general debate of a dossier and the consecutive meetings to a more detailed examination. As a dossier can go quickly through the WP it is important to know in advance when the meetings will be held and to get in touch in due time with the attachés concerned. It is important to keep in mind the fact that about 75% of all dossiers are agreed at this level; therefore from an advocacy point of view, the window of opportunity should not be missed.

Figure 2.7: Working Party level

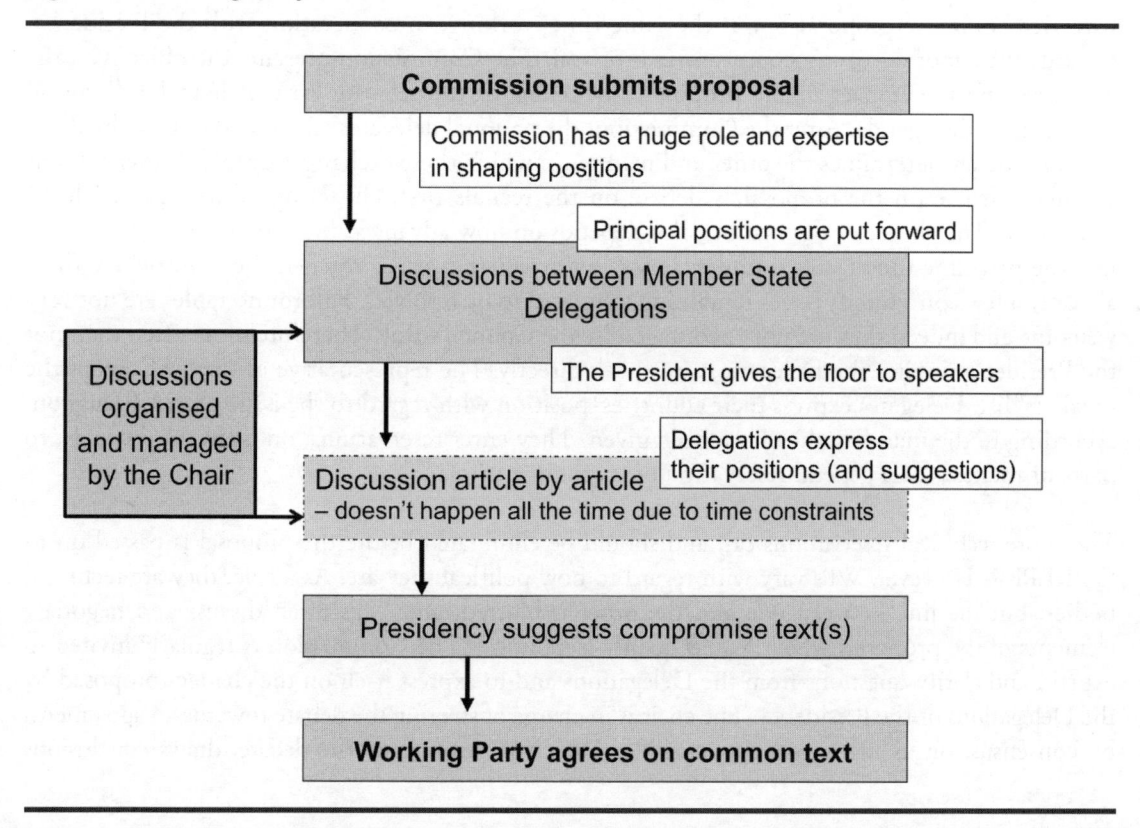

```
                    ┌─────────────────────────────────┐
                    │   Commission submits proposal   │
                    └─────────────────────────────────┘
                            │    ┌──────────────────────────────┐
                            │    │ Commission has a huge role   │
                            │    │ and expertise in shaping     │
                            │    │ positions                    │
                            │    └──────────────────────────────┘
                            ▼
                                 ┌──────────────────────────────┐
                                 │ Principal positions are put  │
                                 │ forward                      │
                                 └──────────────────────────────┘
                    ┌─────────────────────────────────┐
                    │  Discussions between Member     │
                    │        State Delegations        │
                    └─────────────────────────────────┘
                            │    ┌──────────────────────────────┐
                            │    │ The President gives the      │
 ┌──────────────┐           │    │ floor to speakers            │
 │ Discussions  │           │    └──────────────────────────────┘
 │ organised    │           │    ┌──────────────────────────────┐
 │ and managed  │──────────▶│    │ Delegations express their    │
 │ by the Chair │           │    │ positions (and suggestions)  │
 └──────────────┘           ▼    └──────────────────────────────┘
                    ┌─────────────────────────────────┐
                    │ Discussion article by article   │
                    │ – doesn't happen all the time   │
                    │ due to time constraints         │
                    └─────────────────────────────────┘
                            │
                            ▼
                    ┌─────────────────────────────────┐
                    │ Presidency suggests compromise  │
                    │             text(s)             │
                    └─────────────────────────────────┘
                            │
                            ▼
                    ┌─────────────────────────────────┐
                    │ Working Party agrees on common  │
                    │             text                │
                    └─────────────────────────────────┘
```

The WP meeting is chaired by the Presidency, which is assisted by the GSC (whose Legal Service is also present), with the Commission seated opposite to it and the national delegations around, with the previous Presidencies to the left and national delegates of the Presidency and future Presidencies to the right of the chair. Prior to the meeting, usually an hour before, the Presidency, the Commission and the GSC hold a meeting to go over the issues and exchange views on potential problems, to agree on the way to proceed and on the tactics to use. The Presidency opens the meeting and announces how it wants to proceed on an (any) item of the agenda. It is customary for the Commission to be given the floor first to present the proposal. The strength of the Commission is its knowledge of the content of the proposal, its expertise in the subject area and, since it went through the various consultation phases (see Chapter 1.6 and 1.7 on the Commission), also its understanding of Member State positions and the interests behind them. The Commission representative is tasked with defending the proposal but at the same time working, in cooperation with the Presidency, towards the adoption of the compromise proposal. The Commission presents the objectives, the measures and the impact of the proposed document or the relevant part of it to be discussed according to the agenda. After the Commission, the national delegates are invited to take the floor. The Presidency determines the order and manner in which these exchanges unfold. Either it holds a general debate on the proposal, a debate on the recitals first, clustering of articles, article by article, etc. The choice of the manner also depends on how advanced the discussions are, whether it is the first time the dossier is under discussion or whether it has reached the point where there are only a few contentious issues remaining that need to be resolved. Full round tables are not very welcome and indeed they are not encouraged by the Council's RoP. Therefore more often than not the Presidency invites the Delegations to speak directly. The representative of the GSC keeps the speakers' list. Delegates express their countries' position with regard to the issue under discussion, according to the mandate they have been given. They enter reservations, on different grounds, to parts of the text (or a general reservation on a text as a whole).

> **Council Rules of Procedure**
>
> The Council outlines, in detail, all its offices, powers, procedures and much more in its Rules of Procedure.
>
> Pay attention because the Rules of Procedure can change.
>
> It is extremely useful, even necessary, to know these rules if you interact with the Council.
>
> The current Rules of Procedure were adopted on 1 December 2009 (2009/937/EU). The last amendment to incorporate the changes in the qualified majority were adopted on 29 September 2014 (2014/692/EU).

The more technical reservations can and should be eliminated before the proposal is passed on to COREPER. However, WPs vary with regard to how political they are. As a rule, they are technical bodies, but the line between one and the other is blurred, and WPs often discuss and negotiate elements of the proposals which would qualify as political. The Commission is regularly invited to explain and clarify questions from the Delegations and to express itself on the changes proposed by the Delegations or the Presidency. The chair is in charge of steering the debate towards an agreement, by consensus, on as many issues as possible. The chair summarises the debate, draws conclusions and presents possibilities for further proceedings and eventually compromise proposals. A lot of work is done between meetings. The Presidency may ask a specific question and request answers to be sent in writing; it may invite Delegations to submit proposals in writing; it might arrange bilateral meetings with Delegations; and it spends a lot of time on the phone negotiating as well as keeping in contact with its own superiors when it needs a renewed mandate or seeks help. It should be pointed out that the autonomy given to the WP chairs by different Member States holding the Presidency varies – and it also varies with respect to the position of the issue on the Presidency's list of priorities, as well as its relationship to other issues (and therefore the possibility of a 'package deal'). The WP chair also discusses with his or her Mertens or Antici attaché and the (D)PR how to advance the file and when the file is ready to be moved to COREPER. The same item is usually discussed with at least a two week break in between, to allow for the translations and document production and also to allow the Presidency to make progress between meetings.

> **Reservations** the delegates enter on a proposed text can be on linguistic grounds, or because they need to check with their superiors or because they want to verify the effects or because the involvement of a legislator in their country requires that body's primary agreement. Reservations can also be due to a profound disagreement with a part of a proposal, be it in a recital or in the body of the proposal.

If the urgency of a matter requires more meetings, the Presidency has a few alternative ways to advance. It can organise an **attaché-only meeting** which does not require the same interpretation regime as a regular WP. Attaché-only meetings also have different negotiating dynamics: experts' meetings may dwell on technical elements too long, whereas attachés may find solutions employing their negotiating skills and building on their closer relations. It is not unusual for WPs to enjoy an informal social occasion during the term of each Presidency (though we see less and less of them in times of budgetary restraints in the Member States).

On very particular subjects the Presidency may also organise a **Friends of the Presidency group**. These groups are usually set up to discuss big policy-making decisions or especially difficult files. They are equally composed of representatives of all Member States and the Commission, but do not strictly follow the RoP of the Council. They are nevertheless assisted by the GSC.

It needs to be stressed that a WP never votes. They agree by consensus on the common text. If there are still reservations by some Delegations, they are added in square brackets or in footnotes. The chair reports to their (D)PR on the support the proposal has among the delegations based on the discussions in the WP.

2.12 How the Council works: From Working Party to COREPER

Once a WP chair concludes that a common text is ready to be included on the agenda of COREPER, they forward it, together with a written report, to COREPER for examination. The Council RoP requires the WPs to terminate discussions on a dossier within five working days prior to the COREPER meeting (unless urgency requires otherwise). If the dossier does not need any further discussion by COREPER (and is deemed ready for adoption by the Ministers) it enters the COREPER agenda as a **I item** (the 'I' being Roman number one). If however, COREPER is expected to discuss the item it is placed on the agenda as a **II item** (Roman number two).

In preparation of a COREPER meeting, the Antici and the Mertens group meet on the day before to go through the agenda and clarify positions and also see if there have been any developments in between (since the dossier was put on the agenda). COREPER meetings are guided by the same rules as the WP meetings (and so are the Council meetings) and follow the same procedural pattern. Due to the number of issues covered by a single COREPER meeting (be it COREPER 1 or 2) it can resemble organised chaos, with experts from all three institutions exchanging chairs during the meeting depending on the issues under discussion. COREPER meets on Wednesdays and the Presidency, the GSC and the Commission hold a preparatory meeting in the morning prior to the COREPER meeting.

Figure 2.8: From Working Party to COREPER

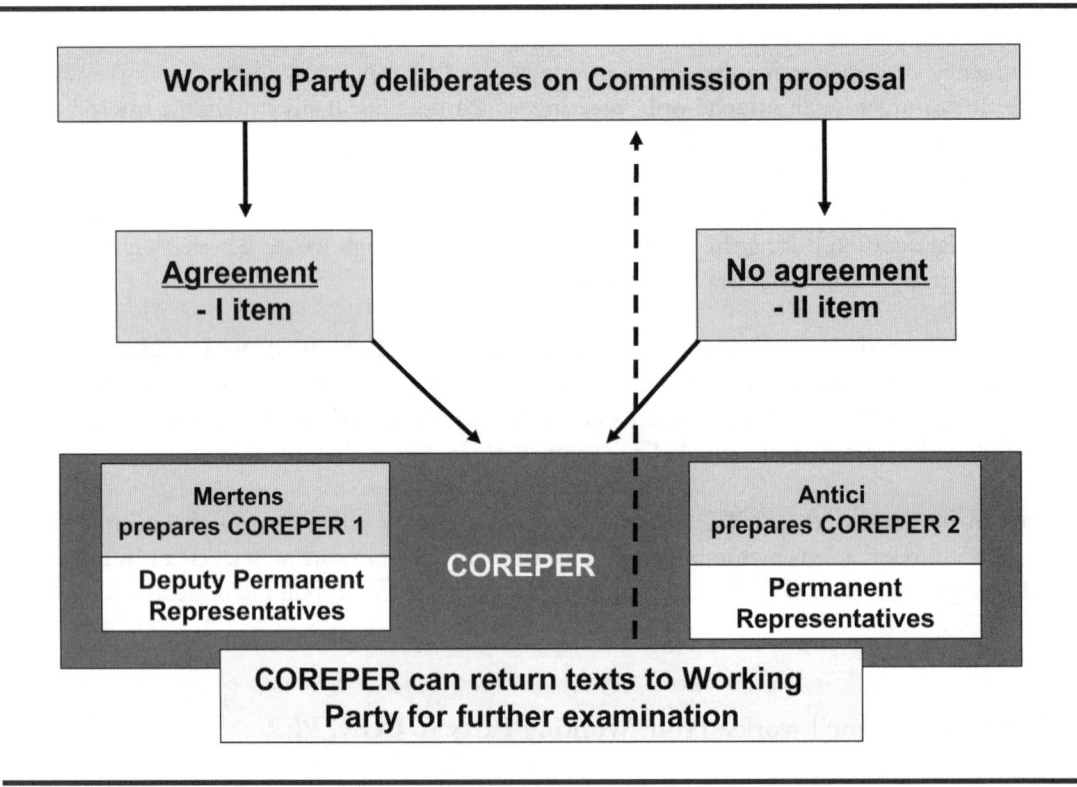

```
                Working Party deliberates on Commission proposal
                    │                           ▲           │
                    ▼                           │           ▼
            Agreement                           │       No agreement
            - I item                            │       - II item
                    │                           │           │
                    └───────────────┐           │   ┌───────┘
                                    ▼           │   ▼
        ┌─────────────────────┬─────────────┬─────────────────────┐
        │      Mertens        │             │       Antici        │
        │  prepares COREPER 1 │             │  prepares COREPER 2 │
        ├─────────────────────┤  COREPER    ├─────────────────────┤
        │  Deputy Permanent   │             │     Permanent       │
        │   Representatives   │             │   Representatives   │
        ├─────────────────────┴─────────────┴─────────────────────┤
        │       COREPER can return texts to Working               │
        │          Party for further examination                  │
        └─────────────────────────────────────────────────────────┘
```

Note: CFSP area is excluded

2.13 How the Council works: From COREPER to Council

Discussions in COREPER are much more political and many of the dossiers under II items are resolved at the level of COREPER and do not require further discussion by the Ministers at the Council meetings. Some items will of course be left for the Ministers to discuss and reach a decision. The statistics suggest that in addition to about 70% - 75% of all issues being resolved at the level of WPs, a further 15% - 20% are resolved by COREPER. Items that do not require discussion by the Ministers at a Council meeting will be placed on the Council agenda as **A items** (to which I items from COREPER's agenda are automatically included), and those requiring discussions are placed as **B items**. However, COREPER can also return dossiers back to the WP for further discussions.

Figure 2.9: From COREPER to Council

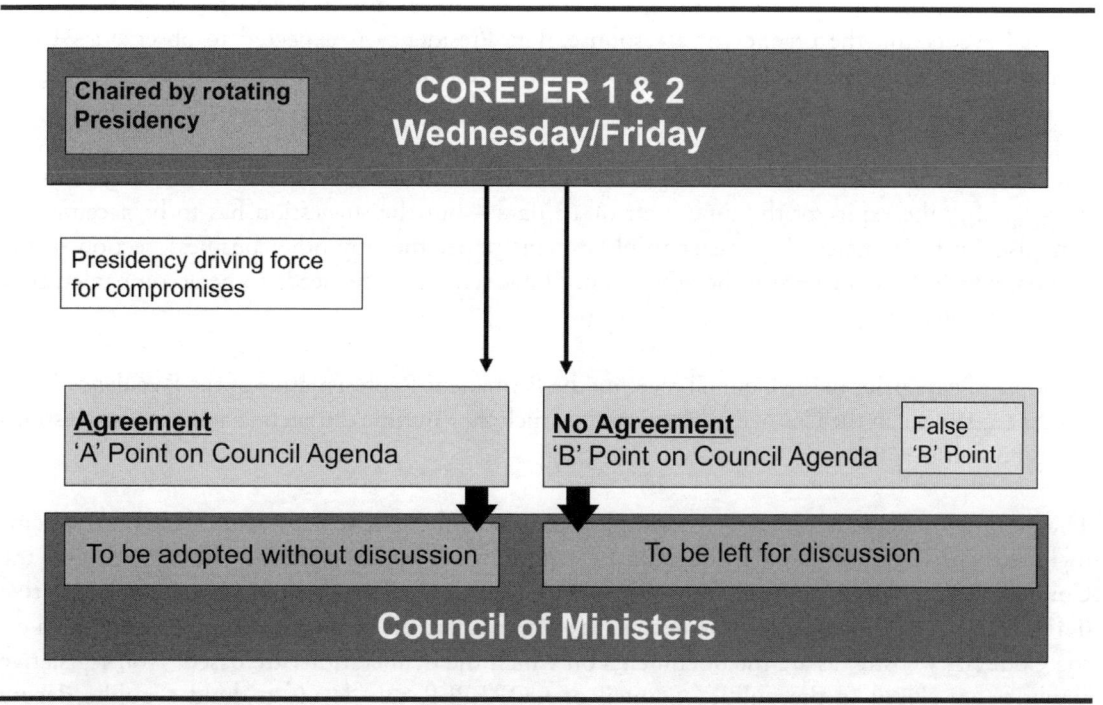

Note: CFSP area is excluded

COREPER is a horizontal body and dossiers which are going onto the agendas of different Council configurations are discussed at a COREPER 1 or COREPER 2 meeting, depending on the Council formation. Provisional agendas of the Council meetings need to be sent to the members of the Council and to the Commission at the latest 14 days before the meeting. This suggests that about three weeks before a given Council meeting COREPER adopts a provisional agenda for that meeting. Requests for inclusion of an item on a provisional agenda of a Council meeting, by the Commission or any Delegation, must therefore reach the GSC at the latest 16 days prior to the Council meeting in question. COREPER can still discuss an item already placed on the Council's agenda.

The decisions prepared by COREPER all have to be formalised by a Council meeting. However, in the case of files in OLP, COREPER can agree, without the need for formal verification by the Council, on the mandate for the Presidency to enter into trilogue discussion with the Parliament.

Provisional dates for Council meetings are communicated by the Presidency several months in advance and the draft agendas, as we have seen in the beginning of this section, are established at the latest one week prior to each Presidency's term in office. Provisional Council meeting agendas are distributed no later than 14 days prior to the Council meeting, with requests for inclusion of an item on the agenda to be received no later than 16 days prior to the meeting. It is generally acknowledged that in the area of foreign affairs these rules cannot always be respected due to external events and the urgency of a response. The Presidency is expected to observe a 21-day deadline for disseminating the agenda, with the entire documentation for the Council meeting, in the case of the Area of Freedom, Security and Justice (AFSJ).

On the other hand it is possible to suggest inclusion of any item on the agenda of any Council meeting after the expiry of the time limit of 16 days – but the suggestion has to be accepted by consensus in the Council. It is easier to place items under the 'any other business' section of the agenda, which does not need to be voted upon; however, a request needs to be accompanied by a written explanation.

A couple of days prior to the Council meeting the Permanent Representative of the Presidency holds a press conference in the Council press centre in which they outline the agenda and answer questions from journalists.

The definitive agenda is adopted by a simple majority in the Council. By a simple majority, items included within the 16-day deadline can be withdrawn from the agenda. The agenda, and the Council meeting itself, are split into two parts. The Council meeting is split into '**legislative deliberations**' and '**non-legislative activities**'. The first are open to the public (web-streamed on the Council's website) as are the documents on which the deliberations are based. Non-legislative activities are closed to the public. Council or COREPER can decide to hold a public debate on an important issue of interest to the EU and its citizens. Such an item is marked as 'public debate' on the Council's meeting agenda, whereas the legislative deliberation is marked as 'public deliberation'. Part A of the agenda includes items which can be adopted without discussion. These are items on which agreement has already been achieved – either at the WP level, at the level of COREPER (or SCA in case of Agriculture and Fisheries Council), or at a previous Council meeting where only an administrative or legal clarification was left over to be made afterwards. They can be adopted item by item or 'en masse', while verifying that the sufficient majority has been achieved (the proof of a necessary majority achieved is displayed on the screen in the meeting room). B items are subject to a discussion in which the Ministers proceed in a way similar to the proceedings explained above in the case of the WP. A so-called '**false B' item** is an item on which an agreement has already been achieved, but on which one, or more, Ministers want to express themselves for mostly domestic political purposes. The process in Council is highlighted in Figure 2.10 below.

Figure 2.10: The Workings in the Council

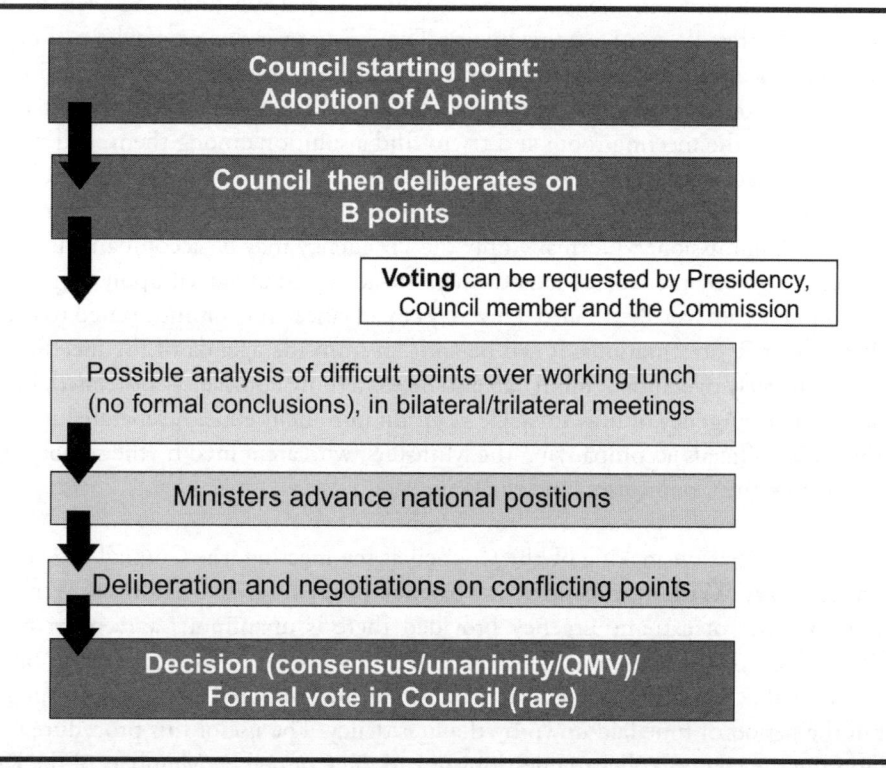

```
Council starting point:
Adoption of A points
   ↓
Council then deliberates on
B points
   ↓           Voting can be requested by Presidency,
               Council member and the Commission
Possible analysis of difficult points over working lunch
(no formal conclusions), in bilateral/trilateral meetings
   ↓
Ministers advance national positions
   ↓
Deliberation and negotiations on conflicting points
   ↓
Decision (consensus/unanimity/QMV)/
Formal vote in Council (rare)
```

Adoption of items normally proceeds without a vote, but a vote can be requested by any Member State or the Commission.

Despite such a high value being placed on the number of votes each Member State has, in fact only about 10% of all decisions which could be taken by qualified majority are actually voted upon. The vast majority of decisions are adopted by consensus. Though more and more decisions can be taken by qualified majority, the consensual culture is so deeply rooted in the Council that decisions adopted without having (almost) everyone on board are still rare, though ever more difficult to achieve. The possibility of the qualified majority vote, which suggests that a country (or more) could be outvoted, changes the dynamics of negotiations. Member States who might be outvoted try to modify a proposal closer to their interests, or they try to prolong the decision-making procedure or to form a **blocking minority** (see Figure 2.1). In the course of the negotiation of a dossier the Member States, and especially the Presidency, pay attention to the blocking minorities being formed; the major negotiation activity on highly contentious files centres on those Member States who are not (yet) with the blocking minority, but whose position seems to be close to it.

Though only about 10%-15% of all decisions taken by the Council are discussed by the Council, this is still enough for vigorous discussions at every Council meeting, for decisions to be taken, or to enable progress on key files. While WP chairs, and also COREPER chairs, are permanently based in Brussels and can therefore stretch their bilateral meetings and plan their work between meetings, Ministers do not have this luxury. They meet over one or maybe two days. If discussions in a Council meeting are not showing any progress, the Presidency has a few options. It can adjourn the meeting in order to meet bilaterally or with a small number of Member States; it can instruct the PRs to leave the meeting room and try to find a solution among them; and it can also decide to discuss the subject over lunch or dinner. While the rest of the Council meeting takes place in a room with about 100 people, in most cases the Ministers' lunch is restricted to Ministers only and the responsible Commissioner. Normally only the Presidency may be accompanied by its PR or another senior official and by the GSC. Many dossiers are advanced or agreed upon during lunch. The lunch discussion items are usually decided a few days in advance and communicated to the Delegations via the Permanent Representations. It can be an item from the agenda of the meeting, with the aim of discussing it freely over lunch, but it can also be something completely unrelated, like a discussion on the seat of a new Agency or how to tackle a certain imminent issue. A separate lunch is also organised for the senior officials accompanying the Ministers, who are joined by the senior officials (Director-General) from the Commission and the GSC.

In addition to decision-making by the Council at the meeting, the Council can also adopt decisions via an **Ordinary Written procedure** or a **Silence procedure**. The Ordinary Written procedure can be used in cases of extreme urgency provided there is unanimous agreement by the Council or COREPER on the use of such a procedure. The simplified Silence procedure can be used on the initiative of the Presidency, where the issue is deemed adopted if no objections have been raised within the period of time laid down by the Presidency. The use of this procedure is seen most often in adopting the text of replies to questions put to the Council by Members of the Parliament.

2.14 Key stages and key actors - The Council

This chapter has detailed the decision-making process in the Council by first explaining how a file gets on the agenda of the Council and then following it through the Council machinery. The chapter has identified all the stages of the decision-making process and the key groups and individual actors that are involved.

The first observation to be made is with regard to the seeming simplicity of the Council workings. Though the process is linear, the content can be subject to many different influences which impact the dynamics of the policy-making process. Given that there is significantly less transparency in the

Council (in comparison to the Commission and Parliament) it is even more challenging to follow the work of the Council.

While the 18-month Trio programme gives only a rough idea as to what the priorities of the Council workings might be during the coming three Presidencies, the operational programmes of each Presidency present a clearer picture as to which files will be worked upon in the Council in the following six months. Even these, however, need to be checked against the actual agenda (for things such as leftovers from the previous Presidency), the Commission's execution of its planning, international events or domestic developments which demand sudden attention. In addition the progress of files depends on factors such as the general mood surrounding the file and the readiness of the Parliament (in case of a Codecision file) to tackle the issue(s) in parallel with the Council. This does not mean that the programme the Presidency set for itself will not be pursued, but it means that due to various factors this or that file may be set aside and another one occupy its place on the agendas.

Council WPs, Committees, COREPER and Council meetings are scheduled well in advance due to logistical constraints with regard to the availability of rooms, interpreters, and the translation of documents and also of officials and Ministers - as well as a desire to avoid surprises as much as possible. With all of this in mind the margin for setting up extra meetings to overcome difficulties or to examine new issues, is limited but not entirely impossible. Management of the Council workings lies in the hands of the rotating Presidency; therefore it is important to watch closely how the Presidency ranks a certain file on its list of priorities and how much of an extra mile it is willing to go to achieve its objectives on the file. The Presidency can advance work during the meetings by inviting the Delegations to submit proposals in writing and by careful preparation of compromise proposals. Though all the Presidency actors are extremely busy and under time pressure, they will have an ear for constructive proposals. This is probably mostly the case at the level of the WP. In principle, political issues with regard to the proposals under examination are not discussed at this level, but the Presidency of course aims at getting a very good sense of everyone's position on the proposal and a possible solution in order to be able to prepare the compromise at this or at any later stage. A WP chair who is well-informed and strong on the substance of a file can be crucial in developing compromise proposals at the later stages.

The linear progress in the Council (passing from the WP/Committee stage to COREPER and finally to the Council) can sometimes be disrupted and reversed in cases of extremely difficult files. Examples of these would be files on which there are divergent positions, due to new developments in positions, or due to the fact that the file is simply not yet ripe for decisions to be taken and more work needs to be done at the technical level. It is up to the Presidency to manage such situations. Its options include referring the file back to COREPER (from a Council meeting), to the Mertens or Antici groups or to the WP itself. It can also propose to set up an ad hoc WP or a meeting of a WP in the composition of attachés only or even invite officials from the national capitals to its own capital for a high-level discussion to find a compromise. Such options are used by the Presidency very carefully, in order not to create the feeling of chaos and haste, but it is precisely with these developments that one can lose track of the progress on a file. Once again, closely watching the steps of the Presidency is important for understanding the dynamics and progress on the file. It is also important to develop a sense of the majorities the Presidency is pursuing for the adoption of a file. Naturally, legal conditions for unanimity are strictly observed, but as explained above, in the vast majority of cases where a decision could be taken by qualified majority, the Council adopts them by consensus. This tendency affects the dynamics of negotiation, the framing of the compromise and eventually the timing of the adoption of the file. However, if consensus does not seem probable and (or) there is time (or peer) pressure, the Presidency can decide to conclude the file with the majority it has obtained. Therefore the voting system outlined earlier in this chapter (see section 2.3 and Figure 2.1) is highly relevant and careful monitoring of majorities throughout the process is still essential.

Following this analysis, the main stages and key actors in the decision-making process in the Council are outlined in Table 2.5.

Table 2.5: Key stages and key actors - The Council

Key stage	Comment	Key Actors
Setting the 18-month Trio-programme	Provides a rough sense of orientation as to what will be tackled in the programmed period.	Permanent Representations and Heads of State or Government + Cabinets of the three countries holding the Presidency
		General Secretariat of the Council and Commission
Setting the operational agendas of the Presidency	Gives a clearer indication as to what will be worked on and with what operational objectives.	Key focus on personnel of the Permanent Representation holding the Presidency
		General Secretariat of the Council
Discussion of a file in a Working Party/ Committee	Rarely only a technical discussion thus this is the stage (and the level) to closely watch for direction in a discussion and for compromise proposals coming from the Presidency.	Attachés/Member State delegates in the Working Party
Discussion of a file in COREPER	Several open issues might be addressed and successfully closed at this stage, or grounds tested for the Ministers' deliberations.	Attachés/Advisors/(Deputy) Permanent Representative
		Antici/Mertens group
Council meeting	Final decisions taken, also in package deals; Presidency to advance compromise; intense negotiations immediately prior and during the meeting.	Ministers, Cabinets
		(Deputy) Permanent Representative

3. The European Parliament

By Alan Hardacre and Joost Mulder

The Parliament is the only directly elected institution in the EU, and as such is the source of direct democratic legitimacy in the Union. Direct elections first took place in 1979, and are held every five years, meaning that in 2014 we started the eighth legislature. Whilst few would have heard of, or worked with, the Parliament back in 1979 it is now a formidable political institution increasingly comparable to influential national parliaments, if not even more powerful. The Treaty of Lisbon, which entered into force in December 2009, has ushered in a new era for the Parliament, the repercussions of which are clearly manifesting themselves - and all of which will be outlined in this chapter. The key facts of the Parliament can be found below in Table 3.1.

Table 3.1: European Parliament - Key facts

Role:	EU legislative body
Established:	1979 (as elected body) 1952 as Common Assembly
Voting system:	Party list and proportional representation
President:	Martin Schulz (Socialists and Democrats) - 2012-2017 Leader of EPP in EP - 2017-2019
Vice-Presidents:	14
No. of MEPs:	751
Term:	5 years (currently 2014-2019 session) - 8th legislative term
Decision-making body:	Plenary
Political Groups: (Figures as of 24 October 2014)	220 European People's Party (EPP)
	191 Socialists and Democrats (S&D)
	71 European Conservatives and Reformists (ECR)
	67 Alliance of Liberals and Democrats (ALDE)
	52 Confederal Group United European Left/Nordic Green Left (GUE-NGL)
	50 Greens/European Free Alliance
	48 Europe of Freedom and Direct Democracy Group (EFDD)
	52 Non-Attached Members (NI)
Internal structure:	20 Standing Committees and 43 Delegations approx. 6,000 officials under Secretary-General
Working languages:	24
Location:	Strasbourg (France), Brussels (Belgium) and Luxembourg

Table 3.1 shows that the Parliament is a body of 751 **Members of the European Parliament (MEPs)** who sit in seven different Political Groups, as well as a number of non-attached MEPs (known by their French acronym NI - for *non-inscrit*). It is within, and between, these Political Groups that the Parliament has to find its position(s) in its decision-taking body - the Plenary session. This chapter will present the Parliament's decision-making process in detail, although trying to explain all the intrigues of such a political body is not an easy task. Whereas the Commission is a public administration with a tightly structured working methodology and process, the Parliament is a political body where two dossiers rarely follow the same path. This makes analysing how the Parliament actually works very challenging and it also makes working with the Parliament very much a case-by-case exercise. This chapter will concentrate on presenting the key players, the key stages and the things to look out for when working with the Parliament. Firstly, it is necessary to start with the macro-view of the Parliament.

3.1 Roles of the Parliament

The Treaty articles that define the general role of the Parliament are Articles 13-14 and 16-17 TEU, and Articles 223-234 TFEU. Within these articles the three main powers of the Parliament can be found: legislative, budgetary and supervisory. Besides these Treaty based formal powers the Parliament also has very important and extensive informal powers.

1. **Legislative power:** The Parliament is the legislative equal of the Council (with a couple of sensitive exceptions). The Parliament has Ordinary Legislative Procedure (OLP) powers over 95% of all legislation across 84 policy areas. This means that the Parliament has an equal say on the outcome of legislation with the Council (see Chapter 5 on the Ordinary Legislative Procedure for more detail). In the seventh legislature, 2009-2014, the Parliament co-decided on 488 acts (an increase from 454 in the sixth legislature).

   Unlike national parliaments, the Parliament does not have the formal right to initiate legislation which, as we saw in Chapter 1, is reserved to the

> **European Parliament Rules of Procedure**
>
> The European Parliament outlines, in detail, all its offices, powers, procedures and much more in its Rules of Procedure.
>
> Everything from Intergroups (Rule 34) to Question Time in Plenary (Rule 129) is explained in the 216 Rules. In addition you will find 21 annexes which range from issues such as a code of conduct for negotiating in Codecision (XIX) to an access to documents annex (XIV).
>
> Pay attention because the Rules of Procedure can change. It only needs one MEP to propose a change followed by an absolute majority in Plenary (Rule 2).
>
> It is extremely useful, even necessary, to know these rules if you work with the Parliament.
>
> You can find them at:
> www.europarl.europa.eu/sides/getLastRules.do?language=EN&reference=TOC

Commission (with Member States on some occasions). This issue is a very sensitive one for the Parliament, and one that some would like to see formally changed. The Parliament does have, under the OLP by virtue of Article 225 TFEU, the right to ask the Commission to submit before it a legislative proposal. To do so the Parliament, as outlined in Rule 45 of its internal Rules of Procedure (RoP), must adopt an Own-Initiative Report (see section 3.5) requesting the desired legislative text. It is then up to the Commission to consider this request, but it is under no legal obligation to bring forward a proposal.

Aside from its substantial powers under the OLP, the Parliament contributes to the legislative process under the Special Legislative Procedures (SLP), notably the Consultation and Consent procedures. For example tax issues still remain under Consultation, and the signing-off of international agreements requires the Consent of the Parliament. These two powers should not be taken lightly because they are important powers that are taken very seriously by the Parliament. This is particularly the case with the Consent procedure, which came to the fore in 2010 when the Parliament withheld its consent on the SWIFT data transfer deal between the EU and the United States. The Consent procedure is a very powerful tool for the Parliament, and one that will gain in prominence in the years to come. As a result of Lisbon, the Parliament also has the right to approve or reject (but not amend) the EU's trade agreements with third countries, such as CETA (Canada-EU) and TTIP (USA-EU).

2. **Budgetary role:** The second major power of the Parliament is its budgetary power. The Council and the Parliament together form the EU budgetary authority, whereby the Parliament jointly agrees the annual Budget with the Council, monitors the execution of the Annual Budget, and finally gives discharge to the budget. The Parliament first gained budgetary powers in 1970, under the Treaty of Luxembourg, and further extended these powers during the following decades. Budgetary powers may thus be regarded as the first real powers the Parliament had and, with the Treaty of Lisbon giving it full equality in budgetary decision-making with the Council, it continues to be a major power (Articles 310-325 TFEU). In fact, the annual budget negotiations offer the Parliament a heavyweight negotiating opportunity because the Parliament has successfully been able to gain concessions from the Council and/or Commission by linking its priority legislative (and other) issues to the Annual Budget negotiations.

> **The Power of the purse**
>
> Since the entry into force of the Treaty of Lisbon, the Parliament shares equal authority with the Council over the EU budget. Its main competences are:
>
> - agreeing the annual budget;
> - monitoring the Commission's execution of the annual budget;
> - giving discharge to the budget.

3. **Supervisory role**: The third major category of powers of the Parliament is the right of supervision and control functions. The most visible of these is its control of the executive power - namely the Commission. The mechanisms for electing a new College, and removing a College, were dealt with in the earlier chapter on the Commission (see Chapter 1.3).

> **The Parliament and the media**
>
> The Parliament is the closest of the EU institutions to the European and national media.
>
> The Parliament, through its MEPs, seeks media coverage of its issues and positions. This is something that should always be taken into consideration when dealing with the Parliament – what are the media opportunities and/or risks?

In addition, the Parliament has further supervisory powers. These include powers to set up Committees of Inquiry to look into violations or wrong applications of EU law by Member States (e.g. mad cow disease, CIA detention flights); to request answers to questions from the other institutions, and ultimately directly petition the Court of Justice of the EU; and to exercise control through its budgetary powers by having a Member State, the Commission, other EU institution or EU Agency appear before its Committees to give account, present annual statements, etc.. In addition the Committee on Petitions hears well over 2,500 public complaints against the institutions a year. The Parliament also has considerable powers of supervision in the realm of 'new' Comitology (see Chapter 6).

Aside from these formal powers, the Parliament also has significant informal powers, notably ones that supplement its powers to supervise and control. As a political body it is able to effectively exert pressure where it feels its formal mechanisms are not being respected, or where they do not exist. For the three formal powers cited above one must consider that all of them are flanked by a vast array of informal powers to try and achieve its objectives. This can be anything from media coverage, events, reports, high-level networking and political connections.

Whilst the powers described above are presented in three separate categories for the sake of clarity, the Parliament often mixes its powers for maximum effect. There is, therefore, always a possibility of an issue you are working on getting tied into other debates and inter-institutional conflicts. It is imperative to never neglect the informal powers of the Parliament because by a simple Own-initiative Report, Written Declaration or Question from MEPs (all covered later) an issue can come alive.

3.2 Internal structure of the Parliament: Outline

The Parliament is made up of MEPs who are elected to represent over 375 million eligible EU voters - making elections to the Parliament the biggest transnational elections in the world. Elections were last held between 22 and 25 May 2014, and all Member States used variations of proportional representation to elect their MEPs. The majority of MEPs are elected from **national party lists**, and there are MEPs from 160-180 national parties who are affiliated to one of the seven European

Political Groups. The implications of this national list system are extremely important when considering the motivations and drive of an MEP in Brussels, and they will be discussed in more detail later in the chapter.

The allocation of seats is done according to the principle of 'degressive proportionality', whereby the size of population alone, while taken into account, is not the sole criterion for the number of MEPs attributed to a Member State. In this way, the smaller Member States are ensured meaningful (actually over-proportionate) representation in the Parliament. For example, an MEP in Germany represents around 800,000 residents whereas an MEP in Malta represents about 80,000 residents. The number of MEPs per country is highlighted in Table 3.2 below.

Table 3.2: Number of seats in the European Parliament by Member State (2014-2019)

Germany	96	Austria	18
France	74	Bulgaria	17
UK	73	Denmark	13
Italy	73	Slovakia	13
Spain	54	Finland	13
Poland	51	Ireland	11
Romania	32	Croatia	11
Netherlands	26	Lithuania	11
Greece	21	Latvia	8
Belgium	21	Slovenia	8
Portugal	21	Estonia	6
Czech Rep.	21	Cyprus	6
Hungary	21	Luxembourg	6
Sweden	20	Malta	6
		TOTAL	**751**

Source: http://europa.eu/institutions/inst/parliament/index_en.htm

The number of MEPs (total and by Member State) is important for several reasons, all of which will become increasingly apparent as the chapter proceeds. In essence the Parliament is all about the numbers game - the number of MEP votes. It is always vital to follow the number of MEPs from a **National Delegation**, within a Political Group, supporting an issue, etc. This issue will be raised on a number of occasions.

Every MEP has one (or several) **assistants** who support their MEP in their tasks. You can find a list of accredited assistants on the Parliament's website at: http://www.europarl.europa.eu/meps/en/assistants.html. The role of an assistant varies enormously from one MEP to another, with some offering solely secretarial support and others offering detailed substance-based assistance with drafting and negotiations. You will only ever discover this through your interactions with MEPs and their office. Irrespective of the previous consideration, an assistant is always a vital gatekeeper to the MEP, privy to a wealth of information about substance, process and procedure.

From these broad areas of competence and power, and the number of MEPs sitting in the Parliament, the next stage is to look at the structure of the Parliament itself, as outlined in Figure 3.1.

Figure 3.1: The internal structure of the European Parliament

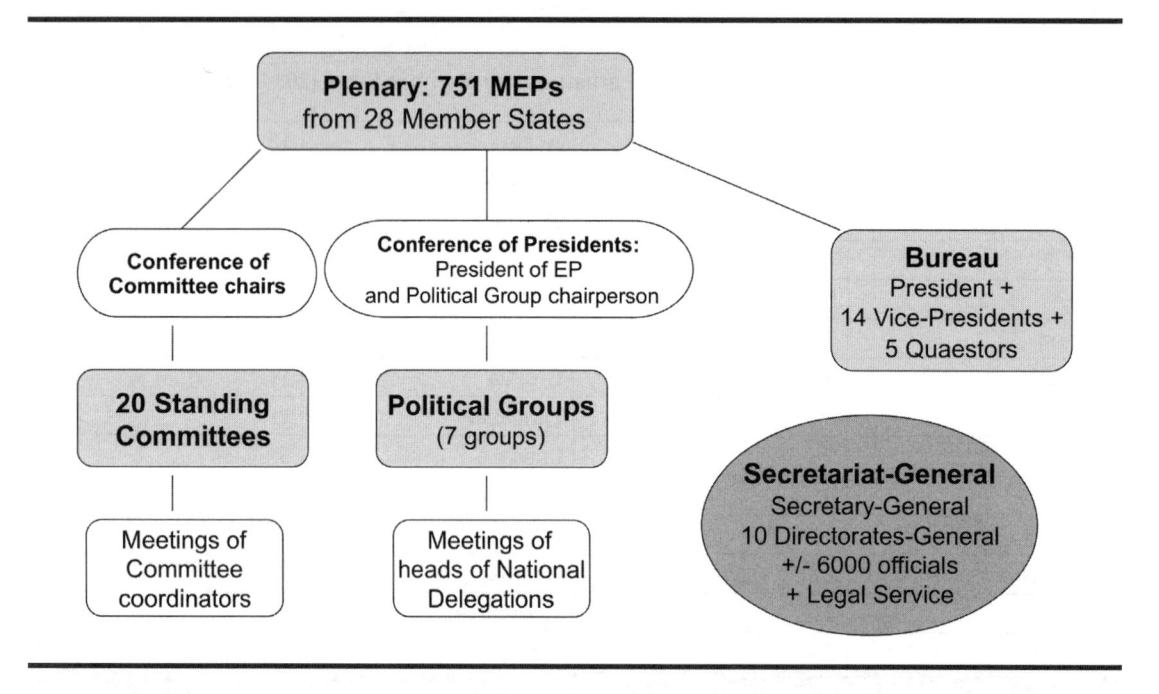

```
                    ┌─────────────────────────┐
                    │   Plenary: 751 MEPs     │
                    │  from 28 Member States  │
                    └─────────────────────────┘
                    /            |            \
      ┌──────────────┐  ┌──────────────────────┐  ┌─────────────────────┐
      │ Conference of│  │ Conference of        │  │       Bureau        │
      │  Committee   │  │ Presidents:          │  │    President +      │
      │    chairs    │  │ President of EP      │  │ 14 Vice-Presidents +│
      │              │  │ and Political Group  │  │    5 Quaestors      │
      └──────────────┘  │ chairperson          │  └─────────────────────┘
             |          └──────────────────────┘
             |                     |
      ┌──────────────┐  ┌──────────────────────┐
      │  20 Standing │  │  Political Groups    │        ┌─────────────────────┐
      │  Committees  │  │    (7 groups)        │        │ Secretariat-General │
      └──────────────┘  └──────────────────────┘        │  Secretary-General  │
             |                     |                    │ 10 Directorates-    │
      ┌──────────────┐  ┌──────────────────────┐        │   General           │
      │  Meetings of │  │    Meetings of       │        │ +/- 6000 officials  │
      │  Committee   │  │  heads of National   │        │  + Legal Service    │
      │ coordinators │  │    Delegations       │        └─────────────────────┘
      └──────────────┘  └──────────────────────┘
```

1. **The Political Group:** MEPs align themselves with one of the seven Political Groups at the European level, or decide to sit as a Non-Attached Member (NI) with no political affiliation.

2. **The President:** Once MEPs have been elected, and have joined their Political Group of choice, there will be a secret ballot of all MEPs for the election of the President and **Vice-Presidents**. Since 1979 there has been a gentleman's agreement between the two main Groups in the Parliament, the European People's Party (EPP) and the Socialists & Democrats (S&D), to divide the five-year term of President into two equal mandates. This system is not without criticism, notably from the other parties which are excluded. Martin Schulz, from the S&D was re-elected President on 1 July 2014, and the EPP and S&D intend to again divide the post for the 2014-2019 Parliament, meaning that the EP presidency will go to a representative from the EPP

Group in early 2017. The exception to this stranglehold on the President's position came in 2002-2004 when Pat Cox, from the ALDE Group, was elected for a two and a half year term.

3. **The Conference of Presidents:** consists of the President of the Parliament and the Presidents of the Political Groups - and as such represents the highest political body in the organisation of the Parliament. It takes decisions on the organisation of the Parliament's work and matters relating to legislative planning; it manages relations with the other institutions and bodies of the EU and with the national parliaments of Member States, and it has responsibility for matters relating to relations with non-member countries and with non-EU institutions and organisations. It meets twice a month to set the agenda for the Plenary sessions. It always aims for consensus although if a vote is required each Political Group President carries the weight of their Group votes.

> **President of the Parliament**
>
> - oversees all of the activities of the Parliament and its constituent bodies;
> - presides over all Plenary sessions, part and full;
> - chairs meetings of the Bureau and Conference of Presidents;
> - represents the Parliament in all external relations;
> - attends meetings of the European Council.
>
> **Recent Presidents**
>
> 2012-2017 : Martin Schulz
> 2009-2012: Jerzy Buzek
> 2007-2009: Hans-Gert Pöttering

4. **The Bureau:** is the highest administrative body for the Parliament, composed of:
   1. the President;
   2. the 14 Vice-Presidents;
   3. the five **Quaestors** (in an advisory capacity only - the five Quaestors are responsible for administrative and financial matters relating directly and personally to MEPs).

The Bureau meets twice a month to deal with financial, organisational and administrative matters concerning MEPs, the internal organisation of the Parliament, its secretariat and constituent bodies. In the event of a tied vote, the President has the casting vote in the Bureau.

5. **The Conference of Committee Chairmen:** it consists of the chairs of all of the Parliament's Committees. It coordinates the activities of the parliamentary Committees, trying to establish horizontal working practices and a forum for the discussion of common issues and problems. It makes recommendations to the Conference of Presidents about the work of Committees and the drafting of the agenda of Plenary sessions.

6. **The Secretariat-General:** The final aspect of the organisation of the Parliament is the Secretariat-General (SG). The head of this body is the Secretary-General who is appointed by the Bureau. The Secretary-General assists the President, the Bureau, the Conference of Presidents and the College of Quaestors in the performance of their duties. The Secretary-General is also the principal authorising officer for the EP budget, and heads a secretariat of about 6,000 officials. The officials

are recruited through open competition and they are assigned to one of the 11 internal administrative structures – such as the Directorate-General (DG) Presidency that is responsible, amongst other things, for the organisation and follow-up from Plenary sittings.

Parliament Secretariat-General

- Secretary-General;
- approx. 6,000 EP staff;
- 11 internal administrative structures - covering procedure and policy.

There is one final, and very important, element of how the Parliament works that needs to be addressed - and that is the multicolour **Parliament Calendar** that most people who work with the EU institutions have to hand. This is a major pre-determined constraint on the individual MEPs and the European Parliament as a whole. There are four main elements of the Parliament's Calendar, although they are not quite as clear-cut as they first seem:

Committee weeks (Pink)	These are held in Brussels when the Committees of the Parliament meet to advance their discussions. Committee meetings can also be held during Plenary weeks in Strasbourg. In a Committee there will usually be between 30-60 MEPs as full members, with an equal number of substitutes. Substitute members can be as, if not more, active in the life and work of a Committee than full members so this needs to be watched on a Committee by Committee basis.
Political Group weeks (Blue)	These are held in Brussels and allow the Political Groups to prepare their positions, notably for the Plenary that is held the week after. Important Political Group meetings are also held in the Plenary week to discuss last minute positions, issues and voting lists.
Plenary weeks (Red)	There are 12 Plenary sessions held in Strasbourg every year. There the full Parliament holds its debates and votes. There are also six red 'mini-Plenary' sessions held in Brussels every year.
Travel and constituency weeks (Turquoise)	These weeks are when MEPs can travel with their Delegations or return to their constituency.

Having a Parliament Calendar close to hand is essential when trying to set-up meetings and work out timetables of action with MEPs. Download the Parliament's calendar from: http://www.europarl.europa.eu/plenary/en/meetings-search.html.

3.3 Internal structure of the Parliament: Political Groups

The individual MEPs sit within the seven Political Groups in the Parliament. The 2014-2019 legislature is presented in Figure 3.2.

Figure 3.2: Political Groups in the European Parliament

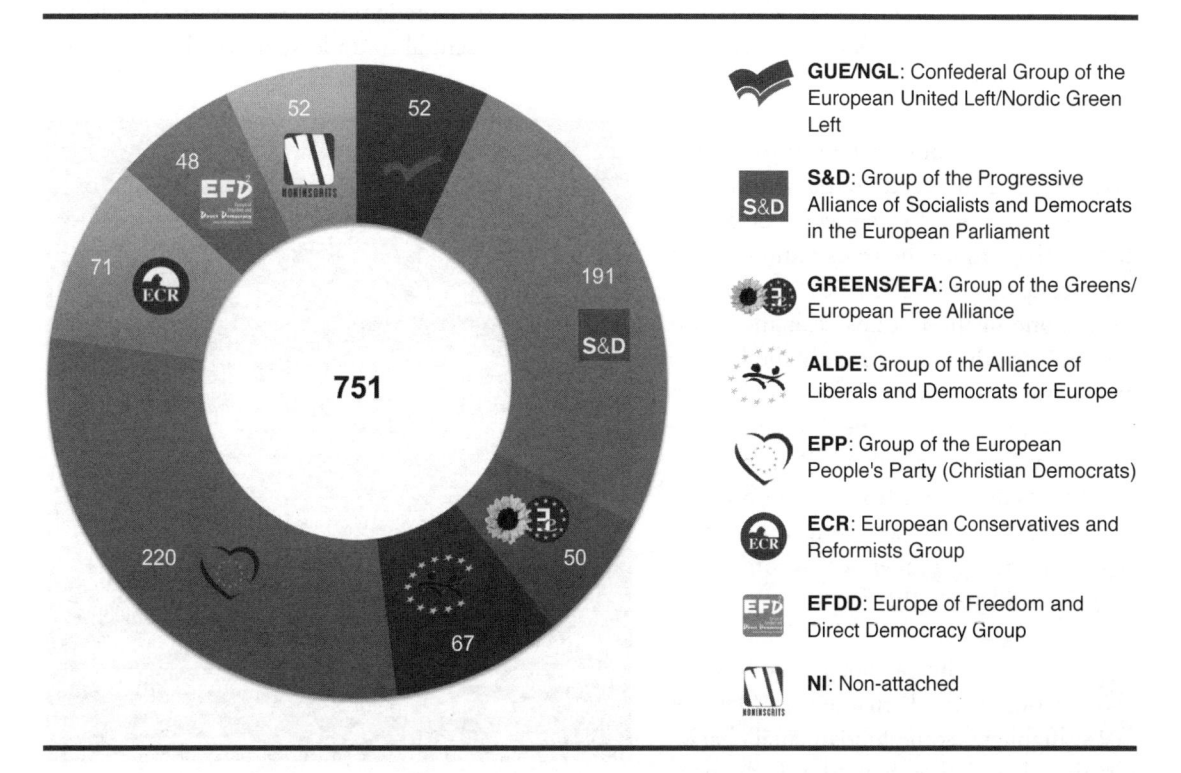

- **GUE/NGL**: Confederal Group of the European United Left/Nordic Green Left
- **S&D**: Group of the Progressive Alliance of Socialists and Democrats in the European Parliament
- **GREENS/EFA**: Group of the Greens/European Free Alliance
- **ALDE**: Group of the Alliance of Liberals and Democrats for Europe
- **EPP**: Group of the European People's Party (Christian Democrats)
- **ECR**: European Conservatives and Reformists Group
- **EFDD**: Europe of Freedom and Direct Democracy Group
- **NI**: Non-attached

Values shown: 52, 52, 48, 71, 191, 220, 67, 50; Total 751.

The Political Groups in the Parliament are very powerful and influential bodies as we shall see through the remainder of this chapter. The politics of the Parliament need to be understood in terms of the interaction between these seven Groups and the numbers they represent. To understand the dynamics of Political Groups in the Parliament it is important to always remember that there is no government, or a stable coalition, therefore the political dynamics are different to what we naturally expect in a Parliament with a government, or governing coalition. A good way to get a thorough understanding of the differences and similarities between the Political Groups is to visit their websites, read their press releases and manifestos and sign up for their newsletters and alerts.

EPP Group	www.eppgroup.eu/home/en
S&D Group	www.socialistsanddemocrats.eu
ALDE Group	www.alde.eu
Greens	www.greens-efa.eu
ECR Group	www.ecrgroup.eu
GUE/NGL	www.guengl.eu
EFDD	www.efdgroup.eu

It is essential to understand the politics between, and within, the Groups and their websites offer an important window into who the Groups are and what they are looking to do in the EU. If you are aiming to engage with the Parliament on an issue it is essential to understand the basic Political Group interplay.

For a Political Group to be formed in the Parliament there need to be at least 25 MEPs from at least seven Member States, criteria that ensure the trans-nationality of the Groups. In the 2014-2019 legislature all but one of the Groups clear these two thresholds with ease, with only the Europe of Freedom and Direct Democracy Group (EFDD) just meeting the Member State minimum figure, with 48 MEPs from seven Member States. Any MEP who chooses not to belong to a Political Group is termed a Non-Attached Member, of whom there were 52 in October 2014.

Figure 3.2, on the previous page, on the composition of the Parliament in October 2014, highlights some fundamental characteristics that define how the Parliament works in general terms. The first obvious point to make is that no single Political Group dominates in the Parliament, meaning that solutions in the Parliament have to be **cross-Group compromises**: there needs to be a coalition to obtain the majorities needed in Committees and Plenary. This basic fact has to underpin every effort to work with the Parliament because there will always be a need to compromise between the largest Groups. A Plenary is always a numbers game within, and between, the Groups - you will always need to follow these numbers because several different coalitions are possible. From this it follows that it is crucial to try and gain the support of the main Groups in the Parliament, and also to avoid neglecting a Political Group, to have the greatest chances of success. This point leads to a second key fact, one that is perhaps a little obscured in Figure 3.2: it is essential to understand the internal dynamics of each individual Political Group to try and ensure their support. For this reason it is important to look a little closer at the composition and functioning of the Political Groups.

A final point of importance relates to the comings and goings of MEPs in the Parliament, both within as they change between Political Groups and Committees, and also outside as a high number of MEPs leave to take up other (usually national) positions. MEPs do not usually have a stringent mandate in their Brussels work and they will have less attachment to their European Political Group than to their national Political Group. The organisation of the Political Groups is presented in Figure 3.3.

Political Group or Political Party?

The Political Groups listed above are all affiliated to one of the ten European Political Parties that operate in the EU - the 'Europarties'.

The *Parties* are funded and regulated by the EU and they operate across the institutions - notably in the Parliament through their affiliated *Groups* and MEPs.

European Political Parties are made up of national parties (from within and outside the EU) as well as it being possible to join on an individual basis. The Parties are very influential over-arching political structures that extend beyond the Parliament - with excellent networks and contacts to influence all aspects of EU business.

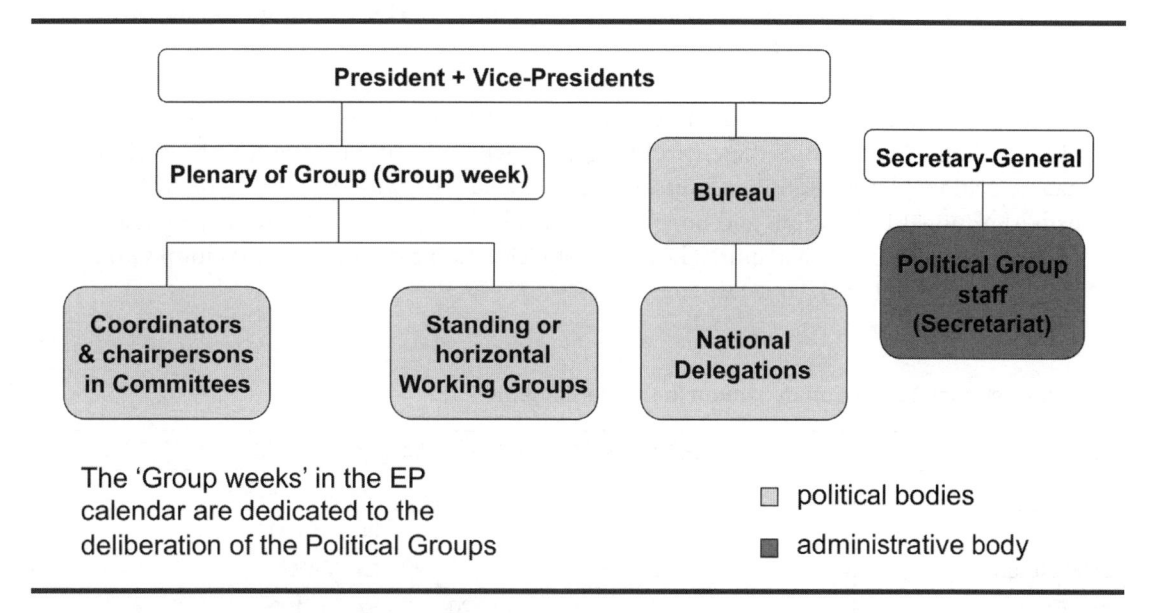

Figure 3.3: Organisation of Political Groups in the European Parliament

```
                    President + Vice-Presidents
         ┌──────────────────┬──────────────┐
   Plenary of Group                    Bureau        Secretary-General
   (Group week)                          │                  │
     ┌───────┴────────┐                  │          Political Group
  Coordinators    Standing or       National            staff
  & chairpersons  horizontal        Delegations      (Secretariat)
  in Committees   Working Groups
```

The 'Group weeks' in the EP calendar are dedicated to the deliberation of the Political Groups

☐ political bodies
■ administrative body

Figure 3.3 provides a general view of the organisation within a Political Group in the Parliament - it is not a replica of any Group in particular, but rather it attempts to pull together the main elements of how all Political Groups are structured and work. Common, and important, features are listed below.

1. **The President:** At the head of the Group are the President and Vice-Presidents (VPs) (normally between three and six VPs), usually elected by secret ballot. The President of the Group normally keeps the post for the duration of the legislature.

2. **The Bureau:** The strategic decisions, creation of Working Groups and the approval of financial decisions of the Political Group is all done by the Bureau of the Group - composed of the President, Vice-Presidents, members of the Political Group who are in the Parliament's Bureau, chairpersons of Committees, former Presidents of either the Parliament or the Political Group and one representative of each National Delegation, usually the head of the National Delegation. The main objective of the Bureau is to set the long-term strategy for the Group.

3. **The National Delegations:** Each Political Group is composed of a number of National Delegations, and these will be very important power players within the Political Group - because depending on their size, they can influence the positions of the Group on everything from high-level strategy to detailed voting lists and specific amendments. Knowing the National Delegations within each Group, and understanding their dynamics, is important to working successfully with the Group as a whole. Each National Delegation can in certain senses represent a separate entity, and National Delegation unity within a Group should never be assumed, as this can change issue by issue. Of particular interest is whether the national party of the National Delegation is

in government in their Member State, in which case they will tend to work closely with their home government positions. It is also important to identify the **Delegation spokesperson** for your particular issue and the **Delegation head**. For example the EPP Group has 27 National Delegations (only the UK is missing), ranging from one MEP (Denmark and Estonia) to the more powerful 34-strong Germans and 23-strong Poles (as of October 2014). When the Plenary of the Political Group votes these two Delegations will obviously be crucial. The S&D Group had 28 National Delegations, the largest being the Italian one, with 31 MEPs. The ALDE Group had 20 National Delegations and none of them made double figures - 8 from Spain and 7 each from France and the Netherlands. The National Delegation dynamics of all Political Groups are highlighted in Table 3.3.

Table 3.3 National Delegation dynamics in the Parliament

Group	No. MEPs	No. Delegations	Largest Delegations
EPP:	220	27	34 - Germany (15%)
S&D:	191	28	32 - Italy (16%)
ECR Group:	71	15	20 - UK (28%)
ALDE:	67	20	8 - Spain (12%)
GUE/NGL:	52	14	11 - Spain (21%)
Greens:	50	17	13 - Germany (26%)
EFDD:	48	7	24 - UK (50%)

What we see in Table 3.3 is that only the S&D have Delegations from all Member States (though the EPP have Delegations from 27 of the 28) and also that, as might be expected, the larger Member States dominate all the Groups. An interesting number is the percentage of the Groups' MEPs represented by the largest Delegations - where we see that the domination of Germany in the EPP and S&D Groups is diluted to 15% and 14% respectively (Italy represents 7% and 16%). The relevance of this is evident when looking at how important Germany is within in the Greens - with 26%, and even more importantly the 50% UK domination of the EFDD Group. These figures help an understanding of the drivers of a Political Group - and should always be kept in mind.

At the European level the Political Groups do not have a strong whip sanction system, whereby members can be sanctioned for not following Group lines, such as by not being placed on the next party lists for elections (which is the power of national parties, not the European Groups). Despite the power of National Delegations and the lack of a strong whip sanction system, Group voting in the Parliament is seen to be very coherent. This trend is very important and makes working successfully with members of the Group vital. For more on Group voting behaviour and coherence, see www.votewatch.eu (which we come back to in more detail later on).

4. **The Working Group:** The proposals that come before the Political Group Plenary are prepared by a Working Group (WG). In some Groups (ALDE for example) any MEP from the Political Group can sit in a WG, irrespective of its Committee or interests, and in others (EPP for example) only MEPs from the relevant Committees can attend. The WG meets the week before Plenary, to discuss and decide on amendments and resolutions to be tabled by the Group, and on any politically sensitive or controversial dossiers that are coming up in the next Plenary. The objectives of WG meetings are two-fold:
   - To form and agree on Group positions from the various Committees whilst keeping a horizontal overview in mind.
   - To find out any sensitive or potentially difficult issues - which would then go to the Group Plenary. This process makes it easier for the Group to be coherent and cohesive when it then comes to full Parliament votes, hence maximising their voting potential.

   The main driving forces in these WGs are the rapporteurs and the Committee coordinators who will try to steer their Committee positions through the WG for full Group Plenary support.

5. **The Plenary or Group meeting:** The main decision-taking body of the Group is the Plenary or Group meeting. It takes place at the end of the Political Group week in the Parliament Calendar, and also during Strasbourg weeks to refine voting positions. It is within this body that the positions of the Political Group will be voted and discussed - hence the importance of working with Political Groups and understanding the internal political and voting dynamics. The Groups usually vote by a show of hands and require a simple majority of members present to adopt a Group position. Given the high level of Group voting cohesion in the Parliament (which we come back to later) the vote within the Group is vital for anyone trying to work with a Political Group. The Group's position is usually strictly followed by all of its MEPs in Plenary, except if a 'free vote' is declared beforehand.

6. **The Secretariat:** Each Political Group has its own secretariat which is led by a Secretary-General. The size of the Secretariat is proportionate to the size of the Group in the Parliament, and all of the staff, or political advisers, can be found on their websites. The Group staff are usually assigned to a Committee (anything from one person covering an entire Committee for a small Group, to three to four advisers per Committee for a larger Group) and they assist their Group MEPs in that Committee by monitoring work, offering research and drafting, liaising with counterparts in other Groups, working on voting lists and keeping important 'work in progress tables'. The Political Group staff is often called into action when an MEP from their Group takes on a rapporteurship - as it will assist with the research, discussions and drafting.

7. **The Group coordinator:** The final key person to highlight within the Group architecture is the coordinator. The full members of a Group who sit in a Committee in the Parliament elect from among themselves a coordinator (and vice coordinator(s) sometimes) for a two and a half year duration - a decision which is confirmed by the Bureau. The coordinator provides political steering and guidance for the Group on the issues that run through their Committee. They will report back to the Group on developments in their Committee and represent Group positions

back in the Committee. A coordinator will also organise the activities of the Group members sitting in their Committee to ensure coherence, consistency and to maximise their efficiency and influence. This will involve nominations of (shadow) rapporteurs, and coordinating any Committee voting. Each Political Group will have one coordinator (and possibly a vice coordinator) in each Committee (if their numbers allow of course).

3.4 Internal structure of the Parliament: Committees, Delegations and Intergroups

There is one final element of Figure 3.1 on the architecture of the Parliament that needs to be explained - the Committees. The Committees are the specialist engines of the Parliament where the technical and detailed work is done, and where the Political Groups develop their positions on an issue, preparing the work of the Parliament Plenary. There are 20 **Standing Committees** in the Parliament, and the list is as follows:

Table 3.4: List of European Parliament Committees

AFCO	Constitutional Affairs	**FEMM**	Women's Rights and Gender Equality
AFET	Foreign Affairs • DROI Human Rights • SEDE Security and Defence	**IMCO**	Internal Market and Consumer Protection
AGRI	Agriculture and Rural Development	**INTA**	International Trade
BUDG	Budgets	**ITRE**	Industry, Research and Energy
CONT	Budgetary Control	**JURI**	Legal Affairs
CULT	Culture and Education	**LIBE**	Civil Liberties, Justice and Internal Affairs
DEVE	Development	**PECH**	Fisheries
ECON	Economic and Monetary Affairs	**PETI**	Petitions
EMPL	Employment and Social Affairs	**REGI**	Regional Development
ENVI	Environment, Public Health and Food Safety	**TRAN**	Transport and Tourism

Source: www.europarl.europa.eu/activities/Committees/CommitteesList.do?language=EN

The list of Committees in Table 3.4 is the configuration within the Parliament in 2014. The list of competences can be found on the website of each individual Committee, along with other very useful information (see box on the next page).

The Committees vary considerably in how they operate, how they relate to the outside world, how much information they make available on their parliamentary websites and generally in how they conduct their business. These differences make it very difficult to generalise about Committee practice in the Parliament as a whole - each Committee often operates in its own separate universe. One thing that is common is the fact that Committees usually meet in Brussels during the two weeks following any Plenary session in Strasbourg, in preparation for the next Plenary. The Committees examine questions referred to them by the Parliament, by debating, preparing reports, opinions and resolutions on legislative and non-legislative dossiers. Committees can also meet, exceptionally, in Strasbourg if the need arises.

> **Committee websites - A wealth of information**
>
> List of members, draft agendas, minutes of previous meetings, calendar of future meetings, work in progress, working documents, reports and opinions of the Committee
>
> *In addition, some Committees have:*
> Newsletters, press releases, details of secretariat staff to contact
> http://www.europarl.europa.eu/committees/en/home.html
>
> Also **follow the Committees live** on your computer with the web-streaming:
> http://www.europarl.europa.eu/ep-live/en/schedule?language=en

Most MEPs serve on one Committee as a full member and on a second as a substitute. It is also possible for an MEP to be a full member of more than one Committee because the number of Committee seats is greater than the number of MEPs. The official process is that Committee positions are assigned through a Plenary vote every two and a half years, when seats are granted according to the size of each Political Group. It is then up to the individual Political Groups to decide which MEPs will fill each of the Committee positions they have received. This process varies across Political Groups but is often done through national party delegations. Each MEP will often specialise within their Committee, usually in one specific area of competence of their Committee - which means nearly all MEPs have a specialist area of competence.

Each Committee has its own Secretariat, usually staffed by around six to ten Parliament officials. These staff will offer dedicated support to the MEPs in the Committee for all legislative and non-legislative activities of the Committee. Secretariat staff assist in the drafting of **reports**, **opinions**, **resolutions** and **working documents** and advise MEPs on questions of substance and procedure. They draw up Committee meeting agendas and voting lists, prepare Committee meetings and assist the chairperson and MEPs in their daily Committee-related duties. Officials of Committees are often allocated to specific dossiers in the Committee, and are hence privy to all information relating to their files.

In addition to Committees, the Parliament also has a plethora of **Delegations to third countries** as listed in Table 3.5 on the next page.

Table 3.5: Conference of Delegation chairs

	Europe	Non-Europe
Joint parliamentary Committees	6	4
Parliamentary Cooperation Committees	4	1
Inter-parliamentary Delegations	1	24
Parliamentary Assemblies		5
Total		45

Find all Delegations at: www.europarl.europa.eu/activities/delegations/home.do?language=en

MEPs make up these Delegations to third countries, regions and organisations. They often hold a few meetings each year, alternately in the Parliament and in the partner country/region. The Delegations are formed in the same way as a Committee with a chairperson, Vice-chairs and a Secretariat. The Delegations have different tasks depending on their partner country or region, so this can be anything from the supervision of the implementation of an accession agreement to an all-encompassing political dialogue. The Delegations are a very good example of the informal powers of the Parliament, especially in the area of external relations, where the Parliament is able to extend its influence. Delegations are vitally important for anyone working with the partner region/country because they offer another avenue and forum for discussion - usually wide-ranging discussion. So while they do not take formal decisions, or formally set agendas, they can bring issues to light and make important statements. It is another way to get your point across to your audience and it can be very useful when your interests correspond to Delegation interests.

There are also **Intergroups** (Rule 34, RoP), which are unofficial groupings of MEPs to hold informal exchanges, usually with industry and civil society, on specific cross-cutting issues. They are not formal Parliament mechanisms, and as such they exist to offer an informal forum for exchange and information. A distinction needs to be made between the Intergroups that are recognised by

---

Recognised Intergroups for 2014-2019 Parliamentary term

Active ageing, intergenerational solidarity & family policies; Anti-racism and diversity; Biodiversity, countryside, hunting and recreational fisheries; Children's rights; Climate change, sustainable development and biodiversity; Common goods and public services; Creative industries; Digital agenda; Disability; Extreme poverty and human rights; European tourism development, cultural heritage, Way of St. James and other European cultural routes; Freedom of religion and belief and religious tolerance; Integrity - Transparency, anti- corruption and organised crime; Lesbian, Gay, Bisexual, Transgender and Intersex rights - LGBTI; Long-term investment and reindustrialisation; Rural, mountainous and remote areas; Seas, rivers, islands and coastal areas; SMEs - Small and medium-sized enterprises; Sky and Space; Social economy; Sports; Trade Unions; Traditional minorities, National communities and Languages; Urban; Welfare and conservation of animals; Western Sahara; Wine, spirits and quality foodstuffs; Youth.

the Parliament, and the plethora of informal gatherings and meetings of MEPs that exist. In 2014 there were 28 recognised Intergroups in the Parliament, as decided in December 2014 for the parliamentary term. They usually meet during Plenary weeks in Strasbourg and are open to the public. They are listed in the box on the previous page.

For full details of each of the Intergroups, including their chairpersons and full lists of members go to: http://www.europarl.europa.eu/aboutparliament/en/00c9d93c87/Intergroups.html.

Both the recognised Intergroups and the non-officially recognised meetings of MEPs are important informal vectors of influence in the Parliament and need to be taken seriously. They are cross-group gatherings of MEPs interested in the same subject dealing directly with stakeholders - thus offering an extremely privileged platform to those stakeholders involved.

3.5 How the Parliament works: From the European Commission into a Committee

Having now outlined the main institutional actors and bodies in the Parliament it is possible to enter into the detail of how the Parliament takes decisions. Decision-making in the Parliament follows a pre-determined path that will be mapped out in the coming pages.

The work of the Parliament that this chapter will base its analysis on is that of **legislative proposals from the Commission** as this is usually the most important. Hence the flow that follows is based on the usual process of dealing with a legislative file. It is, however, entirely possible that the Parliament drafts a report not based on a Commission proposal. The most common type of report here is an **Own-Initiative Report**, of which there are five distinct categories (all of these have to be authorised by the Conference of Presidents):

1. legislative;
2. strategic;
3. non-legislative;
4. annual activity and monitoring;
5. implementation reports (automatic authorisation).

These Own-Initiative Reports can be extremely important documents in their respective fields, as they will be directly targeted at some political objective - usually influencing the thinking of the Commission when it is drafting or working on legislative proposals. They are one of the most direct ways in which the Parliament tries to influence the Commission's right of initiative. These Own-Initiative Reports follow the same path through the Parliament, but will be subject to differing levels of interest and engagement by MEPs and Political Groups and will also receive different levels of amendments and voting attention.

1. The first stage of the process starts when the Parliament officially receives the proposal from the Commission in its Plenary session, as outlined in Figure 3.4.

Figure 3.4: Proposal: From European Commission to a European Parliament Committee

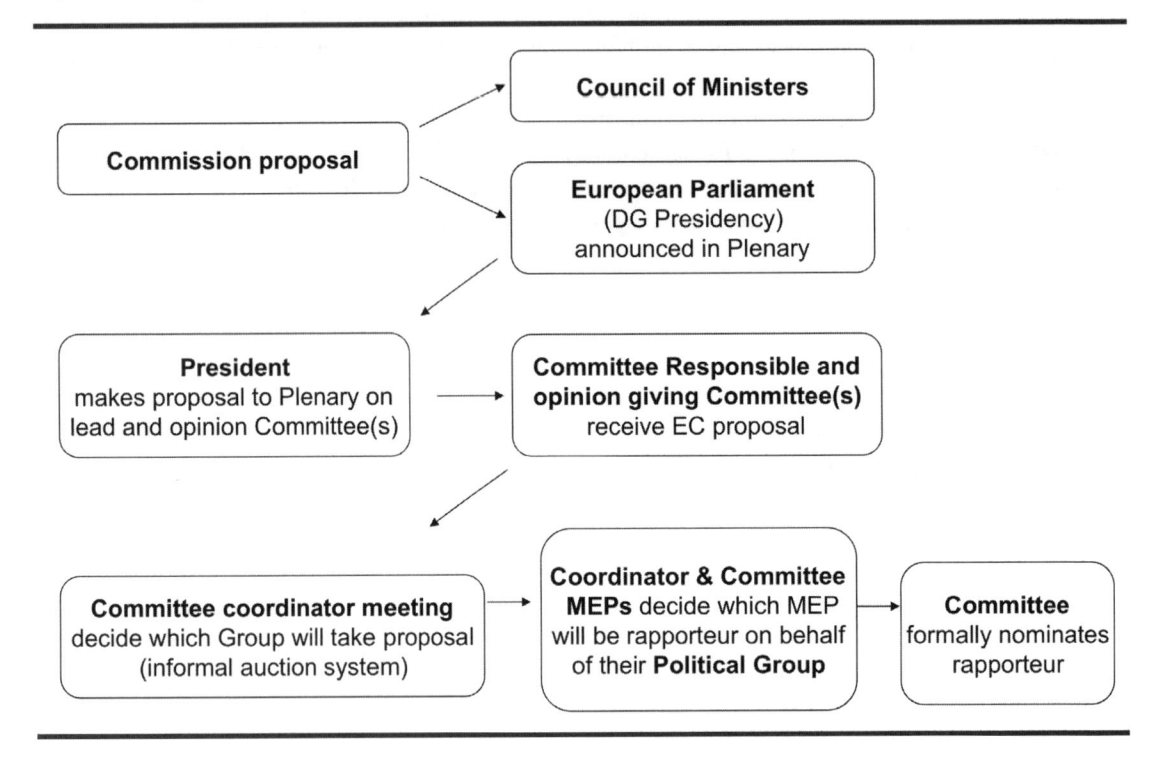

```
                                    ┌─────────────────────┐
                                  ─▶│ Council of Ministers│
                                 ╱  └─────────────────────┘
┌──────────────────────┐        ╱   ┌─────────────────────┐
│ Commission proposal  │───────┼───▶│ European Parliament │
└──────────────────────┘        ╲   │   (DG Presidency)   │
                                 ╲  │ announced in Plenary│
                                  ╲ └─────────────────────┘
                                   ╲        │
┌──────────────────────┐            ▼       ▼
│      President       │    ┌─────────────────────────┐
│ makes proposal to    │───▶│ Committee Responsible and│
│ Plenary on lead and  │    │ opinion giving Committee(s)│
│ opinion Committee(s) │    │   receive EC proposal    │
└──────────────────────┘    └─────────────────────────┘
         ▲                           │
         │                           ▼
┌──────────────────────┐    ┌─────────────────────────┐    ┌──────────────────┐
│ Committee coordinator│    │ Coordinator & Committee │    │    Committee     │
│ meeting decide which │───▶│ MEPs decide which MEP   │───▶│ formally nominates│
│ Group will take      │    │ will be rapporteur on   │    │    rapporteur    │
│ proposal (informal   │    │ behalf of their         │    │                  │
│ auction system)      │    │ Political Group         │    │                  │
└──────────────────────┘    └─────────────────────────┘    └──────────────────┘
```

2. Once the Parliament has received the proposal it must announce it in the next Plenary session, and the official process can start.

> The legislative terms of the Parliament are split into annual session, part sessions and sittings:
> **Annual Session** - Second Tuesday in March.
> **Part-Session** - Monthly meetings of the full Parliament.
> **Sitting** - The daily meetings of the Parliament.

3. DG Presidency will make a suggestion of attribution of the proposal to the relevant Committee(s) through a formal decision of the President and the Conference of Presidents.

4. The normal procedure would be that the President then makes the formal proposal to the Plenary, usually in the minutes to the part-session and not actually during the sitting itself.

5. In 99% of cases this is the end of a straightforward process, but there can be cases of conflict. In these cases the Conference of Presidents can request the Conference of Committee Chairmen to come up with a recommendation, which it will then endorse.

> **Written declarations (Rule 136, RoP)**
>
> Up to five MEPs can submit a written declaration of not more than 200 words. It must be an issue falling within the competence of the EU, and not subject to an ongoing legislative procedure.
>
> They are printed and displayed outside the chambers in Strasbourg and Brussels.
>
> If it is signed by a majority of MEPs, within three months, it is adopted by the Parliament and announced by the President.
>
> Declarations are good ways to raise the profile of an issue and to garner support. They can also be very damaging - so keep an eye out for them.

As it is frequent that more than one Committee has an interest in a proposal the most common nomination is for both a **Committee Responsible** (also known as a **lead Committee**) and up to three (but usually no more) **opinion-giving Committees**. The committee responsible will set the timetable, through the Committee rapporteur, and is where the thrust of the discussion will take place. The opinion-giving Committees will add their expertise on the areas of the proposal that concerns them. This opinion will take the form of amendments and will be submitted for vote in the Committee responsible according to their timetable - and an opinion-giving Committee should never be neglected as their influence can be significant. Sometimes two (or more) Committees have an equal interest in an issue, which can lead to an **associated procedure** between the committee responsible and the opinion-giving Committee(s) - with the difference being that the Committee responsible should accept without a vote the amendments of the opinion-giving Committee (Rule 54 of the RoP - used to be known as the 'Hughes procedure'). In 2010 this led to the first **joint Committee meetings**, with joint votes, between associated Committees, under Rule 55 of the RoP which states that the Conference of Presidents may allow a joint Committee meeting and joint vote on a single draft report. This is a development that is worth keeping an eye on because it alters the dynamics of a dossier.

6. Once the Committees dealing with an issue have been decided, the proposal will be forwarded to them and, usually, announced in the next Committee meeting. The first decision is whether the Committee intends to react or not. After a first discussion of the issue, the chairperson may propose that the Commission proposal be approved without amendment. Unless at least one tenth of the MEPs in the Committee object, the chairperson can present to Plenary a report approving the proposal.

If the Committee decides to react then it is necessary for it to select a rapporteur, from the Committee members or substitutes. The **rapporteur** is the pivotal figure who will steer the dossier through the Committee and into the Plenary. This decision is taken in the **Committee coordinators meeting** – a closed door meeting that usually takes place every few weeks, depending on the individual Committee practice, between the coordinators of all the Political Groups in the Committee. The selection of rapporteurs has taken on rather mythical status due to the complicated, behind closed doors system that is used. Each Political Group receives points for the number of MEPs it has, and it can use these points to bid for reports in these coordinator meetings using a form of 'auction system'. The majority of these decisions are pre-cooked, or subject to negotiated agreement, amongst the Political Groups and the Committee coordinators, and there is rarely prolonged discussion over which Group will take a report. The most straightforward bidding, and the one costing the least points, is to propose a recognised specialist in the field of the dossier itself, perhaps an MEP who worked on the dossier previously. It is also therefore common for coordinators to come to agreements on future reports in the Committee. For frequently recurring reports, such as annual reports (e.g the EU Annual Budget) a rotation system between Groups is set up and announced. The choice of rapporteur is very important because it is a fundamental moment in the life of a dossier in the Parliament - the choice of rapporteur will have a large influence on the development and drafting of a dossier. The majority of politically sensitive files will go to the larger Groups, or expert MEPs.

The majority of report bids that a coordinator places in the Committee coordinators meeting will not have been explicitly discussed by the Group Plenary - it is only the most politically sensitive ones that will come to the attention of the Group as a whole.

7. Once the bidding has taken place within the coordinators meeting and a Group has been accorded the report they will nominate their rapporteur (usually already done in the process of bidding) and the end of the process is that the rapporteur is announced in Committee. The choice of rapporteur will be made by the coordinator and the Group MEPs sitting in the Committee - with the coordinator being the key person involved in this process. For example, in October 2014, in the Environment Committee the ALDE Group had twelve (full and substitute) MEPs, including their coordinator, Gerben-Jan Gerbrandy. This Group of MEPs, under the guidance of the coordinator, will select a rapporteur from their ranks and then meet regularly to agree their positions, voting suggestions and generally refine their strategy in Committee. Once this Group of MEPs has nominated their rapporteur, he or she will be formally nominated by the Committee. The coordinator and the Group in a Committee will also nominate shadow rapporteurs to follow key dossiers and anything of interest to the Group. The process in Figure 3.4, from formal reception of a Commission proposal to the nomination of the rapporteur in Committee, can

> **Political Groups in Committees**
>
> Each Political Group will be represented in a Committee by their apportioned number of MEPs. The key figures will be the Group coordinator, the deputy coordinator (not all Groups have one), any rapporteurs and shadow rapporteurs on specific dossiers.
>
> These MEPs will form the Group positions in Committee under the guidance of the coordinator. They will have preparatory meetings in Committee, and also Group weeks to organise their positions, voting lists, compromise suggestions, etc.
>
> These MEPs will drive their position through Committee, Plenary and their own Group discussions.

take anything from two weeks to six months, depending on the dossier at hand and the importance attached to its speedy resolution. In this sense the Groups will take an overview of the Commission Work Programme and select which reports to go for in advance - something that will lead to strategic choices and strategic negotiations between the Groups. This can lead to rotation systems, more than one rapporteur at a time and other agreements within Committees. There is also the issue of reports that no one wants, or bids for - because these need to be attributed. The practice differs by Committee, but many Committees have a system whereby the Committee chair takes reports that Groups do not bid for.

Before a Commission proposal arrives in the Parliament it is important to have already identified the likely Committees that will be involved and the key MEPs within them. This is possible by looking at past reports, questions, interventions and other activities of the MEPs in the Committees. In this way when the Parliament starts work you are fully prepared and ready to immediately engage with the right MEPs.

3.6 How the European Parliament works: Preparation in Committee

Once a proposal has been attributed to a Committee and a rapporteur chosen by the Political Group responsible for the file, the Committee process can begin. The process in a Committee is outlined in Figure 3.5 below.

Figure 3.5: Process in European Parliament Committee

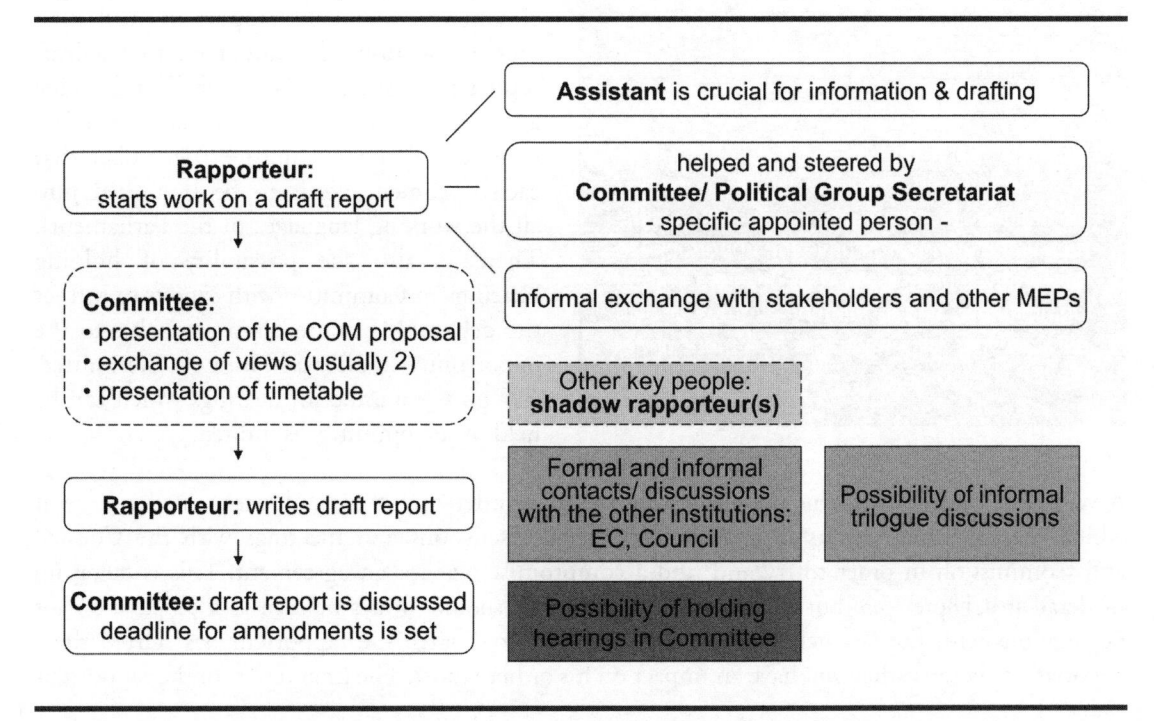

The preparation of a dossier in the Committee stage is not necessarily as linear as Figure 3.5 would suggest, but nonetheless it captures the essence, and the essential elements, of the process. Basically the rapporteur is responsible for bringing before the Committee a draft report on the Commission proposal which should include amendments with justifications and an explanatory statement (optional). Between the nomination of a rapporteur and the issuing of a draft report into the Committee there are a number of ways in which a rapporteur can get information and prepare their work, which will be determined on a case-by-case basis.

> **Own-Initiative Reports**
>
> If the Commission has not published a Communication or a legislative text the Parliament can chose to issue an Own-Initiative Report - which can lead to a motion for a resolution.
>
> These reports are widely used by the Parliament to informally influence the debate around an issue - notably to colour the thinking of the Commission while it is drafting its proposal.

The process in Committee is that the Commission proposal will be outlined in a Committee meeting by the rapporteur with some initial thoughts and ideas. After this, in discussion with the Committee Secretariat, there will be one (or more than one) exchange of views with other Committee members on the proposal at various stages of progress (depending on how sensitive it is). These exchanges take place in the publicly accessible and web-streamed Committee meetings.

> **Following the Parliament online**
>
> European Parliament news and reports are web streamed on EuroparlTV: http://www.europarltv.europa.eu/en/home.aspx
>
> On the Parliament's website, under the 'EP TV' tab you can view live Plenary and Committee meetings, as well as access archived material. You have the opportunity to follow developments on your dossiers both in Committee(s) and in Plenary - from your own desk, in your own language. See more under the 'EP TV' tab.

This will lead to the rapporteur, after guidance from the Committee Secretariat, issuing a timetable for the report (this can be challenged by the Committee chairperson in exceptional circumstances). The rapporteur will first present a **working document** and then a **draft report** for discussion, after which a deadline is set for proposed amendments from other members of the Committee (remember that each document needs to be translated into all the working languages of the Parliament). There is also the possibility of holding **hearings** in Committee with experts to further the debate. MEPs are often amenable to the opportunity to offer a hearing in Committee, though the number of hearings which can be held by a Committee is limited.

A very important part of this process - which will be different for every dossier – is the stage at which the rapporteur enters into informal trilogue discussions and meetings with the Council and Commission in order to try and find a compromise text for an agreement. This is taken up in detail in Chapter 5.3, but discussions in Committee should always be seen as a preparation for negotiations with the Council - and it is crucial to know when the rapporteur has started these negotiations because they will have an impact on his or her report. The final report of the rapporteur that will be voted in Committee will likely be an agreed text with the Council (if agreement was possible in trilogues) - something that is important for the next stages of a dossier in the Parliament. The Committee votes on the text in one of their Committee week meetings, requiring at least a quarter of members to be present (it can be a majority of component members if this is requested by one sixth of the Committee) before voting by simple majority. This is usually done by a show of hands unless, exceptionally, one quarter of the members request a roll-call vote (we will come back to voting technicalities later) - which means there are no records of who voted how from Committee. The only way to know is to actually be in the room when they vote.

As the chapter has shown thus far the procedure for any given individual dossier is relatively strict, although flexibility exists over some of the options and the timeline. This makes it difficult to predict the course of any dossier in advance; however, a key moment to look for is the announcement of deadlines for amendments in Committee, to the draft report once it has been produced. From this moment onwards most dossiers move towards a Plenary vote in the same way. The box on the opposite page outlines how it is possible to follow many of the Committee meetings online. You are also able to follow them in the Parliament itself if you can get an access badge, or get signed in.

Aside from the Committee-based discussions, which represent the tip of the iceberg when it comes to how a rapporteur drafts a report, there are a myriad of less formal and less visible processes at play. First and foremost, it is important to ascertain the influences surrounding the drafting of an individual report - this will include the influences on, and roles of, the rapporteur, their assistants, Political Group Secretariat staff, Committee Secretariat staff and external experts. The Committee Secretariats often play an important hidden role in this process, shaping the work on a report, and the rapporteur will have a Secretariat official nominated to follow their report. Political Group staff are also very influential players, even if there are only usually one to two of them per Committee for each Group. So whilst they might be more pushed for time they are usually quite senior experts in their field with a detailed understanding of the technical aspects of a file and also the political workings of the Parliament. It is not unusual to see a rapporteur supported by a combination of Committee Secretariat officials, their own assistants and Political Group staff.

Opinion-Giving Committee amendments
What happens?

1. If the opinion-giving Committee amendments are submitted *before* the Committee responsible deadline they can be taken up by the rapporteur or MEPs in the Committee responsible, and be tabled as Committee responsible amendments.
2. If the opinion-giving Committee amendments are tabled *close to*, or *after*, the Committee responsible amendment deadline they will need to be inserted into the voting list of the Committee responsible. This can take two forms, either integrated into the voting list article by article alongside Committee responsible amendments, or all put at the end of the voting list.

All opinion-giving Committee amendments will be voted on - therefore the opinion-giving Committee needs to be engaged with - and taken seriously.

In addition to the internal support it is also important to establish which external sources of information the rapporteur is relying on. This will be an entirely personal decision of the MEP in question and will, in many cases, be linked to national and personal networks. The Commission is often called on by rapporteurs to provide technical support and facts and figures. Commission officials can also present MEPs with a state of play from the Council discussions and they are always present in Committee meetings to explain and clarify issues that arise about their proposals. The presence of the Commission in Committee is very important for both institutions, as a source of information for the Parliament, and as a source of political intelligence for the Commission.

The other Political Groups in a Committee can name a **shadow rapporteur** to follow the work of the rapporteur closely. If it is an important file the other Political Groups will name heavyweight MEPs as shadows, and often you can gauge the importance the Group attaches to a dossier through the shadow they have nominated. The rapporteur can then use these shadows to see how much political support their report will garner amongst other Political Groups - because always remember that a coalition is needed. The shadows, for their part, will try to work their Political Group interests into the rapporteur's position. The coalition-building ability of a rapporteur is one of the most important qualities needed for success. It also goes without saying that a rapporteur will have to maintain support for their report within their own Political Group, notably through the coordinator and during Group weeks. In this way the influence of Political Groups on the report will always be very high. One final element that will come to weigh on the work of the rapporteur in the Committee responsible is the report from the opinion-giving Committee(s). The amendments tabled by the opinion-giving Committee(s) will all be voted on in the Committee responsible and are therefore very important to follow, as outlined in the box on the previous page.

3.7 How the European Parliament works: Vote in Committee

Once the rapporteur is ready to table their draft report for vote we enter the second stage of the Parliament workflow - that of a vote in Committee, as outlined in Figure 3.6.

Voting in a Committee is an extremely important stage in the life of a dossier - a time when substantive last minute changes are still possible and when voting can remove or approve positions of different actors.

Once the rapporteur has finalised and presented their draft report to the Committee (having consulted their own Committee Group, shadows and external parties to strike the right balance that they hope will succeed) a deadline for amendments will be set (which varies depending on the Committee and the issue under discussion). At this stage any member, or substitute, can table amendments in writing before the deadline and these will be included in the voting list and be voted on in Committee. The key amendments to keep an eye on are those tabled by Group coordinators, or shadows, as they will usually carry more political weight and be subject to negotiations with the rapporteur.

Once the deadline for amendments has been set there is an indicative timetable leading up to the vote, which is as follows:

Deadline for amendments	Ten working days from the meeting at which announced
Availability of amendments in all languages	Three days after availability of all amendments
Draft voting list	At the latest four working days before the vote
Final voting list	The evening before the vote *(This is the key voting list)*

Figure 3.6: Vote in European Parliament Committee

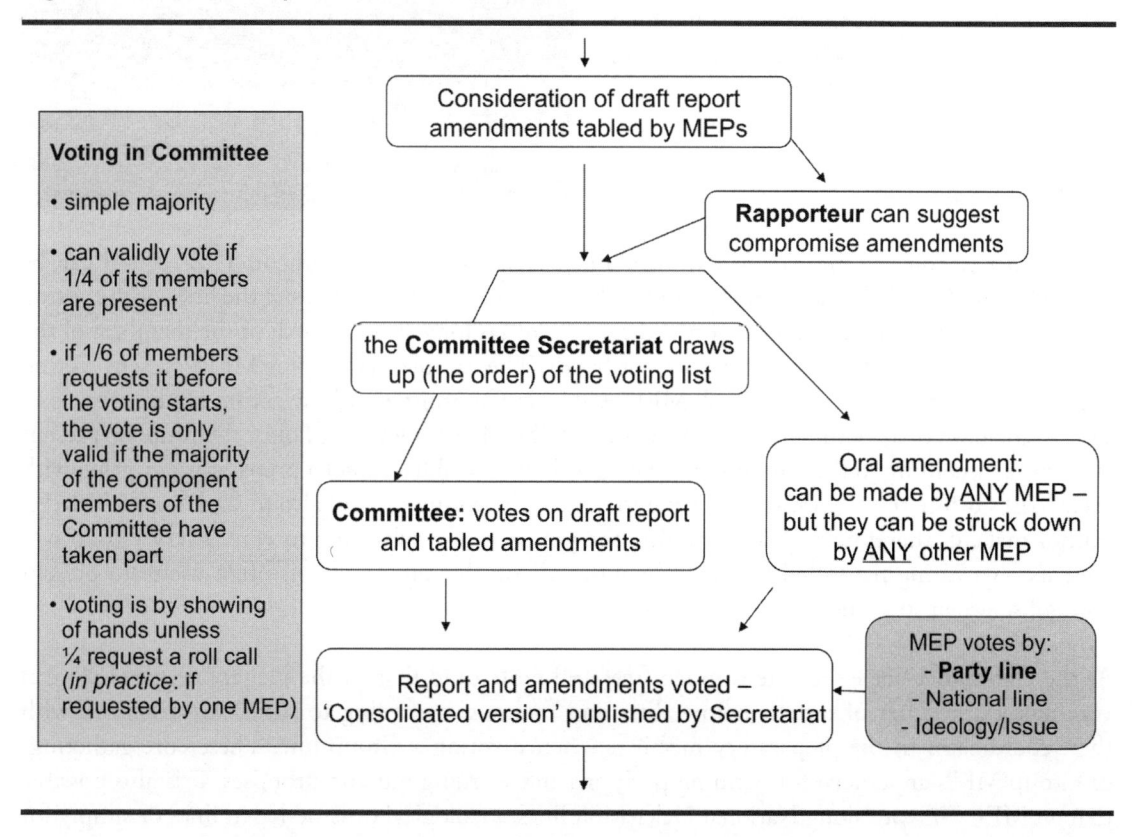

```
                          ↓
            Consideration of draft report
            amendments tabled by MEPs
                    ↓           ↘
                              Rapporteur can suggest
                              compromise amendments
                    ↓           ↙
Voting in Committee
                    the Committee Secretariat draws
• simple majority   up (the order) of the voting list
• can validly vote if
  1/4 of its members
  are present                        Oral amendment:
                                     can be made by ANY MEP –
• if 1/6 of members                  but they can be struck down
  requests it before                 by ANY other MEP
  the voting starts,
  the vote is only   Committee: votes on draft report
  valid if the majority   and tabled amendments
  of the component
  members of the
  Committee have
  taken part                              MEP votes by:
                                          - Party line
• voting is by showing   Report and amendments voted –   - National line
  of hands unless        'Consolidated version' published by Secretariat   - Ideology/Issue
  ¼ request a roll call
  (in practice: if
  requested by one MEP)
                          ↓
```

The rapporteur, through the Committee Secretariat, will receive all the proposed amendments and has the possibility of going to the authors and suggesting compromise amendments to make voting easier in Committee. The Committee Secretariat is responsible for drawing up the final **voting list** - which in itself can be done in a strategic way. The order in which amendments are voted on could have an important impact on the final outcome. There are, however, guidelines as to the order of a vote. Compromise amendments are always first, and amendments from the Committee responsible always precede those of an opinion-giving Committee. Once the amendments have been voted there is a vote on the proposal as a whole (as amended).

For the Committee vote there are a few voting technicalities that can be used, and that can be seen on a voting list. For example, there is a **separate vote** which is a vote on a specific text or paragraph in a report – i.e. if amendments are rejected, the original text shall be deemed adopted unless a separate vote has been requested. According to Rule 58 of the Parliament's ROP, the Committee can request the Commission position on amendments before proceeding to the final vote - something the Commission is usually reluctant to do. Normally a high-ranking Commission official will give a tentative position in Committee.

In the Committee meeting that has been designated as the date of the vote, when the issue comes to vote, an individual MEP can ask to make an oral amendment. This request can be rejected if another MEP makes an objection. The vote will then proceed along the lines of the voting list and is done by simple majority of members present (as long as one fourth of the members of the Committee are present) - usually by show of hands. The 'simple majority of MEPs present' voting rule is vitally important because not all MEPs will be in Committee and the voting can be very close. One of the tasks of a coordinator is to make sure all the MEPs from their Political Group are present and voting according to the Group line. The coordinators will have held a preparatory meeting with their MEPs before the Committee meeting to discuss the voting list and also to find out if any MEP cannot make it, therefore perhaps requiring the presence of a substitute to vote. Every Group will have its own voting list to tell its MEPs how to vote on the day - and it is often useful to present voting lists when speaking with MEPs about forthcoming votes.

> **Voting list - Key document**
>
> The voting list is a key document to get hold of - and more importantly to understand.
>
> A **preliminary** voting list will be drawn up by the Secretariat official and sent to the rapporteur for comments and approval.
>
> After this, a **draft** voting list will be circulated to Political Group Secretariats.
>
> The **final** voting list is usually communicated to the Political Groups the evening before the vote.

At the Committee stage the vote is much freer and more fluid than at the Plenary stage. MEPs can vote along a number of different lines, first and foremost according to what was discussed with their coordinator in the preparatory meetings - hence voting a Group line. These core gatherings of Group MEPs are crucial for defining positions and working out compromises. It is also possible that an MEP will vote along National Delegation lines, ideological or issue-based lines or simply for other personal reasons. It is more likely that you will see an MEP change position, or opinion, in a Committee vote than in a Plenary vote.

Of all the various influences on the vote and preparation of a report in Committee the roles of the Committee Secretariat and Political Group advisers should be firmly highlighted. They will be privy to all developments in substance, procedure and politics - often guiding them due to their experience and influence. They will assist in setting deadlines, drawing up voting lists and (in the case of the Secretariat) finalising the consolidated text after a vote - making them indispensable sources of information.

3.8 How the European Parliament works: From Committee to Plenary vote

After the Committee vote, the final stage of the decision-making procedure within the Parliament is the **Plenary vote** - the final vote to establish the official position of the Parliament as a whole. The Plenary is to the Parliament what the College is to the Commission - the ultimate decision-taking body.

For effective inter-institutional preparation of Plenary sessions there is the so-called '**Inter-institutional Coordination Group**'. This Group is made up of representatives of the secretariats of all institutions. They usually meet once a month on the Tuesday before the Plenary to prepare the forthcoming part-session from an inter-institutional perspective. The vote in the Parliament Plenary is outlined in Figure 3.7.

Figure 3.7: Vote in European Parliament Plenary

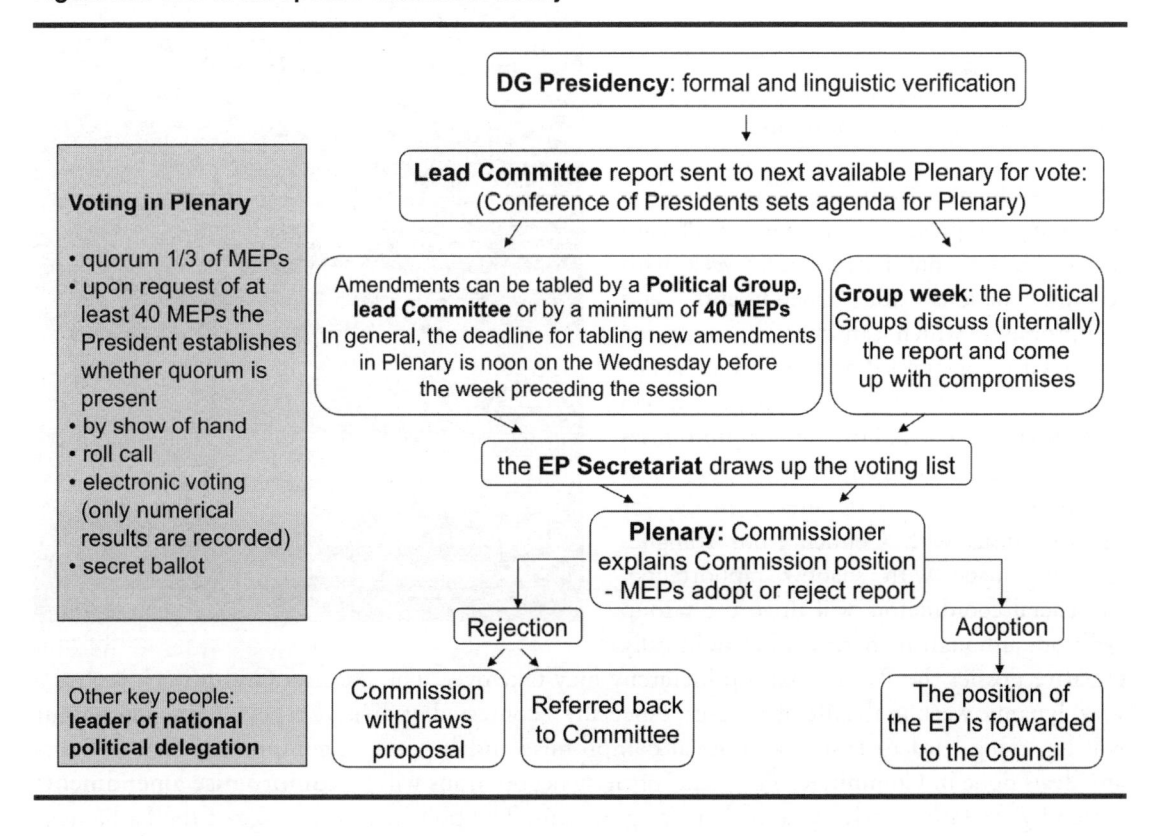

```
                    DG Presidency: formal and linguistic verification
                                        ↓
                    Lead Committee report sent to next available Plenary for vote:
                    (Conference of Presidents sets agenda for Plenary)

Voting in Plenary      Amendments can be tabled by a Political Group,    Group week: the Political
                       lead Committee or by a minimum of 40 MEPs         Groups discuss (internally)
• quorum 1/3 of MEPs   In general, the deadline for tabling new amendments   the report and come
• upon request of at   in Plenary is noon on the Wednesday before        up with compromises
  least 40 MEPs the    the week preceding the session
  President establishes
  whether quorum is              the EP Secretariat draws up the voting list
  present
• by show of hand                        Plenary: Commissioner
• roll call                              explains Commission position
• electronic voting                      - MEPs adopt or reject report
  (only numerical
  results are recorded)         Rejection                         Adoption
• secret ballot

Other key people:      Commission      Referred back       The position of
leader of national     withdraws       to Committee        the EP is forwarded
political delegation   proposal                            to the Council
```

The consolidated version of the report drawn up by the Committee Secretariat is sent to **DG Presidency** as it prepares the next part-session. Normally the text will be placed on the agenda of the next part-session (unless there is political, or technical, reason to hold it back for a future part-session) and this will be made official when the draft agenda is published. From this moment onwards there is the possibility for amendments to be tabled by Political Groups, or a minimum of 40 MEPs, by 12h00 on the Wednesday of the week preceding the part-session. This preceding week is the **Political Group week** and as such is timed for this very reason - to allow the Political Groups to organise themselves for the forthcoming Plenary session. The Political Groups can also meet in Strasbourg on Monday evenings as a preparation meeting, and then again on the Tuesday and Wednesday evenings after the day's proceedings. All of this allows the Group to organise itself and to follow developments closely. As much as the Committee stage of a dossier was all about the rapporteur and the Committee Secretariat, the Plenary stage is all about the Political Groups - they are the drivers of compromise here.

The coordinator from the Committee in question will present to its Group Plenary the issues for vote in the next week with recommendations for amendments and compromises, which can then, if supported by the Group, be tabled on their behalf. A key issue for the coordinator, and rapporteur, will be to keep a tight hold over any compromises that were agreed in Committee voting, so as not to unravel any deals already made (for example deals with Council from trilogues or deals made with shadow rapporteurs). In general coordinators will drive the Group position, although if there is a big politically sensitive dossier the Political Group hierarchy may take over. The Political Group week is thus a very dynamic week in the life of a report, especially a contested or divisive report, as the rapporteur will be trying hard to ensure a political compromise and support, a compromise that honours any deals done in Committee. The result of these negotiations will be **compromise amendments** tabled by the Groups with whom there is agreement. The politics at this stage of the Parliament process take the fore, and a dossier can change radically from the Committee vote. Many of these changes will be done via informal contacts between the rapporteur, coordinators and shadows (and Political Group staff), making it a very difficult week to follow a report on which you are working – which is why previous work and contacts with Political Groups, National Delegations and key Political Group actors is so important.

Voting technicalities

Plenary voting is done by a show of hands unless one of the following is requested/or applies:

Separate vote: vote on a specific text or paragraph in a report, i.e. if amendments are rejected, the original text shall be deemed adopted unless a separate vote has been requested.

Split vote: when an amendment has two or more provisions, or references, that lend themselves to division into two or more parts. This can be used for positioning on very specific (and sensitive) issues.

Electronic vote (EV): The vote is recorded and flashed on the main screen - but individual MEP records are not kept.

Roll-call vote (RCV): The vote is recorded and individual MEP voting records are kept (and published). A RCV is obligatory for the final vote on a Parliament resolution under the OLP.

Any of the above may be requested by a Political Group or at least 40 members. These requests are often politically motivated as one Group tries to split, embarrass or cause problems for other Groups.

One further actor who can have a major influence on the politics of the report to be voted, especially at this stage in the process, is the Council through the Presidency. If the Parliament and Council are trying to find a first reading agreement on a report under the OLP the Council and Parliament will have held a number of trilogue meetings. The Presidency will use the Political Group stage of discussions to intervene and try to maintain any agreement already found with the rapporteur, or to find a compromise agreement. Whilst obviously relevant at the Plenary this aspect of influence in the Parliament will be dealt with explicitly in Chapter 5.3 on the OLP.

Once all amendments have been tabled there will be continued discussion to ensure that whatever compromises were reached are delivered in the Plenary vote. A number of amendments tabled at this stage in the process are simply amendments for the gallery - that is amendments that do not seek to genuinely contribute to the text or have any real chances of success, but that will play well for political and national constituencies at a later stage. DG Presidency will draw up the Plenary voting list for all reports on the Plenary agenda. Here there are further possibilities with regard to the voting list, such as a request for a split vote, or a roll-call vote (Rules 176 and 180, RoP). An example voting list from a Plenary sitting in 2010 is given below - giving a good visual representation of what you need to work with.

Subject	Am No.	Author	RCV etc.	Vote	RCV/EV - remarks
Text as a whole - Block 1 - compromise	63 CP	committee ALDE, PPE-DE, PSE, Verts/ALE GUE/NGL		+	
Block 2 - amendments by the committee responsible - block vote	1-11 13-25 27-37	committee			
Block 3 - 'wild animals'	40-62	UEN		-	
Article 3, § 2	63 CP	committee ALDE, PPE-DE, PSE, Verts/ALE GUE/NGL	EV	+	435,174,20
	39	> 40 Members			
Rectical 13	63CP	committee ALDE, PPE-DE, PSE, Verts/ALE GUE/NGL		+	
	38	> 40 Members			
vote: amended proposal			RCV	+	543,56,39
vote: legislative resolution			RCV	+	550,49,41

Source: Trade in Seal Products Vote, (A6-0118/2009), 2010

This example voting list, from a completed vote, gives you an indication of the main things you will see, and need to look for on a voting list. What is being voted is listed in the first column; in the example we see compromise amendments and individual amendments, with their numbers in the next column. Knowing these numbers at the time of vote can make life much easier for you and your interlocutors. Next comes the author of the compromise or individual amendment and in the example above there is a mixture of different possibilities: the Committee, Political Groups together and also 40+ members. The next column indicates whether a special voting modality has been requested, such as a roll-call vote or an electronic vote (EV). The next column indicated whether the amendment was adopted or not, and the final column shows the numbers if an EV or RCV were used.

The agenda for the part-session is finalised on the Thursday afternoon before the sitting, although last minute changes do occur. A typical Strasbourg ordinary part-session, of which there are obligatorily 12 in the year, starts on Monday at 17h00 and finishes on a Thursday afternoon. In addition there are now six additional part-sessions in Brussels which run from Wednesday 15h00 to Thursday 13h00. The order of a typical Strasbourg session is as follows:

Monday	Adoption of final agenda
	One-minute speeches
	Legislative and non-legislative reports - discussion (until 22h00)
Tuesday	Votes on requests for Urgent procedures
	Legislative and non-legislative reports - major debates
	Votes (12h00 -13h00)
	Legislative and non-legislative reports - major debates
	Communication by Commission on College decisions of their meeting that day (17h00)
	Commission question time (17h30 - 19h00)
	Legislative and non-legislative reports - discussion (21h00 - 24h00)
Wednesday	Major (political) debates
	Votes (11h00 - 12h00 & 12h30 - 13h00)
	Major debates with Council
	Legislative and non-legislative reports - discussion
	Council question time
	Legislative and non-legislative reports - discussion (21h00 - 24h00)
Thursday	Legislative and non-legislative reports - discussion
	Votes (11h00 - 13h00)
	Debates on cases of breaches of human rights, democracy and the rule of law

Watch the Plenary live on http://www.europarl.europa.eu/plenary/en/home.html Find the **'rainbow' verbatim report** (contributions in original languages) on the website the day after the sitting - all speeches, votes etc are in this report.

Strasbourg is a hive of activity as there is the Plenary sitting itself, meetings of the Political Groups, extraordinary Committee meetings (usually on Monday or Tuesday evenings), media activities and events, visiting dignitaries and politicians and a host of informal talks and negotiations. The timings in Strasbourg are extremely important, and trying to work with a dossier that is subject to a vote there can be very challenging.

It is important to keep in mind that the Plenary session is streamed live on the Internet so all the questions and speeches can trigger wider political and media interest. Whilst the majority of the Plenary is well regimented, and speaking time mostly allocated amongst Political Groups, there is one set of questions that are becoming increasingly interesting to follow, those that take place at the end of any debate when an MEP who manages to 'catch the eye' of the President may make a brief contribution. Introduced in 2008 to stimulate debate and generate publicity and interest in parliamentary discussions, the **five minute 'catch-the-eye' debates** have been somewhat disappointing as interventions continue to be prepared in advance and not in response to other MEPs' comments. To make debates more interactive, the Parliament in 2009 introduced a '**blue-card question**' (an analogy to yellow and red cards in football) in Rule 162 that allows MEPs to respond to another MEP immediately after their speech by asking them a follow-up question. While this has helped debates to become livelier, the blue-card questions often are more statements than questions, meant to show divisions rather than asking for further information on an MEP's position.

Before the final vote takes place, the Commission will state its position on all of the amendments tabled by the Parliament - basically whether it would accept them or not. This formal procedure is an important right of the Commission, to guarantee that its right of initiative is not infringed by totally remodelled texts. It is also important for the Council because the Commission's opinion on the Parliament's amendments will determine the applicable voting rules in the Council for that amendment (see Chapter 5.2 and 5.4 for more on this). This opinion of the Commission, expressed in Plenary by the relevant Commissioner, will not be a surprise to anyone in the room as it will have been made known to the Parliament and Council during their trilogue discussions. This exercise again underlines the almost omnipresence of the Commission in the decision-making of the other institutions - because to be able to come to this judgement, the Commission needs to be in on all the negotiations. We come back to this in more detail in Chapter 5.3.

The final stage for the report in the Parliament is during one of the three **voting sessions** in the Strasbourg week. It is worth bearing in mind that during the Plenary week there are a number of press conferences around the topical issues being voted by the Parliament. These are very interesting to follow and also offer opportunities for MEPs to gain media coverage. When the final voting list comes out each Political Group will check to see what voting technicality requests the other Political Groups have tabled, such as split votes or RCV and try to understand the political dynamics behind them. For example, it is often the case that a Political Group will request an EV or RCV in an attempt to highlight divisions in other Groups on sensitive issues. At this stage it is again important to recall the numbers game and the majorities that are required in the Plenary during the vote - as this will have dictated the negotiations within the Parliament in their attempts to find a compromise. The voting requirements are outlined in Figure 3.8.

Figure 3.8: Voting in the Ordinary Legislative Procedure

- **Absolute majority** is needed:
    1. In Plenary in the second reading:
        - to reject the Council position at first reading
        - to adopt amendments

Absolute majority in the Plenary	
751	376 votes

- **Simple majority** is needed:
    1. In Committee votes
    2. In Plenary:
        - for first reading votes
        - in second reading: to approve the Council position at first reading
        - in a third reading: to approve the act in accordance with the joint text prepared by the Conciliation Committee

Simple majority
Majority of the members casting their vote

The key numbers above are the numbers of MEPs and the majorities. If your dossier is to be voted by simple or absolute majority, one factor will be important - the number of MEPs in the room at the time of vote. There are now 751 MEPs, and of these there are usually only around 600 in the room for a vote, according to Votewatch.eu data. This can alter the dynamics of a simple majority vote if the absent MEPs are from a Group that supports you, but it is even more important when an absolute majority is needed. An absolute majority is notoriously difficult to achieve in the Parliament because of the coalitions needed to get 376 MEPs. When the vote comes there are a number of possibilities:

1. **Show of hands:** this is still the most common way to vote on the majority of issues and is used for reasons of time-efficiency given the large number of votes in any voting session. The President calls the issue and takes a look around the room, deciding on the spot whether the majority required has been attained. With this system there is no detailed, or individualised, voting record. If the show of hands is disputed by a Political Group they can request an electronic check, as outlined below.

2. **Electronic votes:** these are used to check disputed and unclear votes. The figures show on the main screen in the Plenary and these aggregated for, against and abstention figures are recorded. In this case individualised voting records are not kept.

3. **Roll-Call:** this is the only category where an individualised voting record is kept. A very interesting addition to the Parliament RoP is the provision that 'when voting on any proposal for a legislative act, whether by way of a single and/or final vote, Parliament shall vote by RCV using

the electronic voting system' (Rule 180, RoP). In addition RCV can be taken when requested in writing by a Political Group or at least 40 MEPs the evening before the vote. RCVs are becoming more and more frequent and have allowed some major developments in monitoring voting behaviour in the Parliament, although due to the fact that they significantly slow down voting it is unlikely they will ever be extended to all votes. This development has allowed the monitoring and analysis of voting patterns by MEPs, Political Groups and the Parliament as a whole. This has been led by Votewatch.eu.

Votewatch.eu

This website is an absolute goldmine of information on the workings of the Parliament. You can find detailed information concerning all voting records, the activity of each MEP such as reports drafted, amended reports, speeches in the Plenary, questions and their attendance records, etc. Votewatch.eu also analyses the voting data to present statistics such as the extent to which an MEP votes according to their European Group line.

Votewatch.eu presents up-to-date complex analysis on how the Political Groups in the EP form coalitions between them, as well as on their internal cohesion. The data is broken down by time intervals and policy areas so that it introduces the reader to the different dynamics of the voting behavior in the Parliament.

The information on the newest votes is processed and published on the website the same day the votes are cast in the EP Plenary and the general statistics are updated following each part-session.

All of this is possible due to the increased number of roll-call votes in recent years. It allows Votewatch.eu to process the official data of the Parliament and show the voting records and statistics of individual MEPs, Political Groups and National Delegations. This rich set of data is essential for anyone trying to work with (even more so on a vote in) the Parliament as it allows all sorts of possibilities that were not available a few years ago.

See all of this at: www.votewatch.eu

Votewatch.eu found the following interesting trends that are likely to be maintained during the 2014-2019 European Parliament:
1. MEPs vote primarily along transnational lines and not along national ones.
2. Political Groups have very high internal cohesion when it comes to voting - MEPs vote on Group lines.
3. The deal-making Group in the Parliament is the ALDE Group - they are the 'king-makers' in coalition deals.

These findings are extremely important for anyone wanting to work with the Parliament. The Parliament is maturing as an institution and this is visible in these changed voting patterns. The fact that the Groups are cohesive voting units, only serves to highlight the importance of working with key National Delegations and coordinators to influence the position of the Groups. These issues will be taken up in more detail in Chapter 8.4 on how to work with the Parliament.

Once the **final vote** on a text has taken place, the Parliament will have either approved the text before it, or will have rejected it. In the first case, for legislative files, the text will be forwarded to the Council so that it can formally engage in its first or second reading. As will be highlighted in Chapter 5.3 on informal trilogues, most legislation is voted by the Parliament after pre-agreement with the Council, leading to a first reading agreement, in which case the text is final and only requires endorsement by the Council. It is also possible that the Parliament rejected the text, in which case it can either be returned to the Committee responsible in question for more work (first reading) or be thrown out altogether (second reading, Conciliation). These voting majorities and requirements will be explained in more detail in Chapter 5.

> **The final vote?**
>
> MEPs can actually change their initial vote, if their voting machine did not work properly at the time of the vote. Sometimes, for this reason, the initial figures (i.e. the number of votes for, against, abstentions) do not match those in the final minutes. However, the initial result (announced by the chair) of the vote cannot be changed, even if, mathematically speaking, after the subsequent individual changes the result would have been reversed.

In the typical Strasbourg session, aside from the key voting time, there are also some final important elements to mention. There is significant time for legislative and non-legislative discussions, which need to be followed carefully. In addition there is also a plethora of opportunities to ask questions, as outlined in the box below.

> **Written and Oral Questions**
>
> 1. **Oral Questions for answer & debate in Plenary**
>   Questions may be put to the Council or the Commission by a Committee, a Political Group or at least 40 MEPs, after submission to the President and Conference of Presidents - who decide whether and in what order Questions should be placed on the agenda.
> 2. **Question time in Plenary**
>   One question may be put to the Council and the Commission by any MEP during each session, after their admissibility has been checked by the President.
> 3. **Questions for written answer**
>   Any MEP can put Written Questions to any other EU institution, who shall respond within three weeks if it is a priority issue, or within six weeks if not.

From 2009 to 2014 the Parliament put nearly 70,000 questions to the Commission, all of which the Commission endeavours to answer within six weeks. This is all managed by the SG of the Commission, and once the responses are sent to the EP they are put on the Parliamentary Questions website at: http://www.europarl.europa.eu/plenary/en/parliamentary-questions.html. This very useful site allows you to search questions and answers by MEP, subject, and sitting, therefore giving you access to a wealth of questions and answers. This information is also automatically integrated into the Votewatch.eu website. These questions should not be neglected because they can lead to political tensions and ultimately to resolutions by the Parliament - it is one way that an issue can find its way onto the agenda of the Parliament.

3.9 Key stages and key actors - European Parliament

The life of a dossier in the Parliament is significantly less linear than the one it will have followed in the Commission or Council. There are, in essence, three main stages with key aspects and actors that need to be highlighted.

1. The first stage of importance is when the dossier is assigned to a Committee responsible and then to a Political Group, and ultimately to the key person who shapes the dossier - the rapporteur. The choice of rapporteur is important and many stakeholders try to secure the most sympathetic and influential personality for their interests. The drivers in this situation will be the Political Group bidding for the report and then the subsequent choice of rapporteur from within the MEPs on the Committee - an issue that can come down to competing National Delegation interests. The choice of rapporteur is also often down to an MEP's interests, their experience, seniority and reputation. So the very early stage of the process can be driven by a Political Group at the level of the Committee - which implies an important role for the Group coordinator. Another key actor at this stage can also be the Committee chairperson.

2. Once the rapporteur has been nominated he or she has to draft a response to the Commission proposal by tabling amendments. The rapporteur has a variety of formal and informal ways to advance their work, but will always need to find a compromise within their own Group, and then with the other Groups. This means the shadows and coordinators can be as important as the rapporteur. The rapporteur can hold exchanges of views in Committee and meet with the shadows to discuss the issues at stake, to ensure support. The majority of this work will take place on an informal basis, with the Committee meetings representing a public airing of the state of internal discussions in the Parliament. An important aspect of this is who the rapporteur chooses to consult and ask for help. Here there are key internal actors such as assistants, Committee Secretariat staff and Political Group staff who will always play important roles and be up-to-date on developments. The MEP will also almost always consult external stakeholders, having probably been flooded by requests for meetings. It is difficult to know in advance who, or how many, external stakeholders an MEP will see - and what influence they will have. The basic nucleus for discussions will be between the rapporteur, their Committee coordinator, the assistants, the assigned Committee Secretariat official, the Political Group official and shadow

rapporteurs. The exchanges of views in Committee will help you gauge the political temperature and to what extent the rapporteur has the support of their own, and other, Political Groups.

Once it comes to voting in Committee, the key players are the Political Groups through their shadows and coordinators in the Committees. Group scrutiny of a Committee report varies widely, depending on the discipline of National Delegations, the salience of the issue for national and European politics and the reputations of the coordinator and rapporteur. Having noted that Political Group voting cohesion is very strong in Plenary, it can be less so in Committee as individual votes can count much more, making them a little less predictable.

3. When the dossier passes from the Committee stage to the Plenary preparation and vote, the dynamics are almost entirely those of the Political Groups and their attempts to find compromise positions that they can all work with. This takes place during the Political Group week that precedes the Plenary and it can often be a turbulent time for a dossier. Bearing in mind the voting patterns in the Parliament, it is essential to secure the support of the main Political Groups during this stage to have any chance of success when it comes to the final vote itself.

From this analysis the main actors (in chronological order) in the elaboration of a Parliament position are as follows:

Table 3.6: Key stages and key actors: The European Parliament

Key Stage	Comment	Key people
Reception of proposal by Parliament & Nomination of Committee (Responsible + Opinion-Giving)	Usually an administrative procedure.	DG Presidency Conference of Presidents
Choice of Group to deliver report	The choice of Group and rapporteur is a crucial moment for any dossier because the political leanings of the Group and the personality of the rapporteur will find their way into the report. For both of these choices the Group MEPs in the Committee, led by the coordinator, are key actors as they will decide whether to bid for a report and who to nominate. **Key** to this process are the priorities of the Groups in Committees which can be driven by the key Delegations or the coordinator.	
Nomination of rapporteur		

Key Stage	Comment	Key people
Preparation of draft report	Each rapporteur, in each case, will turn to different sources for information. The most likely - and the most influential will be those listed to the right. Drafting can also be linked to Presidency/Commission priorities. **Key** here is to understand the dynamics around the rapporteur and shadows from other major Groups.	Rapporteur Shadow rapporteur(s) Key issue MEPs Assistants Political Group staff Committee Secretariat Commission/Council External sources/Network
Exchange of views in Committee	The Committee exchange of views will usually offer an insight into both the technical and political developments of a dossier. It is very useful to follow these closely. **Key** here is to recognise that the exchange will be only a window to the real discussions.	Rapporteur Shadow rapporteur(s) Committee chairperson Coordinators Key issue MEPs
Deadline for amendments in Committee	It is key to know the deadline for amendments. It is very important in the process.	Rapporteur Coordinators Shadow rapporteur(s) Committee Secretariat
Committee vote	Here individual MEPs can make a much bigger difference than in Plenary. **Key** to the Committee vote will be the number of MEPs in the room on the day and the positions of the main Groups - even if individual MEPs have more opportunity to vote for themselves.	Rapporteur Shadow rapporteur(s) Coordinators Committee chair Political Group staff Committee Secretariat **Council - informal trilogues**
Plenary build-up Plenary vote	The Political Groups are the key drivers of both the build up to, and the actual, Plenary vote. The Groups will take their information from the coordinators who will try to keep Committee compromises intact. The Group week that precedes Plenary weeks and the Group meetings in Strasbourg are essential for the formation, or cementing, of compromises. It is **key** to know what agreements have been made with Council through informal trilogues - because if this was already sewn up at Committee vote stage then the text is unlikely to be modified.	

4. Other EU Institutions and Bodies

By Alan Hardacre and Nadia Andrien

The Commission, the Parliament, the Council and the European Council are not the only EU institutions, and they are far from being the only EU bodies. The final chapter in the first section of the book addresses the most important of these other institutions and bodies inasmuch as they impact on the EU policy cycle, or on the workings of the four core institutions outlined in the previous three chapters.

The box on the right outlines the institutions, bodies, offices and agencies after the Treaty of Lisbon. The first thing to notice is that aside from the four institutions we have described thus far in Chapters 1 to 3, there are in fact three further EU institutions. Two of them fall outside the scope of this book as they are not directly involved in the EU policy cycle, or in mainstream EU lobbying strategies. The first of these is the **European Central Bank (ECB)**, which is responsible for administering the EU monetary policy and for supervising the assets of the largest banks in the Eurozone. This powerful financial institution, established in 1998 is based in Frankfurt, Germany.

EU Institutions

- The European Commission
- The European Council
- The Council of Ministers of the EU
- The European Parliament
- The Court of Justice of the EU
- The European Central Bank
- The Court of Auditors

EU Bodies, Offices and Agencies

- European Economic and Social Committee
- Committee of the Regions
- European Investment Bank
- EU Agencies

The second institution outside the scope of this book is the **Court of Auditors (CoA)** because it is likewise not a mainstream EU policy cycle institution. It was created in 1975 and was tasked with auditing the accounts of the EU institutions - notably to scrutinise if the budget of the EU had been correctly implemented, and if all funds had been spent legally and with sound management. This leaves the seventh, and final, EU institution - the **Court of Justice of the European Union (CJEU)**, which this chapter will start with.

Outside of the realm of the seven EU institutions there are a number of other bodies and entities in the EU sphere of activity. The main ones are listed in the box above, and all but one will be dealt with in this chapter due to the roles they play in the EU policy cycle. The only one that will not be dealt with is the **European Investment Bank (EIB)** which was created back in 1958 as a long-term lending institution to support European integration. The **Committee of the Regions (COR)**, the **European Economic and Social Committee (EESC)** and **EU Agencies** all play important roles in the EU policy cycle, therefore they will be detailed in the course of this chapter.

4.1 The Court of Justice of the European Union (CJEU)

The **Court of Justice of the European Union** (the 'Court') constitutes the **judicial branch** of the European Union. The mission of this EU institution is to 'ensure that in the interpretation and application of the Treaties, the law is observed' (Article 19 TEU). The main elements of the Court are outlined in Table 4.1 below.

Table 4.1: Court of Justice of the EU - Key facts

Name:	Court of Justice of the European Union, the Court
Legal basis:	Articles 251 - 284 TFEU
Established:	1952
Jurisdiction:	European Union
President:	• Court of Justice: Vassilios Skouris (since 2003)
	• General Court: Marc Jaeger (since 2007)
	• Specialised Courts (Civil Service Tribunal): Sean van Raepenbusch (since 2011)
Composition:	Sits in chambers of:
	• Court of Justice: 3, 5, 15 or 28 Judges + 9 (11) Advocates-General
	• General Court: 1, 3, 5, 13 or 28 judges
	• Specialised Courts: 1, 3, 5 or 7 judges
Seat:	Luxembourg

The Court comprises three sub-courts: the **Court of Justice** (supreme body), the **General Court** (created in 1988) and the **European Union Civil Service Tribunal** (specialised Court created in 2004). Each has its own responsibilities and ways of working.

The Court of Justice is currently composed of 28 Judges (one per Member State) and assisted by nine permanent Advocates-General (extendable to 11). The General Court also counts 28 Judges (one per Member State) and the Civil Service Tribunal has seven Judges.

The Judges and Advocates-General of the Court of Justice and the Judges of the General Court are appointed for a renewable six-year mandate by joint agreement between the governments of the EU Member States, after consultation of a panel which gives an opinion on the suitability of the candidates (Article 255 TFEU).

Unlike for the first two Courts, the Judges of the Civil Service Tribunal are elected by the Council. All three Courts elect a President from among their members for a three-year term of office.

The role of the Court comes down to guaranteeing that EU law is applied and interpreted correctly by EU Member States and the EU institutions. As part of that mission, the Court reviews the validity of the legal acts adopted by the EU institutions and ensures that the Member States do not fail to act in accordance with the law. It verifies that Member States fulfil their obligations under European law (in terms of legislative instruments and practices) and provides interpretations of Union legislation at the request of the courts and tribunals of the Member States. The Court has the power to settle legal disputes between European institutions, Member States, legal entities and individuals.

The three levels of the Court fulfil very different tasks:

1. The Court of Justice is tasked with interpreting and enforcing EU law. It is the highest court in the EU, outranking national supreme courts. Its judgements can affect both Member States and individuals, and the Court also acts as a referee between the Member States, institutions and individuals in disputes relating to EU law.

2. The General Court judges the disputes brought by individuals and Member States against EU institutions.

3. The Civil Service Tribunal adjudicates in disputes between the EU and its civil services. More specialised courts may be established in the future and their role would be to hear actions in specific areas.

Although the Treaty of Lisbon has considerably extended its scope, the Court still has almost no jurisdiction in the area of Common Foreign and Security Policy (CFSP) and only limited jurisdiction with respect to the Area of Freedom, Security and Justice (AFSJ) (Articles 275 and 276 TFEU). Since their establishment in 1952, roughly 29,000 judgements and orders have been pronounced by the three Courts. Judgements of the Courts are decided by a majority of votes and have binding weight.

While many people working in Brussels will likely never come into direct contact with the Court, it is always useful to understand its powers - they have shaped every EU policy area in some way. The main powers of the Court are outlined in the box below.

Key powers of CJEU

Case Law - The Court creates a system of case law which is often then the established precedent that needs to be followed. You can find the EU case law database at http://curia.europa.eu/jurisp/cgi-bin/form.pl?lang=en

Proceedings for failure to fulfil an obligation (also known as infringement proceedings) - (Article 258 TFEU). The Court can determine whether a Member State has fulfilled its obligations under Union law. These cases are started by the Commission, which - if it deems necessary - can involve the Court. This can lead to the Member State having a fine imposed on them.

Actions for Annulment - (Article 263 TFEU). An applicant can seek the annulment of a measure (usually a Regulation, Decision or Directive) adopted by an institution. The Court can declare a measure void.

Actions for Failure to Act - (Article 265 TFEU). The Court can assess the legality of an institution's failure to act. Where a failure to act is found, the institution concerned must end the failure using appropriate measures.

Application for Compensation (non-contractual liability) - (Article 268 TFEU). The Court can hear compensation claims for any damages caused to citizens and undertakings by the institutions in the course of their duties.

Appeals on Points of Law - (Article 256 TFEU). The Court can hear appeals to judgements given by the General Court if it is on a point of law.

References for a Preliminary Ruling - (Article 267 TFEU). National Courts are the frontline of implementation of EU law - and on occasion they need to turn to the Court to seek clarification on the interpretation of a point of EU law. Once interpretation is given then all Courts in the EU are bound by it.

In sum, unlike several other institutions and bodies, most of the work of the Court takes place after the actual decision-making process; once legal acts have been formally adopted by the institutions and after these have been implemented by Member States. Nonetheless for certain actors, and sectors, appeal to the Court is a very important avenue for clarification of issues and to pursue the correct implementation of EU legislation - all of which will in turn set important precedents for any future actions by the EU.

4.2 The European Economic and Social Committee

The **European Economic and Social Committee (EESC)** is one of the two official **advisory bodies** of the EU (the other being the Committee of the Regions that is addressed next). It was set up to give Europe's civil society actors a formal say on EU legislative proposals.

Table 4.2: European Economic and Social Committee - Key facts

Names:	European Economic and Social Committee (EESC, ESC or unofficially 'EcoSoc')
Legal basis:	Articles 300 - 304 TFEU
Established:	1957
Type:	EU body
Role:	Formal: Consultative (non-binding opinions)
	Informal: Involve civil society in EU affairs, promote creation of consultative structures
Members:	353 (will be reviewed before 20 September 2015)
Groups:	I Employers, II Employees, III Various Interests
Represents:	Social and economic interests
President:	Henri Malosse (since 2013)
Seat:	Delors building, Brussels (shared with Committee of Regions)

Founded in 1957 under the Treaty of Rome, the EESC was created with the aim of involving social and economic interest groups in the establishment of a common market, by allowing them to represent their interests in the EU decision-making process. The Committee, among other things, represents the interests of consumers, trade unions, employers and farmers. Serving as a bridge between the Union institutions and its citizens, it encourages participation of civil society in EU decision-making. By informing, and involving economic and social interest groups, it enhances the effectiveness of the EU and strengthens its democratic legitimacy, leading to a more integrated Europe. Besides a representation, information and integration role, the Committee also plays an advisory role. The Treaty makes the EESC an integral part of the EU decision-making process by obliging the Council, the Commission and the Parliament to consult the EESC before taking decisions on topics that affect economic and social actors. The institutional triangle must consult the EESC when the Treaty so provides, but it may also consult it on a voluntary basis whenever it deems it appropriate. Moreover, the Committee may also issue **own-initiative opinions** (approx. 5 per year) or **exploratory opinions** at the request of one of the institutions. The box below provides an overview of the areas where consultation of the EESC is compulsory.

European Economic and Social Committee consultation - Policy areas

Agricultural policy; Free movement of persons and services; Transport policy; Harmonisation of indirect taxation; Approximation of laws on the internal market; Employment policy; Social policy, education, vocational training and youth; Public health; Consumer protection; Trans-European networks; Industrial policy; Economic, social and territorial cohesion; Research and technological development and space; Environment.

The Committee advises the three main decision-taking institutions by issuing **non-binding opinion documents**. It delivers an average of 50 opinions each year. EESC statistics show that although the opinions are non-binding, the Commission acts on four out of five EESC opinions. Among the success stories where elements of EESC opinions have featured in legislation are the agricultural policy reforms, the Employment recovery plan and the 1989 Charter of Fundamental Social Rights.

The Committee enters into play in the decision-making procedure as early as the pre-legislative phase. It is during this phase, as was described in Chapter 1, that the Commission evaluates policy options, conducts an Impact Assessment (IA) and prepares a legislative proposal. It is usual that the EESC collaborates with the Commission on Impact Assessments.

Once the Commission's proposal is adopted by the College of Commissioners it is forwarded simultaneously to the Parliament, the Council, the national parliaments and, where appropriate, to the EESC and/or the Committee of the Regions. The EESC is then requested to issue a non-binding opinion on the Commission proposal. As soon as the EU institutions start discussing the legislative proposal, the Parliament and the Council are obliged to consult the EESC, which can in turn submit its views on all amendments tabled to the initial Commission proposal. In case a legislative proposal is altered during the legislative procedure, the EESC may also adopt a revised opinion on the legislative proposal. This however occurs very infrequently. The views of the EESC are non-binding and can only be taken into account if they are timely and integrated with the Parliament and Council timelines.

The provisions governing the functioning, and the composition, of the EESC are contained in Articles 301 to 304 TFEU and in its Rules of Procedure. The Council is responsible for determining the number of seats allocated to each Member State. These seats will be occupied by representatives of economic and social interest groups who will be appointed to one of the following three Groups:

1. Employers (Group I);
2. Employees (Group II);
3. Various Economic and Social Interests - such as professional associations, farmers, consumer groups, environmental organisations, NGOs, etc. (Group III).

The Council formally appoints the members for a renewable five-year term of office, following nominations made by the respective national governments. Once appointed, the members work in a personal capacity in complete political independence. They, moreover, mostly continue to live and work in their own countries and only come to Brussels for meetings. The selection criteria for members are technical expertise and capacity to represent diverse social and economic groups. Since the accession of Croatia in July 2013, the EESC is made up of 353 members. This number is, however, only temporary since it is incompatible with the provisions contained in Article 301 TFEU which stipulates that the number of members of the Committee may not exceed 350. This number will need to be adjusted and allocation of seats adapted by a Council decision before 20 September 2015 at the latest (Article 301 TFEU), taking into account potential economic, social and demographic developments within the Union. Until the entry into force of the decision referred to in Article 301 TFEU, the allocation of members of the EESC shall be as follows:

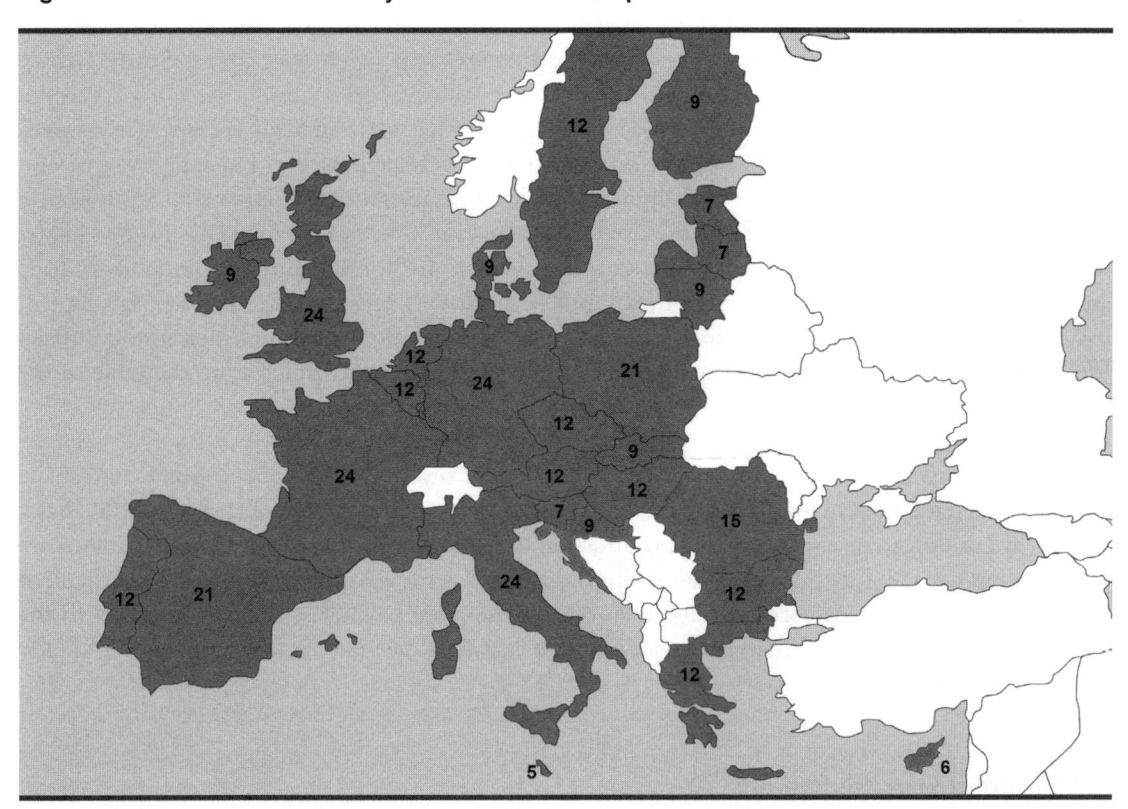

Figure 4.1: Breakdown of seats by Member State: European Economic and Social Committee

Every two and half years the EESC elects, from its midst, a **Bureau** consisting of a President, two Vice-Presidents, the three Group presidents, the section presidents and a number of directly elected members (no more than the number of Member States) (Rule 3 (1d) RoP). The Bureau is currently composed of 40 members. The Bureau is mainly tasked with the general management of the Committee and its work. The full EESC meets in **Plenary Assembly** nine times a year. The Plenary formally adopts, or rejects, the texts and decisions of the Committee prepared by its '**Sections**' (**Commissions**).

Table 4.3: The Sections/Commissions of the European Economic and Social Committee

ECO	Economic and Monetary Union, Economic and Social Cohesion
INT	Single Market, Production and Consumption
TEN	Transport, Energy, Infrastructure and Information Society
SOC	Employment, Social Affairs and Citizenship
NAT	Agriculture, Rural Development and Environment
REX	External Relations Section
CCMI	Consultative Commission on Industrial Change

When the EESC is asked to produce an opinion or information report by the institutions, the Bureau designates the Commission that will be responsible for the work in question. The Commission concerned then appoints a **rapporteur** (+ **co-rapporteur**) and when necessary a **Study Group** or **Drafting Group** which may be set up from among its members to study the question under consideration and collect the views expressed. To gather the views of civil society, the sections organise meetings, conferences, hearings, cultural activities, publications, etc. The rapporteur(s) and the Study Group then draw up the draft opinion which they transmit to the responsible Commission within the EESC, in order for it to be discussed and voted on. Once the opinion has been voted by this Commission it is transferred to the Committee Plenary for formal adoption. In general, texts and decisions of the EESC are adopted by a simple majority of votes cast. As soon as it is adopted, the opinion is forwarded to the Union's decision-making bodies and then published in the Official Journal of the EU. The EESC is also assisted by a Secretariat-General which is accountable to the President.

The EESC is often forgotten by many stakeholders, except those with specific economic and social interests, when it comes to lobbying strategies. As this short section has highlighted, the EESC has a privileged position to give opinions on Commission legislative proposals. Whilst these opinions are non-binding the ideas within them can easily filter into Commission, Council and/or Parliament thinking. Beyond this advisory capacity, members of the EESC also have privileged access to the other institutions and to information - making them extremely useful contacts and partners for any work in Brussels.

4.3 Committee of the Regions

The **Committee of the Regions (CoR)** is the EU's second advisory body. In many ways the CoR is similar to the EESC. Consisting of representatives of local and regional authorities, the CoR was created in order to provide local and regional interests with a voice at EU level.

Table 4.4: Committee of the Regions - Key facts

Names:	Committee of the Regions (CoR)
Legal basis:	Articles 300, 305 - 307 TFEU
Established:	1994
Type:	EU body
Role:	Formal: Consultative (non-binding opinions)
	Informal: Voice for regional and local interests in Brussels
Members:	353 (will be reviewed before 20 September 2015)
Principles:	Subsidiarity, Proximity, Partnership
President:	Michel Lebrun (since 2014)
Seat:	Delors building, Brussels (shared with EESC)

The CoR was formally established by the Treaty of Maastricht which entered into force in 1993. The rationale behind the creation of this body was two-fold: firstly, an important percentage of EU legislation is implemented at the sub-state level which makes it important for local and regional representatives to have their say in European policy-making; and secondly, the EU needed a solution to bridge the perceived widening gap between its institutions and its citizens. Involving locally elected officials, who represent a direct link between Brussels and the EU citizens, was expected to serve this purpose. Besides representing local and regional interests, the Committee also serves as an information source; it channels information from the European institutions to the local authorities (and vice-versa) and as a result brings Europe closer to the people.

While the Committee is a source of information, and a representative of local and regional administration interests, it is also another policy advisor for the European institutions along with the EESC. Article 300(1) TFEU stipulates that the Commission, the Council and the Parliament must consult the CoR before taking decisions. In exactly the same way as there is a Treaty obligation to consult the EESC, there are obligations to consult the CoR. While its consultation is mandatory, its opinions also have no binding weight. The CoR must be consulted on proposals made in areas that directly affect local and regional interests. The box below provides an overview of the policy areas concerned.

> **Compulsory Committee of the Regions consultation - Policy areas**
>
> Transport; Employment; Social policy; Education, vocational training and youth; Culture; Public Health; Trans-European Networks; Economic, social and territorial cohesion; Environment and climate change; Telecommunications and Energy.

The CoR, similarly to the EESC, may also issue **exploratory opinions** and **own-initiative opinions** whenever it judges this appropriate. The latter enables the CoR to put issues on the EU agenda. Moreover, when the EESC is consulted, the CoR may also issue an opinion on the matter if it considers that specific regional interests are likely to be affected. The functioning and the role of the CoR in the EU decision-making process are very similar to that of the EESC. It however plays two additional roles: firstly, in monitoring the compliance of the EU institutions with the principle of subsidiarity after the formal adoption of EU legislation, and secondly, in monitoring the implementation of EU legislation at national, regional and local level. As a result of the entry into force of the Treaty of Lisbon, the CoR may now initiate **infringement proceedings** at the Court of Justice if EU legislative acts still do not respect the subsidiarity principle after being formally adopted. The CoR is thus heavily involved throughout the entire legislative process.

The composition and organisation of the CoR are regulated by Articles 305 to 307 TFEU and by its Rules of Procedure. The members of the CoR, who are elected by and/or politically accountable to an elected regional or local assembly (holders of executive office), are appointed for five years by the Council on a proposal of the respective national governments. These officials may, for example, be local Council members, Regional Parliamentarians or Regional Ministers, City or County Councillors and Mayors. Since the accession of Croatia in July 2013, the CoR is made up of 353 members. This number can however only be temporary since it is incompatible with the provisions contained in Article 305 TFEU which stipulates that the number of members of the Committee may not exceed 350. This number needs to be adjusted and the allocation of seats adapted by a Council decision before 20 September 2015 at the latest (Article 305 TFEU), taking into account potential economic, social and demographic developments within the Union.

The breakdown of seats by Member State is the same as for the EESC (see Figure 4.1).

Again, as for the EESC on which the CoR is to a large extent modelled, the constituent bodies of the CoR are the **Plenary Assembly**, the **Bureau** and the **Commissions**. The Bureau, which is elected by the Plenary Assembly for two and a half years, is currently composed of 63 members, comprising the President, the first Vice-President, one Vice-President per Member State (28), 28 other members (the number per Member State reflects national and political balances) and the chairmen of the political groups. The Plenary Assembly meets on average five/six times a year. Its role is to formally adopt or reject the texts and decisions of the CoR prepared by its seven Commissions. These Commissions mainly prepare the discussions of the Plenary in terms of content, i.e. they draw up the draft versions of opinions and reports. The CoR may also institute temporary sub-Committees, for particular matters. These sub-Committees are comparable to the Commissions in functioning and role.

The way in which the CoR drafts its opinions is similar to the way in which the EESC works, as described in the preceding section. The Commissions of the CoR are as follows:

Table 4.5: Commissions of the Committee of Regions

COTER	Territorial Cohesion Policy
ECOS	Economic and Social Policy
ENVE	Environment, Climate Change and Energy
EDUC	Education, Youth, Culture and Research
CIVEX	Citizenship, Governance, institutional and External Affairs
NAT	Natural Resources
CAFA	Commission for Financial and Administrative Affairs

One element of the functioning of the CoR differs markedly from that of the EESC in that it is a much more political body. Within the CoR, five of the major Political Groups we saw in Chapter 3 are represented: the European People's Party (EPP), the Party of European Socialists (PES), the Alliance of Liberals and Democrats for Europe (ALDE), the European Alliance Group (EA Group) and the European Conservatives and Reformists Group (ECR Group). Members of the CoR can affiliate with one of these Political Groups, which like the Political Groups in the Parliament, are major actors in the life of the Committee.

4.4 Key stages and key actors - EESC and CoR

As with the core institutions in the preceding three chapters it is again useful to highlight the key stages and actors within the EESC and CoR. Before drawing this list, it is important to list their key formal and informal powers. The key powers of the EESC and the CoR are as follows:

1. Giving non-binding opinions - parts of which find their way into Council, Parliament and Commission texts;
2. Interaction and networks within the EU institutions;
3. Recognised voices of economic, social, and regional interests;
4. Privileged access to Commission, Parliament and Council officials;
5. Privileged access to information.

These key powers should not be underestimated and any lobbying strategy should ensure that it takes the two consultative bodies into consideration. The key stages and roles of the EESC and CoR are summarised in Table 4.6 below.

Table 4.6: Key stages and actors - The EESC and CoR   = CoR only

Decision-making phase	CoR/EESC role
Pre-legislative phase: European Commission evaluates policy options and prepares legislative proposal	• EESC rapporteur (+ co-rapporteur) and its study group, organise consultations with civil society organisations. Find consultations here: http://www.eesc.europa.eu/?i=portal.en.take-part; • CoR rapporteur (+ co-rapporteur) organises consultations with local and regional authorities. Find consultations here: http://cor.europa.eu/en/activities/stakeholders/Pages/stakeholder-meetings.aspx; • CoR rapporteur (+ co-rapporteur) assisted by its commission, cooperates with the EC on Impact Assessments; • EESC rapporteur (+ co-rapporteur) assisted by its study group, cooperates with the EC on Impact Assessments (EC Cooperation Agreement).

Decision-making phase	CoR/EESC role
European Commission adopts legislative proposal and must consult both Committees	• CoR rapporteur (+ co-rapporteur) organises consultations with local and regional authorities in order to incorporate their views; • CoR rapporteur in cooperation with the Subsidiarity Steering Group and the Subsidiarity Expert Group analyses compliance with the subsidiarity principle and must ensure that subsidiarity is respected from the point of view of regional and local authorities. The CoR rapporteur also consults with National and Regional Parliaments ('Early Warning Mechanism'); • EESC rapporteur (+ co-rapporteur) assisted by its study group organises consultations with civil society organisations in order to incorporate their views.
EU institutions start discussing legislative proposal. The EP and the Council are obliged to consult the Committees	• EESC rapporteur (+ co-rapporteur) assisted by its study group cooperates with associations representing economic and social interests to incorporate their views on amendments tabled; • CoR rapporteur (co-rapporteur) assisted by its commission cooperates with associations representing local and regional authorities and with the Subsidiarity Monitoring Network to incorporate their views on amendments tabled; • CoR/EESC rapporteurs and their commissions/study group draft opinion on legislative proposal.
In cases where a legislative draft is significantly altered during the legislative process	CoR/EESC rapporteurs assisted by their commission/study group may adopt revised opinions on a legislative proposal.
Council and Parliament have adopted EU legislation	The President of the Committee or the commission responsible for drawing up an opinion initiates infringement proceedings at the European Court of Justice if adopted EU legislation still does not comply with the subsidiarity principle.
Implementation of EU legislation at national, regional and local level	CoR monitors implementation of EU legislation.

4.5 EU Agencies

The last section of this chapter deals with **EU Agencies**, one of the most important groups of actors in the EU policy cycle. EU Agencies come in a variety of forms, shapes and sizes and they perform different tasks in different policy areas, but it is essential to understand their role, especially if your policy field involves an EU Agency in some way. This section will detail what EU Agencies are, why we have them, what they do and how they do it.

Table 4.7: EU Agencies - Key facts

Names:	EU Agencies
Legal basis:	Secondary legislation creating each individual Agency
	Own legal personality
	Independent (administratively & financially)
Categories:	Decentralised Agencies (35)
	Executive Agencies (6)
	EURATOM (2)
	European Institute of Technology (EIT)
Staff:	Approx. 6-7,000 (subject to EU rules)
	From under 50 in Community Plant Variety Office (CVPO)
	To over 650 in Office for Harmonisation in the Internal Market (OHIM)
Annual budget:	Approx. €1.96 billion (2013 figure)
Basic typology:	Regulatory/decentralised
	Executive
Website:	http://europa.eu/about-eu/agencies

EU Agencies are not mentioned in the Treaty (with the exception of the European Defence Agency) and they are not EU institutions. They are EU bodies governed by European law, set up by secondary legislation, operating within the EU policy cycle to fulfil specific tasks. Agencies exist essentially to assist the Commission, and the Member States, in fulfilling various specific tasks. It is for this reason that the majority of Agencies are closely linked to, if not reporting directly to, the Commission.

The first Agencies appeared in the 1970s, two of them in fact, both created to improve effectiveness in specific policy objectives -the European Centre for the Development of Vocational Training (Cedefop) and the European Foundation for the Improvement of Living and Working Conditions (EUROFOUND). The possibility of creating Agencies stemmed from the ability of the Commission to delegate tasks to a separate body - something that was established in the Meroni case of 1958 - now known as the '**Meroni doctrine**'. It is from this case that the Commission has proposed, and received Member State support for, the creation of a series of Agencies. It must be noted that the exact interpretation of the Meroni case is still, over 50 years later, highly disputed. The key aspects of the case are highlighted in the box below.

It was not until the 1990s that more Agencies appeared, with 11 further Agencies being created in this decade. This wave of Agency creation was linked to the objective of completing the internal market - notably with attempts to increase technical harmonisation and deliver very specific technical and scientific knowledge in certain sectors. An example of these Agencies is the Office for Harmonisation in the Internal Market (OHIM) which deals with Trade Marks and Designs. The final wave of Agency creation came in the last decade with the appearance of a further 22 Agencies, created for a variety of reasons, such as improving the quality of EU policies, enhancing responsiveness to crises, providing impartial expertise and technical know-how, and for reasons of efficiency. An example here is the European Food Safety Authority (EFSA) which gives independent scientific advice on all aspects of food safety.

> **Meroni Case**
> **(Case 9-10/56 Meroni v. High Authority)**
>
> - The Commission cannot delegate broader powers than it enjoys itself
> - Only strictly executive powers may be delegated
> - No discretionary powers may be delegated
> - The exercise of delegated powers cannot be exempted from the conditions to which they would have been subject if they had been directly exercised by the Commission
> - The delegated powers remain subject to conditions determined by the Commission and subject to its continuing oversight

From the preceding short historical digest of Agencies, it is important to stress that the numbers have grown for a variety of reasons - all linked to very specific circumstances, needs or objectives. The rationale for the creation of Agencies also helps us understand what Agencies do. In the box below is a list of some of the main reasons why Agencies have mushroomed since the 1970s.

> **Rationale behind Agencies**
>
> - Assist in carrying out Community activities
> - Reduce the workload of the European Commission
> - Lack of expertise & human resources in the European Commission
> - Flexibility: day-to-day management of projects
> - Independent expertise and advice
> - Increase transparency within policy fields, and across EU decision-making
> - Facilitate European-wide cooperation between stakeholders
> - Enable more efficient and flexible implementation of EU legislation

It is clear from the above rationale behind Agencies, that each Agency is a very specific entity serving specific needs within its policy sector. In this sense no two Agencies are the same - and every Agency is an extremely important actor within its field of competence/speciality. The development of Agencies can be seen by listing the Agencies that existed as of October 2014, in Table 4.8.

Table 4.8: List of EU Agencies

Name	Acronym	Location	Created
Community Agencies			
Agency for the Cooperation of Energy Regulators	ACER	Ljubljana Slovenia	2010
Body of European Regulators for Electronic Communications	BEREC	Riga Latvia	2009
Community Plant Variety Office	CPVO	Angers France	1994
European Agency for Safety & Health at Work	EU-OSHA	Bilbao Spain	1994
European Agency for the Management of Operational Cooperation at External Borders	FRONTEX	Warsaw Poland	2004
European Union Agency for large-scale IT systems in the areas of freedom, security and justice	eu-LISA	Talinn Estonia	2011
European Asylum Support Office	EASO	Valetta Malta	2010
European Aviation Safety Agency	EASA	Cologne Germany	2002
European Banking Authority	EBA	London UK	2011
European Centre for Disease Prevention & Control	ECDC	Solna Sweden	2004
European Centre for the Development of Vocational Training	Cedefop	Thessaloniki Greece	1975
European Chemicals Agency	ECHA	Helsinki Finland	2006
European Environment Agency	EEA	Copenhagen Denmark	1990
European Fisheries Control Agency	EFCA	Vigo Spain	2005
European Food Safety Authority	EFSA	Parma Italy	2002

Name	Acronym	Location	Year
European Foundation for the Improvement of Living and Working Conditions	EUROFOUND	Dublin Ireland	1975
European GNSS Supervisory Authority	GSA	Prague Czech Republic	2004
European Institute for Gender Equality	EIGE	Vilnius Lithuania	2007
European Insurance and Occupational Pensions Authority	EIOPA	Frankfurt am Main Germany	2010
European Maritime Safety Agency	EMSA	Lisbon Portugal	2002
European Medicines Agency	EM(E)A	London UK	1995
European Monitoring Centre for Drugs & Drug Addiction	EMCDDA	Lisbon Portugal	1993
European Network and Information Security Agency	ENISA	Heraklion Greece	2004
European Police College	CEPOL	Hampshire	2005
European Police Office	EUROPOL	UK	1992
European Public Prosecutor's Office (in preparation)	EPPO	The Hague	Unknown
European Railway Agency	ERA	Netherlands	2004
European Securities and Markets Authority	ESMA	Paris France	2011
European Training Foundation	ETF	Unknown	1994
European Union Agency for Fundamental Rights	FRA	Vienna Austria	2007
Office for Harmonisation in the Internal Market (Trade Marks and Designs)	OHIM	Alicante Spain	1996
Single Resolution Board (in preparation)	SRB	Brussels Belgium	2014
European Union Judicial Cooperation Unit	EUROJUST	The Hague Netherlands	2002
Translation Centre for the Bodies of the European Union	CdT	Luxembourg Luxembourg	1994
European Defence Agency	EDA	Brussels Belgium	2004
European Union Institute for Security Studies	EUISS	Paris France	1990
European Union Satellite Centre	EUSC	Madrid Spain	2001

Executive Agencies			
Education, Audiovisual and Cultural Executive Agency	EACEA	Brussels Belgium	2006
Executive Agency for Small and Medium-sized enterprises	EASME	Brussels Belgium	2013
European Research Council Executive Agency	ERC Executive Agency	Brussels Belgium	2007
Consumers, Health and Food Executive Agency	CHAFEA	Luxembourg Luxembourg	2005
Research Executive Agency	REA	Brussels Belgium	2007
Innovation & Networks Executive Agency	INEA	Brussels Belgium	2006
EURATOM Agencies			
EURATOM Supply Agency	ESA	Luxembourg	1960
European Joint Undertaking for ITER and the development of Fusion Energy	Fusion for Energy	Barcelona Spain	2007
European Institute of Innovation and Technology (EIT)			
European Institute of Innovation and Technology	EIT	Budapest Hungary	2008

Source: data taken from http://europa.eu/about-eu/agencies

Table 4.8 shows very clearly how Agencies operate in very different and specific areas. It also shows how Agencies are geographically spread throughout the EU, with almost all Member States being home to at least one Agency. The final aspect of this section on EU Agencies will look, in more detail, at the tasks that Agencies carry out i.e. what they do. This question is a very difficult one to answer because Agencies have mushroomed over time within no specific uniform framework and are based on different reasons and circumstances. As each Agency is created by secondary legislation it can be given very different tasks and powers - so taking a look at the basic act of any Agency in your field is fundamental to know what they do. The main types of Agencies are listed below in Table 4.9.

Table 4.9: Different Types of EU Agencies

> There are two broad types of agency, each with different characteristics and raising different issues: 'Regulatory' Agencies (today more commonly known as decentralised agencies) and Executive Agencies.

Executive Agencies
- Set up under a Council regulation (2002).
- Tasks related to the management of Union programmes.
- Created for limited periods of time.
- Located close to European Commission in Brussels or Luxembourg.
  Examples: EAR, ETF

Regulatory/decentralised Agencies
- Have their own sectoral basic act.
- Spread around Europe.
- Independent bodies with their own legal personality.
- Most are funded by the EU Budget.

Different types:
- Agencies adopting individual decisions which are legally binding on third parties.
  Examples: CVPO, OHIM, EASA and ECHA
- Agencies providing direct assistance to the Commission and, where necessary, to the Member States, in the form of technical or scientific advice and/or inspection reports.
  Examples: EMSA, EFSA, ERA and EMEA
- Agencies in charge of operational activities.
  Examples: EAR, GSA, CFCA, FRONTEX, EUROJUST, EUROPOL and CEPOL
- Agencies responsible for gathering, analysing and forwarding objective, reliable and easy to understand information/networking.
  Examples: CEDEFOP, EUROFOUND, EEA, ETF, EMCCDA, EU-OSHA, ENISA, ECDC, FRA and European Institute for Gender Equality.
- Services to other agencies and institutions.
  Examples: CDT

Source: Communication to the European Parliament and the Council: EU Agencies - The Way Forward' (COM (2008)135 final)

Table 4.9 shows the main tasks that Agencies undertake, again highlighting the variety and differences that exist. There is a big distinction between Regulatory Agencies and the others. **Regulatory Agencies** are actively involved in executive functions by enacting instruments to regulate sectors and some of them have their own decision-making powers. This type of Agency is thus a very powerful and important player in the EU policy cycle in its sector of competence. The Agency will of course be involved in assisting, informing and working with the Commission on all proposals, legislative or Delegated and Implementing Acts, throughout the drafting and decision-making phases. The Agency will also be called on to share its expertise with the Council and Parliament.

An **Executive Agency** on the other hand is created, strictly supervised and dissolved by the Commission - and they are all Brussels or Luxembourg-based. These Agencies are set up for specific time periods to do a fixed job - which is that of managing and implementing a programme.

In an attempt to clarify and standardise the functioning and working methods of the decentralised Agencies which had significantly grown in number and diversity, the Commission adopted the 'Communication to the European Parliament and the Council: EU Agencies - The Way Forward' (COM (2008)135 final) in 2008. This document signifies the recognition of the importance of EU Agencies and is an expression of the need to adopt a common approach to the governance of Regulatory Agencies. Several years of inter-institutional discussions on ways of improving the efficiency, effectiveness, transparency and accountability of the Agencies, eventually resulted in the endorsement in 2012, of a Common Approach and a Roadmap that translates the approach into concrete implementing initiatives. Implementation of this Roadmap will continue into 2015 and beyond, in accordance with the deliverables and deadlines set in it. From a stakeholder's point of view, it is worth keeping an eye on these developments since these may change the way of interacting with Agencies.

Agencies are vitally important sector-specific actors in the EU policy cycle and the box below highlights how and why Agencies are important for all stakeholders to understand, and if necessary engage with:

> **Importance of engaging with EU Agencies**
>
> 1. An Agency is often the main EU source of technical/scientific expertise on specific subjects - their voice counts.
> 2. The work of Agencies will directly, or indirectly, influence the work of the Commission and the co-legislators.
> 3. Agencies will develop their own stakeholder networks - through contacts, events, sub-Committees, open hearings, etc.
> 4. Agencies are frequently requested to assist the Commission as it drafts legislative texts and Delegated and Implementing Acts.

Section 2

How EU Decision-Making Works

5. The Ordinary Legislative Procedure

By Alan Hardacre and Nadia Andrien

European decision-making has often been criticised as being too complex and difficult to understand. This is because the processes of decision-making in the EU traditionally involve a multitude of actors and vary according to the policy area concerned and the nature of the act to be adopted. It is also the mixture of formal procedures, informal practices (that have arisen over time) and the evolving inter-institutional relations that are difficult to follow and understand. So whilst the EU decision-making procedures may appear complex, this and the next chapter, show that in fact they are approachable and that it is possible to get to grips with not only the formal procedures, but also the informal practices. In addition, it should also be highlighted that EU decision-making is not necessarily more complex than any national bicameral legislative system. Before looking in specific detail at the Ordinary Legislative Procedure (OLP), this chapter starts with a general overview of decision-making in the EU.

5.1 EU Decision-Making: The Basics

The first place to start when trying to understand EU decision-making and how it works, is to consider the typology of EU legal norms as outlined in Figure 5.1.

The figure shows the basic hierarchy of EU legal norms, and it helps us understand the decision-making procedures we detail in this and the next chapter. The Treaty of Lisbon is the basic document that lays down which decision-making procedures should be used in different areas of EU activity. Included within the Treaty are specific provisions for where the EU can legislate, and according to which procedure. On the basis of this Treaty provision, which, for example, allows the EU to legislate in the field of the environment, the Commission can come forward with a proposal to start the Ordinary Legislative Procedure, the result of which will be the adoption of a Regulation, Directive or Decision - **EU secondary legislation**. This level is the most visible level of EU decision-making because it is here that the political objectives of the EU are laid down - and it will be the focus of this chapter. The level below secondary legislation, **Implementing and Delegated Acts**, will be dealt with in the next chapter because it is derived from EU legislation. The Treaty provides for the possibility of EU legislation and in its turn, EU legislation provides the possibility of Implementing and Delegated Acts.

Figure 5.1: Typology of EU legal norms

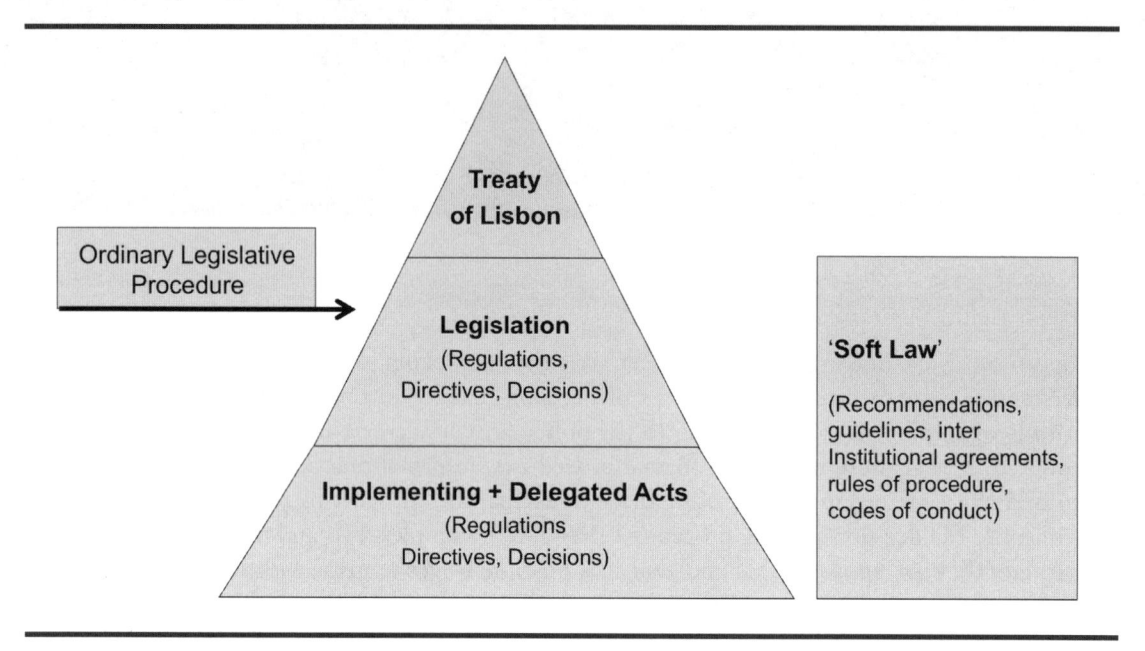

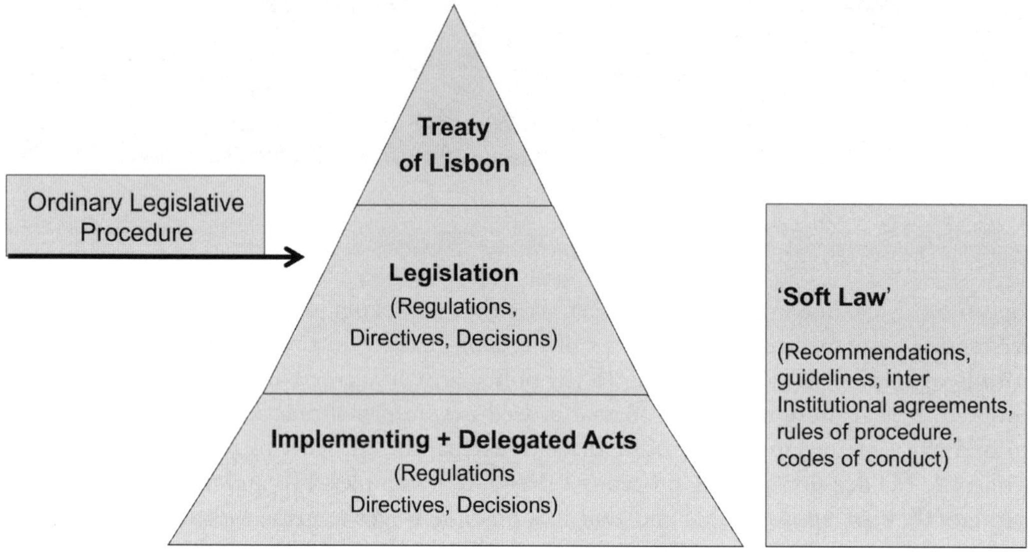
Treaty of Lisbon
Ordinary Legislative Procedure
Legislation
(Regulations, Directives, Decisions)
Implementing + Delegated Acts
(Regulations Directives, Decisions)
'Soft Law'
(Recommendations, guidelines, inter Institutional agreements, rules of procedure, codes of conduct)

For the adoption of EU secondary legislation, the Treaty of Lisbon provides for two types of procedure: the **Ordinary Legislative Procedure** (**OLP**, also known as Codecision) which 'consists in the joint adoption by the European Parliament and the Council of a Regulation, Directive or Decision on a proposal from the Commission' (Article 289(1) TFEU) and the **Special Legislative Procedures (SLPs)** which consist in 'the adoption of a regulation, directive or decision by the European Parliament with the participation of the Council, or by the latter with the participation of the European Parliament' (Article 289(2) TFEU). The policy area under consideration is decisive in determining which one of the two procedures will be followed, and this is always specified in the relevant Treaty article.

With the entry into force of the Treaty of Lisbon in 2009, the Codecision procedure was renamed Ordinary Legislative Procedure, but the name Codecision continues to be used because it is a derived term and has established currency - and it will be used inter-changeably with OLP in this chapter.

Main EU Decision-Making Procedures

1. **Ordinary Legislative Procedure**
   Commission proposal, Council (QMV) and Parliament co-decide in up to three readings.
   Example: Roaming Charges Regulation

2. **Special Legislative Procedure(s)**
   Consultation Commission proposal, Council (unanimity) decides after consulting Parliament (non-binding opinion).
   Example: Competition Law

3. **Special Legislative Procedure(s)**
   Consent
   Role of Commission and Council vary, Parliament has to give its consent.

The scope of the OLP was significantly extended by the Treaty of Lisbon, making it the rule for passing EU legislation. Considering that this is the most inclusive and arguably the most democratic decision-making procedure in the EU, this was an important development. Before looking at the OLP in detail it is important to first address the main forms of SLP.

The SLPs cover the Consultation, the Consent and some very specific individualised procedures.

1. **The Consultation procedure**
   In the Consultation procedure, the Council, acting either by unanimity or by qualified majority, adopts acts based on a Commission-initiated proposal after having consulted the Parliament. An important power that the Parliament has under the Consultation procedure is similar to the US-style filibuster principle, because even if the Parliament's opinion is non-binding the Council still has to wait for it to issue one before it can act itself - meaning that the Parliament can delay giving its opinion.

2. **The Consent procedure**
   In the Consent procedure, the Council, acting either by unanimity or by qualified majority, adopts acts based on a Commission-initiated proposal only after obtaining the explicit approval of the Parliament. As noted in the chapter on the Parliament, the Consent procedure came to prominence in 2010 when the Parliament failed to give its consent to the SWIFT agreement on data transfers from the EU to the US. This procedure notably applies to international agreements, an area in which the Parliament has considerable power. Giving its consent to these agreements is a significant role for the Parliament and can have important consequences.

There are two main differences between the Consent and the Consultation procedure; firstly, under the Consultation procedure the Parliament can table amendments, which is not possible under the Consent procedure; and secondly, under the Consultation procedure the Council is not bound by the Parliament's position, but it is however obliged to consult the Parliament.

Even though these are the two most important SLPs, a variety of other procedures are used in very specific cases, for example in sensitive areas such as Justice and Home Affairs, EU Budgetary Affairs and for specific aspects of certain policies such as social protection for workers. For these procedures it is necessary to look into the specific Treaty articles for more detail.

This chapter will now focus explicitly on the main legislative decision-making procedure: the OLP. The majority of lobbying work in Brussels is concentrated on the OLP, making it the procedure that external stakeholders work the most with.

Table 5.1: Ordinary Legislative Procedure - Key facts

Names:	Ordinary Legislative Procedure (OLP), Codecision
Established:	1992 - Treaty of Maastricht (entry into force 1 November 1993)
Legal basis:	Article 294 TFEU
Scope:	85 Treaty articles
Key actors:	European Commission (proposal), European Parliament (legislator), Council of EU (legislator)
Process:	Up to three readings as follows:
	First reading (2009-2014: 85% of legislation adopted at this stage)
	Unlimited in time
	All amendments possible
	Voting: Parliament - Simple Majority, Council - QMV
	Second reading (2009-2014: 13% of legislation adopted at this stage - including early second-reading agreements)
	Limited to 3 and maximum 4 months for each legislator
	Amendments limited
	Voting: Parliament - Absolute Majority, Council - QMV
	Third reading/Conciliation (2009-2014: 2% of legislation adopted at this stage)
	Limited to 3 times a maximum of 8 weeks
	No amendments possible
	Voting: Parliament - Simple Majority, Council - QMV

While previous chapters analysed legislative decision-making from a micro perspective inside the core EU institutions, this chapter will adopt a macro level approach, situating the previously studied internal decision-making systems in a broader context. As a result, the focus will shift from intra-institutional dynamics to inter-institutional dynamics.

After briefly tracing the origins of Codecision, this chapter will set out the formal steps of the procedure, the informal practices and the evolving inter-institutional dynamics, allowing for the identification of opportunities and challenges when working with OLP.

> **Basic premise of the OLP**
>
> The Commission presents a legislative proposal. The Parliament and the Council both have to agree to, and adopt, the same text. This is usually done through inter-institutional negotiations to find a compromise.

The functioning of the OLP is laid down in Article 294 TFEU. The main characteristics of this procedure are that the Commission, or a number of Member States or other institutions (in very specific Treaty-based cases), present(s) a legislative proposal that is then subject to negotiation and adoption by the Parliament and the Council (by qualified majority voting in the Council).

Thus under OLP, the Parliament and the Council benefit from **equal legislative powers**, consequently a legislative act cannot be adopted as long as the two institutions have not reached a compromise agreement.

5.2 The rise of Codecision

The Codecision procedure has undergone a number of changes since its introduction in 1993. The procedure, and the balance of power between the EU institutions, has developed over time with each treaty modification. Although it was the Single European Act, with the adoption of the Cooperation procedure, that paved the way towards 'equal bicameralism', it was the Treaty of Maastricht that formally introduced the Codecision procedure in 1993.

Originally, the Codecision procedure applied to a limited number of 15 legal areas, primarily related to the internal market. The procedure consisted of a minimum of two, and a maximum of three stages (first reading, second reading, and third reading/Conciliation). In 1999, the Treaty of Amsterdam extended the scope of the procedure to 39 legal areas, with the main new ones being public health, social exclusion, the environment and transport. Moreover, it also simplified the Codecision procedure by introducing the possibility to adopt a proposal at first reading; the so-called '**first reading agreement**'. These agreements are based on informal negotiations (called **trilogues**) between the Council, the Parliament and the Commission (acting as a 'broker'). These trilogues will be discussed later in this chapter because they are the main informal mechanism for finding agreement in OLP. The development of this early agreement mechanism was seen as a logical next step in the evolution of Codecision since the compulsory second reading had become superfluous in a majority of cases. Indeed, in 64 out of 99 dossiers concluded at second reading between 1993 and 1999, the Parliament left the Council common position unchanged.

First reading deals accounted for 85% of all secondary legislation concluded under Codecision between 2009 and 2014, which is 13% more than the number registered in the period 2004-2009 and 39% more compared to 1999-2004. The stages of agreement in 2009-2014 can be seen in Figure 5.2 on the next page.

The Treaty of Nice, which entered into force in 2003, added five more legal areas to the realm of Codecision, the bulk of which were in the area of Justice and Home Affairs. The Treaty did not, however, change the substance of the procedure. With the entry into force of the Treaty of Lisbon in 2009, the number of legal bases subject to the OLP almost doubled, reaching 85 articles – the biggest increase since the introduction of the procedure in 1993. Unlike Nice, the Treaty of Lisbon also proposed an important number of amendments to the provisions governing legislative decision-making.

Table 5.2 captures the areas covered by the Ordinary Legislative Procedure and the main areas still not subject to the procedure.

Figure 5.2: When agreements were made in Codecision: 2009-2014

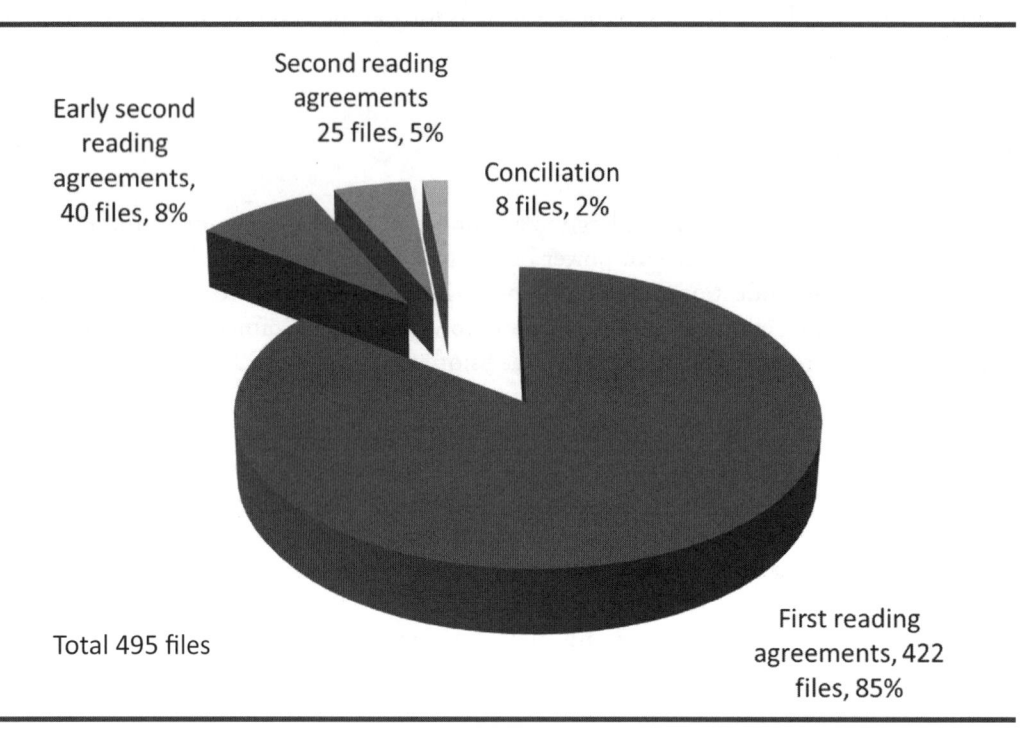

- Early second reading agreements, 40 files, 8%
- Second reading agreements, 25 files, 5%
- Conciliation, 8 files, 2%
- First reading agreements, 422 files, 85%

Total 495 files

Table 5.2: Policy areas covered by the Ordinary Legislative Procedure post-Lisbon

Ordinary Legislative Procedure	
• Services of general economic interest • Intellectual property rights • Public health (common safety concerns) • Exclusion of certain activities from right of establishment • Liberalisation of services in specific sectors • Implementation of European Research Area space • Sport/tourism/civil protection/ administrative cooperation • Economic, financial & technical assistance to third countries	• Humanitarian aid • Services of general economic interest • Citizens' initiative • Statute of Court of Justice (most) • Statutes of ESCB and European Central Bank • Modalities for control of implementing acts • European administration • Financial rules • EU Staff Regulations • Fisheries • Trade Policy (aspects of)

Special Legislative Procedures

- All of CFSP / CSDP
- Parts of agriculture ("measures on fixing prices, levies, aid and quantitative limitations and on the fixing and allocation of fishing opportunities")
- Specific R&D programmes
- Detailed rules on electoral rights
- Action to combat discrimination
- Strengthening citizens' rights
- Uniform procedure for EP elections
- System of own resources
- Tax harmonisation, approximation of laws, measures in energy having a fiscal character
- Sensitive areas of social policy
- Family law with cross-border implications
- Operational police cooperation
- European Public Prosecutor's Office
- Parts of Fisheries

The highlights of the new areas subject to OLP after Lisbon are clearly aspects of agriculture, fisheries and EU trade policy. These long-standing reserves of the Council finally became subject to the Codecision procedure, in essence the last major policy areas that had remained outside its grasp. In addition to agriculture, Table 5.2 shows the other areas that were also changed with Lisbon. The table also highlights the main areas still not subject to Codecision, such as CFSP, some specific elements of agriculture, tax harmonisation and certain areas of social policy - all of which are extremely sensitive domains for the Member States. For example the elements of fisheries that have remained outside Codecision (Article 43(3) TFEU) require that the Council, on a proposal from the Commission, adopts measures on fixing prices, levies, aid and quantitative limitations and on the fixing and allocation of fishing opportunities.

The progressive increase in the number of legal bases covered by the Codecision procedure was matched by a parallel growth in the number of launched, and adopted, Codecision files (see box), making an understanding of its inner workings more important than it was before.

> **Number of Codecision acts adopted**
>
> Maastricht era (1993-1999): 165
> Amsterdam and Nice Treaties (1999-2004): 403
> 6th parliamentary term (2004-2009): 447
> 7th parliamentary term (2009-2014): 495

Having outlined the rise and spread of Codecision, and before looking in detail at the step-by-step process, it is important to emphasise certain key defining elements:

1. The first reading stage has become the main part of the action for all Codecision files, and produces a final agreement in 85% of cases.

2. An understanding of the first reading stage provides the key to understanding the whole procedure, as the later stages cover the same material and use the same formal and informal negotiating processes, just adding constraints as they proceed.

3. For these reasons, the first reading stage, before the Parliament has voted, is the only realistic point of entry for efforts from stakeholders to influence the content of the legislation, as the later stages are limited by the baselines drawn at first reading.

With these three fundamental points about Codecision in mind, the chapter will now go through the procedure in detail - with a clear focus on the first reading.

5.3 Ordinary Legislative Procedure: First reading

Table 5.1 highlighted that in the previous legislature 85% of legislation was agreed in first reading, making it essential to understand why, and how, legislation is agreed at the first stage of the process. This section will outline the formal procedure, but more importantly the informal processes that have been created to facilitate agreement at the earliest possible stage. Figure 5.3 outlines the process of first reading.

Whilst first reading is unlimited in time there are usually political, or technical, reasons to want to conclude the dossier early. In the 2009-2014 legislature the average time required to find agreement at first reading was 17 months.

First reading formally begins when the Commission, through the College, adopts and forwards a legislative proposal to the Council and Parliament. The procedure may also be launched on the initiative of one quarter, or more, of the Member States. This allows a group of like-minded Member States to make a legislative initiative that they wish to pursue. For example, in January 2010, at the request of 12 Member States, an initiative was launched for the European Protection Order. Likewise in 2013, 25 Member States requested the amendment of Regulation 2005/681/JHA establishing the European Police College.

Before looking at how the legislators deal with a proposal in OLP we also need to consider the other actors who receive the legislative draft - and the roles they play. At the same time as the legislators, the draft is sent to national parliaments (see Chapter 1.8) and, where required by the Treaty, to the Economic and Social Committee (EESC) and the Committee of Regions (CoR) (see Chapters 4.2 and 4.3).

The Ordinary Legislative Procedure 153

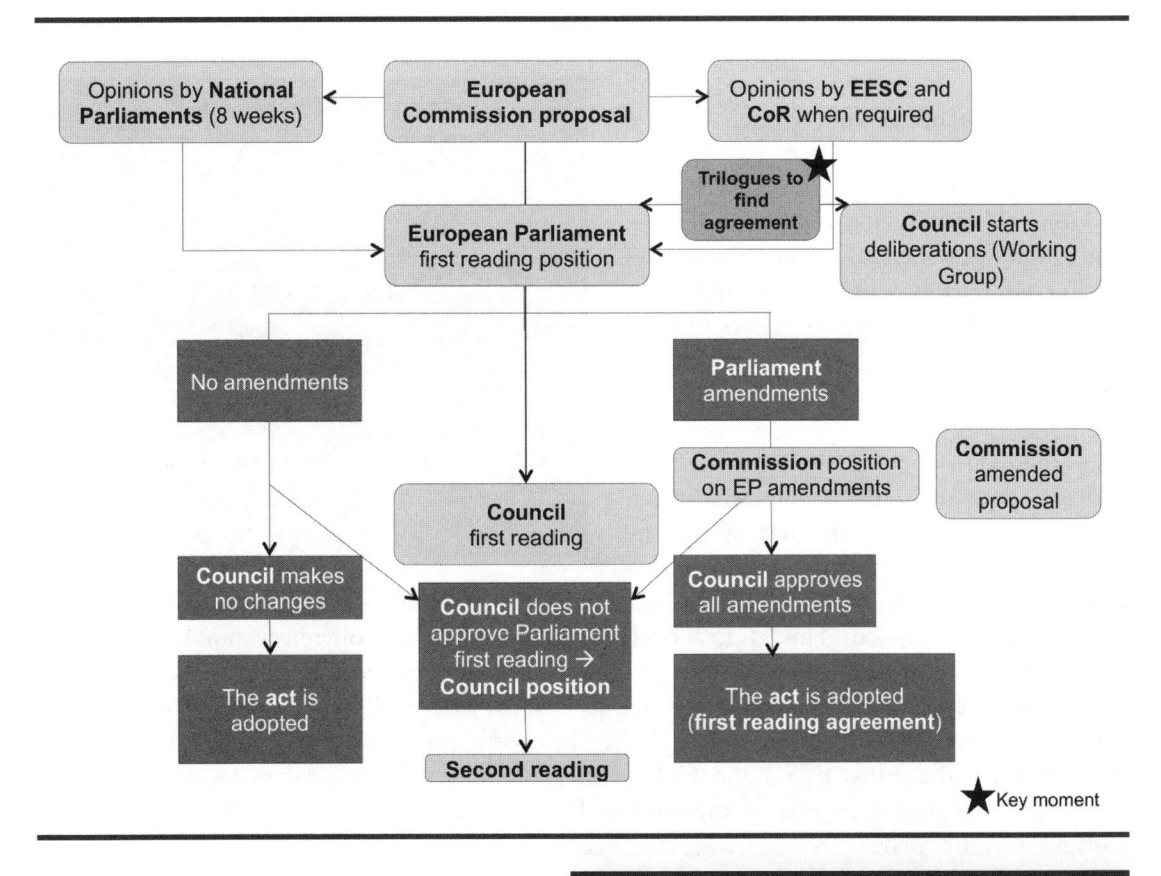

Figure 5.3: First reading of Ordinary Legislative Procedure

```
Opinions by National          European             Opinions by EESC and
Parliaments (8 weeks)  ←   Commission proposal  →   CoR when required
                                                         ↓
                                               Trilogues to ★
                                               find
                                               agreement
                          European Parliament   ←
                          first reading position  ←     Council starts
                                                        deliberations (Working
                                                        Group)
                                  ↓
         ┌────────────────────────┼────────────────────────┐
    No amendments                                    Parliament
                                                     amendments
                                                         ↓
                                              Commission position      Commission
                                              on EP amendments         amended
                                                                       proposal
                            Council
                            first reading
    Council makes                                 Council approves
    no changes          Council does not          all amendments
                        approve Parliament
         ↓              first reading →                  ↓
    The act is          Council position            The act is adopted
    adopted                                        (first reading agreement)
                              ↓
                        Second reading
```

★ Key moment

National parliaments have eight weeks to scrutinise Commission legislative proposals to give a reasoned opinion on **subsidiarity** (Article 12 TEU and Protocol 1). If one third opposes a draft (one quarter for Police and Judicial Cooperation in Criminal Matters) ('**yellow card**'), then the draft must be reviewed by the Commission, who must explain any changes, or lack of changes, it decides to make. If a simple majority opposes the draft ('**orange card**') then it must be reviewed by the Commission. If the Commission decides to maintain the proposal, the Council and Parliament can take account of the position of the national

National Parliaments

Pay attention to the process of scrutiny and the opinion voiced by National Parliaments. Not because it is likely to lead to objections on the grounds of subsidiarity, but because it will be a good indicator of how the Parliament will pressure its own government and MEPs. Some EU Member States get negotiating mandates from their National Parliaments, and none of them can ignore the opinion of their Parliament(s).

Find out more information via the Conference of Community and European Affairs Committees of Parliaments of the European Union (COSAC): www.cosac.eu/en

The Ordinary Legislative Procedure

parliaments during their first reading and either of them can stop the Codecision procedure by a 55% majority in Council or by a simple majority in the Parliament.

A further element of obligatory consultation is that of the CoR and the EESC. Both of these consultative Committees are sent the proposal and are then free to submit their opinion, albeit a non-binding opinion. The opinions of the two consultative bodies are not always followed by stakeholders, as they are non-binding, but elements of their thinking, or their ideas, can be taken up by the legislators.

The subsidiarity check by the national parliaments, and the opinions from the CoR and EESC, do not delay the start of the Codecision procedure - these procedures run in parallel to, and feed into, the start of the internal procedures in the Parliament and Council. This said, a Codecision procedure can obviously not be concluded within these eight weeks (also bearing in mind that the eight weeks scrutiny only actually starts when each national parliament receives the documents in its own language - which can add a few more weeks to the process). It can be worth keeping an eye on developments in the national parliaments, EESC and CoR in the early stages of the process to see if anything important is taking place, even if the obvious focus of the first stage of Codecision is on the co-legislators themselves.

> **First reading - Negotiating mandates**
>
> The early stages of first reading are when each legislator develops its position and identifies its interests. This process is all about preparing a **negotiating mandate** (formal or informal) for inter-institutional negotiations.
>
> Legislation is *always* the outcome of inter-institutional negotiation. This means it is always necessary to work with both legislators and to understand the actual, and potential, negotiation dynamics.

In the formal process of Codecision it is the Parliament that will have to deliver its position first, so the focus of attention is naturally drawn to the Parliament - but this should not mask the fact that the Council also starts work at exactly the same time to find its position for negotiation with the Parliament in their attempts to find a first reading agreement. So whilst the Parliament acts first, it usually only does so after informal negotiation with the Council (the Parliament can, and sometimes does, of course adopt its first reading position without any negotiation with the Council if it wants an undiluted position, to make a strong statement), making it essential to consider both legislators at the same time.

The internal decision-making system of the Parliament was covered in Chapter 3.5-3.8, the key elements of which will be covered again here. The Parliament has to nominate its **responsible** and **opinion-giving committee(s)** and a **rapporteur** from the Political Group that 'wins' the dossier. The rapporteur then drafts a **report** that needs to go through Committee and to Plenary for final adoption. In Codecision, the Parliament has three options in Plenary (all by simple majority voting), it can:

1. Approve the Commission proposal without amendments.
2. Adopt its own position with amendments to the Commission proposal.
3. Reject the Commission proposal (not foreseen in the Treaty, but in the Parliament's Rules of Procedure, RoP).

It should be clarified that normally a rejection in Plenary would result in the proposal going back to the Committee. The Committee would then try to persuade the Commission to withdraw its proposal, which is the only legally acceptable way to close the file at this stage of the procedure under Treaty rules. This is, however, something that the Commission is reluctant to do, unless it is sure that the EP's negative views are shared by the Council. It does, however, mean that the legislative proposal is, for all intents and purposes, politically dead. The explicit rejection by the EP is not formally foreseen in the Treaty of Lisbon, but neither is it explicitly prohibited - and the Parliament has adapted this into Rule 60 of its Rules of Procedure. Such a rejection happened in January 2006 when the Parliament opposed the Port Services Directive and the Commission withdrew the text. Likewise, in March 2014, the Parliament voted down a proposal for a new Plant Reproductive Material Law. The most common outcome is that the Parliament approves the Commission proposal with amendments. At this stage the Commission may accept some, or all, of the Parliament's amendments and incorporate them into a '**modified**' **proposal** and forward this to the Council (although there have been very few modified proposals up to now).

> **Commission Inter-institutional Relations Group (GRI)**
>
> **Who:** Members of all Cabinets in charge of relations with other institutions - meets at least three times a month (Fridays).
>
> Prepared by Parliament/Council coordinators in each DG (Thursdays).
>
> **Why:** Main tool of Commission to coordinate its relations with other institutions.
>
> **What:** All inter-institutional relations, such as OLP and MEP questions.

Internally there is a clear structure for the discussion and adoption of positions on Codecision developments in the Commission - which is spearheaded by the **Inter-institutional Relations Group** (known by its French acronym **GRI**). This group prepares all Commission positions on inter-institutional relations for the College, notably therefore on Codecision files - and it is the GRI that will establish coherent Commission positions on all aspects of Codecision files. These internal deliberations in the Commission are formally aimed at empowering a Commissioner to take a position on behalf of the Commission. The power of this position, which is Treaty-based, is that the Commission can require the Council to act by unanimity at first and second reading when the Commission disagrees with Parliament amendments. The strength of the disciplined internal Commission procedures is the enhanced credibility, and hence political influence, of the Commission in the negotiations, with a view to eventually exercising its power to block a decision by QMV in the Council.

When the EP's **first reading position** is forwarded to the Council, the Council formally has two possibilities, it can:

1. Approve all the amendments made by the Parliament (first reading agreement). To do this, the Council must vote by qualified majority on the text as a whole (or by unanimity if the Commission did not accept any amendments).
2. Not approve the Parliament's first reading position.

> **Council first reading position - Adoption**
>
> As a general rule, the Council adopts its position by qualified majority voting. However, when the Council's position differs from the Commission's position, unanimity is required.

In the first case, the act is adopted and the Codecision procedure is finished. In the second case, the Council has to proceed to adopt its own first reading position which may, or may not take the Parliament's first reading position into account and which it will return to the latter to launch the second reading.

Just like the European Parliament, the Council does not have the formal (Treaty-based) power to reject a text - but unlike the EP it has never actually used or foreseen such an outcome. In practice however, the Council has the power to block a text by taking no action at first reading. What allows the Council to do so, is the absence of time limits at this stage of the procedure. As a result, a dossier becomes pending and will remain so until the Council decides to take action. A withdrawal of the proposal by the Commission would be the only legally acceptable way to close the file at this stage of the procedure. In a majority of cases however, the formal procedures of the first reading will end either with an agreed legislative text or the need to go into a second reading with the Council position as the basis for continued discussions. Given that 85% of legislation is now agreed in an average of 17 months in the first reading stage, more consideration needs to be given to what happens within, and between, the institutions to reach these **early agreements**.

On the next page Figure 5.4 illustrates the separate processes that are taking place at the same time within the Parliament and Council - as already identified in the respective chapters on the Parliament and Council.

Figure 5.4 highlights the intra-institutional procedures during the OLP first reading stage. What is of importance now, is to understand how they work together towards first reading agreements - and how they interlink and influence each other.

Figure 5.4 Processes in OLP First Reading

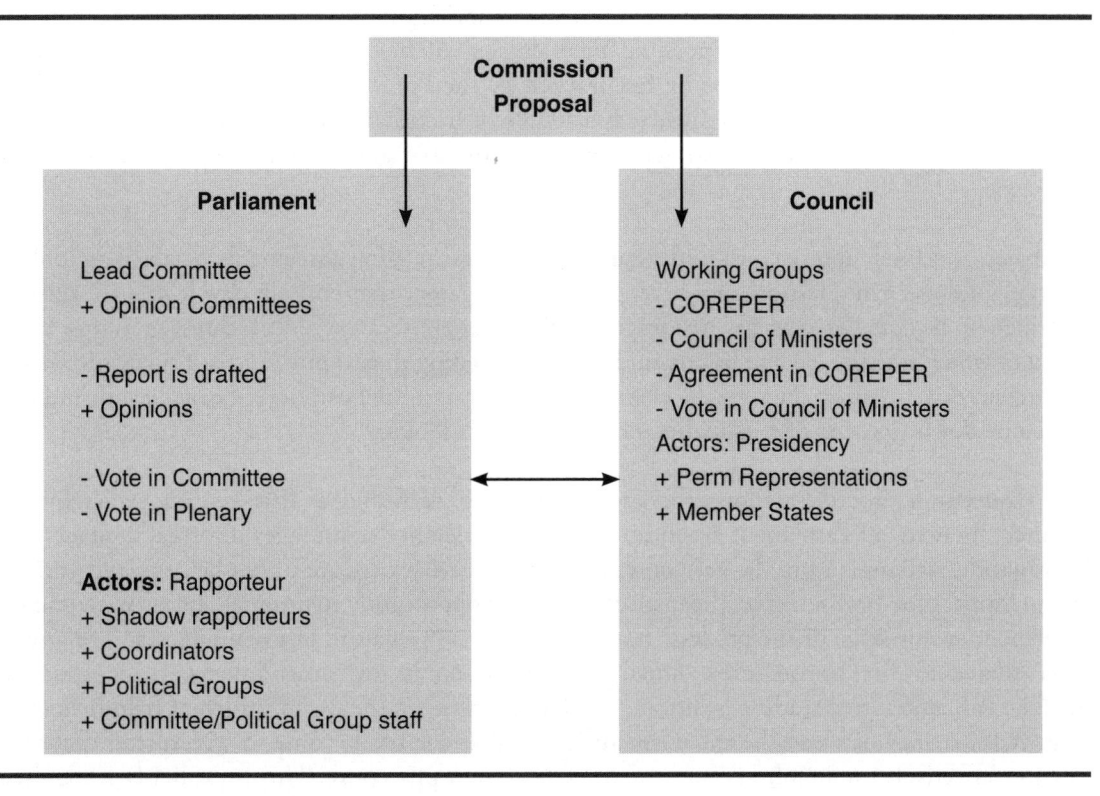

```
                    Commission
                     Proposal
                    ↓        ↓
    Parliament                      Council

Lead Committee                Working Groups
+ Opinion Committees          - COREPER
                              - Council of Ministers
- Report is drafted           - Agreement in COREPER
+ Opinions                    - Vote in Council of Ministers
                              Actors: Presidency
- Vote in Committee    ←→     + Perm Representations
- Vote in Plenary             + Member States

Actors: Rapporteur
+ Shadow rapporteurs
+ Coordinators
+ Political Groups
+ Committee/Political Group staff
```

5.4 First reading agreements - Informal trilogues

Before looking at these 'interlinkages' it is important to consider when first reading agreements are likely to be pursued and/or achieved. The only reference to this matter is made in the European Parliament Rules of Procedure, Annex XX, where point 2 states that the 'decision to seek to achieve an agreement early in the legislative process... shall be politically justified in terms of, for example, political priorities; the uncontroversial or "technical" nature of the proposal; an urgent situation and/or the attitude of a given Presidency to a specific file'. The following paragraphs will address these elements in more detail.

Urgency can be determined by external shocks (e.g. financial crisis or a health care or environmental disaster) in combination with institutional factors, especially the end of a Member State Presidency of the Council, elections in a Member State or the end of the legislative term of the EP. Two of these factors are very important and need to be highlighted.

Firstly, the end of a legislative term usually sees a large spike in Codecision activity, but this is once every five years. Secondly, many Presidencies favour a fast-track approach to legislation in line with the needs of the dossier, their own political interests and also in the drive to operate a 'successful' Presidency - which is a practice that happens every six months as the Presidency rotates. An incoming Presidency will always announce its priorities in advance, which will, in part, be based on an assessment of what is possible. Each dossier will be evaluated in political and practical terms - which could result in it being fast-tracked by the Presidency. This dynamic will be dealt with again later in the chapter because it is a source of friction between the institutions, notably because the Parliament can often strategically decide to fast-track, or not, the proposals from the Presidency.

A further, and final, approach to understanding why first reading agreements occur, is to look at the type of dossier in question, and here it becomes apparent that entirely new legislative acts are less likely to be concluded in first reading than files that are recasts, codifications, revisions, etc. - many of which actually have to be concluded in first reading due to inter-institutional agreements setting out this intention. Finally, the element of negotiation itself can never be neglected, and this can come down to issues of personality, nationality and ideology.

The Codecision procedure allows for an agreement to be found at first reading, whereby the Council approves all Parliament amendments. This possibility encourages informal contacts and information exchanges from the very onset of the legislative procedure (if not before), and as there are no formal time-limits, it gives the institutions ample opportunity to negotiate towards a common agreement at this stage of the process. It also determines the nature of the interaction because as the Parliament is first to vote, the Council has to make sure its own amendments are incorporated into the Parliament first reading position. This has given rise to the use of **informal trilogues** – the informal meetings between the three institutions. Their use has become so widespread that they are now effectively an established part of any Codecision procedure. This is explicitly recognised in the 2007 'Joint Declaration on practical arrangements for the Codecision procedure' (2007/C 145/02), which codifies the best practice of Codecision and how the institutions interact. Points seven and eight address the processes of informal cooperation between the institutions, recognising the importance that these meetings bring to the ability to find first reading agreements in a flexible and cooperative spirit. This is then expanded by points 12, 13 and 14 on the process of trilogues in first reading, which is captured in Figure 5.5 on the next page.

The informal trilogue process is fundamental to the passage of every legislative dossier because they will all go through the early stages of the process above. To understand Codecision is to understand the dynamics of trilogues. Figure 5.5 highlights the fact that both legislators start work at the same time as they individually try to establish their respective positions, which will eventually form their **negotiating mandates**. For this reason it is essential to stay abreast of developments in both legislative institutions and to understand what the potential sticking points could be - as there will always be negotiating chips created and used as collateral. Once each institution has advanced sufficiently to enter into discussions, informal trilogues will be planned. Trilogues take place with:

1. **The Council:** it will be represented by the Presidency, usually the official chairing the Working Party and/or the COREPER Chair and representatives from the Council Secretariat (usually from the Directorate dealing with the file, the Legal Service and the Codecision Unit).

Figure 5.5: The informal trilogue process

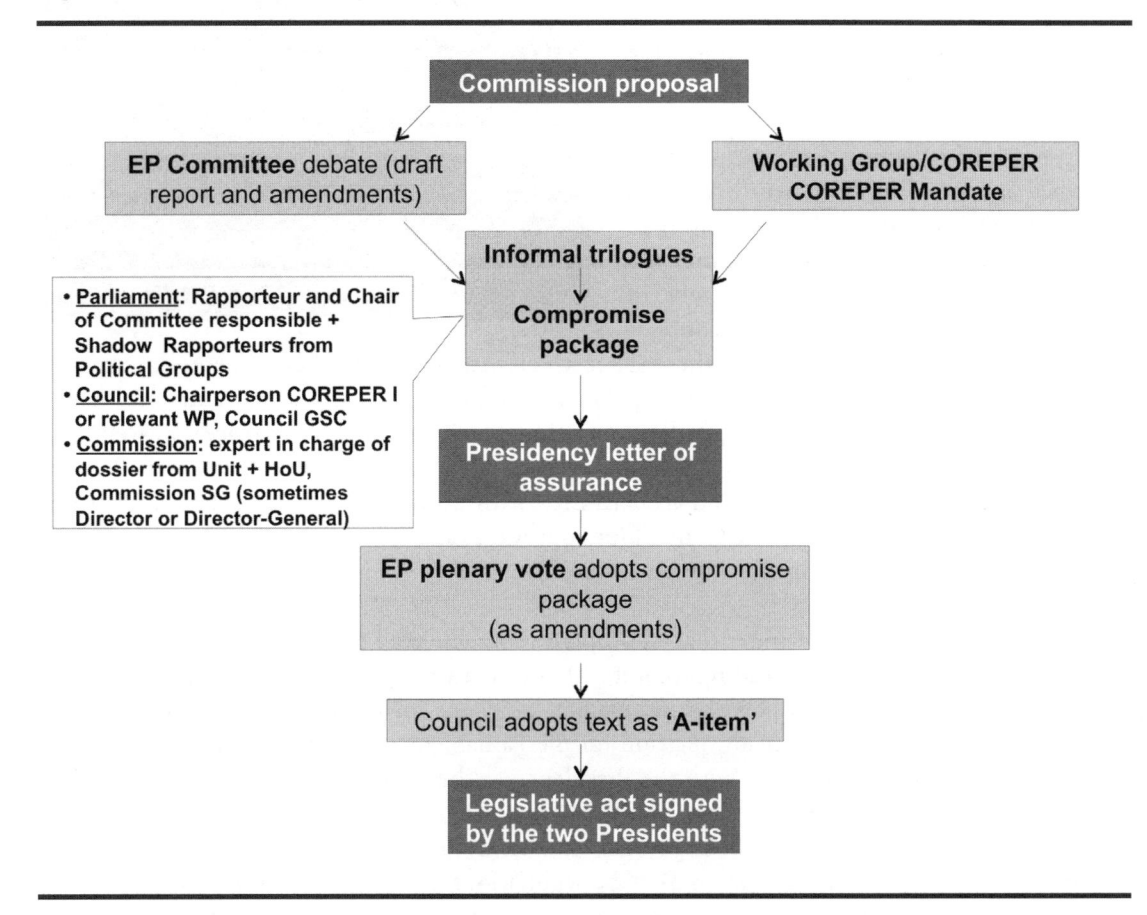

```
                        Commission proposal
                       ↙                  ↘
  EP Committee debate (draft)      Working Group/COREPER
  report and amendments)           COREPER Mandate
                       ↘          ↙
                      Informal trilogues
                            ↓
  • Parliament: Rapporteur and Chair      Compromise
    of Committee responsible +            package
    Shadow Rapporteurs from
    Political Groups                          ↓
  • Council: Chairperson COREPER I
    or relevant WP, Council GSC         Presidency letter of
  • Commission: expert in charge of     assurance
    dossier from Unit + HoU,
    Commission SG (sometimes                  ↓
    Director or Director-General)
                                     EP plenary vote adopts compromise
                                             package
                                           (as amendments)
                                               ↓
                                     Council adopts text as 'A-item'
                                               ↓
                                     Legislative act signed
                                     by the two Presidents
```

2. **The Parliament:** the EP negotiating team will always at least comprise the rapporteur who will lead the team, a shadow rapporteur from each Political Group and the Chair of the Committee responsible (or the Vice-Chair designated by the Chair) who will preside over the team.

3. **The Commission:** it will be represented by the Head of Unit (HoU) in charge of the dossier within the Directorate-General (DG) responsible, as well as by representatives of the Secretariat-General (SG) and the legal service. It is also possible that a Director, or even Director-General is involved in the Commission delegation.

These representatives will hold as many trilogue meetings as are required, with the inevitable need to return to their institutions to validate proposals and negotiated texts, until they are able, or unable to find an agreement. If an agreement is found, the Presidency, via the chairperson of COREPER, will forward a **letter of assurance** that has been approved by COREPER to the chairperson of the relevant Parliament Committee, in which the Council indicates its willingness to accept the text as agreed if it is voted by the Parliament Plenary. This means that the Council promises to adopt as an **A point** the agreed trilogue text.

The process of trilogues that has just been described is not quite as straightforward as it appears. The text that has been agreed in these closed-door meetings still requires the formal approval of the two institutions in their internal decision-making procedures -

> **Following trilogues**
>
> A good way to try and keep up with trilogues is to follow the agendas of COREPER - because you often find points marked 'follow up on trilogue' - and although no detail is provided you at least know that the trilogues are happening - and to contact the key actors involved to find out more.

which can be awkward depending on the stage at which the trilogues find agreement. For example an agreed text could still need to be subjected to a vote in Parliament Committees and Plenary (and on occasion just in Plenary depending on when the negotiations took place), as well as in COREPER and Council. This means the compromise text has to be steered through Political Groups, a Plenary (or Committee) and COREPER - with no changes, for it to stay valid. If it is approved then it is forwarded to the Council for approval as an A point, after which the legislative act can be signed by the two institutions and enter into law.

The Joint Declaration of 2007 states that 'appropriate contacts shall be established to facilitate the conduct of proceedings at first reading' (Point 12) and that the Commission 'shall facilitate such contacts' (Point 13). There is, however, no explicit guidance on when or how trilogues should start. This was a particularly difficult question for the Parliament. The Council had its discussions in the Working Group (WG) and, with the Presidency in the chair, it was usually able to deliver some form of negotiating mandate (after COREPER clearance) with a reporting system via the Presidency. This process in the Parliament was significantly more complex. Questions soon arose within the Parliament about the transparency of negotiations and the guidance and accountability of the rapporteurs involved in trilogues. Parliament therefore took a step towards improving its working methods on inter-institutional negotiations in 2009, by fine-tuning its Rules of Procedure. These rules were further amended and supplemented in 2012 and are constantly being reviewed.

Under the rules as they stand in early 2015, a formal Committee decision is required before negotiations are opened. There are two different procedures:

1. A **standard procedure** (Rule 73), under which negotiations can start immediately on the basis of the report adopted in Committee;

2. An **exceptional procedure** (Rule 74), which applies to negotiations that start prior to the adoption of a report in Committee, and involves the Plenary.

Both procedures apply to all stages of all legislative procedures for which negotiations are planned, and include important binding elements (see also *Activity Report on Codecision and Conciliation 14 July 2009 - 30 June 2014*):

- the case-by-case decision to enter into negotiations requires an absolute majority of Committee members, and must define the mandate and composition of the negotiating team;
- documentation (in the form of a four-column document) indicating the respective positions of the institutions involved and possible compromise solutions must be circulated to the negotiating team in advance of the trilogue in question;
- the negotiating team must report back to the Committee responsible after each trilogue;
- documents reflecting the outcome of the last trilogue must be made available to the Committee, which may update the mandate in the light of the progress of the negotiations;
- any decision by a Committee on the opening of negotiations prior to the adoption of a report in Committee shall be included in the draft agenda of the part-session following the announcement for consideration with a debate and vote, and a deadline shall be set for the tabling of amendments where a Political Group or at least 40 Members so request within 48 hours after the announcement.

These rules are complemented by Annex XX of the EP RoPs (see box).

Annex XX of the European Parliament Rules of Procedure - Code of Conduct for negotiating in the context of the Ordinary Legislative Procedures

The nine-point annex outlines how the Parliament should approach trilogues. The main issues that it addresses are the following:

- **Decision to enter into negotiations:** The rapporteur in the responsible Committee should get the approval of the full Committee by broad consensus or, if necessary, by a vote (2).

- **Composition of negotiating team:** The decision by the committee to enter into informal negotiations shall also include a decision on the composition of the EP negotiating team. (3)

- **Mandate of the negotiating team:** The amendments adopted in committee or in plenary shall form the basis for the mandate of the EP negotiating team. The committee shall also determine priorities and a time limit for negotiations. In the exceptional case of negotiations on a first reading agreement before the vote in committee, the committee shall provide guidance to the EP negotiating team. (4)

- **Organisation of trilogues:** Trilogues should be announced in advance. Negotiations should be based on one joint document distributed in advance, indicating the position of the institutions on all amendments (this is the four-column document) and also including any compromise texts distributed at trilogue meetings. (5)

- **Feedback and decision on agreement reached:** After each trilogue the negotiating team of the Parliament should report back to the Committee with all documents. The committee shall consider any agreement reached or update the mandate of the negotiating team in the case that further negotiations are required. (6)

The revised Rules of Procedure have increased the political accountability and the inclusiveness of the inter-institutional negotiations in legislative procedures. Furthermore, they have enhanced the visibility of mandates and the transparency of proceedings in Committee and of the negotiation process in trilogues, strengthened the role of the Committee Chair (who plays an important coordination role), and have contributed to a more uniform application across Committees of internal working methods on legislative files (see also *Activity Report on Codecision and Conciliation 14 July 2009 - 30 June 2014*).

However, the fear remains within the Parliament that a file could be closed to negotiation before the Committee has voted, the Political Groups have deliberated and the Plenary has taken a decision. This concern is accentuated by the fact that first reading agreements have become so common, meaning that a major part of the Parliament's legislative work could be as good as finalised at an early Committee stage, because Political Groups and the Plenary normally adopt the compromise agreements presented to them. This is an important issue for both the Parliament and for those trying to work with it. It means that in certain cases, parliamentary Committees are considerably more powerful than the subsequent two stages of parliamentary decision-taking: Groups and Plenary.

First reading agreements are the only texts that come from a Committee in the Parliament that are normally not amended by the Political Groups, and that are often adopted in Plenary without modification. This section has made it clear that working with the Parliament has to take place *before* it enters into negotiations with the Council, especially as the resulting text could simply be rubber-stamped by the Coordinators meeting, the Committee vote, Political Group week and the Plenary vote.

Having introduced the difficulties that the Parliament faces, it should also be made clear that a Presidency also has constraints - heavy time pressure, difficulties finding agreements in Working Groups and potential problems steering dossiers through COREPER. In addition, the Presidency now only comes around once every 14 years so a Presidency often faces a steep learning curve. It can also be a challenge for a Presidency when it is tasked with negotiating with a coherent delegation from the Parliament that includes long-standing MEPs who were former Ministers, Prime Ministers, etc. So while the Presidency, representing the Council, is usually able to get an explicit negotiating mandate from COREPER (having been through the WG), enjoys internal transparency and is well-placed to know where its limits and lines are, it will also encounter time pressure, internal negotiating problems between Member States and possibly some negotiation imbalances with the Parliament. For example, the interests of the two legislators can be strongly opposed when the drive of a Presidency to conclude a file at first reading within its Presidency is countered by the desire of the Parliament to take time to consider its position. Presidencies also have challenges in identifying and driving forward priorities, organising all the trilogues, and also in agreeing to the substance and mandate they take into negotiations. For the most part these problems can be avoided through the interaction of an incoming Presidency with the Parliament, well before it takes over its role, to discuss what dossiers can be taken forward together.

A final problem that is common to both institutions is the fact that neither the Parliament nor the Council is in fact negotiating with a definitive position, so changes can occur. For example the Parliament negotiators have to steer any agreed text through either/or the Committee, the Political Groups and the Plenary.

> **Presidencies and trilogues**
>
> - Presidencies are tempted to try conclude as many dossiers as possible in first reading.
> - Presidencies need to set priorities - what is feasible in six months.
> - The Presidency will get in touch with the people it needs to collaborate with (Parliament and Commission) on forthcoming dossiers as soon as possible.
> - At the start of the term, the Presidency will meet with the Parliament Committee chairpersons on all OLP files to see how they stand and on which files they are ready to have trilogues.

It is usually the Presidency that organises the practicalities of trilogues, such as the venue, the times and the languages to be used - although it must be noted that most trilogues take place in the Parliament (Strasbourg and Brussels). Many trilogues take place in Strasbourg, due to the fact that almost all MEPs are there and usually available. A good day to organise trilogues in Strasbourg is the Tuesday because it is often the most convenient day of the week for MEPs to find time. After a trilogue meeting, the Presidency can go back to COREPER to report on discussions and, if necessary, get a new negotiating mandate/clarification. Obviously as COREPER meets every week this can take place within a few weeks in Council. Sometimes a Presidency will bring a Minister to trilogues to show the importance that it attaches to a certain dossier, to push negotiations in a specific direction or simply to match the level of seniority presented by the MEPs in the negotiation. It is also possible that the Presidency could bring along the next Presidency, to ensure a smooth handover, although when the next Presidency comes to trilogues it can give the impression that the incumbent Presidency has given up on the file and does not intend/wish to try and finish it (although it can also be a tactic to pressure the Parliament). In addition to the relative ease of getting amended mandates from COREPER, the Presidency, especially from larger Member States, has an additional advantage because it can use its MEPs to get inside information from the Parliament.

Although trilogues have been formalised over time, making them more traceable and transparent, there is still a transparency issue from a general stakeholder perspective. These informal meetings occur behind closed doors, do not figure on any agenda, do not generate any formal minutes, and only disclose a limited number of documents - so it is difficult to follow them and understand what is happening (before it is too late). Points can be modified, new issues emerge and texts can undergo significant changes, so it is essential to have good contacts within one of the institutions taking part in these informal meetings: what is agreed in the informal trilogues has a tendency to be ratified untouched by the respective legislative institutions.

Another way to try and keep up with trilogues is to follow the agendas and minutes of the parliamentary Committees and COREPER meetings - you will often find points marked 'follow up on trilogue' - and although in a majority of cases very little or no detail is provided you at least know that the trilogues are happening. It is also important to pay attention to the different documents adopted by the Council and the Parliament and published in their respective document registers in preparation and in follow-up of trilogues. These documents provide relevant information regarding the composition of the negotiating team, their mandates, the outcome of discussions, compromise texts and next steps. These documents are however not systematically drafted and made available to the public. The key document in trilogues that was mentioned earlier in relation to the Parliament Code of Conduct is the so called '**four-column document**', an example of which is presented in Table 5.3.

Table 5.3: Example trilogue four-column document

Proposal COM	EP Committee position	COREPER position	Possible Compromise Text
Article 12	Article 12	Article 12	Article 12
Text of Commission Proposal	Text of Parliament Committee report or of Parliament position	Text of Council position	Text of possible compromise position

Source: Own creation generated from variety of four-column documents - this is not a standard format document and each trilogue can use a different variant of something similar to the example presented here

This document forms the basis of discussions and negotiations. With regard to the format, the position of each institution is put into the grid, so that differences and similarities can be highlighted. The obvious prerequisite of the compilation of such a document is that the Parliament and Council have a position in the first place. Once the positions are established, work will begin on column four for a possible **compromise text**. There can also be a final column for other comments and remarks - a kind of commentary or institutional memory for future meetings. It is through this process of trying to complete the compromise text box that the trilogues move towards a final text that can be ratified by both institutions.

The dynamics of trilogues within, and between, the Parliament and Council are vital to understand and follow for the simple reason that this is where the majority of compromises come from in Codecision. The success, and institutionalisation, of the informal trilogue system has brought with it a number of challenges for all the actors involved. It has also increased the risk of the creation of even more informal meetings between the key actors on files. These can be used, for example, to exclude some unwanted actors - making it all the more difficult to keep up with the developments that take place in these meetings.

Whilst this trilogue system is the default for adopting legislation in the first reading stage, it is also a process that continues throughout the further stages of the process should it not prove possible to conclude legislation in the first reading. It is now important to consider what happens to legislation that passes onto the further stages of the Codecision procedure.

5.5 Ordinary Legislative Procedure: Second reading

The second reading of Codecision can lead to three possible outcomes:

1. An early second reading agreement - in which the Parliament approves the Council first reading position.
2. The Parliament proposing amendments to the Council first reading position - which the Council can accept (leading to adoption), or not accept (leading to third reading).
3. The Parliament rejecting the Council first reading position - in which case the proposed legislative act lapses.

This section will detail these three possibilities in more detail, starting with the early second reading agreements.

Early Second Reading Agreement
If the Council was not able to agree with all the amendments of the Parliament through the informal trilogues in first reading, then the Parliament will proceed to its first reading vote and adopt its position. This position will then be forwarded to the Council which will have to proceed to establish its own first reading position with an accompanying statement of reasons which, when accompanied by the Commission's communication is published and transmitted to the Parliament, launching the second reading. If the Parliament has voted amendments that the Council did not accept in their first reading negotiations, the next chance of agreement in Codecision is an **early second reading agreement** - but this has to be prepared in the first reading stage. In essence the dynamics of Codecision simply switch from the original attempts of the Council to get its views into the Parliament position, to attempts by the Parliament to get its views into the Council position so that it can lead to a successful early second reading agreement. And it will be the same key actors, again in the trilogues, seeking to further the process. OLP second reading is captured in Figure 5.6.

The Parliament and the Council will generally try to avoid having to go to a **full second reading** because procedurally it changes quite drastically from the first reading. For example, politically sensitive dossiers and major inter-institutional fights will be taken into second reading (along with other issues on which no agreement could be found). As there are no time limits in first reading it is mostly preferable to continue negotiations there rather than pass into second reading, until it becomes evident that there is no possibility of a first reading agreement. This is why further informal trilogues between the Council and the Parliament frequently take place before the Council adopts its first reading position, in an attempt to find an early second reading agreement.

As this is still in first reading there is no time limit to the continuation of trilogues and discussions to find an agreement that the Parliament can ratify in its second reading. If the Parliament successfully finds a compromise with the Council at the Council's first reading stage by managing, in trilogues, to bridge the difficulties that were not resolved before the Parliament's first reading position was established, the Parliament will send a **letter of assurance** (from the Chair of the committee responsible) to the Council to state that they will support the Council position in their second reading. In this case it will be possible for the Parliament to adopt an early second reading agreement by simply ratifying the Council position with no changes at a Plenary session within the three (or four, see below)-month deadline (voting by simple majority to accept the Council first reading position). The early stage of the second reading in this case becomes an extension of the first reading. Failing this there is the more 'classical' full second reading.

Figure 5.6: Second reading of Ordinary Legislative Procedure

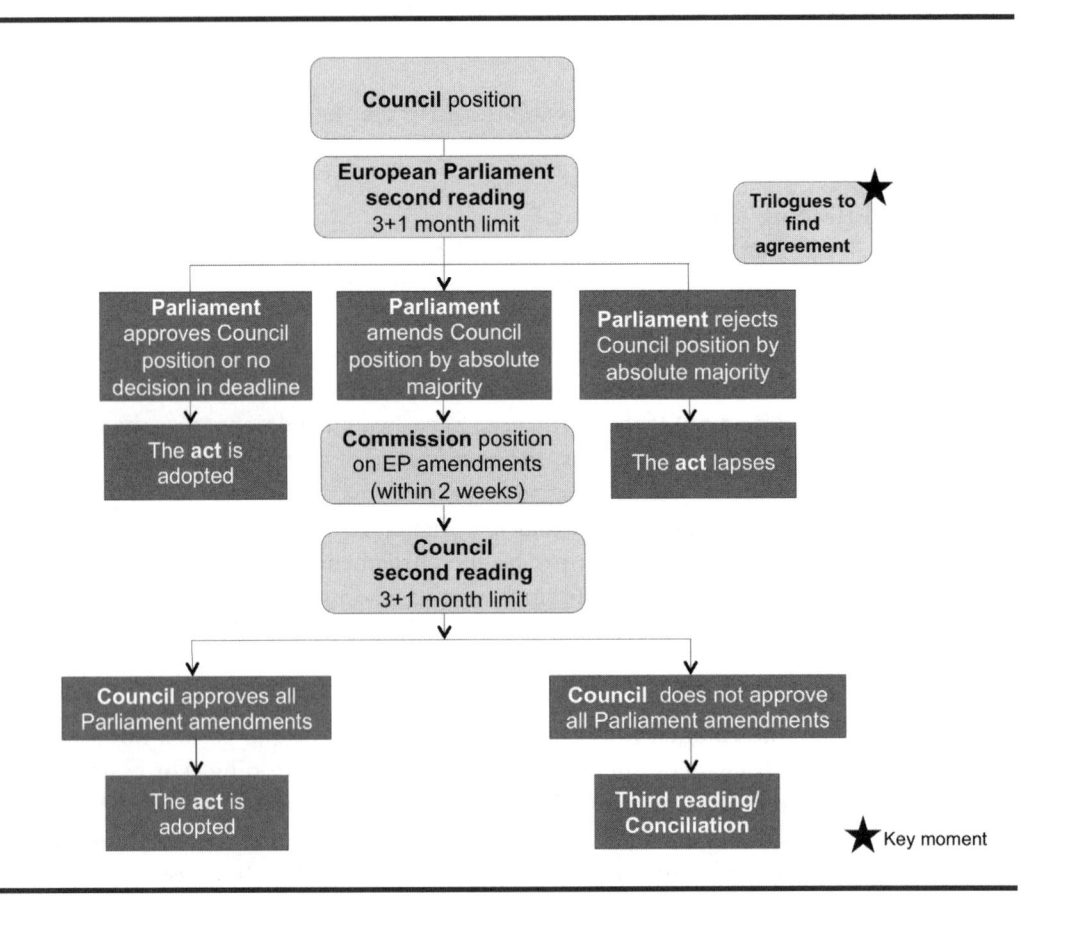

Classical Second Reading
The Parliament only has three months (extendable by one month to a maximum of four, if required) to enact its second reading, which is a very short time limit within which to react, and while the Treaty provides for the adoption of the Council position, should the Parliament fail to deliver an opinion within the three months (max. four), the Parliament has never missed a deadline. While the Treaty deadline appears very tight, in reality there is often room for manoeuvre. For example the second reading only formally starts when the President of the Parliament announces the Council position in a Plenary session - having received the Council position in all its working languages. There is often, therefore, a period of a month (or months) between Council adoption of its position and the formal start of second reading. This period can be used for very informal contacts between the Council Presidency and the rapporteur, with or without the Commission, but not for trilogues as such, to advance the work on finding a compromise.

The Parliament does have the option of extending the second reading by an extra month, on the request of the committee responsible chairperson, if this is required (Article 294 TFEU, Rule 65 Parliament RoP). Early second reading agreements in the 2009-2014 legislature represented 8% of Codecision agreements, the full second reading representing a further 5%, and with the average time for a full second reading agreement at 33 months. In second reading it is only the Committee responsible that continues with a file within the Parliament - any opinion-giving Committees that were consulted in first reading are no longer included. It is also usually the same rapporteur from first reading who continues with the file - and the trilogues will continue as they did in first reading (although perhaps the Presidency will have changed between readings).

> **Second reading**
>
> In second reading the debate becomes inter-institutional and the room for new elements is very limited.
>
> Second reading requires an understanding of the first reading and of the issues that were raised then.

It is possible at this stage, if the Parliament has real objections to the Council position, that the Parliament rejects the Council position (by absolute majority), in which case the legislative proposal lapses. This has only happened once, in 2005, when the Parliament voted by 648 to 14 to throw out the Council position on the directive 'Patenting of Software Inventions for Computers'.

If there was not an early second reading agreement, or an outright rejection of the Council position, the final possibility in second reading is that the Parliament, within their three months (max. four), **proposes amendments to the Council position** (by absolute majority), in which case it is forwarded to the Council for its second reading. The tabling of amendments in second reading is subject to **strict admissibility criteria** which severely restrict the margin for manoeuvre and the discussions that take place in second reading. Second reading amendments are only admissible if:

1. They seek to restore, wholly or partly, a position adopted by Parliament in first reading.

2. They seek to amend a part of the text of the Council's position which was not included in, or that differs in content from, the proposal submitted in first reading.
3. They seek to take into account a new fact or legal situation which has arisen since the first reading (such as an election for the Parliament).
4. They are a compromise deal between the Council and Parliament.

These amendments are all subject to **absolute majority** in the Plenary which, as Chapter 3 stressed, is very difficult to attain. These strict conditions on a second reading amendment, in terms of content and voting rules, have very important consequences for the Codecision procedure, notably because amendments focus on the key differences between the positions of the Council and the Parliament. Whilst in first reading there are many more amendments due to the less strict admissibility criteria and the fact that a simple majority can carry them through Plenary, it is often true that many amendments are simply 'Christmas tree amendments' - there is something for everybody. In second reading the admissibility criteria restrict what can be tabled and the absolute majority voting rule ensures that only serious amendments with a chance of support will be tabled. While the theory is that new, or different, issues are not introduced at this stage it is not unusual that the Parliament tries to introduce new amendments - though for the most part the rules above are well-adhered to.

The discussions in second reading will therefore focus on the sticking points inherited from first reading, issues that the Parliament will likely have already debated. The fact that the Parliament also has to vote by absolute majority at second reading means there are significantly fewer amendments tabled, and those that are tabled carry heavy political and institutional weight. As a result of these content and voting limitations and the fact that the Council position stands unchanged if the Parliament does nothing in its allotted 3-4 months, the latter has never failed to meet these tight deadlines.

The Commission prepares its opinion on the Parliament's second reading position and plays a crucial role by giving an opinion on all Parliament amendments before the Plenary vote - exactly as it did in first reading. Again the importance of this stage is that if the Commission opposes a Parliament amendment, and it is voted by the Parliament, this will oblige the Council to vote by unanimity on this amendment in its second reading. This is again not to be taken lightly as unanimity is an onerous voting requirement in the Council. The Commission position is reviewed and ultimately agreed by the GRI, and then the College, as was outlined earlier. The Commission will go to the Plenary of the Parliament before the vote on amendments to state which ones it is able to accept in full, or partially, and which not.

This Parliament position, with its voted amendments, is forwarded to the Council for their three (max. four) months second reading. The Council at this stage only has two choices:

1. To accept all the amendments tabled by the Parliament - which is something that again will have been pre-agreed in a trilogue meeting before the vote of the Parliament - in which case the act is adopted.

2. If, however, the Council is unable to approve all the amendments of the Parliament it will inform the Parliament that it has not accepted its position - therefore the President of the Council, in agreement with the President of the Parliament, will convene a meeting of the Conciliation Committee within six weeks (may be extended by two weeks) - the beginning of the third reading. An important point at this stage is the fact that the Council usually does not indicate to the Parliament which amendments it has not supported in the Parliament's second reading position, as this is not a formal requirement laid down by the Treaty. The Council does this to maximise its negotiating position in the subsequent third reading, although the previous trilogue meetings will have usually made all the points of discord clear.

The second reading stage of Codecision is therefore, as we have seen, very different to the first reading. The procedure is similar, and the use of trilogues (with the same actors) remains, but it is the time limit, amendment admissibility rules and voting changes that constrain discussions to only the most important inter-institutional points of discord.

5.6 Ordinary Legislative Procedure: Third reading/Conciliation

When the Council and the Parliament do not manage to come to an agreement in second reading, the institutions have to go through a **third and final reading** which can effectively be split into three distinct stages;

1. **Stage 1:** Council second reading (as highlighted in the previous section) is often used to prepare for third reading because it is by this stage obvious that no agreement has been found in second reading. For this reason the Council second reading can actually be more important to prepare for the third reading than it is for second reading itself.

2. **Stage 2:** The convening of and the actual meetings of the Conciliation Committee and the Conciliation trilogues that prepare their work.

3. **Stage 3:** The approval of any joint text agreed within the Conciliation Committee.

This means, in reality, that third reading is actually three stages of six to eight weeks to find an agreement. This section will detail each of these three stages in turn.

Stage 1: Informally, **third reading starts** as soon as the Council knows in second reading that it will not be able to find an agreement with the Parliament. This allows extra time to prepare what are usually very difficult negotiations. In the 2009 to 2014 period only 2% of Codecision files made their way through to this stage. This is in comparison to 5% in the previous legislative period. The average time for a dossier to be completed, if it gets to Conciliation, is 30 months. There is a series of important stages in the third reading procedure, as highlighted in Figure 5.7.

Stage 2: The second stage in the third reading process concerns the convening of the **Conciliation Committee**, which should happen within six, or if necessary eight weeks from the time of the Council's formal decision to reject the Parliaments second reading position. Once the first formal Conciliation Committee meeting takes place the Committee is deemed to have been convened and the formal six to eight weeks of negotiations start. The first six to eight weeks are spent preparing the negotiations that will take place within, and between, the three institutions in the second phase, so here again there are a series of informal trilogues that bring together small teams of negotiators from the institutions. The **delegations** are usually as shown in the boxes below.

Parliament delegation - 28

- **Chair** 1 of 3 Vice-Presidents responsible for Conciliation (all in delegation)
- **rapporteur** and **Chair** of the Committee responsible
- 23 other MEPs, mainly from Committee responsible

The composition of the whole delegation must reflect the political balance of the Parliament

Council delegation - 28

- **Chair:** Minister or Secretary of State from Presidency
- **COREPER 1 or 2**

Commission

- **Commissioner** + support staff

The Commission is there to help 'reconcile' positions

These are the delegations that will take part in the full Conciliation Committee that has to take the final decisions on a text. It is, however, much like first and second readings because it is again within the reduced informal trilogues that the text will be elaborated. In these conciliation specific trilogues it is usual to have:

1. The chairperson of COREPER and the chairperson of the Working Party from the Council.
2. The Director-General or Director, and experts from the Commission.
3. The Vice-President of the Parliament heading the Parliament delegation, the Committee chairperson and the rapporteur from the Parliament.

This reduced group will try to agree on a compromise text to be presented to the full Conciliation Committee, as outlined above. They will usually have started their meetings during the second

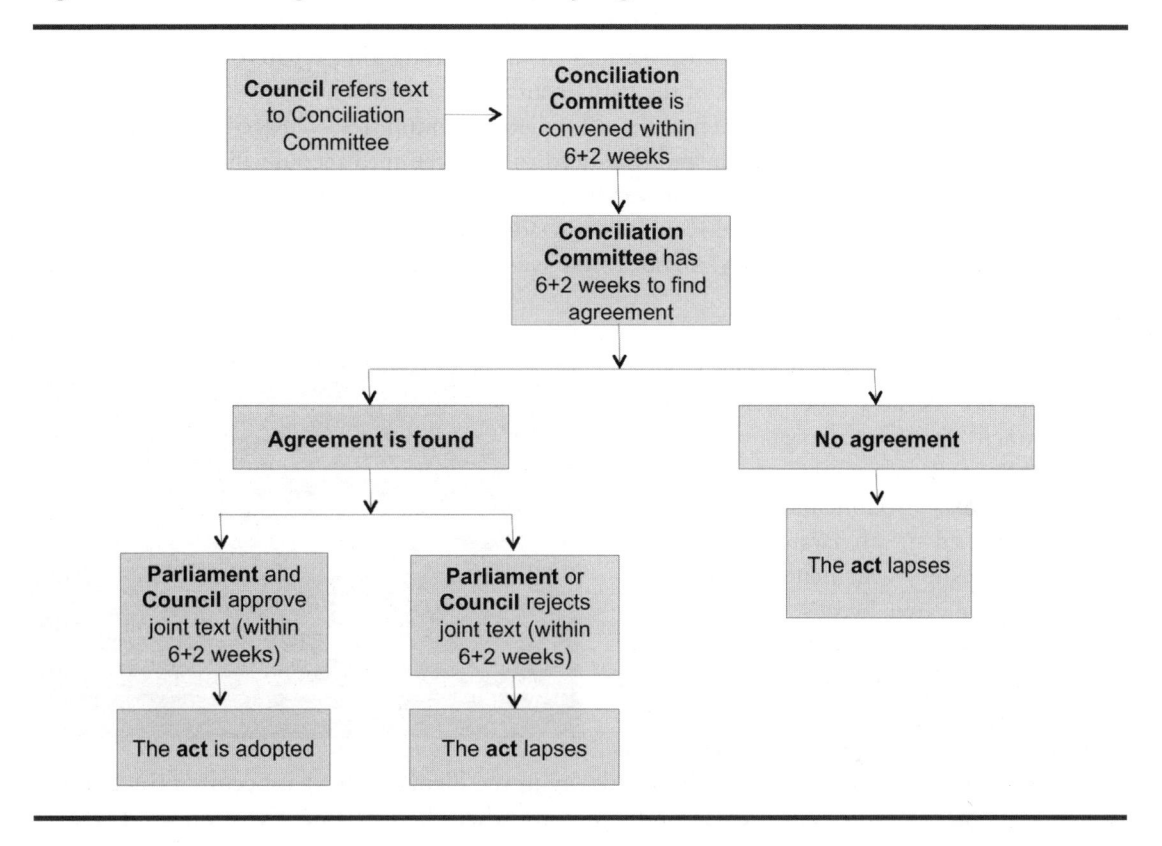

Figure 5.7: Third reading/Conciliation of Ordinary Legislative Procedure

```
┌─────────────────┐      ┌─────────────────┐
│ Council refers  │      │  Conciliation   │
│ text to         │─────>│  Committee is   │
│ Conciliation    │      │  convened within│
│ Committee       │      │  6+2 weeks      │
└─────────────────┘      └─────────────────┘
                                  │
                                  v
                         ┌─────────────────┐
                         │  Conciliation   │
                         │  Committee has  │
                         │  6+2 weeks to   │
                         │  find agreement │
                         └─────────────────┘
                           │             │
                           v             v
                  ┌──────────────┐  ┌──────────────┐
                  │ Agreement is │  │ No agreement │
                  │    found     │  │              │
                  └──────────────┘  └──────────────┘
                    │         │           │
                    v         v           v
         ┌──────────────┐ ┌──────────────┐ ┌──────────────┐
         │ Parliament   │ │ Parliament   │ │ The act      │
         │ and Council  │ │ or Council   │ │ lapses       │
         │ approve joint│ │ rejects joint│ │              │
         │ text (within │ │ text (within │ │              │
         │ 6+2 weeks)   │ │ 6+2 weeks)   │ │              │
         └──────────────┘ └──────────────┘ └──────────────┘
                │                │
                v                v
         ┌──────────────┐ ┌──────────────┐
         │ The act is   │ │ The act      │
         │ adopted      │ │ lapses       │
         └──────────────┘ └──────────────┘
```

reading stage as identified earlier - meaning that they will be advanced before the six to eight week preparation phase during which the full Conciliation Committee has to be convened. Any agreement that comes from these discussions is usually a delicate package that has been laboriously negotiated. Remember that if a file has arrived in Conciliation it has not proved possible to find agreement at either first or second reading, meaning that positions will be well entrenched.

If an agreement is found within these informal conciliation trilogue discussions, it will be presented to the two legislator delegations individually - not as a whole Committee. The Council delegation votes by qualified majority and the Parliament delegation by simple majority. It is possible that one, or both, Conciliation delegations will reject the text. This occurred in 2011, when the EP delegation decided with 15 votes against (no votes in favour and 5 abstentions) to reject the final compromise proposal on the revision of the Novel Food Regulation. It can also happen that a joint text is not found within the time limits. The trilogues preparing the Conciliation Committee have failed to find a joint text to present to the full Committee on only one occasion: in 2009 under the Czech Presidency, when no joint text was found on the Working Time Directive. In both cases, the legislative proposal lapses (see box 'no agreement' in Figure 5.7).

Stage 3: If an **agreement on a joint text** has been reached in the Conciliation Committee there is an exchange of letters between the co-Chairmen of the Conciliation Committee. From here the General Secretariat of the Council, or the Parliament Secretariat, will prepare the draft legislative text to be forwarded to the Presidents of the Parliament and Council. The text will be accompanied by a letter signed by both co-Chairmen of the Conciliation Committee - the letter will outline any important statements that were made and that need to be taken into account in the final stage of the third reading - the votes on the joint text by the two legislators. This stage of the procedure is limited to six to eight weeks. The Council must adopt the text by qualified majority and the Parliament by simple majority - they are both simple accept or reject votes (i.e. there is no chance to make amendments).

For the Council, this stage has never posed any problems because the delegation of the Council to Conciliation is usually COREPER, and when they have agreed to the joint text in Conciliation they have always approved it afterwards within the Council. For the Parliament the situation is more complicated because the 28-strong delegation to Conciliation is not necessarily representative of the position of the full Plenary. For example a small majority in the Parliament Conciliation Committee vote (simple majority) may not turn out to be a majority in the Plenary. This has occurred three times, first in 1995 on the Biotech dossier, secondly in 2001 when the Parliament vote on the Takeover Bids Directive resulted in a tie - meaning that after 12 years of negotiating, the Directive was thrown out. The final case concerned Port Services in 2003, when the Parliament voted 229-209 against the Conciliation joint text, ending the legislative procedure.

> **The Paradox of transparency**
>
> The lack of transparency of the Conciliation Procedure highlights a paradox in the OLP. Council meetings, for legislative files, and Parliament Committee and Plenary meetings are all screened live on the Internet. The main arena for compromises and decisions is that of trilogues - which remain totally outside of any public scrutiny.

For the few dossiers that arrive in Conciliation it is very difficult to follow proceedings as they take place within the restricted trilogues. Of all the parts of the OLP the Conciliation stage is the least transparent and the most difficult to work with. All of the meetings take place behind closed doors and there are no public information sources on the content or direction of negotiations because there are no minutes, or summaries published. In addition the dates and times of these Conciliation trilogues are difficult to find out in advance so it is not easy to know when the negotiations are happening.

5.7 Key stages and key actors - Ordinary Legislative Procedure

Like previous chapters, this one ends with a table of the main stages and actors in Codecision, along with key comments. The key stages and actors are in Table 5.4.

Table 5.4: Key stages and key actors: Ordinary Legislative Procedure

Key stage	Comment	Key actors
Preparation of legislative proposal	The Commission has the right of initiative and changes to Commission texts require significant majorities within and between the legislators.	Unit within Commission Commissioner Cabinets *(see Chapter 1)*
Opinions of national parliaments, CoR, EESC	Whilst none of these opinions are binding, the discussions and ideas can easily transfer to the legislators - therefore they need to be monitored carefully.	Opinion rapporteurs for both CoR and EESC European Committees of national parliaments *(see Chapter 4)*
First reading Parliament Committee Council Working Party & COREPER	Whilst Parliament acts first, the Council deliberates at the same time - making it essential to monitor and work with both at once. The formal processes are quite straightforward to follow, although it is easier to access documents and discussions of the Parliament. Each institution needs to be engaged with to build into their position - notably their negotiating mandate for the next stage.	Parliament Committee: Rapporteur Shadow rapporteurs Group coordinators Opinion-giving Committee *(see Chapter 3)* Council Working Party and COREPER Commission DG, SG and GRI
Informal trilogues Valid for all stages of Codecision hereafter - trilogues continue until an agreement can, or cannot, be reached	The key fora for inter-institutional negotiations, where the legislators work with their respective mandates to find a compromise text. It is very difficult to find information on trilogues, especially ongoing ones. Knowing who sits in them is one way to access information. The key document here is the four-column document that is used to find agreement.	EP: Rapporteur, shadows of Political Groups and Committee Chair Council: Working Group chair DP or DPR Commission: officials from DG + (SG/Legal Service possible)
First reading - Plenary	Any agreement from a trilogue has to be passed by the Political Groups and the Plenary vote **(simple majority)**. Note that pre-agreed trilogue compromises usually get 'ratified' without change.	Rapporteur Shadow rapporteurs Group coordinators Political Groups

First reading - Council	In 85% of cases the Council approves the Parliament position, usually as an A item on the Council agenda. The Council can also vote by **QMV** - unless the Commission did not accept EP amendments, in which case the Council votes by **unanimity** on those amendments. If the Council does not agree with the Parliament position then working with the Presidency on the Council position is the objective of all stakeholders - including of course the Parliament.	Presidency Key Member States *If required:* Rapporteur Shadows Key MEPs Commission
Second reading - Parliament Early Second Reading Agreement Classical Second Reading	In 8% of cases, the Parliament approves the Council position with no changes. In other cases it will be necessary to go back to all the key positions from first reading - noting that now there are strict time-limits, amendment admissibility and voting rules - making it more difficult to reach agreement in second reading. The Parliament votes by **absolute majority** of its members.	Parliament Committee: Rapporteur and shadows Coordinators Political Groups
Second reading - Council	The Council in second reading only has two possibilities; to agree to the Parliament text with no changes or to reject the Parliament position. This leaves very little room to work with the Council. The Council votes by **QMV** unless the Commission does not accept EP amendments, in which case the Council votes by **unanimity**.	Presidency Member States Commission
Third Reading Council Second Reading prepares third reading Conciliation Committee and trilogues Votes on joint text by both legislators	Third reading has three phases as outlined below - but all three are very difficult to engage with, find out about or influence because the battle lines have already been well drawn at the first and second reading stages. 1. Preparation/Negotiation in Trilogues 2. Discussion at the Conciliation Committee 3. Ratification in Parliament and Council	EP: Rapporteur and Chair of Committee responsible Vice-Presidents responsible for Conciliation Council: Minister or Secretary of State from Presidency COREPER 1 or 2 EC: Commissioner Support staff

6. Delegated and Implementing Acts: 'New Comitology'

By Alan Hardacre and Michael Kaeding

The second category of decision-making that needs to be considered in this section of the book is that of **non-legislative acts**, which can be either '**Delegated Acts**' (Article 290 TFEU) or '**Implementing Acts**' (Article 291 TFEU). These two articles of the TFEU have introduced major changes to the old system of **Comitology** - creating two new worlds of delegated powers for the Commission. This level of decision-making can be seen more clearly with reference to Figure 5.1 (at the start of the previous chapter) where Delegated and Implementing Acts ('**D&I Acts**') clearly come after co-decided secondary legislation in the typology of EU legal norms.

It is almost impossible to work in, or with, Brussels these days and not come across a reference to Comitology - it seems to be everywhere. Comitology has developed a longstanding reputation as an opaque procedure that is difficult to understand, follow, and find out about - let alone work with. This reputation has been changing slowly in recent times due to innovations in transparency, the growing involvement of the Parliament and an increasing awareness on behalf of stakeholders that Comitology is something that they simply have to engage with. The Treaty of Lisbon, which represents the latest in a long line of adaptations to the Comitology system, is without doubt the most significant reform there has been in terms of legal basis, procedures, institutional balance and openness for interested stakeholders. It has also split Comitology into two new worlds, making use of the word Comitology itself more difficult (see box). So what exactly is it and why do we hear so much about it?

What is Comitology?

Comitology is the name given to a system of Committees since the 1960s made up of representatives of the Member States, chaired by the Commission. Their job is to assist (and control) the Commission as it drafts implementing measures on technical aspects of EU legislation. Examples include:
- Taking decisions on the detail of the implementation of legislation (e.g. Capital Requirements Directive).
- Taking decisions to implement EU policies, such as how much to spend on what (e.g. FP7 programmes).
- Taking decisions to adapt or update EU legislation in order to take account of technical, or scientific, developments (e.g. Driving License Directive).

Changing name?
The Treaty of Lisbon creates two avenues for implementing legislation; one of them no longer uses Committees - **making the use of the term Comitology partly redundant. This chapter will therefore refer to Delegated and Implementing Acts (D&I Acts)**.

D&I Acts are all about the Council and Parliament delegating tasks to the Commission in secondary legislation (the process of which was described in the previous chapter). This is the EU equivalent of systems that exist in all EU Member States whereby during the course of agreeing legislation the executive is granted powers to implement or change the legislation - which it can subsequently use to propose subordinate legally binding measures. It is therefore indispensable to understand the 'new Comitology': the two systems of D&I Acts.

This chapter will start with a short recap of why the legislators delegate tasks to the Commission. It will then explicitly address why and how Comitology has become so important in European affairs - for all stakeholders interested in European decision-making. The chapter will then outline the two categories of D&I Acts in turn. These sections will explain in detail what D&I Acts are and how the new decision-making procedures work. The key facts on the 'new Comitology' can be found below in Table 6.1.

Table 6.1: Delegated and Implementing Acts - Key facts

Names:	Comitology
	Delegated & Implementing Acts since 2009
Established:	Informally: 1961
Formally:	Single European Act (entry into force 1987)
	Article 290 TFEU - Delegated Acts - Common Understanding
	Article 291 TFEU - Implementing Acts - Regulation
Key actors:	European Commission, European Parliament, Council,
	Comitology Committees, Expert Groups, Agencies
No. Committees:	2013 - 302
No. meetings:	2013 - 718
No. IA:	2013 - 1,716
No. RPS/PRAC:	2013 - 171
DA:	2013 - 57
Procedures:	***Delegated Acts***
	1. Commission prepares and drafts Delegated Act
	2. Commission presents draft act directly to EP & Council
	3. EP and Council have two months to object (or approve)
	4. If no objection, or approbation, act adopted
	5. EP (absolute majority) or Council (QMV) can object to an individual act (on any grounds) - act rejected
	6. EP (absolute majority) or Council (QMV) can revoke (partially or fully) the delegation of powers to the Commission
Procedures:	***Implementing Acts***
	1. Commission prepares and drafts Implementing Act
	2. Commission presents draft act to Comitology Committee
	3. Committee (Member State representatives) discuss act

> 4. Committee votes according to one of two procedures:
>   - Advisory (Simply majority, non-binding)
>   - Examination (QMV needed to approve act)
>
>   If Committee approves act by QMV - Commission adopts
>   If Committee rejects act by QMV, or has 'no opinion' -
>   sent to Appeal Committee or act not adopted

Historical Overhang: The Third Procedure... Regulatory Procedure with Scrutiny

The Regulatory Procedure with Scrutiny (RPS) was established in 2006 to provide the co-legislators with more control over very sensitive modifications of basic acts that were already taking place in comitology. It was used when amending non-essential elements of secondary legislation, such as adding substances to an annex. It was applicable under two requirements: first the basic act needed to be adopted by codecision; and second, the measure needed to be of general scope and considered as 'quasi legislative'.

Quasi-legislative was code language for politically sensitive issues that the legislators wanted to keep a closer eye on, notably in the areas of environment, financial services, public health, and law enforcement cooperation. These items are now dealt with by Delegated Acts - but a number of acts still foresee the RPS as the procedure has not been replaced in all existing legislation.

There are two levels of control for the Commission here. First there is the usual committee voting (as per Implementing Acts) and then the European Parliament (by AM) and the Council (by QMV): both have a right of veto on the proposed measure. If the Comitology committee delivers a positive vote (by QMV) then the Parliament and Council each have three months to use one of three legal grounds to object to the measure.

The three legal grounds apply if the draft measure:
• exceeds the competences laid out in the basic act
• is not compatible with the aim or content of the basic act
• does not respect the principles of Subsidiarity and Proportionality

If either legislator objects, using one of these criteria, then the measure is rejected. In the case of a negative opinion, or the absence of an opinion, of the Comitology committee, the Commission refers the measure first to the Council, which has two months to take a decision on what to do. The Council can oppose the proposed measure by QMV, in which case it goes back to the Commission (and the Parliament does not have any rights). The Council can also envisage adopting the measure or not find any opinion by QMV within its two months, in which case the Commission submits the measure to the Parliament, which in turn has a further two months to perform the same legal checks outlined above. The Parliament does not enjoy the same status as Council under the RPS procedure - which was a major source of tension prior to the introduction of Delegated Acts.

Examples: Body scanners in airports, Loop-belts in airplanes, detailed implementing rules in Financial Services, Lists of products and substances in the environmental field.

Comitology has risen from very obscure beginnings in the agricultural markets in the 1960s to gaining ever-increasing importance and visibility in EU policy-making. From the delegation of tasks such as setting prices and fixing export restitutions to the Commission in the 1960s, Comitology has evolved so that the Commission is now delegated far more sensitive tasks such as supplementing and amending technical annexes of legislation, for example in the Financial Services or Environment policy areas. It is this changing nature of the tasks delegated to the Commission that has required numerous modifications to the decision-making procedures used for the Commission to adopt its Comitology measures - the latest of which was the Treaty of Lisbon and the introduction of D&I Acts. This introduction of D&I Acts split the 'Comitology world' into two parts and each has a very different procedure for taking a decision. A Common Understanding on Delegated Acts and a Regulation on Implementing Acts were negotiated under the Spanish and Belgian Presidencies in 2010 to bring these two new systems fully into force. We will see later in the chapter that Delegated Acts are a sharp deviation from the past practice of Comitology, whereas Implementing Acts are the continuation of the 'traditional' Comitology system.

From Table 6.1 we can also notice that D&I Acts involve a significant number of actors, meetings, and ultimately implementing measures. Indeed we see that in 2013 there were 1,716 Implementing Acts - a significant number of legal acts with important localised consequences. It has been, and is increasingly, a crucial decision-making arena of the EU, not only because of this large volume but more importantly because of the fact that many of these acts have important localised impacts and implications - the devil is often in the detail. A legislative act, as developed and adopted in Codecision/Ordinary Legislative Procedure (OLP), might frame overall objectives and the broad structure to achieve these, but it is through D&I Acts that the details will be outlined - and it is here that many stakeholders will see their interests directly impacted. For example a Chemical Company will be impacted by secondary legislation on the quality of the environment, but it will be more impacted by a Delegated Act that bans specific chemical products from the EU market. It is for this reason that stakeholders need to be able to work with D&I Acts in the same way, and with the same confidence, that they work with the OLP. Figure 6.1 displays the process of delegating powers to the Commission.

Figure 6.1: Delegating implementing powers to the Commission

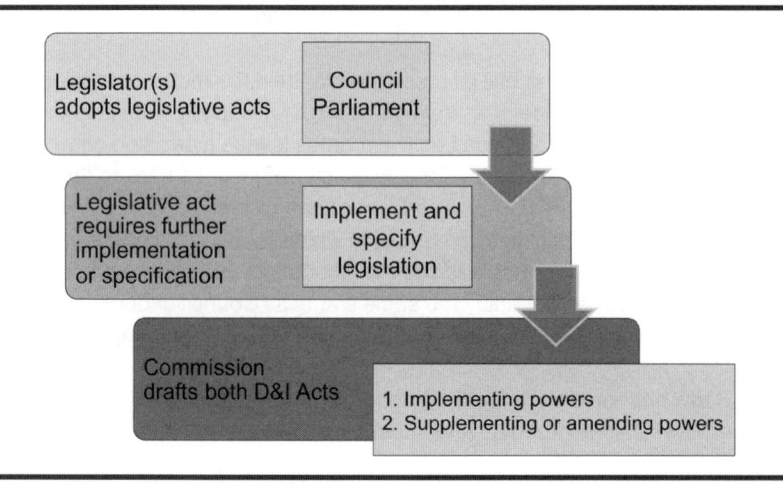

Delegated and Implementing Acts: 'New Comitology'

The Lisbon Treaty stipulates that Member States shall adopt all measures of national law necessary to implement legally binding Union acts. But the Council, along with Parliament in most cases under OLP, can decide to delegate certain powers to the Commission to either implement or further specify the legislative act. With the Lisbon Treaty this can be done in two different ways: Delegated Acts and Implementing Acts. These two categories represent two different types of tasks and two different procedures for taking decisions once these tasks have been delegated to the Commission:

1. Firstly supplementing and amending non-essential elements of legislation.
2. Secondly purely implementing the provisions of the legislation.

These two categories of powers can be delegated to the Commission and form the basis of this chapter's discussions of D&I Acts. Before looking at why we have such an extensive system of D&I Acts it is important to clarify an often neglected point - D&I Acts need to be engaged with throughout the EU policy-making cycle and not just when it comes to the Commission stage of presenting an individual D&I Act. This can be seen more clearly in Figure 6.2.

Figure 6.2: D&I Acts in the EU policy cycle

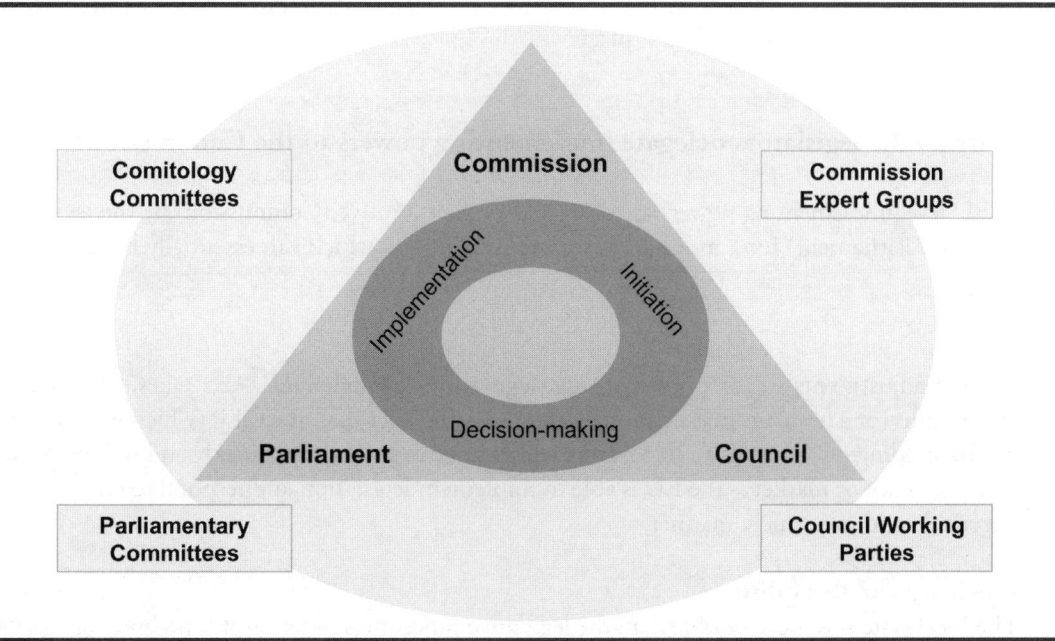

The D&I Acts procedures are decision-making procedures with the objective of applying or specifying particular technical matters of EU legislation that were agreed by the co-legislators. From a sequential perspective, D&I Acts come at the end of the EU policy cycle as seen in Figure 6.2, but practically speaking D&I Acts will already have formed part of the negotiations between the co-legislators and their scope will have been subject to discussions within the Commission when presenting their legislative proposal. It is therefore crucial to highlight that all D&I Acts will have:

1. Been developed by the Commission in their legislative proposal - meaning that (all) elements of D&I Acts were likely discussed in Commission Expert Groups, within the Commission Inter-Service Consultation (ISC) and with stakeholders via consultation (formal and informal). The resulting D&I Acts dispositions in the legislative text are the ones that the Commission will have found to be the most suitable to undertake the tasks identified and in line with past practice.

2. Been subject to negotiation in OLP. The legislators take a very keen interest in the tasks delegated to the Commission and their oversight of these tasks, so D&I Acts are often present in OLP negotiations.

Since D&I Acts are present in most legislative acts they are a practically constant subject of discussion in legislative preparation and decision-making. This means that, firstly, it is essential to work on D&I Acts throughout the whole policy-making cycle and that, secondly, working with a legislative file will often involve an appreciation of the D&I Acts elements within it. Having outlined the key elements of D&I Acts and the importance they play throughout the EU policy cycle it is now useful to address the question of why Council and Parliament delegate implementing powers to the Commission in the first place.

6.1 Why do the legislators delegate implementing powers to the Commission?

At the EU level implementing powers are delegated to the executive (Commission) by the legislator(s) (Council and Parliament) for a number of important reasons - which can essentially be stated as the following:

1. **Speed**
   Making adjustments to, or implementing, legislation through D&I Acts takes, on average, a few months (or a few days in exceptional cases) - much faster than the OLP (which has an average for first reading of 17 months). In this way legislation can be updated quickly and in keeping with events, science or markets - the EU is able to implement legislation and respond to circumstances effectively and in a timely manner.

2. **Efficiency and flexibility**
   The D&I system is more flexible than the legislative procedures in terms of time-lines, obligations, etc. Technical expertise is provided by Member State specialists who assist the Commission in the drafting of its acts based on their respective national experiences - an exercise that subsequently facilitates implementation by the national capitals.

3. **Technical nature of work**
   D&I Acts concern technical aspects of legislation. The Commission will draft the acts but will be assisted by Member States and other sources of expertise (Expert Groups, EU Agencies, etc.).

The D&I decision-making procedures allow the legislators to concentrate on their core legislative work and move technical work to the level of technical experts - where updates can be adopted more quickly and with greater ease.

4. Oversight and control

D&I Acts are also about Member State control over the Commission while it is exercising the implementing powers. In essence, they are a series of different decision-making procedures for the approval of Commission drafted acts - with increasing oversight and control by the legislators the more sensitive and political the acts become. This oversight and control of the legislators is in particular a counter-balance to the first two points. Speed, efficiency and flexibility are crucial for the EU to get the right information into D&I Acts to be able to respond to policy challenges, markets, events, science, etc. - but there needs to be a political oversight mechanism to ensure this works properly and within the agreed legal boundaries.

The first two reasons were sufficient for Comitology to spread very quickly over the last decades, and across policy areas, such that now there is virtually no area of EU activity that does not have some D&I Acts. This fact is highlighted in Table 6.2 below.

Table 6.2: Number of Comitology Committees 2007-2013

Policy sector	2007	2009	2013
Enterprise and Industry (ENTR)	33	39	33
Environment (ENV)	35	36	33
Health and Consumers (SANCO)	17	16	26
Agriculture and Rural Development (AGRI)	31	15	20
Mobility and Transport (MOVE)	35	39	32
Taxation and Customs Union (TAXUD)	11	12	13
Research (RTD)	5	7	8
Europe Aid (AIDCO)	9	7	6
Other	88	95	131
Total	**264**	**266**	**302**

Source: Report of the Commission on the working of Committees during 2007/8 COM(2008) 844 final, 2008/9, COM(2009) 335 final, COM(2010) 354 final, COM(2014) 572 final

Table 6.2 shows the number of Comitology Committees by policy sector. It reveals that, in terms of numbers, the majority of Committees are found in only a handful of sectors - with the top five sectors accounting for approximately 50% of the Committees. It is worth bearing in mind a couple of things at this stage. Firstly, a **Comitology Committee** is established by a legal act, the secondary legislation, so all of the Committees above have a legal basis. The second thing to remember is that a legislative act can refer to an existing Committee if the tasks delegated by the legislation are similar (or the same) as tasks delegated by other pieces of legislation. One Committee can therefore be dealing with several legislative acts at once - a fact that makes the statistics in Table 6.2 a little misleading because the number of Committees is no indicator of the volume of work, or the nature of the actual decisions being taken. This is more accurately reflected in Table 6.3, which shows the number of Comitology measures per sector.

Table 6.3: Number of Comitology measures by policy sector 2007-2013

Policy sector	2007	2009	2013
Enterprise and Industry (ENTR)	269	207	29
Environment (ENV)	62	88	36
Health and Consumers (SANCO)	331	278	605
Agriculture and Rural Development (AGRI)	963	460	202
Mobility and Transport (MOVE)	39	76	39
Taxation and Customs Union (TAXUD)	63	147	106
Research (RTD)	57	202	250
Europe Aid (AIDCO)	388	224	127
Other	281	408	322
Total	2,453	2,091	1,716

Source: Report of the Commission on the working of Committees during 2007/8/9, COM(2008) 844 final, COM(2009) 335 final, COM(2010) 354 final, COM(2014) 572 final

Table 6.3 shows Health and Consumer protection led in the number of Implementing Acts adopted in 2013, and Agriculture & Rural Development led in 2007 and 2009. But in each year there were significant numbers of Implementing Acts adopted across a wide range of policy areas.

6.2 The rise and spread of Comitology

The history of Comitology has been characterised by inter-institutional tensions and by changes in legal basis, procedures and institutional roles. Comitology was not foreseen in the original Treaty of Rome, something that caused the Council a few headaches when it had to start implementing the Common Agricultural Policy (CAP) at the beginning of the 1960s. Implementing the CAP required the regular setting of prices, tariffs and quotas, which due to the legal architecture of the Treaty of Rome had to be done by the legislator - the Council. The Commission seized the initiative in 1961 and proposed to the Council that it should delegate these technical implementing tasks to the Commission as this was the classical role of an executive. The Council was only too happy to agree to such delegation of tasks, but only on the condition that one representative of each Member State, in a Committee, could check the measures that the Commission was proposing: this was the birth of the Comitology system whereby the Commission was granted the power to adopt technical implementing measures under the control of these Member State Committees. This was in many senses a natural development because aspects of EU legislation needed to be implemented at the EU level - and this practice was already well enshrined in Member States and their executive branches.

The new Committees proved to be very successful fora for cooperation between the Commission and Member States, and they spread quickly through the field of agriculture as the CAP was expanded and deepened. In the 1970s and 1980s, as the EC project spread into new areas and continued to develop, these Committees likewise spread across policy areas. This growth in the number and functioning of Committees did not, however, take place in any systematic way with, for example, horizontal rules. Due to this there were many different variations of Comitology Committee procedures. At this time there was also no centralised record of how many Committees there were, what decisions they were taking and how they operated - this effort would not come until much later. There were also no horizontal rules about what types of tasks were delegated to the Commission, and as Comitology covered many policy areas there had been evident moves away from the straightforward technical measures of the 1960s.

History of Comitology

1961	First Committee starts work in field of CAP
1970	Köster case at ECJ validates practise of Comitology
1970s	Expansion of Committee system
1987	Single European Act gives legal basis (Article 145 EEC)
1987	First Comitology Decision
1999	Treaty of Amsterdam gives new legal basis (Article 202 TEC)
1999	Second Comitology Decision
2006	Third Comitology Decision
2009	Treaty of Lisbon Articles 290 and 291 TFEU
2012	Schengen border case (C-355/10)
2014	Biocide case (C-427/12)

It was not until 1987, and the entry into force of the Single European Act, that Comitology was given formal legal recognition, through Article 145 EEC. This came some 26 years after the first Committee started working, and some 17 years after the landmark Köster case in which the European Court of Justice legitimised the Comitology system in 1970 in the face of a claim it was not legal and disturbed the institutional balance. Back in 1987, Article 145 of the Single European Act required secondary legislation to set out, for the first time, some horizontal Comitology procedures. The Council adopted a Decision, later in 1987, which created seven different procedures. The different procedures were rather complicated, and in addition, the Parliament had no role at all in the new system until 1992.

In 1992 the Treaty of Maastricht created the Codecision procedure which vastly increased the powers of the Parliament in co-deciding legislation. This development set the stage for a series of inter-institutional clashes over the Parliament's role in Comitology. Simply put, the Parliament wanted a role that was proportionate with its role in Codecision. If the Parliament delegated tasks that were sensitive, it wanted the right to make sure they were being dealt with correctly - otherwise the Parliament could be circumvented by using Comitology. These tensions were only partially resolved in 1999 with a new Comitology Decision, which represents the basis for much of what we see, and understand, in Implementing Acts. It reduced the number of procedures from seven to three; it created Rules of Procedure for Committees; it created an obligation for the Commission to issue an annual Comitology report; and finally it increased the rights of the Parliament. These changes were almost entirely driven by the Parliament and its desire to find out what was happening in Comitology and to get involved. In part the Parliament was waging a symbolic fight with the Council to have equal status as a legislator.

The power granted to the Parliament in 1999 was the **right of scrutiny** (which is described in more detail later in this chapter), which has only been used on a handful of occasions. This meagre power, a series of inter-institutional tensions and a political crisis over the non-transmission of Comitology documents from the Commission to the Parliament in 2005, led to further calls for reform from which a new Comitology Decision arose in 2006. The 2006 revised Comitology Decision added one new procedure, the **Regulatory Procedure with Scrutiny (RPS)**, to grant the Parliament more rights in the Comitology system on measures that were deemed to be more sensitive (quasi-legislative). At this stage, therefore, under the new Decision there were five different Comitology procedures, all of which engendered the use of a Comitology Committee: Advisory, Management, Regulatory, RPS and the Safeguard procedure. The new RPS granted the Parliament increased powers over a very specific category of implementing measures - those deemed to be the most sensitive and quasi-legislative.

These Comitology procedures were a mechanism to create different levels of control for different types of implementing measures - with more control for those that were more sensitive for the legislators. This brings us to two fundamental questions in Comitology that relate to the procedures and the differing levels of control required by the legislators. Firstly, what are technical and more politically sensitive implementing acts and how should they be dealt with; and, secondly, how much should the efficiency of the system be compromised by political oversight and control?

'Old' Comitology procedures
(1999/468/EC as amended by 2006/512/EC)

Article 3	Advisory procedure
Article 4	Management procedure
Article 5	Regulatory procedure
Article 5a	Regulatory procedure with scrutiny
Article 6	Safeguard procedure

There is in fact no definitive answer to these questions. In the first case, on whether a measure is political or technical, it is always the prerogative of the legislators to decide in the legislative act. While the legislators retain this right, what has become apparent over the years is that there are clearly different categories of tasks being delegated to the Commission - including a grey zone between what is technical and political. It is clear that deciding on the price of an export restitution for barley should not be treated in the same way as modifying an annex of banned substances in the field of the environment.

The second issue is whether the system of deciding implementing measures should lean more towards efficiency in terms of getting measures decided in an appropriate timeframe, or towards legitimacy such that all decisions taken are carefully checked by the legislators to make sure the system is not being abused.

Efficiency or Legitimacy?

When matters were purely technical, the legislators required very little control over the Commission - which allowed measures to be taken very quickly. Over time, as more areas came under Comitology, and as the measures became increasingly quasi-legislative, there was a call for more control and legitimacy of the system. This increased control takes time - making the system of D&I Acts less efficient in terms of speed.

Technical or Political?

Comitology in the early days was purely concerned with technical matters. Over time, however, it has taken on more and more **quasi-legislative** tasks i.e. ones that could have been dealt with by the legislators. The issue of technical or political is at the heart of D&I Acts - essentially at the OLP phase when the legislators have to decide whether to use an Implementing (pure implementation) or a Delegated (amend/modify) Act - or to take the decisions in OLP themselves.

These two questions have framed the debate on Comitology for many years and the system that has been created with Lisbon is the latest attempt to answer them. Let us therefore now consider these two issues in more detail.

The two boxes above highlight the two key questions outlined earlier. Both of these questions have a major influence on the decision-making procedures that have developed for adopting D&I Acts. Examples of technical and political matters in the boxes below will help complete our understanding of what D&I Acts are.

Example: Technical matter

Policy area:	Common Agricultural Policy
Issue:	A price needs setting, an export restitution needs modifying.
Technical or political:	The Commission is simply implementing the provisions of the legislative act. This is a very straightforward technical matter (which does not mean it is not important).
Control and oversight:	The Commission act does not need to be subject to extensive scrutiny because the Commission's margin for manoeuvre is extremely limited. The use of a Comitology Committee is sufficient (it is an Implementing Act).
Other examples:	Market authorisations, allocation of grants.

The Commission implements and applies the legislative act respectively.

> **_Example_ Political matter**
>
> **Policy area:** Air Safety.
> **Issue:** Establish the criteria for a 'Black List' of air companies that cannot fly into, or over, EU airspace. The list of individual air companies is established by implementing the criteria that all airlines have to comply with.
> **Technical or political:** Because of technical and scientific progress the criteria for the list might need to be updated regularly. The impacts of these updates can have serious repercussions for airlines around the world.
> **Control and oversight:** This is very sensitive and has important impacts so the legislators require significant oversight and control (in return for delegating the power to the Commission). Here Commission measures to change the criteria need to be evaluated by the legislators (it is a Delegated Act).
> **Other examples:** Adaptation of annexes, definitions of minimum/maximum requirements.
>
> **The Commission supplements or amends non-essential elements of the legislative act.**

6.3 The Treaty of Lisbon and the 'new Comitology'

As mentioned earlier, with the entry into force of the Treaty of Lisbon on 1 December 2009, the Comitology world was split into two: Delegated Acts and Implementing Acts. The Treaty of Lisbon thus provided the legislators with two legal avenues to use when delegating tasks to the Commission. This change is nothing more than the continuation of developments that had been taking place in the Comitology system for some time. It is an explicit recognition that there are two fundamentally different types of activities (technical/application vs. political/modification) taking place in Implementing and Delegated Acts - and it creates two separate systems to deal with them. These two avenues are as follows:

> **Implementing Acts (Art. 291 TFEU)**
>
> - Traditional Comitology with Committees.
> - Rules laid down in new Regulation (Regulation 182/2011).
> - Used for general or individual measures.
> - A measure of individual scope is always an Implementing Act.
> - Implementing Acts cannot add, insert, delete or modify anything.
> - An Implementing Act gives effect to the rules laid down in the legislative act.

> **Delegated Acts (Art. 290 TFEU)**
>
> - New system created - **without Committees.**
> - Rules in Treaty of Lisbon - with a new **Common Understanding.**
> - A measure of individual scope is **never** a Delegated Act.
> - Delegated Acts are for measures of general scope that **add, insert, delete or modify** non-essential elements of the legislative act.

From these short descriptions it becomes clear how the Treaty of Lisbon, and its subsequent implementation under the Spanish and Belgian Presidencies in 2010, split the old Comitology world into two different procedures - notably through the abolition of Committees for Delegated Acts. Both of these avenues will be explored in detail in the following two sections, starting with Implementing Acts.

6.4 The 'new' procedures: Implementing Acts

Article 291 TFEU designates Implementing Acts as one of the two categories of acts that can be delegated to the Commission (and in exceptional circumstances to the Council). It is here that we find the 'traditional' Comitology measures and the Committees that were in operation before Lisbon. Whilst Delegated Acts did not need any legislation to be implemented, Article 291 TFEU for Implementing Acts explicitly required a Regulation to lay out the new decision-making procedures - and this time the Regulation had to be co-decided. The negotiation of this Regulation took 12 months to complete and it entered into force on 1 March 2011 (Regulation 182/2011). The new Regulation modified the 'old' Comitology procedures - notably by reducing them to only two: the Advisory procedure and a new Examination procedure (which we describe in detail in this next section). The process for Implementing Acts is as follows:

1. The legislators (in OLP) decide to delegate implementing powers to the Commission.
2. There must be uniform conditions of implementation.
3. The legislators decide what level of control they want to impose on the Commission.
4. The legislators decide which procedure is best suited.
5. The legislators create a new Comitology Committee, or refer to an existing Committee.
6. The secondary legislation is published in the OJ and enters into force.

Through this process the delegation of powers is set into the legislative act, which once adopted forms the legal basis for the Commission to adopt Implementing Acts.

As the box on the right shows, the Commission drives the process of Implementing Acts, from drafting the text, calling and chairing meetings, finding compromises and modified texts, trying to ensure a positive vote and then finally adopting the Implementing Act. As stated above, there are now two procedures under which the Commission can operate for Implementing Acts. The first procedure, the Advisory procedure (Article 4) is shown in Figure 6.3.

Role of Commission for Implementing Acts

1. Drafts the Implementing Act.
2. Organises Comitology Committee meetings.
3. Sets agenda, organises minutes, chairs meeting, ensures secretariat.
4. Finds compromises, organises vote.
5. Adopts the final Implementing Act voted upon by Member States in Committee.

188 Delegated and Implementing Acts: 'New Comitology'

1. **The Advisory procedure**

Figure 6.3: The Advisory procedure

Draft implementing act of the Commission

The Committee adopts an opinion, if necessary, by simple majority vote

↓

The Commission takes the utmost account of this opinion
Legally, it is <u>not obliged</u> to follow this opinion

Figure 6.3 shows the Advisory procedure (Article 4), which remains exactly as it was laid out in Council Decision 1999/468/EC as amended by 2006/512/EC - it has not been changed by the new Implementing Acts Regulation. This procedure is used when the changes being made are not politically sensitive - because it is the least binding on the Commission, and also the quickest for taking decisions. The process is that the Commission presents a draft Implementing Act to the Committee which has to deliver an opinion 'if necessary by taking a vote' (by simple majority) with each Member State having one vote. The Commission then has to take the 'utmost account of the opinion delivered' and inform the Committee of the manner in which its opinion has been taken into account. Legally, the Commission is not obliged to follow the Committee's opinion (although for political reasons the opinion of the Comitology Committee will carry significant weight).

2. **The Examination procedure**

Next to the unchanged Advisory procedure is the Examination procedure (Article 5), which has merged the previous Management and Regulatory procedures, as shown in Figure 6.4.

The Examination procedure has some interesting innovations. Like the Advisory procedure, the Commission presents a draft Implementing Act to the Committee, but for the act to be adopted the Commission has to obtain a qualified majority in favour of its draft.

Committee voting

55% Members States
65% EU population
Blocking minority must comprise at least 4 MS

Or if requested old QMV system (until 31 March 2017):
Positive opinion (QMV) = 260 votes for
Negative opinion (QMV) = 260 votes against
No opinion = no QMV for or against

For more information see *Chapter 2*

Figure 6.4: The Examination procedure

Draft implementing act of the Commission

The Committee must adopt an opinion by qualified majority

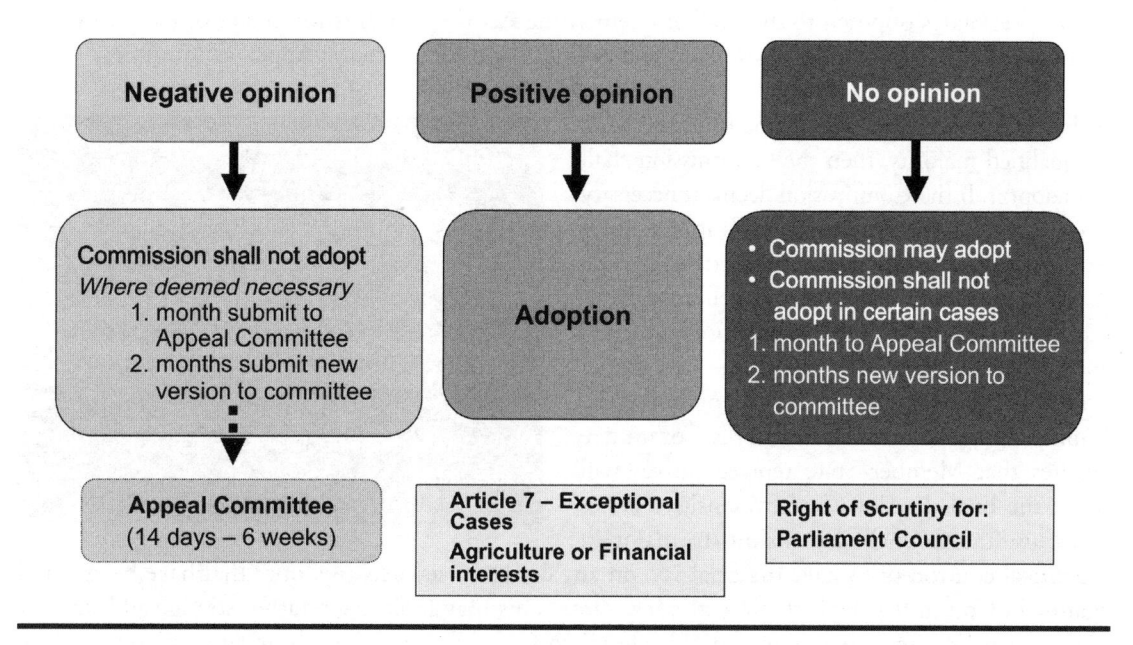

- **Negative opinion**
  - Commission shall not adopt
  - *Where deemed necessary*
    1. month submit to Appeal Committee
    2. months submit new version to committee
  - → Appeal Committee (14 days – 6 weeks)

- **Positive opinion**
  - Adoption
  - Article 7 – Exceptional Cases
  - Agriculture or Financial interests

- **No opinion**
  - Commission may adopt
  - Commission shall not adopt in certain cases
    1. month to Appeal Committee
    2. months new version to committee
  - Right of Scrutiny for: Parliament Council

If the Commission is unable to find a qualified majority in support of the draft, or if the Committee finds a qualified majority against the draft, the Commission either has to refer the matter to the Appeal Committee (see below), or it has to start again in the Committee. Hence, under the Examination procedure the Commission can only adopt Implementing Acts if they obtain a qualified majority in the Committee - this is the element of Member State control over the Commission.

The Parliament (and the Council) benefits from one right here - the right of scrutiny. This means that for legislative acts adopted under Codecision either legislator can pass a non-binding Resolution if they feel that the Commission, in the draft Implementing Act, has gone beyond its powers. As such resolutions are non-binding, the Parliament has hardly ever used this right of scrutiny - and given that the Member States have both the Comitology Committee and the Appeal Committee, it is unlikely that this right will be exercised too often.

If the Committee is unable to find a qualified majority for, or against, the Commission's draft Implementing Act it issues 'no opinion'. In this case the Commission is not obliged to adopt the act - which is an important change from the old Regulatory procedure in which the Commission was obliged to adopt (something that was happening with GMO authorisations and putting the

Commission in a difficult position). Now the Commission is able to reconsider and resubmit a new Implementing Act to the Committee, or to send it to the Appeal Committee. This allows the Commission greater flexibility where the Member States are divided themselves - making sure that any final decision has the support of the majority of Member States (a further control mechanism). In certain specific cases when there is no opinion, such as taxation, financial services, health and safety and safeguard measures, the Commission shall not adopt. Likewise if there is a simple majority of Member States opposed to the draft Implementing Act the Commission shall not adopt. In both of these cases it is likely the Commission will present the draft act to the Appeal committee.

If the Committee votes against the draft measure, by qualified majority, then the Commission shall not adopt it. If the Commission deems it necessary it can forward the rejected draft Implementing Act to the **Appeal Committee** (Article 6). The Appeal Committee has one representative from each Member State (at the appropriate level) and is chaired by the Commission. It has the power to vote changes to, adopt, or reject the Implementing Act referred to it. This Committee ensures that Member State representatives will make the final decisions on any sensitive issues – because the Council was anxious to maintain a political control, or to have the final say, on any controversial acts (i.e. ones that have been voted against in Committee - which are extremely rare). This may look like a rather strange addition, or like a cosmetic name change to the old referral to Council, but it simply reflects the outcome of negotiations between the Parliament and the Council where the Member States wanted to have a political instance to look at controversial measures (i.e. ones that have been voted against, or in specific cases that received no opinion, in Committees - which are not significant in number). The Appeal Committee is like a high-level Comitology Committee that covers political sensitivities.

> **Appeal Committee**
>
> Committee of MS representatives 'at the appropriate level' (foremost COREPER level).
>
> Meets to deal with sensitive files that the Comitology Committee voted by qualified majority to reject.
>
> Can take final decisions on the content of the files.

The Examination procedure is used for (amongst others) Implementing Acts of general scope, programmes with substantial budgetary implications, measures related to the CAP and fisheries, taxation and the Common Commercial Policy (CCP).

> *Examples:* **Market authorisations (GMOs for example), setting of limits and classifications.**

3. The Regulatory Procedure with Scrutiny (RPS)

The Regulatory Procedure with Scrutiny dates back to 2006, allowing the legislators more control and oversight over very sensitive modifications of basic acts - where the implementing measures took on a quasi-legislative character. Between its introduction in 2006 and the entry into force of the Treaty of Lisbon in December 2009, the procedure was written into many legislative acts. Next to the (priority) alignment of the existing acquis throughout 2007 and 2008, any new legislative proposal needed to be tested for potential implementing measures of a 'quasi-legislative' nature. RPS, as a procedure, has not been inserted in any new legislation since the entry into force of the Treaty of Lisbon as it has been replaced by Delegated Acts. Due to pre-Lisbon legislation though, in 2013, 171 RPS measures entered into force. The RPS procedure will now be gradually replaced i.e. slowly phased-out in the coming years (we come back to this later). The RPS procedure is outlined in Figure 6.5.

Figure 6.5: The Regulatory Procedure with Scrutiny

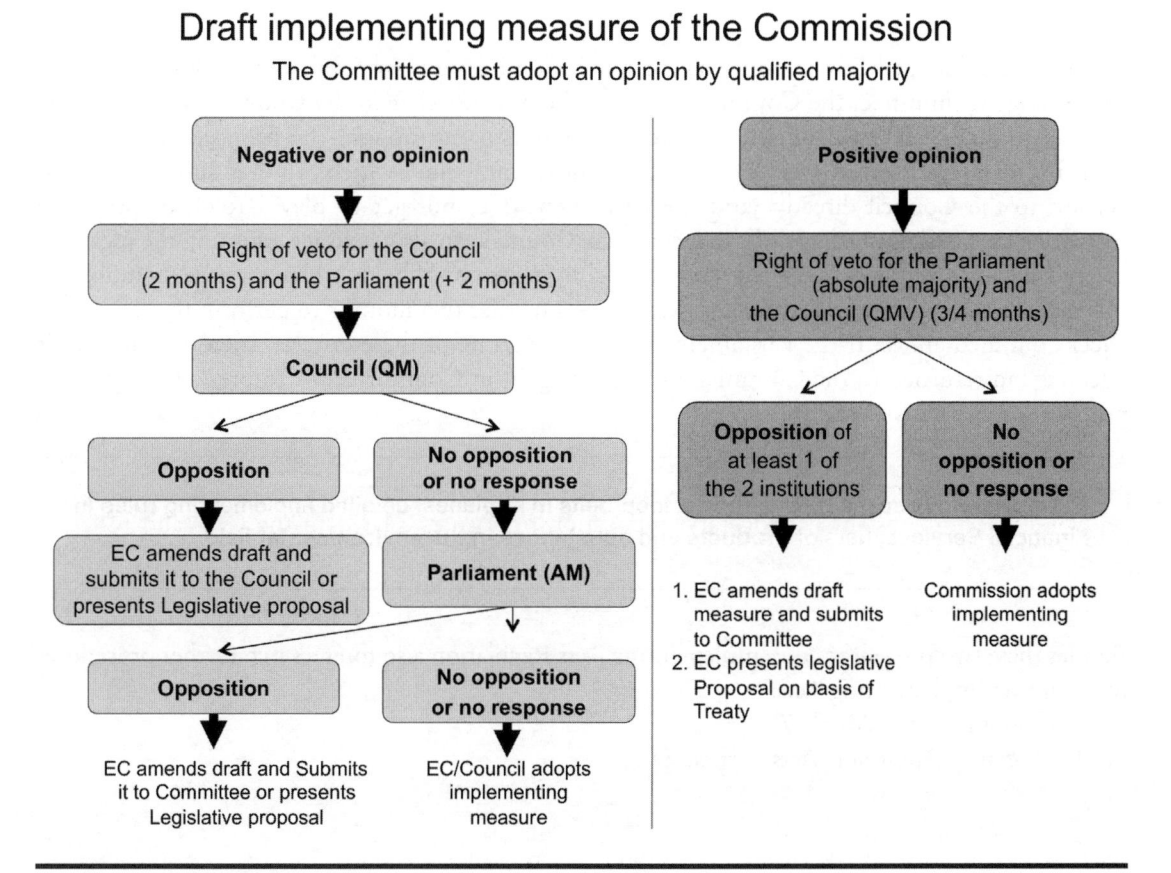

Draft implementing measure of the Commission
The Committee must adopt an opinion by qualified majority

Negative or no opinion
- Right of veto for the Council (2 months) and the Parliament (+ 2 months)
- Council (QM)
  - Opposition → EC amends draft and submits it to the Council or presents Legislative proposal
    - Opposition → EC amends draft and Submits it to Committee or presents Legislative proposal
    - No opposition or no response → EC/Council adopts implementing measure
  - No opposition or no response → Parliament (AM)
    - No opposition or no response → EC/Council adopts implementing measure

Positive opinion
- Right of veto for the Parliament (absolute majority) and the Council (QMV) (3/4 months)
  - Opposition of at least 1 of the 2 institutions
    1. EC amends draft measure and submits to Committee
    2. EC presents legislative Proposal on basis of Treaty
  - No opposition or no response → Commission adopts implementing measure

The RPS was the most constraining procedure for the Commission before the Treaty of Lisbon entered into force because there are two levels of control for it to deal with.

The RPS is a two-tier system of control with firstly a Committee vote and secondly the Parliament and the Council both having a right of veto on the individual measure. So both the Comitology Committee and the legislators have to review the individual measure. The way this works is that if the Committee delivers a qualified majority in favour of the RPS measure then the Parliament and Council each have three months to object to the measure based on three legal grounds. The three legal grounds are if the draft measure:

1. exceeds the competences laid out in the basic act;
2. is not compatible with the aim or content of the basic act;
3. does not respect the principles of subsidiarity and proportionality.

If either legislator objects, using one of these criteria, then the measure is rejected and returned to the Commission to start again in Committee, or to present a legislative proposal on the basis of the Treaty.

In the case of a qualified majority against the Commission proposal, or no opinion in the Comitology Committee, the Commission refers the measure first to the Council, which has two months to take a decision on what to do. The Council can oppose the proposed measure by qualified majority, in which case it goes back to the Commission, which can then submit a revised version to the Council directly (and the Parliament does not get to play a role), or present a legislative proposal on the basis of the Treaty. The Council can also envisage adopting the measure, or not find any opinion by qualified majority within its two months, in which case the Commission submits the measure to the Parliament, which has a further two months to perform the same legal checks outlined above. If the Parliament objects, using one of these criteria, then the measure is rejected and returned to the Commission to start again in Committee, or to present a legislative proposal on the basis of the Treaty.

> *Examples:* **Body scanners in airports, loop-belts in airplanes, detailed implementing rules in Financial Services, lists of products and substances in the environmental field.**

Besides these two procedures the Implementing Acts Regulation also foresees two further procedures for adopting Implementing Acts:
1. Exceptional Cases (Article 7)
2. Immediately Applicable Acts (Article 8)

Under these procedures the Commission is empowered to adopt acts for immediate application. For exceptional cases if there has been a negative opinion, or no opinion, from an examination procedure committee the Commission may adopt the Implementing Act against the wishes of the committee if the Commission needs to do so to avoid significant disruption in agricultural/financial markets. In this case the Commission shall immediately submit the measure to the Appeal Committee which must vote by qualified majority - with a negative vote meaning the Commission has to repeal the Implementing Act. The logic behind this is that, for reasons of urgency in the two specific areas, the Commission might need to proceed to immediate application of an act against the will of the Comitology Committee.

For immediately applicable acts the Commission is empowered, if it has been stated explicitly in the legislative act, to adopt Implementing Acts that have immediate effect i.e. without first going to the Committee. In this case the Commission must submit the adopted Implementing Act to the Committee within 14 days to get their opinion. The Committee can force the Commission to repeal the act by voting by qualified majority against it - otherwise it will remain in force. Many legislative acts foresee the possibility of immediately applicable acts, just in case an emergency requires the Commission to act, but they are seldom employed in practice.

> *Examples:* **Health and safety measures (avian flu influenza for example), emergency measures in financial, agricultural markets etc.**

Automatic alignment to Implementing Acts took place on 1 March 2011

1. Advisory procedure was maintained (only article number changed)
2. Management and regulatory procedures were replaced by Examination Procedure
3. Regulatory Procedure with Scrutiny remains in existing legislation

---

As highlighted in the box above, the new Implementing Acts Regulation foresaw an automatic alignment process whereby all existing Management and Regulatory procedures were converted to the Examination procedure - so that these new procedures are common currency in old and new legislative files alike.

The new system created by Article 291 TFEU, and the Implementing Acts Regulation, is not such a big break with past practice. The key elements are still in place, notably the Comitology Committees and the 28 Member State representatives, although they only operate under two main procedures now. Referral to the Council has been replaced by an Appeal Committee but this is the Council in everything but name and the Commission has been granted flexibility over the obligation to adopt acts that a majority of Member States do not support.

6.5 The 'new' procedures: Delegated Acts

Unlike Article 291 TFEU, Article 290 TFEU did not require any implementation and was therefore immediately applicable. This is because Article 290 TFEU explicitly moved away from a horizontal framework, so the legislators are free to set the modalities, such as objectives, scope, duration and the conditions to which the delegation is subject in each and every legislative act. In this sense there was no requirement to have secondary legislation to set a legally binding horizontal framework - the legislators were empowered to decide case-by-case. While no legislation was needed to implement Article 290 TFEU there was a concern that it could lead to a piecemeal approach and to more difficult, i.e. longer, negotiations of Delegated Act provisions in the Codecision phase. Therefore, the institutions sought to develop a '**Common Understanding**' on how to apply and work with Delegated Acts. Delegated Acts are almost identical to the RPS that was outlined in the previous section. They have been created to deal with the same sensitive quasi-legislative matters where the legislators are granting extra powers to the Commission for the sake of speed and efficiency - but where they require extra control in return. Delegated Acts, like RPS, grant the Commission the power to **supplement or amend** non-essential elements of the legislative act.

Whilst Delegated Acts cover the same sensitive tasks that were dealt with by RPS measures, there are a number of significant procedural changes to the oversight of the Commission that need to be detailed. Figure 6.6 displays the new procedure for Delegated Acts.

Figure 6.6: Delegated Acts - The procedure

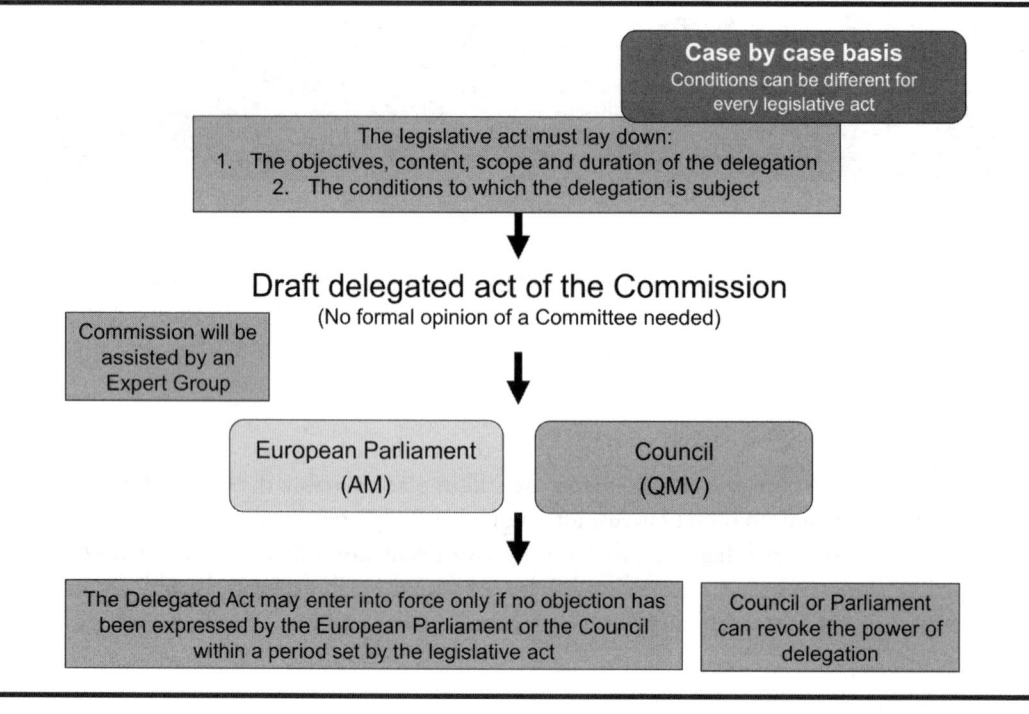

```
                                              ┌────────────────────────────┐
                                              │   Case by case basis        │
                                              │ Conditions can be different │
                                              │   for every legislative act │
                                              └────────────────────────────┘
          ┌─────────────────────────────────────────────────────┐
          │   The legislative act must lay down:                 │
          │   1. The objectives, content, scope and duration     │
          │      of the delegation                               │
          │   2. The conditions to which the delegation is       │
          │      subject                                         │
          └─────────────────────────────────────────────────────┘
                                  ↓
                    Draft delegated act of the Commission
                  (No formal opinion of a Committee needed)

  ┌────────────────────┐                    ↓
  │ Commission will be │
  │   assisted by an   │
  │    Expert Group    │
  └────────────────────┘
                           ┌─────────────────┐    ┌─────────────┐
                           │European Parliament│    │   Council    │
                           │      (AM)         │    │   (QMV)      │
                           └─────────────────┘    └─────────────┘
                                           ↓
  ┌───────────────────────────────────────────────────┐  ┌──────────────────┐
  │ The Delegated Act may enter into force only if no │  │ Council or       │
  │ objection has been expressed by the European      │  │ Parliament can   │
  │ Parliament or the Council within a period set by  │  │ revoke the power │
  │ the legislative act                               │  │ of delegation    │
  └───────────────────────────────────────────────────┘  └──────────────────┘
```

This process is a sharp deviation from past practice, and from the Implementing Acts (notably the RPS) outlined in the last section. It becomes immediately apparent that the two-tier control of RPS has been simplified, because the Commission presents its Delegated Act directly to both legislators simultaneously. As Figure 6.6 highlights, both legislators have a time determined by the basic act (two + two months) to object to the act on any grounds, or to revoke the delegation altogether. There is also the possibility that the legislators can give their approval to a Delegated Act so that the Commission can adopt it faster (so-called 'early non-objection'). Whilst the new one-tier procedure is simpler, each legislative act can set out different conditions for Delegated Acts on a case-by-case basis due to the lack of a legally binding horizontal framework. The Common Understanding between the institutions on how to use Delegated Acts includes some model articles - but this is far from being a binding framework.

There are already many examples of legislative acts that foresee Delegated Acts (as well as Delegated Acts themselves). By the end of the last legislative term (April/May 2014) 196 legislative acts included Delegated Acts provisions which had led to the adoption of 166 Delegated Acts. Having a look at these examples will give you a clearer indication of how the conditions for the procedure can change from one case to another. The fact that all of these conditions can be changed in each and every legislative act means that work on Delegated Acts has to start as early as possible - because these conditions can be very important to address.

The procedure for Delegated Acts is very different from past practice and there are a number of innovations in this process that need to be stressed:

1. **No horizontal legally binding framework:** The first major innovation to highlight is that there is no horizontal framework to cover Delegated Acts, so the legislators are free to set the objectives, scope, duration and the conditions to which the delegation is subject in each and every legislative act. The Common Understanding on how to use Delegated Acts includes some model articles - but it is not a binding framework. Have a look at Regulation No. 438/2010 on the animal health requirements applicable to the non-commercial movement of pet animals - this was the first time provisions for Delegated Acts were inserted into a text.

2. **Absence of Comitology Committee:** The next, and perhaps most noticeable, change is the absence of a Committee and the lack of any requirement for the Commission to obtain an opinion. The Committee stage has been abolished in favour of much greater control by the legislator (right of veto and revocation). Whilst there is no longer a formal requirement for the interaction and vote with a Comitology Committee, the Commission will still need to consult with Member States whilst drafting a Delegated Act, something that is done via Expert Groups.

3. **Right of veto on any grounds:** The third major change is a very important one because of its likely effect on the practice of oversight by the legislators. Council and Parliament have the power to object to an individual Delegated Act on any grounds whatsoever. They no longer need to find one of the three legal justifications outlined under the RPS. This significantly increases the powers of the legislators over individual Delegated Acts and will likely lead to closer scrutiny and more objections.

4. **Right of revocation:** The final change that needs to be highlighted is that in addition to the right of veto to an individual Delegated Act the legislators are also granted the ultimate control mechanism - the right to revoke the delegation to the Commission altogether. If either legislator becomes so dissatisfied with how the Commission is using its power to issue Delegated Acts it could vote to revoke fully or partially the delegation. Whilst this seems somewhat drastic, and unlikely, it is possible that the threat to revoke the delegation will become more of a negotiating tactic used in inter-institutional relations - should either the Council or Parliament become very dissatisfied with the Commission.

In sum the procedure for adopting Delegated Acts is fundamentally different to that used to adopt RPS measures. Working with these new Delegated Acts has to start early in the EU policy cycle, given that the objectives, scope, duration and the conditions to which the delegation is subject can change in every legislative act - meaning that there is more scope to change these modalities on a case by case basis. The process of drafting a Delegated Act involves identifying the relevant Expert Groups, and other actors assisting the Commission. These detailed discussions are vital for the Commission to get the technical expertise of the Member State experts, and to test the political temperature of the Council and the Parliament before presenting a Delegated Act directly to the legislators. The Commission does not want to present Delegated Acts to the legislators without having consulted them in some way before - otherwise it risks having the Delegated Acts rejected.

Ultimately it is likely that there will be an increased number of objections to individual Delegated Acts from the legislators because they can now object to anything they do not like. Whilst it is easier to object to a Delegated Act it remains difficult to get the required majorities to do so in either legislator. One final factor related to attempts to reject a Delegated Act is the fact that to do so means working against the Commission. Experience with the RPS shows that when there was a risk of an RPS measure being rejected, the Commission lobbied intensely at both technical and political levels to avoid the rejection of the measure.

> **Progressive alignment to Delegated Acts beyond 2014**
>
> There was no automatic alignment from RPS to Delegated Acts. Instead, basic acts will be revised progressively, meaning that RPS will continue to exist as a procedure in Comitology Committees, albeit one that will slowly but surely shrink over the years. The progressive approach will guarantee that all provisions referring to RPS will have been removed from all legislative instruments in the years to come.

Table 6.4 makes a direct comparison of the main changes that have been ushered in by Article 290 TFEU and the introduction of Delegated Acts.

Table 6.4: Delegated Acts compared to the Regulatory Procedure with Scrutiny

Regulatory Procedure with Scrutiny (RPS/ PRAC)	Delegated Acts
A framework; Article 5a of the Comitology Decision	No binding framework Case by case basis
Necessity to obtain an opinion from a Comitology Committee	No compulsory consultation of Committees BUT consultation at expert level
EP and Council are not completely on an equal footing	Perfect equal footing between EP and Council
Limited grounds for the right of opposition	No limited grounds for the right of opposition
	Right of revocation

Source: Based on Council Decision 1999/468/EC as amended by 2006/512/EC and Regulation 182/2011 of the European Parliament and Council

6.6 Delegated and Implementing Acts - The new worlds of delegated powers

This chapter has shown how Comitology has been fundamentally changed by the Treaty of Lisbon and its subsequent implementation through the co-decided Regulation and an inter-institutional Common Understanding. The name Comitology is now partially redundant because of the creation of two separate regimes: Delegated and Implementing Acts. For both of these categories the procedures are simplified and information is more accessible - making understanding (and working with) this new world of Comitology less difficult than before. The key aspects to retain are that:

1. **Delegated Acts** are an entirely new world, notably with the abolition of Comitology Committees - instead the Commission uses Expert Groups and EU Agencies. The powers of the legislators are now considerable with a discretionary right either to object to an individual act or to revoke the delegation itself. Whilst the objection of an individual act is a drastic decision to take, the fact that the legislators can now object on any grounds has opened the doors to an increased number of objections. Note that existing RPSs have not been automatically aligned to Delegated Acts, so the RPS will continue to be used in Comitology Committees until the basic act is revised - a process which will go on beyond 2015.

2. **Implementing Acts** retain the requirement on the Commission to pass through Comitology Committees by submitting draft acts for discussion and vote. As this entered into force on 1 March 2011, there was an automatic alignment that guaranteed an immediate switchover from the old procedures. All of the information on Implementing Acts is available on the Comitology register (although there is usually a time-lag that means for proactive Implementing Acts work, the register is not to be over-relied on as a source of information). For Implementing Acts the main changes are that there are only two full procedures: Advisory and Examination. The Commission retains its right of initiative and the chairing of the Comitology Committees, and the Parliament, now joined by Council, still only has the limited (but not to be neglected) right of scrutiny (*'droit de regard'*). Finally the referral to Council has been replaced by referral to an Appeal Committee - which is COREPER in everything but name.

6.7 Case Law Developments

The importance of choosing the right instrument - Delegated or Implementing Acts - matters considerably to safeguard the prerogatives of each institution and to respect the Treaty's intentions with regard to the inter-institutional balance. Where the basic legislative act provides for Delegated Acts the legislators have the power to veto. In the case of Implementing Acts the powers of the legislators are more limited.

In 2014 the Court of Justice of the European Union (ECJ) handed down the first decisive judgment regarding the application of both articles 290 and 291 TFEU (Case C-427/12 - the so-called 'biocide case'). It ruled that Implementing Acts can only be used if the power is well framed in the basic legislative act. However, it did not provide general guidance on other criteria for choosing between both instruments.

A further case came before the ECJ on the matter of Implementing and Delegated Acts: the so-called 'Schengen border case' - C-355/10. In this case it was clarified that essential elements of a basic legislative act are those that 'entail political choices falling within the responsibilities of the European Union legislature, [by requiring] the conflicting interests at issue to be weighed up on the basis of a number of assessments.' It made clear that this assessment of certain elements as being essential, or not, is not just a choice of the legislators [the EP and Council], 'but must be assessed on objective factors amenable to judicial review'. In practice this implies that what is important is an assessment of the actual nature of the instrument concerned, not its title.

While these two cases do not give guidance in exact terms as to what constitutes an Implementing or Delegated Act, they start to further our understanding of where the line between the two types of acts stands. We should expect further cases to be put to the European Court of Justice in the coming years - because this grey zone between Implementing and Delegated Acts will continue to cause friction between the legislators.

> In its communication 'Better regulation for better result', from 19 May 2015, the Commission announced that it will present the draft texts of delegated acts to the public at large on the Commission's website for four weeks in parallel to the consultation of experts in the Member States. The same will apply to important implementing acts which are subject to Committee opinion. Stakeholders should closely follow how the Commission implements these commitments in practice.

6.8 Key stages and key actors - Delegated and Implementing Acts

It is possible, in two separate categories, to now present the main stages and actors in D&I Acts. It must be remembered that it is vital to work with OLP on the insertion of delegated and implementing provisions into texts, in which case the previous chapter is applicable - Table 6.5 only deals with the actual D&I Acts themselves.

Table 6.5: Key stages and key actors: Delegated and Implementing Acts

Key stage	Comment	Key actors
Implementing Acts		
Drafting of Implementing Act	The Commission will likely require technical assistance in drafting the act. The most common source of assistance for the Commission is the Comitology Committee.	Commission Unit/DG Comitology Committee
Commission Inter-Service Consultation (ISC)	A draft Implementing Act has to get approval in ISC.	Lead DG Consulted DGs
Discussion in Committee	The Commission will discuss the Act in Committee to evaluate support - which can lead to major modifications.	Commission Unit/DG Member State representatives Third Parties invited to Committee meeting
Vote in Committee	Adoption is almost always by consensus.	Commission Unit/DG Member State representatives
Appeal Committee	Only for very sensitive and political issues that had problems in Committee.	Member State representatives - but of a more political level COREPER Commission Unit/DG
Commission adoption	The College will adopt the final Committee text as voted (usually by Written procedure).	College Cabinet(s)
Right of scrutiny	Parliament & Council (under Codecision acts) have the right of scrutiny at any time.	Parliament
Delegated Acts		
Drafting of Delegated Act	The Commission will likely need technical assistance in drafting the Act. The most common source of information will be Expert Groups.	Commission Unit/DG Expert Group Agency
Commission ISC	A draft Delegated Act has to get approval in ISC	Lead DG Consulted DGs
Commission adoption	The College will adopt the Delegated Act - but the Cabinets have more margin for changes than under Implementing Acts because they are not going against a Committee opinion in this case.	College Cabinet(s)

Key stage	Comment	Key actors
Parliament veto **Parliament revocation**	The Parliament will have a period of time (usually two plus two months) to scrutinise the Delegated Act to see if it objects (to anything). An objection can come from a variety of sources and there is no horizontal approach. Any objection needs to start early to have a chance of success.	Committee responsible Committee responsible chairperson Coordinators Rapporteur from Codecision Secretariat Political Groups staff
Parliament draft Resolution	The draft Resolution is important as it will state what the Parliament objects to - which can influence the voting in Committee and Plenary.	Rapporteur Coordinators Committee MEPs Secretariat
Parliamentary Committee vote	A simple majority is needed to pass the draft Resolution. There will likely be heavy pressure from the Commission to maintain the Delegated Act.	Rapporteur Coordinators Committee MEPs Secretariat
Plenary vote	An absolute majority is needed to carry the draft resolution.	Rapporteur Coordinators Political Groups
Council veto **Council revocation**	Usually a number of the same experts who will have assisted the Commission in an Expert Group will be in the Working Group in the Council.	Working Group Key Member States Council Secretariat
COREPER discussion	The political level of Council might see different things in the Delegated Act to their technical colleagues. Any decision to object needs to be endorsed in COREPER.	Presidency COREPER
Council decision	The Council has to vote by qualified majority to reject a Delegated Act or revoke the Delegation.	Presidency Council Key Member States

Section 3

How to Work with the EU Institutions & Decision-Making

7. Ethics and Transparency in the EU

By Robert Mack

Having read the earlier chapters of this book, you will have a good understanding of the institutional framework of the EU, its key actors, the principal decision-making processes, and some practical ideas on developing and implementing a lobbying strategy. The purpose of this chapter is to review the context of lobbying itself - the current and future 'regulatory' framework for lobbying, other rules and practices inside the EU institutions that impact the lobbyist and the implications for lobbying best practice. All lobbyists must be aware of this evolving environment for the reasons listed in the box below.

1. Since 2005 there has been a significant debate in Brussels about how to frame lobbying at EU level to ensure it is transparent.
2. This debate has resulted in a voluntary register for lobbyists, which has already evolved significantly since first introduced in June 2008.
3. In June 2011 the European Commission and European Parliament launched the joint Transparency Register, and started to pursue a number of other measures that impact the way the institutions interact with lobbyists.
4. In April 2014 the European Commission and European Parliament announced a number of additional changes to the Transparency Register, following an extensive review. The revised Transparency Register was launched on 27 January 2015, introducing a number of changes not only affecting how lobbyists must register activities, but also how they must conduct them.
5. Moreover, European Commission President Juncker has committed to pursue the introduction of a mandatory Transparency Register.
6. Consequently, there is great focus on how lobbyists interact with the institutions, both from politicians and officials inside the EU institutions and activists outside of them.
7. Good lobbyists must comply with the obligations and expectations placed upon them and be respected for engaging with the institutions transparently and ethically.
8. The debate about lobbying will continue and will influence how individuals - and the organisations they represent - are perceived by those they lobby. Understanding this context is essential to being able to work with the EU Institutions in a positive and effective way.

While the Commission, in particular, has taken many steps to increase the transparency of how it operates, this chapter will focus on those developments which have an impact on how lobbyists interact with the EU institutions. The chapter puts the emphasis on developments within the Commission and the Parliament, the two EU institutions which are most developed in their efforts to enhance transparency per se; it will not focus on the Council because, as an institution, it has not yet taken any specific steps to address the issue of its interaction with lobbyists. (That said, the regulation of lobbying has been addressed at the national level in several EU Member States and is under discussion or active review in several more.)

Over the course of the EU's development, the institutions of the EU have steadily and progressively taken on more collective responsibility for policy development that directly impacts the citizens of the EU in a wide range of areas. These policies not only affect individual citizens but a wide range of stakeholders including companies that are operating in the single market or governments of third countries that are dealing with the EU. Indeed, as the areas of activity of the EU have expanded, so too has the web of interests affected by decisions taken in Brussels and Strasbourg.

> For an overview of developments in the field of transparency and lobbying the OECD is an excellent source of information. You can find more at: www.oecd.org/governance/ethics/lobbying.htm

At the same time, the EU institutions have become more sophisticated in their dialogue with interested stakeholders. In 2015 there is genuine recognition that stakeholder dialogue is an essential component of policy development and, following the entry into force of the Lisbon Treaty, it is even recognised as a democratic principle in Article 11 of the Treaty on European Union, which states that 'the institutions shall, by appropriate means, give citizens and representative associations the opportunity to make known and publicly exchange their views in all areas of Union action'. In other words, good balanced policies cannot be developed without input from interested stakeholders. Earlier chapters of this book have explained and highlighted several different examples of the mechanisms through which this consultation and dialogue with stakeholders takes place.

Consequently, lobbying is - and should be seen as - an important part of the policy development process in a modern democracy. Politicians and officials need input from a wide range of stakeholders in order to understand better the impact that their decisions will ultimately have and to make the best informed decisions possible. Legislation and regulation adopted by the EU institutions impacts multiple interests and getting the balance right requires healthy debate and dialogue with all interested parties. Necessarily, this input must be legally correct, ethical and transparent.

To reflect this increased public interest in European policy development, the Commission has gradually and progressively taken a number of steps to improve the overall transparency of its interactions with lobbyists. Since 1999, it has implemented a number of reforms including in the area of access to EU documents, launching databases about consultative bodies and expert groups, improving stakeholder consultation and Impact Assessments (IAs), and adopting codes related to the behaviour of Commission staff. On 9 November 2005, the Commission launched its **European**

Transparency Initiative (ETI) as the next important phase in these ongoing efforts to ensure the professionalism and legitimacy of its work. The three key elements of the ETI are in the box below.

> 1. Fuller information about the management and use of Community funds (which will not be addressed in this chapter).
> 2. Professional ethics within the European institutions.
> 3. The framework within which lobby groups and civil society organisations operate.

It is the last of these three which has received the most sustained interest from the media and other stakeholders - and the one that with time has been developed the most, as this chapter will now detail.

7.1 The Register of Interest Representatives

Perhaps the most widely recognised legacy of the ETI was the European Commission Register of Interest Representatives, the precursor to and basis of today's EU Transparency Register. The Commission Register was a voluntary online listing of lobbyists and provided information about organisations lobbying the EU and the level of resources they allocated to these efforts.

The Commission Register was launched on 23 June 2008. Although it was voluntary, the Commission made great efforts to ensure that all organisations engaging with the EU institutions felt the need to participate in the Register. As such, participation in the Register fast became an expectation for any organisation that wished to be seen as a responsible, transparent interlocutor of the EU institutions. In its first two and a half years, more than 3,500 organisations participated in the voluntary register.

With the Register of Interest Representatives established, answers to several important questions had to be provided. These are presented below. These questions and answers continue to play a significant role in the debate on ethics and transparency in the European Union.

1. What is a lobbyist?

The first question to address was who exactly a lobbyist was. For its part, the Commission chose not to define the term 'lobbyist' - or rather what it called an 'interest representative'.

> **Lobbyist vs interest representative**
>
> For the most part in this chapter we will use the terms 'lobbying' and 'lobbyist' and avoid the Commission's terms of 'interest representative' and 'interest representation'. Even though there is a range of views on the words themselves, transparent ethical lobbying is a constructive and necessary part of the policy development process. The word 'lobbyist' does not imply specific standards since these standards are set by the system in which a lobbyist functions. The Commission also freely uses the terms 'lobbyist' and 'lobbying' in the debate on ethics and transparency.

Instead, the Commission focused on defining the act of lobbying (also termed 'interest representation'), taking the view that lobbying is a term that can be applied to activities undertaken by NGOs, trade associations, consultancies, law firms, etc. While several lobbyists, in the course of the debate surrounding the ETI, tried to argue that they were not in fact lobbyists by virtue of the fact that they were employed by a law firm, an NGO, a religious organisation, a think-tank or some other body, the Commission has never accepted this line of reasoning.

In its **Code of Conduct for Interest Representatives** the Commission defined lobbying as all 'activities carried out with the objective of influencing the policy formulation and decision-making processes of the European institutions'. It is important to note at the outset that this definition raised a fair amount of discussion and debate. The Commission intentionally did not make it specific because it wanted to try to capture a broad view of how much resource was being spent on lobbying by each individual registrant.

> **Commission definition of lobbying**
>
> 'All actions initiated with the aim of influencing European policy formulation or decision-making processes, irrespective of the communication channel or medium it is using.'

When it conducted its assessment of how the Register functioned in its first year, published in a Communication on 28 October 2009, the Commission addressed any confusion over what was to be considered lobbying by referring to all actions 'initiated with the aim of influencing European policy formulation or decision-making processes, irrespective of the communication channel or medium it is using'. In other words, the clear message from the Commission was that anything you did, whether it was directly aimed at the institutions (such as a meeting with an official or a Member of the European Parliament) or in a broader communication (such as an advertisement intended to be seen by policy-makers or sponsoring an event in Brussels) should be considered as lobbying for the purposes of the Register.

It is also important to note that the Commission, in its Code of Conduct, explicitly excluded certain kinds of activities from its definition of lobbying for the purposes of registration. These included:

1. Legal and other professional advice, when they related to the exercise of the fundamental right to a fair trial of a client, including the right of defence in administrative proceedings.

2. Activities of the social partners as actors in the social dialogue (trade unions, employers' associations, etc.).

3. Activities in response to the Commission's direct request, such as ad hoc or regular requests for factual information, data or expertise, invitations to public hearings, or participation in consultative Committees or in any similar fora.

The Commission clearly indicated, however, that while these activities would be exempt from registration, other activities carried out by the same actors may indeed be considered lobbying and require registration.

2. What kind of lobbyists are there?

If a lobbyist decided to participate in the voluntary Register, they quickly needed to determine what kind of lobbyist they were. It is important to note that the Register only required the registration of *organisations* involved in lobbying, not the names of *individuals* acting as lobbyists.

Any registrant had first to classify their organisation into one of the following categories:

1. **Professional consultancies/law firms** involved in lobbying EU institutions - divided into the sub-categories of: law firm; public affairs consultancy; independent public affairs consultant; other (similar) organisation.

2. **'In-house' lobbyists** and **trade associations** active in lobbying - divided into the sub-categories of: company; professional association; trade union; other (similar) organisation.

3. **Non-governmental Organisations (NGOs)/think-tanks** - divided into the sub-categories of: non-governmental organisation/association of NGOs; think-tank; other (similar) organisation.

4. **Other organisations** - divided into the sub-categories of: academic organisation / association of academic organisations; representative of religions, churches and communities of conviction; association of public authorities; other (similar) organisation.

It is important to note that for the purposes of the Register the Commission did not provide definitions for any of these categories, but instead said in published guidance that it was up to each registrant to decide to which category their organisation belonged. While for some organisations - such as professional consultancies - self-categorisation may have been straightforward, for others it was less so. For example, there were discussions about whether an organisation should be considered an NGO or a think-tank.

3. What information should lobbyists provide?

Having decided for yourself to which category of lobbyist your organisation belonged, you could consult guidance from the Commission on how to complete your registration. The nature of the information required from each category of registrant was somewhat different. Nonetheless, some important general principles applied.

First, the main objective of the Register was to shed light on the interests being represented and the magnitude of resources being deployed. Therefore, all categories of registrants were required to provide some form of financial disclosure and the Commission tried to adapt the requirements to the nature of the organisations in each category. Also, for categories such as NGOs or law firms and consultancies, the Commission structured the requirements so as to reveal the nature of the constituencies represented. In this vein, note that:

1. For **professional consultancies**, the core requirements included the provision of a list of clients, the total 'lobbying turnover' (i.e. turnover 'related to representing interests to EU institutions on behalf of clients'), and the rough attribution of this turnover by client.

2. For **in-house lobbyists** and trade associations, an estimate of the costs related to the direct representation of interests to EU institutions by the organisation had to be included (which could include the compensation costs for individuals involved in these activities, operating costs of Brussels offices, travel, etc.).

3. For **Non-governmental Organisation (NGOs)**, they needed to provide the number of individual members or the number of member organisations and their respective memberships and their overall budget and funding sources.

For the most part, the Commission gave significant latitude to registrants to decide how to make the proper determinations on these matters. It issued answers to 'Frequently Asked Questions' to guide registrants in the process. But overall, it avoided giving specific guidelines on too many detailed matters and instead encouraged industry associations to draft guidelines to help their corporate or consultancy members to analyse the myriad of specific questions that had to be addressed to complete a responsible submission. However, the wide range of approaches to registration suggested that these guidelines were not useful.

The Commission did not take any proactive steps to control or enforce the accuracy of submissions in the voluntary Transparency Register during its first two years of operation. In October 2010, the attention was drawn to obvious errors such as one organisation reporting €247,000,000 of lobbying expenditure in 2008 (probably a human error), a law firm listing one obviously fictitious client and no lobbying turnover (an act of defiance) and certain NGOs having failed to identify any members whatsoever - either as natural persons or member organisations.

According to the Secretariat-General (SG) of the Commission, the Commission subsequently began to take steps with regard to checking the quality of registrations through random checks, but only to identify and correct obvious aberrations. The SG explained that the purpose of the checks was to ensure the overall credibility of the Register, not to audit or validate the accuracy of any of the specific information in it. When the Commission identified something that didn't seem right, an official would contact the registered organisation to raise the issue. The Commission would not go in and 'check the books' of an organisation to determine the accuracy of its financial disclosure. In most cases randomly checked, the aberrations proved to have been due to human error or a misunderstanding about the requirements of registration.

The process of development of the Register was firmly underway - and we will return to this a little later on in describing the new Register. For now, however, we will turn our attention to other developments that started at the same time as the first Register.

7.2 The European Commission's Code of Conduct

In addition to the obvious implication of registration, i.e. making information about your lobbying activities available for all to see, registrants were also required to sign up to the European Commission's Code of Conduct - or declare that they had signed up to a code of conduct with equivalent effect and provide the name thereof (for example, the European Public Affairs Consultancies' Association, EPACA, had a Code of Conduct for its members that included all the provisions of the Commission Code and was therefore accepted as a Code having equivalent effect).

The Commission's Code after outlining its definitions, listed two general principles and seven specific rules that lobbyists must respect. The Commission Code of Conduct included the following:

Table 7.1: Commission Code of Conduct

The principles

1. Interest representatives are expected to apply the principles of openness, transparency, honesty and integrity, as legitimately expected of them by citizens and other stakeholders.
2. Similarly, members of the Commission and staff are bound by strict rules ensuring their impartiality. The relevant provisions are public and contained in the Treaty establishing the European Community, the Staff Regulations, the Code of Conduct for Commissioners and the Code of good administrative behaviour.

The rules

Interest representatives shall always:
1. Identify themselves by name and by the entity(ies) they work for or represent.
2. Not misrepresent themselves as to the effect of registration to mislead third parties and/or EU staff.
3. Declare the interests, and where applicable the clients or the members, which they represent.
4. Ensure that, to the best of their knowledge, information which they provide is unbiased, complete, up-to-date and not misleading.
5. Not obtain or try to obtain information, or any decision, dishonestly.
6. Not induce EU staff to contravene rules and standards of behaviour applicable to them.
7. If employing former EU staff, respect their obligation to abide by the rules and confidentiality requirements which apply to them.

Source: Taken from the Commission Code of Conduct - the full code is available at; https://webgate.ec.europa.eu/transparency/regrin/infos/codeofconduct.do

The Commission Code of Conduct also specified that breaches of the rules may lead to suspension or exclusion from the Register following an administrative process. Anyone could lodge a complaint about a suspected breach of the rules if it was substantiated by material facts.

Registrants were also informed that:
1. Their contributions to public consultations would be published on the Internet together with the identity of the contributor, unless a valid objection was made on the grounds that publication would harm their legitimate interests.
2. The Commission could, upon request and subject to the provisions of the Regulation on access to documents (see below), have to disclose their correspondence and other documents concerning their activities.

7.3 Registration in the European Parliament

The Parliament tackled the issue of its interaction with lobbyists long before the Commission. In 1996, the Parliament adopted Rule 9 of its Rules of Procedure (RoP) which specifically stated: 'The Quaestors shall be responsible for issuing nominative passes valid for a maximum of one year to persons who wish to enter Parliament's premises frequently in order to supply information to Members within the framework of their parliamentary ma ndate in their own interests or those of third parties'.

Its main objective was to make lobbying more transparent. Interestingly, lobbyists were simply defined as persons wanting access to the building in order to share information. In return for the access card, which had to be renewed annually, lobbyists were required to:

1. Respect the Parliament's Code of Conduct, published in the RoP.
2. Sign a register kept by the Quaestors.

The key provisions of the Parliament's Code of Conduct are in Table 7.2 below.

Table 7.2: Parliament Code of Conduct

1. Require lobbyists to: state the interest(s) they represent in contacts with Members of the European Parliament, their staff or officials of Parliament.
2. Refrain from any action designed to obtain information dishonestly.
3. Not claim any formal relationship with Parliament in any dealings with third parties.
4. Not circulate Parliament documents for profit.
5. Lobbyists must comply with other relevant rules, e.g. Annex I to the Rules of Procedure on transparency and members' financial interests.
6. Lobbyists must comply with the European Parliament's Staff Regulations when recruiting former officials.
7. Lobbyists must comply with relevant rules on the rights and responsibilities of former members.
8. Any breach of the Code could lead to the withdrawal of the access pass for individuals or their firms.

Source: Taken from the Parliament Code of Conduct

This system had a positive impact on the dialogue between the Parliament and lobbyists. As of 31 January 2011, a few months before the Parliament merged its system with the Commission Register, there were 1,829 organisations and 2,872 long-term individuals registered. The Parliament had taken a very practical approach based on the recognition that it needed to receive views and information from a wide range of interested stakeholders, and that those external lobbyists needed to act ethically in accordance with the principles outlined in the Parliament's Code of Conduct. By establishing a system giving those stakeholders access to the premises of the institution, it had helped to make the conduct of Parliament's business more transparent.

7.4 Review of the Commission Register

The Commission launched a public consultation in July 2009 to review the functioning of the Register during its first year. On the basis of that consultation and its own work, the Commission published on 28 October 2009 a Communication outlining the changes it would make to the Register to improve its implementation.

One such change was **clarification of the definition of lobbying** to ensure, as noted above, that it caught any actions intended to influence the development of EU policy. During its consultation, the Commission received comments from organisations in several different categories about what types of activities were intended to be covered by the financial disclosure requirements. The Commission took the opportunity to be very clear on the question:

> 'Registrants should disclose all expenditures covering actions initiated with the aim of influencing European policy formulation or decision-making processes, irrespective of the communication channel or medium it is using (whether direct or indirect, using outsourcing, media, contracts with professional intermediaries, think-tanks, 'platforms', fora, campaigns, etc.). Social events or conferences fall within the scope of the Register if invitations have been sent to staff or members of European institutions.'

The Commission Communication continued:

> 'The activities to be declared for the financial disclosure of the Register are those aimed at all European institutions and bodies, their members, and their services, as well as European agencies and their personnel. These activities also include activities directed at the Permanent Representations of the Member States, including the Council Presidency. However, activities aimed at influencing Member States' authorities in the capitals or any sub-national authority are deemed to be outside the scope of the Register.'

The Commission also clarified its position on the issue of '**double-counting**', e.g. counting funds paid by a company to its association under both the company's registration and the association's. When the Commission Register was first launched, the guidance given was that double-counting should be avoided and only the recipient of the funds should declare them for purposes of financial disclosure under the Register. In other words, if a client hired a consultancy, the fees paid would be reflected in the financial disclosure of the consultancy, not of the client, and dues paid to an association would be reflected in the financial disclosure of the association, not in that of the member paying the dues. The Commission clarified in its Communication that double-counting was no longer excluded. Registrants were expected to ensure transparency by describing such situations in their declaration, using the text fields of the declaration in particular to provide 'specific explanations', e.g. to identify funds paid to consultancies, membership fees paid to associations, or in-kind contributions of staff from one organisation to another. The Commission went on to clarify an important point: 'the aim of the Commission's policy is not to achieve a consolidated analysis, but to provide transparency at the level of each individual registrant'. Therefore 'double-counting' does not 'affect the Register's basic purpose, which is to provide information on how much each individual entity spends on lobbying'.

At the same time, the Commission took the opportunity to:

1. Be more precise about the **scope of the exemption** on legal advice and assistance, in the hope of encouraging law firms to register for the activities they undertook and which fell under the definition of lobbying.

2. Tighten the **financial disclosure requirements** that consultancies must use to detail the breakdown of their 'lobbying turnover' by client. Moving forward, these would be based only on ranges denominated in euros, where the size of the range depends on the 'lobbying turnover' of the consultancy in question; in the past, consultancies could choose to classify clients in brackets by percentage of their overall 'lobbying turnover' (<10%, 10-20%, etc.).

3. Divide **NGOs and think-tanks** into two separate categories to reduce the risk of confusion between the two.

4. Ask each registered organisation to include an estimate of the overall **number of people involved in lobbying** (while not requiring them to identify them by name).

5. Indicate that it would clarify in a separate explanatory note the functioning of the administrative process around **monitoring and enforcement**.

7.5 The Establishment of a Joint Transparency Register

In December 2008 the High Level Group of the Parliament and the Commission, consisting of the responsible European Commissioner and designated MEPs from each of the main Political Groups in the Parliament, met for the first time to begin consideration of how the two institutions could work together to integrate their efforts on lobbying transparency. The talks were re-launched in May 2010 (after EP elections in June 2009 and the investiture of the Barroso II Commission in February 2010) at the initiative of Commission Vice-President Maroš Šefčovič and European Parliament Vice-President Diana Wallis, leading the Parliament delegation composed of MEPs

Carlo Casini, Jo Leinen and Isabelle Durant. After a series of meetings, the Group concluded its discussions on 10 November 2010, reaching consensus on a draft agreement on the establishment of a joint 'Transparency Register' for the Commission and the Parliament, which combined and replaced both the Commission's and Parliament's existing registers.

Consensus was reached in the High Level Group by early 2011 and the agreement was endorsed both by the Parliament and the Commission through their respective processes. On 23 June 2011, the **Inter-Institutional Agreement (IIA) between the European Parliament and the European Commission** on a common **Transparency Register** was signed in the EP Plenary by then EP President Jerzy Buzek and EC Vice President Maroš Šefčovič thereby launching the new Transparency Register.

Structurally, the new register remained based on the Commission Register and took on the proposed changes to the Register published by the Commission in its October 2009 Communication. Several other changes were also introduced as an outcome of the IIA reached between the Commission and the Parliament. On the whole, these changes introduced more structure and clarity into the entire process surrounding registration and transparency.

Despite the preference in the Parliament for mandatory registration, the Register remained voluntary and became a joint register of the Commission and Parliament. It also received a new name, becoming known as the 'Transparency Register' (and no longer as the 'Register of Interest Representatives'). This name change, it was said, better reflected the purpose of the Register but it was also hoped that it would help to encourage the participation of certain categories of lobbyists - such as lawyers, think-tanks and representatives of religious communities - who did not participate in the voluntary Commission Register because they didn't want to be known as 'interest representatives' or 'lobbyists'.

Importantly, as the new Transparency Register became a register of both institutions, anyone holding an access card to the Parliament had to participate in the new Register or give it up. In other words, simply subscribing to the Parliament Code became no longer sufficient to have access to the European Parliament. This was a significant change to the status quo, and Commission officials and MEPs closely involved in the process began referring to the Transparency Register as 'quasi-mandatory', as for many lobbyists in Brussels access to the Parliament is essential for their work.

In 2011, many individuals held access cards to the Parliament even though the organisation for which they worked may not have been participating in the Commission Register. Consequently, this change significantly increased 'voluntary' participation in the Transparency Register compared to the participation levels in the Commission Register, as many lobbyists did not want to lose their access passes for the Parliament. In practice, the Transparency Register identifies both registered organisations and individuals from each organisation listed by name if they hold an access pass to the Parliament.

The scope of activities covered by the joint Transparency Register became the refined definition of lobbying activities outlined by the Commission in its October 2009 Communication. However, the IIA went further in its attempts to clarify the important principle of a level playing field.

It stated: 'All organisations, irrespective of their legal status, engaged in activities falling under the scope of the Register are expected to register', and noted that only Member State governments, third country governments, international intergovernmental organisations and their diplomatic missions were excluded.

At the same time, the IIA was much more explicit about the definition of the situations where professional advice was protected and could be excluded from the Register. This was intended to address the 'problem of the lawyers', who had thus far been very reluctant to participate in the Commission Register even for their lobbying activities, raising many concerns linked to client confidentiality and barriers put in place by bar associations. It chose to do so by defining the activities that can be excluded from the Transparency Register as *'legal and other professional advice*, in so far as they relate to the exercise of the fundamental right to a fair trial of a client, including the right of defence in administrative proceedings, such as carried out by lawyers or *by any other professionals involved therein*' [italics added]. The choice to present it this way is important because it emphasised the principle of a level playing field. The relevant paragraph then went on to provide a detailed and specific description of what could be excluded from the Register on these grounds.

For all the types of activity excluded from the Transparency Register, the IIA aimed to clarify that these exclusions were meant to be narrow - and for all categories benefiting from specific exclusions, it made clear that other lobbying they did would indeed be subject to declaration in the Transparency Register. For example, activities of the Social Partners were only excluded from the scope of the Register when they were 'acting within the role assigned to them in the Treaties' and the exclusion related to activities in response to a request for information was also more precisely worded.

The IIA clarified that religious communities, political parties, and local, regional and municipal authorities were not expected to register, but any organisations that represented them towards the EU institutions were expected to register. These provisions were intended to address the reticence to participate in the Register demonstrated by such organisations since the Commission's Register was launched in June 2008, while clearly reinforcing the principle of a level playing field and establishing very narrow, specifically defined exclusions.

The IIA also attempted, in its Annex I, to provide descriptions for the different categories of lobbyists who registered. As noted above, there had been confusion over whether certain organisations should be considered NGOs, think-tanks or even part of the media. These descriptions have helped ensure that all registrants take an approach as similar as possible to their registration thereby enhancing the credibility of the Transparency Register.

Interestingly, the agreement also clearly addressed the issue of ad hoc groups and coalitions, by noting that 'networks, platforms and other forms of collective activity without a legal status or legal personality but which constitute de facto a source of organised influence, and engaged in activities falling within the scope of the Register are expected to register. In such cases, its members should identify one of their number as its responsible contact person for their relations with the administration of the Register'. A number of ad hoc coalitions do exist where, for example, smaller groups of like-minded companies work together on an issue about which consensus may be difficult to reach inside a trade association with a large and diverse membership. While it was already expected that such groups had to be clear about the interests they represented, the IIA introduced a clearly articulated expectation that such groups should register as well.

The IIA also clarified and explicitly listed the obligations of registrants. All registrants were required to agree that the information they provided was public and guarantee that it was correct; agree to act in compliance with a **new common Code of Conduct**; accept that a complaint against them would be handled based on that Code of Conduct; accept the measures that would be applied in case of a breach of the Code; and take note of the application of the EU Regulation on access to documents. The new common Code of Conduct was based on the existing codes of conduct of the Commission and the Parliament. It did not contain any significant new provisions but rather combined and streamlined the provisions of the existing Commission and Parliament codes - as seen in Table 7.3.

Table 7.3: Code of Conduct for Joint Register

Common Code of Conduct

In the context of their relations with the EU institutions and their Members and staff, registered entities shall:

a. always identify themselves by name and, by registration number, if applicable, and by the entity or entities they work for or represent; declare the interests, objectives or aims they promote and, where applicable, specify the clients or members whom they represent;
b. not obtain or try to obtain information or decisions dishonestly or by use of undue pressure or inappropriate behaviour;
c. not claim any formal relationship with the European Union or any of its institutions in their dealings with third parties, or misrepresent the effect of registration in such a way as to mislead third parties or officials or other staff of the European Union, or use the logos of EU institutions without express authorisation;
d. ensure that, to the best of their knowledge, information, which they provide upon registration, and subsequently in the framework of their activities covered by the Register, is complete, up-to-date and not misleading; accept that all information provided is subject to review and agree to co-operate with administrative requests for complementary information and updates;
e. not sell to third parties copies of documents obtained from EU institutions;
f. in general, respect, and avoid any obstruction to the implementation and application of, all rules, codes and good governance practices established by EU institutions;
g. not induce Members of the institutions of the European Union, officials or other staff of the European Union, or assistants or trainees of those Members, to contravene the rules and standards of behaviour applicable to them;
h. if employing former officials or other staff of the European Union, or assistants or trainees of Members of EU institutions, respect the obligation of such employees to abide by the rules and confidentiality requirements which apply to them;

> i. obtain the prior consent of the Member or Members of the European Parliament concerned as regards any contractual relationship with, or employment of, any individual within a Member's designated entourage;
> j. observe any rules laid down on the rights and responsibilities of former Members of the European Parliament and the European Commission;
> k. inform whomever they represent of their obligations towards the EU institutions.

Source: Taken from http://ec.europa.eu/transparencyregister/public/homePage.do

The Transparency Register, like the Commission's Register before it, had an enforcement mechanism in the case of non-compliance. Anyone could lodge a complaint against a registrant about suspected **non-compliance** with the Code of Conduct as long as it was substantiated by material facts. Annex IV to the IIA, however, much more clearly described the complaints procedure and the range of measures available in case of non-compliance than did the Commission's Register. Punishments could include deletion from the Transparency Register for up to two years, mention of the disciplinary measures in the Transparency Register itself for all to see, and revocation of Parliament access cards.

While both the Commission and the Parliament retained their respective authority to deal with issues applying uniquely to one institution or the other (such as the issuance of access cards or any other range of decisions about interaction with lobbyists), a joint operational structure was set up to oversee the implementation of the new system. The **Joint Transparency Register Secretariat (JTRS)** consists of a group of officials drawn from both the Commission and the Parliament and final decisions are taken by the Secretaries-General of the Commission and the Parliament by mutual accord. The responsibilities of the JTRS include enforcement - or random checking of registrations to ensure their accuracy, as begun by the Commission for its Register in autumn 2010. It was a significant new development and was indicative of the ambition the Commission and Parliament had to run a serious, professional Register.

7.6 Review of the Transparency Register

In June 2013, the Commission and Parliament launched a review of the IIA conducted by a high-level group co-chaired by the Vice Presidents of the Commission and Parliament then responsible for transparency, Maroš Šefčovič and Rainer Wieland respectively. The group, which included MEPs from all political groups and an observer from the Council, held nine meetings. External stakeholders were consulted during the process.

As a result, a **new Inter-Institutional Agreement** was adopted by the Commission on 9 April 2014, approved by the Parliament on 15 April 2014, and signed by both institutions the following day.

> The 2014 IIA can be found at: http://eur-lex.europa.eu/legal-content/EN/TXT/PDF/?uri=CELEX:32014Q0919(01)&from=en

For the most part, the new IIA respects the structure and approach of the previous one, which it replaces. It does, however, make several improvements to the clarity and specificity of the language used in the IIA and a few substantive changes as well. Most of these changes reflect problems experienced with the operation of the Transparency Register during its first two years, many of which were brought to the attention of the high-level group by stakeholders.

The **key changes** of which the practising lobbyist must be aware are outlined below.

1. **Clarifications to the categories of registrants:** the high-level group felt that in the past not all registrants selected the correct category when they registered. Consequently Annex I to the IIA has been slightly amended.

    Concerning 'in-house lobbyists and trade/business/professional associations' the following have been added to the new IIA:

    - descriptions of what is meant by 'trade and business associations' and 'trade unions and professional associations';
    - specific examples in the 'other organisations' subsection including: 'event-organising entities (profit or non-profit making)'; 'interest-related media or research oriented entities linked to private profit making interests'; and 'ad-hoc coalitions and temporary structures (with profit-making membership)'.

    For NGOs, the description of an NGO has been expanded to note that any NGO 'including profit making elements among its membership' must register in the category of 'in-house lobbyists and trade/business/professional associations'.

    Finally, concerning 'organisations representing local, regional and municipal authorities, other public or mixed entities, etc.', the subsections have been expanded from two to four and the descriptions have been clarified. Now the subsections include:

    - 'Regional structures', meaning associations or networks created to represent regions collectively (as regions themselves and their representative offices may register but are not expected to do so);
    - 'Other sub-national public authorities' such as cities, local and municipal authorities, or their representation offices, national associations or networks;
    - 'Transnational associations and networks of public regional or other sub-national authorities';
    - 'Other public or mixed entities, created by law whose purpose is to act in the public interest'.

2. **Overhauling the complaints procedure:** The complaints procedure of the old IIA was criticised as cumbersome and not sufficiently protective of the rights of registrants who are the subject of a complaint. To address this a number of changes were made.

Notable among them was to transform the procedure into an alerts and complaints procedure comprised of two different components. 'Alerts' have been introduced to allow any person to notify the JTRS about what they believe to be inaccurate information in the Transparency Register or an ineligible entry. Following an alert, the registrant concerned will be asked either to update the information or explain why no update is required.

At the same time, anyone can lodge a formal 'complaint' if they feel a registrant has failed to abide by the Code of Conduct in any way other than an error of fact subject to an 'alert'. The procedure for handling complaints has been clarified and, notably, the right for a complainant to be represented by a professional organisation has been included.

3. **Strengthening the Code of Conduct:** minor changes to the Code of Conduct have been introduced to make it more clear and complete. For example, in its introduction, the Code of Conduct now makes it explicitly clear that all lobbyists are expected to abide by the Code of Conduct, whether or not they choose to participate in the Transparency Register. It also states that when contacting EU institutions or their Members, lobbyists shall identify themselves not only by name and affiliation, but also by their Transparency Register registration number.

In addition the following two new clauses have been added to the Code of Conduct:

- 'f. in general, respect, and avoid any obstruction to the implementation and application of, all rules, codes and good governance practices established by EU institutions';

- 'i. obtain the prior consent of the Member or Members of the European Parliament concerned as regards any contractual relation with, or employment of, any individual within a Member's designated entourage'.

4. **Committing to introduce more incentives to encourage registration:** An issue that emerged during the high-level group's dialogue with stakeholders concerned incentives. In the past, registrants were only 'rewarded' for their participation in the Register by receiving email notifications from the Commission about public consultations in their policy areas of interest, which many felt was insignificant. At the same time, Commissioners and other senior officials would regularly speak at events or otherwise support organisations that were not participating in the Transparency Register. To address this a new section of the IIA on 'measures applicable for compliant registrants' has been added.

It states that the Commission and Parliament shall offer incentives to encourage registration in the Transparency Register. For the Commission, in addition to notifications about consultations, these may include measures with regard to expert groups and other advisory bodies, specific mailing lists and 'patronage by the European Commission'. On this last point, the Commission has said that 'Commissioners will no longer accept to be patrons of events where the event organisers should be registered but aren't'.

For its part, the Parliament has used this section of the IIA to formalise its policy on access passes to the Parliament, which will only be issued to individuals representing or working for registered organisations. It is noted, however, that registration does not confer automatic entitlement to an access pass and that the process for granting such passes remains an internal procedure of the Parliament.

Additional incentives offered by the Parliament may include: further facilitation of access to its premises, Members and their assistants, officials and other staff; authorisation to organise or co-host events in the Parliament premises; facilitated transmission of information; participation as speakers in committee hearings; and patronage by the European Parliament.

5. **Introducing a level playing field for all registrants concerning financial disclosure:** In the past, registrants in all categories have had to make some form of financial disclosure but it has been structured differently based upon their category. Now, all registrants must provide an estimate of the annual costs related to activities covered by the Register. The aim is to provide a level playing field and improve comparability of data across categories.

In addition, the different financial disclosure requirements per category will be maintained and, in certain cases, slightly adjusted. For professional consultancies, law firms, and self-employed consultants:

- A new band has been added for turnover attributable to lobbying. Before, the first band was €0 - 499,999; now the first band is €0 - 99,999 and the second band is €100,000 - 499,999.

- Likewise new bands have been introduced for client revenue. Before, the first band was below €50,000; now there are bands for €0 - 9,999, €10,000 - 24,999, €25,000 - 49,999, and €50,000 - 99,999. After that, bands progress in €100,000 increments, with the last band being for amounts greater than €1,000,000.

6. **Explaining better the scope of activities covered, thereby encouraging the registration of law firms:** The low level of registration by law firms in the Transparency Register has been an issue of concern frequently cited by the Commission. To address this, the new IIA expands the language in its section on 'Activities not covered' concerning lawyers and spells out specifically what activities undertaken by lawyers are covered 'where they are intended to influence the EU institutions, their Members and their assistants or their officials or other staff'.

On 27 January 2015, a **new Transparency Register website** was launched to implement the changes outlined above while also improving the functionality, ease of use and information available on the site.

> The website of the Transparency Register can be found here:
> http://ec.europa.eu/transparencyregister/public/homePage.do

7.7 Access to documents

On 3 December 2001, Regulation (EC) No. 1049/2001 regarding public access to Parliament, Council and Commission documents entered into force. Its main objective was to introduce greater transparency into the work of the EU institutions by creating a process through which any citizen of the Union or any natural or legal person residing in or having its office in the EU could request access to documents of the Parliament, Commission and the Council.

It is important to note that the Regulation concerns all documents held by an institution concerning all matters falling within its sphere of responsibility in all areas of activity of the EU. That means access to document requests can be made by just about anyone to EU institutions for just about anything, including any form of written communication received by an EU institution or a Member State government on an EU issue. In other words, EU institutions can receive requests for the information you submit when you lobby them, including the text of emails. Of course, every lobbyist should bear this in mind when preparing information to be provided to the EU institutions.

The Regulation identifies a number of exceptions to this general principle:

1. **Absolute exceptions** - Access must be denied.
   - Public security
   - Defence and military matters
   - International relations
   - Financial, monetary or economic policy
   - Environment (e.g. breeding sites of rare species)
   - Privacy and integrity of the individual (notably on data privacy)

2. **Relative exceptions** - Access must be denied unless there is an overriding public interest in disclosure.
   - Commercial interests including intellectual property rights
   - Legal rights and legal proceedings
   - Purpose of inspections, investigations and audits
   - Would undermine the EU decision-making processes

When an EU institution receives a request for a third party document, the institution must consult the third party that provided the document unless it is clear that the document should - or should not - be disclosed. During that time period the institution consults the third party to determine, for example, if any of the documents requested contain commercially sensitive information, are related to legal proceedings, or qualify for any other defined exception. The affected third party can then identify which documents, or parts of documents, should not be shared with the applicant.

If the institution totally, or partially, refuses the applicant's request, the applicant has 15 days to ask the institution to reconsider its decision. Ultimately, the case can be referred to the European Ombudsman or Court proceedings can be launched.

Data published (http://ec.europa.eu/transparency/access_documents) on requests for access to documents provides interesting insights into the use of these procedures. The first, and perhaps unsurprising, observation is that the number of access to document requests to the EU institutions has grown dramatically over the years. In 2001, there were 450 such requests and in 2013 there were 6,525. While, as noted above, it is important to be aware that the EU institutions can be made to turn over documents received from third parties, it is also important to be aware of the opportunity that the Regulation on access to documents creates for all lobbyists. It places an obligation of transparency and openness upon the EU institutions which creates a useful source of information - through access to document requests - about the deliberations of the EU institutions on a wide range of policy issues.

Following a public consultation in 2007, the Commission on 30 April 2008 made a **proposal to amend the Regulation on access to documents**. Its reasons for doing so were multiple: the Commission promised to review the Regulation when it launched its ETI in 2005; the Parliament, in a Resolution adopted on 4 April 2006, asked the Commission to come forward with proposals for amending the Regulation; the EU's decision to apply the Århus Convention on access to justice in environmental matters necessitated some change to the existing Regulation; significant case law had developed and the European Ombudsman had settled several complaints which revealed the need for revisions; and the Commission wanted to incorporate lessons learned from its practical experience.

Consequently, the Commission's proposal puts forward several significant modifications to the Regulation. One is the clarification of who can benefit from the Regulation, which would be simplified to 'any natural or legal person'. At the same time, the Commission proposal would clarify exactly what is meant by the word 'document' for the purposes of the Regulation. The new definition would be much more encompassing than the old one; it clarifies that just about anything received by an institution, even in electronic form, is a document if it can be extracted. Moreover, the criterion about relevance to a matter falling within the 'institutions' sphere of responsibility would be dropped. While in most cases lobbyists should be contacting the EU institutions about matters for which they are responsible, this change would establish the principle that anything produced or received by an institution is potentially accessible (as long as no exception, e.g. for commercially sensitive information, applies to it). A number of other more technical changes to the scope of the Regulation and its definitions have also been proposed.

The exceptions to the general principle of access to documents for the most part would be clarified - but not fundamentally altered - by the Commission proposal. The Commission proposal would, however, add a new exception intended to protect the objectivity and impartiality of selection procedures of the European institutions, for example in the areas of recruitment, or the awarding of contracts.

At the same time, in order to reflect jurisprudence from the Court of Justice of the EU, the rules on consultation would be clarified with respect to the procedures for documents originating from a Member State and the initial deadline to provide documents following a request would be extended from 15 to 30 working days, as experience has shown it to be near impossible for the EU institutions to respect that deadline.

As of February 2015, the Commission proposal is blocked over a wide variety of specific issues and it remains unclear how this will move forward. However, it is important for the lobbyist to note that this debate is ongoing, and whilst it is not expected to be resolved anytime in 2015 it is a key dossier that will likely be revisited in the not too distant future. It is hard to speculate on the potential implications - but suffice it to say that any changes will need to be closely monitored and considered by all lobbyists.

7.8 Rules in place for European Commission officials and Commissioners

As part of the European Transparency Initiative, the Commission is very focused on professional ethics within the Commission as an institution. For the lobbyist, it is important to have some understanding of the rules that govern how Commission officials can act when dealing with individuals from outside the institutions, even if some believe these rules are not yet as developed as they should be.

The relevant rules can be found in Articles 11 to 17 of the **Staff Regulations of Officials of the European Communities** (http://ec.europa.eu/civil_service/docs/toc100_en.pdf). These articles fall into the part of the Staff Regulations that addresses the rights and obligations of officials. As such, they establish a number of principles that guide the Commission official's interaction with lobbyists, some of which mirror the expectations placed on lobbyists via the Code of Conduct. These can be seen in Table 7.4.

Table 7.4: Rules for Officials of the European Communities

1. Professional duties must be carried out solely with the interests of the EU in mind and officials may not seek or take instructions from any interest (including governments) outside his or her institution.
2. An official shall not accept gifts from any source outside his or her institution without permission (see below for more details).
3. An official must not deal with issues in which he or she has some personal or financial interest.
4. An official must behave with integrity and discretion when accepting appointments after leaving the employ of the Commission. He or she must inform the Commission of any occupational activity for two years after leaving, and the Commission may either forbid the proposed activity or approve it subject to conditions.
5. An official shall refrain from any unauthorised disclosure of information received in the line of duty that is not already in the public domain.

Source: http://ec.europa.eu/civil_service/docs/toc100_en.pdf

The Commission has trained nearly all its staff regarding the behaviour that is considered appropriate and ethical. For new officials attending the training on ethics and behaviour is obligatory. The Commission also issued a booklet on this issue for its staff members.

1. Gifts, meals/entertainment, and travel

In addition to the Staff Regulations cited above, Commission officials are subject to more specific rules on gifts, meals and entertainment, and travel. The rules for European Commissioners on gifts, travel and a wide range of other issues are quite detailed and are enumerated in a Code of Conduct for Commissioners (see http://ec.europa.eu/commission_2010-2014/pdf/code_conduct_en.pdf). Amongst other things, this Code of Conduct obliges each Commissioner to complete a declaration of interests. The declarations for all Commissioners can be found online on the individual pages of the Commissioners.

The Commission has also put in place a register of gifts received by Commissioners whose value exceeds €150. This list is regularly updated. The majority of gifts that Commissioners receive are from governments, Heads of State and parliaments that they meet in relation to their work activities.

Other Commission officials must seek permission for gifts with a value greater than €50 but are allowed, in principle, to accept gifts with a value up to €150 (http://ec.europa.eu/transparency/docs/sec_2012_0167_f_en_communication_to_commission_en.pdf). Meals and entertainment are considered gifts for the purposes of this rule.

The rules with respect to travel are slightly more complicated. For every trip (or 'mission' in Commission speak), the official must receive an authorisation. In the process of asking for that authorisation, he or she must declare whether the travel costs would be paid for by the Commission or by a third party, which of course must be identified. When such costs are paid by a third party, the tendency is for the Commission to accept this when the purpose of the trip is useful to the Commission official in the discharge of their duties. Therefore, if it was the intention of an organisation to invite a Commission official to any sort of an engagement (e.g. a conference or site visit) requiring travel, the organisation would have to demonstrate, at the time the invitation is made, how the engagement will provide information to the official that will help them with their work.

According to the SG all Commission officials will make personal choices on whether to accept meals, trips or speaking engagements, guided only by the rules and principles noted above. In practice, therefore, lobbyists will be confronted with different standards of accepted behaviour. The training being given to Commission officials is structured in order to help them confront such practical situations. It gives them scenarios intended to represent practical situations they are likely to face and encourages them to exercise their judgment - not necessarily to refuse the contact. Commission officials are encouraged to uphold a standard of 'healthy scepticism', meaning that the case for why you need to meet the official must be strong. At the same time, officials are encouraged to keep written records of requests for meetings and the decisions made to grant them, and ensure that other colleagues are aware of any meeting with an external lobbyist (which, in practice, means it is rare to get a one-on-one meeting with an official). They are encouraged to meet a standard which avoids even the appearance of impropriety. Of course, Commission officials are encouraged to ask if the lobbyist's organisation has joined the Register and are free - but not required - to refuse a meeting if it has not. Such enquiries are increasing, as more Commission officials are trained and begin to change their behaviour, but do not yet seem to be universally applied across the entire Commission.

2. Public consultations

The Commission conducts a number of public consultations to obtain input from interested stakeholders on policy ideas it is considering or developing. These consultations can often represent a good opportunity for lobbyists to ensure that their organisations' views are clearly communicated to the Commission. It is important to know, however, that all submissions will be published online by the Commission, unless you make a convincing case when you submit your response to the consultation that you qualify for an exemption specified in the Regulation on access to documents.

The Commission has established the '**Your Voice in Europe**' website (http://ec.europa.eu/yourvoice/index_en.htm), which serves as an entry point for citizens to share their views with the Commission on European policy initiatives. When you click on the tab for consultations, you will arrive at a page where it is possible to see all the open consultations with their respective deadlines for input. A list of closed consultations is only one click away and from there it is easy to click to the actual text of responses received from all stakeholders who participated in these past consultations. It is the practice of the Commission to classify the inputs received as being from 'Public Authorities', 'Registered Organisations' (i.e. participating in the Commission's Register), or 'Citizens and Others' (where you will find the submissions of organisations who are not yet participating in the Commission's Register). While the policy of the Commission is to segregate the publication of all responses to consultations along these lines, according to the SG, this practice is not yet uniform across all Directorates-General of the Commission.

The Commission does not yet publish responses to targeted consultations (i.e. when the Commission seeks input from a specific set of identified stakeholders) but these responses are of course still subject to the Regulation on access to documents. Likewise, this approach does not apply to procedures where specific rules on consultation have been defined in EU legislation, e.g. in the area of competition policy.

7.9 Rules in place for Parliament officials and Members of Parliament

Officials of the Parliament, like their colleagues in the Commission, are subject to the Staff Regulations of Officials of the European Communities. Consequently, Parliament officials must respect the same rules as Commission officials when dealing with individuals from outside the EU institutions, the relevant elements of which are discussed in detail above.

In July 2009, a new employment and payment system was adopted for MEPs' assistants, creating a system of common rules to replace the 28 different approaches taken previously under national law of each Member State. As a result, MEPs' assistants are also subject to these same provisions of the Staff Regulation - see Table 7.4 above.

For MEPs, the rules they must respect are spelled out in the Rules of Procedure of the Parliament. In particular, Rule 11 - the same rule that governs access passes - obliges the Parliament to lay down specific rules on the transparency of members' financial interests. The specific rules that are listed in Annex I to the RoP are outlined in Table 7.5.

Table 7.5: Rules for MEPs

1. Must declare any direct financial interest in a subject under debate before speaking on it in Parliament or if proposed as rapporteur.
2. Must complete a financial declaration annually (which is posted on the Parliament's website as part of the profile of each MEP) covering their professional activities and any other remunerated functions, any salary received for the exercise of a mandate in another Parliament, and any financial or staff support granted by third parties.
3. Should refrain from accepting gifts or benefits.

Source: http://www.europarl.europa.eu/sipade/rulesleg8/Rulesleg8.EN.pdf

7.10 The outlook for transparency and ethics in the EU

The launch in January 2015 of the new, improved Transparency Register, based on an updated IIA, and the operational changes to be implemented by the JTRS as a consequence thereof, will catalyse a number of improvements to lobbying transparency in Brussels.

The changes outlined above should lead to a Transparency Register comprised of clearer and more consistent, comprehensive and comparable data. The new system of 'alerts' is an important part of this. Several NGOs that actively campaign on lobbying have spent a fair amount of effort attacking the quality of the data in the Register. The alert system should allow those complaints to be managed more efficiently and lead to changes in data where required without penalising registrants who change their data accordingly.

The commitment to improved incentives is also significant, as the principle is now established that the Commission and Parliament should do business differently with registered and non-registered lobbyists. It will, however, be important to see how this is implemented in practice. Some of the incentives listed in the IIA are significant, while others are not.

Both institutions, however, have given themselves the freedom to go further in this regard. For example, on 25 November 2014, in only its fourth week in office, the new European Commission of President Juncker took a decision that from 1 December 2014 the Commission would make public the meetings with lobbyists of all Commissioners, their Cabinets, and the Directors-General of Commission services. Within two weeks of each meeting, the Commission would publish on its website the dates, locations, names of the organisations or self-employed individuals met, and the topics of discussion. President Juncker has also clarified that in principle they should only meet lobbyists who are registered in the Transparency Register.

> **New mandatory Lobbying Register?**
>
> Keep an eye out in the course of 2015 & 2016 for a new mandatory lobbying register.

Indeed the Juncker Commission has from the outset prioritised ethics and transparency. It has committed to preparing a proposal for an Inter-Institutional Agreement creating a mandatory lobby register covering the Commission, the Parliament and the Council, which it has said will be done in 2015. One of the longstanding criticisms of the Transparency Register by a wide range of stakeholders has been that it is not mandatory. The inclusion of the Council, which does not participate in the current Transparency Register, is also important. While it remains to be seen how this proposal will be structured and whether it will be truly mandatory, the fact that the Commission has now committed to proposing a mandatory register is a significant step forward.

These developments in part reflect growing public pressure for the EU institutions to improve how they conduct their business. That pressure will continue to manifest itself not only in institutional advances on transparency, but also in more ad hoc efforts by elected politicians, officials and other stakeholders, so that actions such as publishing a record of meetings with lobbyists on their individual websites will increasingly become the norm.

At the same time, the intensity of campaigns on lobbying issues by NGOs has only increased. Several NGOs, led by Greenpeace, Friends of the Earth and a few others, formed in July 2005 the **Alliance for Lobbying Transparency and Ethics Regulation (ALTER-EU)**, an informal coalition active on such issues. While their motives are more focused on 'exposing the power of corporate lobbying in the EU' (www.corporateeurope.org) than necessarily ensuring the equitable pursuit of the best policies on transparency, they have successfully used the EU debate on transparency issues as a platform to promote their agenda. They have a long list of objectives they still want to achieve, including a 'high-quality', mandatory, lobbying transparency register; full transparency and 'safeguards against corporate capture' of Commission expert and advisory groups; 'closing the revolving door between the European Commission and industry lobbies'; 'effective conflicts of interest rules' for Commissioners, Commission officials and Special Advisers; independent monitoring and enforcement; upgrading of Parliament's transparency and ethics rules; and more. This list may be a decent indication of the kinds of issues that may get greater attention in the years ahead.

7.11 Key practical conclusions on Ethics and Transparency

For those individuals actively involved in lobbying the EU institutions, there are a number of conclusions that can be drawn - and these are listed in Table 7.6.

Table 7.6: Transparency, Ethics and Lobbying - Key Points

1. Transparent behaviour in all contacts with the EU institutions is a non-negotiable requirement of credible and professional public affairs engagement with the EU.
2. Even though the current Transparency Register is voluntary, there is a clear expectation that responsible organisations will register. Indeed the language of the new IIA goes very far to make registration feel mandatory even though it is not. The focus on 'incentives' in the new IIA and the requirement to register in order to obtain an access pass to the Parliament are significant in this regard.
3. While this chapter has focused principally on the Commission and Parliament as that is where the key action has been so far, the trend towards transparency spans across the EU institutions. For example, the Regulations on access to documents and Staff Regulations both apply more widely.
4. Many of the standards of behaviour discussed in this chapter represent a minimum standard. Parliamentarians and officials across the institutions can, and often do, impose a higher standard of transparency when you approach them for meetings or other requests.
5. Assume all information you provide in writing could be shared with just about anyone who asks for it.
6. Don't forget that all responses to formal consultations are published on the Internet, unless submitted together with a valid request for confidentiality complying with the standards set in the access to documents Regulation (e.g. commercially sensitive information).
7. If you want any information you submit in writing to an EU institution to be kept confidential, provide a written argument when you submit it, outlining why it should be covered by the terms of the access to documents Regulation.
8. The standards themselves are changing. The implementation of the new IIA and the updated Transparency Register, the commitment to propose a mandatory register in 2015 which would include the Council, and the pressure from NGOs for the institutions to continue to act on a range of other specific points means there will be an environment of constant debate and changing expectations.

8. Practical Guide to Working with the EU Institutions

By Alan Hardacre

The first section of this book detailed how the EU institutions work, outlining all the key stages and key actors within each institution. Those chapters are fundamental building blocks to understand how to work with the EU institutions. This chapter builds on them by explicitly detailing how to work with each of the core EU institutions. Knowing how an institution works, albeit vital, is only the first step to working effectively with it. The next step is to put this knowledge to practical use by translating it into operational activities and guidelines - all of which must respect a series of institutional 'do's' and 'don'ts'. The objective of this chapter is to set out in clear and user-friendly language a series of guidelines, recommendations and best practice ideas on how to engage with the Commission, the Council and the Parliament. Combining the relevant sub-sections of this chapter with the institutional chapters from Section one, and the other chapters in this section of the book, will provide you with an in-depth knowledge of what to provide, to who, when, how and within what context.

There is a paucity of developed guides on how to work with the EU institutions, in part due to the difficulties of trying to elaborate such a guide. There is no magic formula for how to work with an institution, and what works in one case might not work in another. Given that the activity of working, or engaging, with the EU institutions is more an art than a science, opinions differ when confronted with the question of how to approach different institutions in different circumstances. This chapter recognises the limitations of trying to outline how to work with the institutions, and does not aspire to be a definitive approach. Much like other chapters in this section of the book, the objective is to present the current state of the art in working with the institutions which will serve as a spring-board for anyone wanting to effectively engage with the EU institutions.

> There is no magic formula for how to work with an EU institution - what works in one case might not work in a second. **BUT** there are fundamental things that you should always try to do, fundamental rules you should always respect, and ways to do things to be more efficient, effective and ultimately successful - both for you and for the officials and politicians you interact with.

8.1 Working with the EU institutions: The fundamentals

Some general points, and principles, about working with the institutions are fundamental to all of them so they will be addressed in this first section, before moving to an institution by institution approach in the following sections. In essence the basics of good engagement in the EU are drawn not just from the EU context, but from a variety of different national, international and local contexts because they are all applicable in Brussels as well. This chapter will call these the Fundamentals for Working with the EU Institutions because they are now widely accepted and applied in Brussels - by all stakeholders, whether they do this consciously or not. Despite the fact that the EU environment evolves quickly - which it often does, meaning that what was not possible last year could be imperative next year - these fundamentals remain valid. They are outlined in Table 8.1.

Table 8.1: Fifteen Fundamentals for Working with the EU Institutions

1. **The earlier the better** - It is easiest to work with the Institutions from the very beginning, allowing you to follow developments closely.
2. **Be transparent/professional** - Being honest about who you are and what you represent is essential. Integrity is valued highly in the Brussels 'village'.
3. **Understand the institution/process** - To get the right message to the right person at the right time you need to know the institutions and their decision-making processes.
4. **Understand the people** - To make the most impact with an interlocutor it is essential to know them as well as possible so do your homework.
5. **Political/Technical** - It is always necessary to balance between the two and the way you present them; it will invariably change.
6. **Evidence** - Independent, reliable, evidence/case-studies/facts are always in demand in Brussels - as long as they are presented in the right way.
7. **Provide solutions** - Be proactive and constructive in all engagements.
8. **Identify your key audience** - Know who you need to contact about what, at the right time with the right arguments.
9. **Communicate with your audience in mind** - Your messages need to be tailored to the audience each time and in Brussels you will have more than one audience.
10. **Communicate using all channels** - There are many ways to interact with decision-makers: know what they are and use them.
11. **Always follow up** - Sending a paper, or having a meeting, is only the beginning. Everything should be followed up properly.
12. **Be European** - National or individual positions and arguments do not work well in Brussels so generate broader/European positions/arguments/angles.
13. **Be flexible/prepared** - Always be prepared to change strategy or approach as your issue/circumstances change; learn as you develop.
14. **Compromise** - Be ready to compromise as you will very rarely get 100% of what you want. You are never working alone on an issue.
15. **Long-term** - Activity in Brussels should always be viewed from a long-term perspective. All contacts, messages, papers and communications need to keep this in mind. Always build for the future

The 15 fundamentals in Table 8.1 offer broad guidance for working with the EU institutions - they are guidelines that cover all of the EU institutions, bodies and agencies, and they are the fundamental basis for any attempt to work with them. Table 8.1 is not an exhaustive list and the guidelines are not prioritised in any specific order. Without entering into the detail of all of the points listed above, as many are self-explanatory, a few necessitate further explanation:

1. **The earlier the better**
   This principle is one of the golden rules of working in Brussels and is vitally important. The sooner you are active and visible on an issue, the more chance you have of influencing proceedings, being identified as a key stakeholder, and building lasting contacts and networks. Like many of the fundamentals listed above this is often easier said than done - and will rely on a number of other factors that are covered in Chapter 10. Being able to work early on an issue pre-supposes an ability to invest in your engagement work which is often very difficult: many stakeholders are only activated when an issue is 'live' and moving.

2. **Be transparent & professional**
   The importance of being open and honest about who you are and what you represent is increasingly a necessity in Brussels. Being in the Transparency Register, adhering to a code of conduct and showing integrity in your dealings with the EU institutions are now prerequisites to successful engagement. No longer is transparency something that is nice to have - it is now a must have. In addition to transparency it is also important to be professional in your dealings with the EU institutions. This means keeping your word, respecting deadlines, respecting your promises and those of others, sending additional information when required/promised, ensuring follow-up from meetings, and responding promptly to requests, etc. This is particularly important given the long-term nature of working with the EU institutions and the 'village' character of Brussels decision-making circles.

3. **Communicate with your audience in mind**
   It is essential to always prepare your communication with a clear target audience in mind. Each audience will need to be addressed in different ways. The fundamentals about political/technical and facts/evidence (points 5 and 6 in Table 8.1) are rendered useless if they are not presented correctly for each target audience. Facts and evidence need to have political context and as such the right message for each target audience needs to be packaged in the right way.

4. **Be European**
   The importance of this fundamental needs to be stressed because engaging with the EU institutions will require a minimum acceptance of the goals of EU integration. National positions will have some traction in national circumstances (the Council or national MEPs for example) but they will need to be re-packaged for the European arena. European angles, ideas, solutions, compromises, issues and propositions should always be sought out. The notion of further European integration should underpin the work you are seeking to do.

5. **Long-term**
Any attempt to engage with the EU institutions should always be done with the long-term in mind. This has a number of practical implications - notably on maintaining open and constructive dialogue with the institutions and other stakeholders - because you will likely have to work with the same people on other (or the same) issues in the future. It needs to be accepted that one cannot win them all and that the European arena is characterised by continual compromises. In this sense scaremongering, hostility, non-constructive, extreme and anti-European positions are highly detrimental to long-term strategic engagement. Ultimately they are the fastest ways to discredit yourself.

From these 15 broad Fundamentals for Working with the EU Institutions - which act as over-arching guidelines for everything else that comes in this chapter - a number of other key horizontal aspects need to be addressed in this opening section.

1. **Brussels presence:** The need, or not, to have a Brussels presence is the first issue of importance. Can engagement or other activities be undertaken with the EU institutions in a 'virtual' format only – i.e. from a distance? Whilst this is an equation that will need to be weighed up on a case-by-case basis, it is clear that a physical presence in Brussels will be required, at least from time to time. MEPs and officials always prefer to hear messages in person from the stakeholders themselves. All the work of monitoring, message development and campaign strategy can obviously be done at a distance - but conveying the messages needs to be done in person via actual meetings. A Brussels office offers a significant number of advantages such as networking, intelligence gathering, attending events, building visibility and presence, ability to react to ad hoc situations quickly, and a general better understanding of the Brussels environment that can only come by working there on a daily basis. So while not a requirement a Brussels Office, although at a cost, offers significant advantages to EU work that you would not otherwise benefit from.

2. Tied into the previous point is **membership of think-tanks and European and national associations/federations**. Obviously, if you are not based in Brussels, these fora can offer vital channels for information (both directions), networking and influence in Brussels. Even if you are based in Brussels they can offer exactly the same advantages - as they are usually plugged into their specific sectorial work better than anyone else in the field. The EU institutions also prefer, when possible, to hear from European associations and federations, to get a feel for a European-level industry position - so being within these groups is important.

3. The next issue to address is that of **nationality and culture**. Nationality is important in Brussels for a number of reasons that go beyond simple issues of contacting people of the same nationality - because nationality has implications in terms of language and also culture, to mention but two important aspects. There is always a natural tendency to approach officials, MEPs and other stakeholders of our own nationality - which can be very beneficial and enriching - but this needs to be part of a wider approach to all nationalities in the EU. This links to the issue of culture, because when meeting and interacting with people in Brussels one will be confronted by

very different norms and expectations. An official of German origin will likely express themselves differently, and have different preferences for interaction, than an official of Spanish origin for example. While being careful not to stereotype, it is important to be aware of cultural differences and the role they play in your EU work.

4. The final horizontal issue that is important to address in this first section concerns the **media** and the evolution into social media in your engagement. The media will come back in the following sections, notably on the Parliament, but it needs to be addressed more broadly here. Brussels is home to one of the world's largest press corps: this peaked at some 1,300 accredited journalists after the 2007 enlargement, before dropping to a still very impressive total of around 1,000 in 2014. The Brussels media landscape is essentially made up of journalists looking to report their stories back home in their own country, and as a consequence many journalists, by the nature of the Brussels posting, are generalists. This is important to bear in mind because it is an opportunity for stakeholders to engage with them and become trusted and honest brokers of information. Brussels journalists also have to compete for space with specialists back home - which can mean they tend to focus on EU specialist subjects, as opposed to other issues. Working with social media has become much more of a necessity since the first edition of this book - with many companies opening online channels of communication - and at the very least monitoring social media developments. It is something that should form part of any holistic EU strategy.

Working with the media is imperative for all stakeholders trying to get their messages across to EU policy-makers and other influential stakeholders - it should not be excluded from any strategy. There are some general rules for working with the EU media that are horizontal to all work in Brussels - these are outlined in Table 8.2.

EU media landscape

- Newspaper correspondents
- Wire services
- Online only media services
- TV and radio journalists
- Freelancers
- Bloggers
- Social Media
- Brussels leaks - www.brusselsleaks.com

Table 8.2: Working with the EU media

Guiding rules for working with EU media

1. Establish target audience very carefully
2. Identify right media for this audience - Online? National?
3. Make the message clear and easy to understand - EU issues are complicated
4. Translate into clear and easy to understand facts for the target audience
5. Be short, to the point, use short sentences and use easy language (with examples to bring issues to life for the reader)

6. Have clear EU perspective/angle - and if national then create national angle / implication / resonance for readers
7. Have new insights into EU policy implications
8. Do not be alarmist or scaremonger in the story - try to engage positively in your media relations
9. Regulatory stories are a harder sell - they need to have a very specific industry emphasis
10. Consider the use of infographics to better tell your story
11. Arrange background briefings - informally raise awareness
12. Build long-term relationships of trust - try to become a reliable source of information to whom journalists turn when in need
13. Offer insights and information on an on-going basis - without immediate expectation of coverage

Source: Based on 'Analyzing the Union' by Turner, L. & Eilert Pignal, E., Brunswick Review Issue 3 Winter 2010, available from; www.brunswickgroup.com

The key aspects of working with the media in Table 8.2 outline the broad picture of how to try and engage with the media in Brussels. A few aspects should be highlighted given their importance. Firstly, it is always useful to engage proactively with journalists for the long-term - which means contacting them regularly and not just when you have a live issue. When you have a live issue you need to get your positions out quickly in clear and easy to understand language - often posting these on your website can be sufficient (as long as you keep your website updated). You need to have a good message (story) that is well written, comes at the right time and is reader friendly.

A further aspect of media and communications is worth a little extra attention. This is the phenomenon of **blogging**. In essence blogging gives someone with a computer, and the will to engage, an opportunity to influence the news cycle. It is a very cheap and easy way to interact with an audience. Blogging is common currency in the United States and an integral part of the political process there, yet in Brussels blogging is only just coming to life. There are new websites offering platforms for debates and discussions as well as increasing numbers of specialist EU specific blogs. It is very likely that this culture of blogging and online discussion will gain ever more credence and importance in Brussels, so it is worth keeping an eye on.

> **Keep updated on your iPhone**
>
> Follow all EU developments and have the EU at your fingertips with **EUssentials iPhone app**.
>
> Find more information on the Apple Store.

This section of the chapter has outlined the Fundamentals of Working with the EU Institutions and some other key horizontal issues for how to work with the EU institutions. From these broad perspectives it is possible now to move to the level of each institution and address more specific recommendations and guidelines for how to work with them individually. The analysis of how to work with each of the three institutions that will be addressed in the following sections will be done under four key headings:

> 1. General strategic
> 2. Decision-making
> 3. People
> 4. Communication

1. **General strategic:** This section will concentrate on the overarching guidelines for interaction with each institution. The recommendations will relate to the institution in a broad sense.
2. **Decision-making:** The decision-making guidance will relate to the internal decision-making procedures of each institution - and to the key stages and actors tables found in Chapters 1 to 3.
3. **People:** The people section of the recommendations will relate directly to the officials, MEPs, Ministers, etc. who you will be trying to work with - giving guidance on how to approach the different actors within each institution, and what they need, why they need it and when they will most likely need it.

> **How to find people?**
>
> 1. The online directory EU WhoisWho
> 2. Online staff directories of institutions and political groups
> 3. Networking and events
> 4. Stakeholder.eu publication
> 5. European Union & Public Affairs Directory 2015

4. **Communication:** The final section of each set of institutional recommendations will look at the methods and types of communication that work best.

These four different categories will allow for a set of key recommendations for each institution to be established - again not as an exhaustive list, but as an indicator of best practice and guidance for how to interact with each individual institution and its staff.

8.2 Working with the European Commission

8.2.1 General strategic

The Commission is likely to represent the most important interlocutor you have in Brussels, simply by the nature of its roles, importance and influence. Engagement with the Commission will be necessary, irrespective of the issue or the stage in the policy cycle - as the Commission has a role across policy areas and the entire EU policy cycle. In terms of long-term engagement strategies, the most important institution to which this applies is without doubt the Commission. Whatever you do, you will need to deal with the officials from the Commission again in the future - often the not too distant future.

> The so-called rule of '**the earlier the better**' in relation to influencing a proposal cannot be stressed enough in relation to the Commission - it is the institution that develops all proposals. Not getting something into, or out of, a proposal will mean an intensive uphill struggle later in the process with the two legislators. The earlier the better nearly always means working directly with the Commission at the earliest stages of policy thinking and preparation. The earlier the involvement, the better for the Commission as your information could help them craft a better proposal. The best time for engagement is at the conceptual stage, before ideas are formalised and set on paper.

It is important to ensure that there is a regular flow of information to the Commission, irrespective of whether you are active on a dossier or not. Once you have identified your key interlocutors you should keep in touch with them, sending them any analysis, reports, studies, annual reports or company/organisation information that you think could be useful. You never know what might be useful for them - and it is helpful to keep in touch this way. It allows you to stay visible, keep the dialogue open, be constructive and engaged with the Commission for a long-term durable relationship - and it allows the Commission to gather information that might be useful to it. Keep the Commission informed of your positions and of any issues you are having with legislation or policy.

The Commission will expect nothing less than total transparency in any interaction with stakeholders. This is covered extensively in Chapter 7 on Transparency and Ethics but a few key points can be recalled here. Commission staff increasingly check the Transparency Register before accepting a meeting. They may also check for any consultation responses, registrations for open hearings, and correspondence with the Commission before meetings; this means they could be well-informed and able to distinguish long-term engaged stakeholders from one-off requests - and will have an obvious preference and inclination to meet the former and not the latter, especially when they receive so many meeting requests.

Effective engagement with the European Commission has some important prerequisites:

1. First and foremost, the Commission is the institution most in need of, and actively seeking, **evidence and facts** - it needs them to understand the differing situations it is trying to deal with and to create the best possible solutions. This is not to say that the Commission is a purely technical institution - it has to craft proposals that will survive Brussels politics - but the Commission is the most in need of technical information, case-study material and evidence to support its positions, proposals and ultimately decisions.

2. Secondly, the Commission is the most 'European' of all the institutions. The Commission is tasked with **promoting the European good**, as noted in Chapter 1, and this needs to be translated into working with the Commission. In this sense European arguments and positions are more widely accepted by the Commission. The opposite is also true in that it is the least tolerant of all the institutions to overt national, or blocking, positions.

3. Directly linked to the 'European' aspect is that of **positive/constructive engagement**. Irrespective of your point of view it should always be expressed in a positive and constructive way. If there are problems, do not just highlight them - provide possible solutions and answers. With the other institutions it may be possible to be more openly critical, but with the Commission it is always better to be constructive and positive with officials.

4. The Commission will have a plethora of information at its disposal - it will be the **ultimate policy expert**. The Commission works on proposals and then follows them very closely through the other two institutions - meaning that the Commission is usually right on top of the technical and political aspects of its dossiers, more so than the other institutions. This can be very useful and you can always ask the Commission its opinion on where work is needed or where a dossier is moving.

8.2.2 Decision-making

Table 1.5 drew the main conclusions from the Commission chapter with regard to key stages and actors. That table is a very useful place to start when engaging with the Commission decision-making process. Follow that process as closely as you can from start to finish. Things can change very quickly and you need to read the signs as soon as possible, to be able to act accordingly. It is worth at this point breaking down the Commission decision-making process into stages and identifying what is needed and appropriate at each stage.

1. **Political Guidelines & State of the Union**
   These are very important documents as they frame the work of the Commission for the coming years. It is important not to neglect them as 'unattainable' documents that can't be influenced. They can - but it is always a question of the channels to do this. At this high political level in the Commission the most effective way to work in influencing its future agenda is through Member States, European associations/federations and MEPs - who can all place key issues on the Commission agenda. Internally these documents are most shaped by the President, the President's Cabinet and the Secretariat-General (SG). Working on these documents requires big picture thinking, long-term engagement and European political objectivity.

2. **Commission Work Programme**
   The second stage in the internal decision-making process is the Commission Work Programme (CWP), which is again a high-level document - though now a more technical and practical translation of the political priorities identified by the Commission in its Guidelines and State of the Union. Working with this document will again require work at the highest levels of all Directorates-General (DGs) and Services. Remember that the CWP will give rise to other key documents such as Management Plans (MPs). By assessing how your issue is being dealt with by the Commission you can give yourself a vital institutional context - looking through how an issue will be dealt with by the Commission in a DG MP will be very instructive. It will tell you the objectives and indicators of success, which you should use when working on that issue with the Commission - you will be working in the same direction as them on the issue, reinforcing their work.

   > **Context of your issue**
   >
   > Check:
   > - How does it relate to the Political Guidelines and State of the Union?
   > - Is it a strategic or flagship issue?
   > - Is the issue in the Work Programme?
   > - How is the issue presented in the DG Management Plan?
   > - What objectives are in the Management Plan?

3. **Impact Assessment**
   It is very important to try and engage with the Commission during Impact Assessments (IAs). This will usually be part of the IA process because the Commission needs to consult. The best way to successfully engage with an IA is to read some IAs and understand the process, logic and flow within them and take a look at completed IAs in your field - this very useful exercise will

help you understand the type of information, evidence and facts that the Commission needs at this stage of its thinking and preparation. On occasion the Commission uses consultants, in which case it is important to identify them and try to meet with them if possible. Some suggestions for working with the Commission at this stage include:

1. propose alternatives to the questions through the public consultation;
2. be as concrete as possible in your engagement;
3. set your points into the broader political context and objectives behind the IA;
4. remember that every IA has to consider economic, social and environmental impacts;
5. provide your own IA material and evidence;
6. provide concrete issues and supporting facts, figures and arguments from the field;
7. work with the lead DG drafting the IA and also the Steering Group for the IA.

Working with an IA is very much a technical exercise, but it should also be done with an awareness of the broader political context and the DG objectives as stated in the Management Plan. Interaction will mostly take place at the level of the Unit undertaking the IA itself and the Steering Group which has been set up to help it. It is important to work your ideas into the IA process through as many avenues as possible, so leverage other DG contacts as much as possible.

4. **External consultation (formal)**
The Commission needs responses to formal consultations as a basis for its own arguments - potentially for those involved to support and bolster their own position internally if need be. Bear this in mind when responding to the Commission or sending in position papers. Also bear in mind that your consultation response will be posted online for everyone else to see - closed consultations offer a goldmine of information about the state of play on an issue and are often the source of many mapping activities (see Chapter 10).

It is very hard to justify to the Commission why you want to meet them on an issue if you did not respond to their formal consultation - they will keep records of this and be aware of your responses and meeting requests. It is therefore important to engage in this process with the Commission with a constructive, creative and solution-based approach. The mentality of only responding to point out bad things is not constructive. Submitting a formal response to a consultation is a very good basis to organise a follow-up meeting to explore some of your points in further detail.

Expert Groups are perhaps the single most important source of information for the Commission so they need to be understood, identified and engaged with. Use the Expert Group Register to identify the group you are interested in, but always also check with the Commission Unit in question to see if anything else exists, as not all groups are registered. If one exists in your area of work you need to find out what they are working on, their timetables and who is sitting in the group (usually possible from the Commission or a Permanent Representation). From there it is important to try and engage with the experts in the group.

5. **Inter-Service Consultation**
While this is an entirely internal process, the Inter-Service Consultation is a very important stage in the life of a dossier and it needs to be followed attentively. Despite its internal nature, ISC texts have a habit of finding their way into wider circulation. Every Cabinet prepares its spokesperson on key issues going into ISC because they anticipate that their text will leak out from somewhere at this stage. The lead DG will open the ISC and wait for responses from other DGs, although much of the debate will already have taken place within the Inter-Service Coordination Groups. Get good contact information of who is in the Inter-Service Coordination Group as they will usually also be responsible for responding to the ISC. Like before with the IA, it is again worth leveraging all possibilities that exist within other DGs involved, especially if the lead DG is not as supportive of your case as you would like. There are different perspectives and interests at play in the Commission and the internal decision-making procedures give different internal actors the opportunity to make changes - something you need to be aware of. Proposals can get modified here and it is important to watch out for this and to understand where the changes came from and why, as this will help you later.

6. **Cabinets**
The next stages of the internal decision-making of the Commission all revolve around the activities of the Cabinet. The Cabinet will ultimately prepare the final decisions, make final changes or ask for additional information before adoption by the College. In the Oral procedure this takes place within the weekly Special Chefs and Hebdo meetings; it otherwise takes place electronically for the Written procedure. In both cases, therefore, it is useful to keep the relevant Cabinet member aware of your concerns: you can find all Cabinet members and their areas of work on the Commissioners' websites. Your interaction with Cabinet members does not need to be constant: well-timed interventions will likely be more successful in this sense. Bear in mind that at this level dossiers can become more political and a Cabinet is looking out for the interests of their Commissioner, which will involve a complex mix of political, national and policy preferences.

7. **College**
The final stage of decision-making is the College meeting of Commissioners. It is very difficult to exert meaningful influence on these meetings given their high-level political nature and should be a last resort on a highly political dossier. Access to Commissioners at this level of decision-making is restricted to their Cabinets, Head of Cabinet in particular, and Member State interventions (usually to their 'home' Commissioner).

There are a number of key elements to retain from the stage-by-stage view of Commission decision-making taken above:

1. Engage in the process as early as possible. This will give you an advantage in terms of potential influence, presence and visibility, and credibility on the issue as an engaged stakeholder - it will also help you build up a picture of what you are working on.
2. Follow the whole process to the end. Things can change very quickly and from the most unforeseen actors - these need to be monitored and understood. Knowing how and why something changed can be very useful for you later in the process.

3. There is a dichotomy between the technical and the political in the Commission, both of which need to be appreciated and engaged with.
4. Remember that engagement is for the long-term and constructive solutions-driven interventions will be better for developing long-term credibility.

8.2.3 People

1. **Civil Servants**

   At the level of people in the Commission it is possible to make some more specific comments about different groups of actors, how to approach them and what they need. The first useful tool to assist this work is the EU Whoiswho website, which offers a quick and easy way to find the person you are looking for and all their contact details. The best ways of finding and contacting Commission officials can be found in the box below.

   It is worth trying to map out all your actual and potential contacts in the Commission at the earliest possible stage and across all DGs. This will enable you to contact the right people at the right time according to your needs and positions. As highlighted in the last section it is always advisable to try and maintain two levels of contact in the Commission, with both the technical (Unit) and political (Cabinet) levels.

   > **EU Whoiswho**
   > http://europa.eu/whoiswho/public/
   >
   > **European Commission Switchboard**
   > +(32) 2 299 11 11
   >
   > **E-mail**
   > Firstname.Familyname@ec.europa.eu

2. **Cabinet**

   The importance of the Cabinet has already been established and it will thus appear prominently on any mapping of key Commission contacts. Key points to consider when working with Cabinet members are:

   1. A key role of Cabinets is to work on internal coalitions to push points, issues and modifications. This is a very active political role of the Cabinet - and highlights the fact that Cabinet members spend a lot of time meeting and discussing with other Cabinet members.
   2. Most Cabinet members can get between 40 and 60 e-mails per day with information, meeting requests, etc. These can come from European associations down to individual citizens. The policy is to try and answer all of them although through prioritisation this can take some time to get through the backlogs.
   3. A general policy of Cabinet staff is not to meet individual companies or stakeholders - they prefer to meet European associations and federations to get a broader picture. Only in specific cases, where the issues are localised, would they consider more individual meeting requests.
   4. The Cabinet has an excellent overview of work going through the entire Commission machinery and also of the internal politics of the dossiers: the only other people with such a (political) overview are Director-Generals and Directors.

3. **Unit**
    The Unit is the standard partner when people speak of working with the Commission. It is at this level that the long-term engagement strategy is so important. Further points are:

    1. Get to know the members of the Unit. Try to find out their nationality, working language and background and any other information you think will help you communicate with them.
    2. Identify any Seconded National Experts (it is also possible to do this through a Permanent Representation) as they will be technical experts in the field of the Unit.
    3. Always be honest and transparent in your interests and positions, and respect anything said or given in confidence. Commission officials will talk to each other within Units, as well as within and across DGs and between DGs and Cabinets, as well as to officials from the other institutions. Information can travel very quickly, in both positive and negative ways.
    4. Understand which other stakeholders engage with the Unit in question on your key issues. This is a key piece of stakeholder mapping (see Chapter 10 for more on this subject) as this will help you understand the drivers and dynamics and allow you to tailor your information better.

8.2.4 Communication

The final aspect of working with the Commission to look at is the types and forms of communication that are best used. As a general rule the preferred means of communication is meetings and written briefing materials. Communicating with the Commission needs to follow the key points below.

1. As identified in this chapter and Chapter 1, the Commission is often in need of hard facts to support its proposals - so the more technical and factual information that can be supplied, the better.
2. The more the position you are advocating represents a general EU position, the better. An individual company can provide good data but it needs to be of a general nature because the more specific, the less value it will have - especially when you get to the political levels of the Commission.
3. Convincing always needs arguments - a good tool to do this is a case-study with effective cost-benefit data. In addition, it brings a regulatory issue to life in a way that can be understood and supported by all.
4. When answering consultations, be constructive and positive and use facts and figures. Make sure your responses are well crafted and drafted.
5. Remember to carry out a two-fold communication, covering the political as well as the technical level.
6. Informal contacts should follow formal contacts and consultation to stress a point, refine an argument, bring extra support, etc.
7. Dinners, lunches and other such events are usually declined by Commission officials and do not offer very conducive environments to establish positions and convey your points.

From the preceding sections it is possible to resume the key points of working with the Commission in Table 8.3:

Table 8.3: Working with the Commission: Key points

1. Maintain contacts with Commission officials throughout the decision-making process. The Commission has a key role as 'technical advisor' and 'facilitator' during the discussions between the EP and the Council.
2. Seek to reduce the detrimental features of a Commission proposal rather than to reject the proposal altogether. Be vocal in support of a Commission proposal where applicable; and respect the consensual approach and the most realistic ways of approaching things.
3. Follow the entire Commission decision-making procedure to be of assistance as required, and to spot any changes/modifications that concern you.
4. Respond to, and engage in, consultations, Impact Assessments and hearings.
5. Follow the work of Expert Groups very carefully.
6. Make sure you are in the Transparency Register.
7. Provide technical solutions and information, case-studies and information from the field.
8. Remember there is natural hierarchy of access to the Commission starting with European associations or federations, moving through national associations or federations down to individual stakeholders.
9. Leverage all possibilities across DGs to get information and stress your points.
10. Map all your actual and potential contacts as early as possible.

8.3 Working with the Council of Ministers

8.3.1 General strategic

As Chapter 2 showed the powers of the Council have been extended to include more and more areas - making it a real driving force in EU affairs. The Council will, however, likely represent the most difficult institution that you will have to deal with in Brussels, for four main reasons:

1. Working with the Council in effect means working with national capitals.
2. The Council is the representation of national interests in Brussels so is more nationally focused.
3. Member States in the Council will work more closely with their own national key stakeholders.
4. Of all the EU institutions the Council is the *least* in need of technical information.

The first point is perhaps the most important to stress because the national level is a key driver when it comes to working with the Council. Whilst it is essential to work with the Permanent Representation in Brussels, the majority of the substantive decisions of the Council, as shown in Chapter 2, are taken back in the national capitals and through the experts they send to the Working Group meetings. The key work, positions, mandates and decision-makers within the Council structure are thus to be found back in Member State capitals. This can present advantages if you are based in a national capital and represent a national interest as it will be easier to engage with the key national officials. On the other hand understanding the different political systems and contexts of other Member States, and being able to find all the relevant national decision-makers can be very challenging. For this reason many stakeholders limit their work to Permanent Representations and the national experts coming to Brussels for meetings.

> **Follow the Council**
>
> 1. List of Permanent Representations
>   http://europa.eu/whoiswho/public/index.cfm?fuseaction=idea.hierarchy&nodeid=3780&lang=en
> 2. Council website, including press room
>   http://www.consilium.europa.eu/1
> 3. Presidency websites - agendas/priorities

The second and third points relate to the fact that there is a natural tendency, when working with the Council, to concentrate solely on one's own nationality, especially if based in a national capital. Successful work with the Council will involve much wider efforts and engagement, while always bearing in mind that the Permanent Representatives and national officials of other Member States that you meet will all be assessing their own national interests - something that will be outlined in more detail later in this section.

The fact that the main decisions are taken nationally means they are usually done so using national networks and trusted advisors - a difficult circle to enter into from abroad. Secondly there will be very important linguistic and cultural barriers to entry in these domains, making working with them more difficult. Member States all have a civil service of experts at their disposal, so their need for expert factual input is less than that of the Commission and Parliament, although they still need information. Moreover, each national capital has clearly defined objectives in terms of its own national positions and interests. And finally, the Council does not openly publish all its documents, although many Member States share documents with key national stakeholders. It is this combination of geographical, linguistic and national interests that makes working with different Member States very challenging.

The **key general strategic points to consider when working with the Council** are as follows:

1. The Council is the least open and transparent of all the EU institutions, bodies and agencies - making it more difficult to find out what is happening, what is needed and who to speak to. It is also generally the most difficult institution to access and work with. To successfully work with the Council you need good long-term contacts.
2. The national factor: it is less open to working with other nationalities. The key national decision-makers are generally based in national capitals.
3. Understand the national political agenda and priorities, and how these can be linked to your issue.
4. Identify national decision-makers and their agendas, usually through the Permanent Representation. For example, try to find out which experts the Member State is sending to Commission Expert Groups.

5. The national connection: identify and explain how a national sector is affected or how your issue supports a national cause. What is your national angle?
6. Understand the national press and how to work with them as well as what to expect from them. The national press can play an important role on EU issues.
7. Work in both Brussels and the national capitals: it is essential to have a two-fold communication and engagement. While the decisions might be taken in the national capital, the Brussels antenna, the Permanent Representation, will always be involved in the process and will probably have to communicate and negotiate the outcome (with possible room for manoeuvre).
8. Understand devolved powers - meaning that working with regions (Länder in Germany for example) can be as important, if not more, on certain issues. Sometimes Member States send Regional Ministers to Council meetings. They will often also have a representative office in Brussels, so working with both their home base and their representations in Brussels is important.

These key general strategic recommendations can be supplemented by a set of more specific suggestions when it comes to working with the Council:

1. Raise awareness of your case in other Permanent Representations not just your national one: the national route is usually the first but should not be the only one.
2. Work with the Presidency: they have all the procedural and content information and they are trying to broker compromise solutions. Be aware that a Presidency, as described in Chapter 2, has a very specific role of compromise finder.
3. Work with the GSC - again they are well placed and have information to hand on national positions and the state of play.
4. Build coalitions with other nationalities via European associations/federations or on an ad hoc basis.
5. Big countries count but small Member States can also be influential and may be more open to discussion and assistance.

The Council on Votewatch.eu

Votewatch.eu has opened a very useful section on its website dedicated to the Council. In this section they have an easy-to-use database of all votes on Codecision issues, as well as explanatory statements made by the Member States with regard to their votes. You can search by individual Member State as well as by issue. You can also access information on coalitions and minority positions. Whilst still a work in progress, when compared with the data available on the Parliament, it is an excellent source of information.

Find all of this at www.votewatch.eu

8.3.2 Decision-making

Table 2.5 drew the main conclusions from the Council chapter with regard to key stages and actors. That table is a very useful place to start when working with the Council decision-making process. Follow the entire Council decision-making process as closely as you can from start to finish - although this can be very challenging and will depend on very good long-term contacts within the Council structures. Things can change very quickly and you need to read the signs as soon as possible to be able to act appropriately.

1. **Council**

    Working with a Council of Ministers vote, or discussion, is a very difficult task - much like trying to work with a College meeting in the Commission. This will require high-level political contacts in the national capitals or with Permanent Representatives. In essence, trying to work at this level is usually a last resort for highly politicised issues with national salience. Council conclusions are very important documents and they exert a significant influence on the other institutions - notably the Commission when the Council asks for a report, proposal or makes suggestions.

    In this way a single Member State, irrespective of its size, can have the power to put issues onto the European agenda. So when a Council meets it is important to try and discover all the elements that will be presented, formally and informally.

    > **Council Voting Calculator**
    >
    > A very useful tool to see how voting is shaping up in the Council and to familiarise yourself with the workings of the Council voting is the online Voting Calculator:
    > http://www.consilium.europa.eu/en/council-eu/voting-system/voting-calculator/

    When it comes to Council voting, the smaller Member States are often forgotten or ignored, which is a mistake. While the big countries have a larger voting weight, the Council tries to work by consensus, so it usually attempts to accommodate all Member States in some way. Some smaller Member States are also very influential, persuasive and good compromise generators, making them important in the negotiations as well as when it comes to a vote.

It is vital to familiarise yourself with the Council voting matrix and all the permutations on your particular dossier; this will be crucial throughout the process. The box above refers to a very useful calculator for this purpose. In Council voting there are also certain types of ad hoc and standing coalitions, which again you should understand if you are working with the Council. This will help you know when there are coalitions at play and how majorities are moving in Council, for which you need to follow the political discussions very carefully.

Coalitions are an intriguing part of Council dynamics and they need to be monitored carefully on a case-by-case basis. There are traditional loose groupings of countries such as France, Italy and Spain along with other Mediterranean countries in one group, or the UK, Netherlands and Nordic countries in another. Such coalitions arise from natural affinities and shared interests, but they should not be taken as a given. Coalitions are very fluid and can form and disappear quickly in the Council on an issue-by-issue basis - and in many cases they can depend on who is in government in the respective Member States.

Council meetings are very important due to their decision-taking power and the high-level political decisions being taken, so engaging in discussions with the people attending them can prove to be very difficult. In the same sense it is very difficult to engage with the Presidency around these meetings because they are so busy trying to organise everything, including all the possible compromises and decisions to be taken. Getting in touch with the aforementioned actors, without having high-level political contacts in the respective Member States, and their Permanent Representations, is thus challenging and should only be attempted if the particular issue is really significant for you - and them.

A final aspect of working with the Council relates to the fact that the single biggest external source of influence on the Commission is the Council itself. This is particularly the case when the Commission is in its preparatory phases, or even before. One of the main vehicles to influence the Commission is the **Council Conclusions** because they are one of the most important sources of direction and suggestion to the Commission. At all stages of the EU policy cycle it is worth remembering that the Council, as a body, has a very strong power of persuasion vis-à-vis the Commission and this should be monitored and is also something that can be worked with. This argument also holds true for the Council in relation to the Parliament - but here more as individual Member States and their relations with their national MEPs. In this sense the Council is very well-positioned with information and influence.

In sum for Council:

- Engagement with Council is very difficult and usually via PR, DPR and national capitals.
- Subjects for discussion at Council level tend to be only the most sensitive dossiers in which national positions are not aligned, making engagement on these issues difficult.
- Trying to work with the Council should be a last resort given the difficulties of getting to the right people and the subsequent chances of success.
- Always keep an eye on blocking minorities and coalition formation in the Council - something that should have become apparent earlier in the Council decision-making (WP level).
- Council discussions are imminently national and political, so any material designed to work with the Council needs to take this into account.
- Working with the Council will require senior management engagement.
- Working with one, or several, Member State(s) to try and get issues into Council conclusions can be very useful and is something that needs to be monitored.

2. COREPER

The Permanent Representative (PR) and Deputy Permanent Representative (DPR) are the Brussels-based antennas. Whilst they might not have a key role in national policy formation given that many of the key decisions are taken back in the national capitals, the PR and DPR usually have some room for manoeuvre and they will also usually be briefing the national capital on the state of negotiations and what is possible (or not) in Brussels. It is for this reason that a double line of communication is always important, with both national capital and Brussels. The PR and DPR will often be the ones doing the negotiating and communicating in Brussels, via COREPER. The PR and the DPR have an extremely good overview of everything on the table at any given moment in time, of the politics surrounding files and the likely coalitions and majorities that are forming. They are also the key conduits of information from the Permanent Representation back to the national capital.

COREPER is the key level of Council decision-making as it oversees all the Working Parties and prepares all the work for Ministerial meetings - meaning that many of the deals and decisions are made at this level. It is important to know if COREPER is giving any steer and guidance to the work of a Working Party and it is important to remember that COREPER will always look at the work of the Working Party before it goes for Ministerial approval or discussion. For this reason it is important to keep engaged with COREPER and to know what is going on. COREPER can modify Working Party work, request changes, or it can agree without changes - but the key is that it has all these options. Looking at COREPER agendas is also a very good indication of what is on the table at any one time in the Council. COREPER is a closely-knit family as its members meet frequently and often have very good contacts.

For obvious reasons the PR and DPR are usually busy and more inclined to engage with national stakeholders than with other nationalities and European Associations and Federations. It is useful to identify, in each Permanent Representation, the official(s) in charge of your dossier - at every level. Usually a Permanent Representation will have several attachés each focused on a specific issue so it is quite straightforward to identify who is in charge of your dossier. Nearly all Permanent Representations have clear and user-friendly websites that allow you to find this information, otherwise the EU Whoiswho is very useful for this task.

The key elements of working with COREPER are as follows:

- COREPER will see all dossiers and have an influence on all of them - so it needs to be monitored and engaged with.
- PR and DPR will be working very closely with their national capitals.
- Working with a Permanent Representation requires an appreciation of the national position and politics on an issue.
- COREPER is an inherently political body and will require political input and arguments, mostly related to the Member State in question.
- Working with COREPER requires senior management activity and engagement.

3. **Mertens and Antici groups**
Between the Working Group and COREPER are the two key preparatory bodies, the Antici and Mertens groups, presented in Chapter 2. These are attachés based in the Permanent Representations who play an organisational and political filtering role for the PR and DPR. They have an extremely

good overview of all dossiers on the table at any given moment - and also of the evolving political climate in COREPER. They become invaluable contacts when your dossier is being negotiated by COREPER.

It is important to establish contact with the Mertens and Anticis as they can provide detailed and up-to-date information about the position of their, and other, Member States with regard to all proposals before COREPER at any given point in time. They will also have key information when it comes to the discussions taking place in the European Council. These key roles are shown below in Figure 8.1.

Figure 8.1: Roles of Antici and Mertens Attachés

Antici	VS.	Mertens
• They are usually more senior – from the Ministry of Foreign affairs in the capital • They perform business planning functions • They have an important role during the European Council – to inform the National Delegation on other MS positions		• They play mainly a reporting function; they handle the process of Council workings • They send political messages to the capital • They clarify positions and signal points of contention that could arise during negotiations • They act as a 'point of contact' for personnel in the Perm Rep (they know what is on the mind of the Ambassador)

4. **Working Groups (or Working Parties)**
Working Groups are usually attended by experts from national capitals, hence the importance of working via national capitals. It is often possible to identify the national experts by contacting their Permanent Representation, the Commission Unit responsible for the proposal being discussed (as it will be running the Working Group too) or the General Secretariat of the Council. As Chapter 2 identified, a significant percentage of all dossiers are agreed at WG level, making it the key decision-making level to work with from the start. Statistically it is therefore likely that your dossier will be agreed at this level, making it imperative for you to work with the national experts in the WG. You should identify who 'your' national expert is and provide them with facts and evidence, formulated as arguments that can be used in negotiations. A WG is all about negotiation - and this should be reflected in the material you communicate. From working with 'your' own national expert (if indeed you have one) you need to identify the other members of

the WG and try to set up meetings with them. You need to bear in mind that the officials in WGs are national experts so the information and evidence you present them should take this into account.

In almost all cases the attachés/experts taking part in the different Working Parties get to know each other very well by virtue of working together on a frequent basis. This means they often meet on an informal basis as well, so one needs to deliver a coherent and consistent message when engaging with them. It is very likely that they will talk to each other between the meetings and it can prove to be counterproductive to deliver contradicting messages to attachés/experts on the basis that they represent different Member States. The key elements of how to work with Working Groups are:

- They are mostly technical experts from national capitals so they will need to be engaged with on a technical level.
- The WG is where the majority of dossiers find technical agreement so working with the WG, or monitoring its progress, is very important.
- From WG discussions you will already get a very clear idea of the chances of success of the dossier in Council as positions, coalitions and key issues become apparent.
- Working with a WG means identifying the national experts who sit in the WG, the attachés in the Permanent Representation who deal with the dossier, the officials in the General Secretariat of the Council and the officials from the Commission who also attend.

Having briefly assessed the different stages in the Council decision-making process, and what is needed to work with each level, it is useful to turn to the issue of people.

8.3.3 People
The first potentially difficult element of working with the Council is in finding the right contacts and their details. The best sources are below.

EU Whoiswho
http://europa.eu/whoiswho/public

List of MS Permanent Representations to the EU
http://brussels.cta.int/dnload/en/liste_rep_permanentes_en.pdf

For the details of MS officials working in Working Groups the best sources of information are:
1. A Permanent Representation (attaché in charge of the subject area)
2. The National Ministry in the MS in question
3. General Secretariat of the Council officials
4. The Commission official who sits in the Working Group (the desk office/HoU from the relevant Unit)

The limitation of the EU Whoiswho and the websites of the Permanent Representations is that they will only help you identify the Brussels-based Council actors. It will then be through these actors that you have to try and map the other key officials - the national based power players and technical officials. It is for this reason that a mapping of key contacts in the Council can be much more elaborate and difficult to finalise. In general the Permanent Representations are the best sources of information about their own national colleagues, structures and driving forces.

At the level of people in the Council it is possible to make some more specific comments about different groups of actors, how to approach and best work with them.

1. **National capital based officials**
   Member State officials back in the national capitals are important actors to work with if you are really trying to change the content and substance of a Member State position. For this the following recommendations are useful:

   1. Identify national decision-makers and their national political agendas.
   2. Know the national political structures and decision-making fora - you need to identify where the national positions are coming from within the national administrations. This information can usually be obtained from a Permanent Representation.
   3. Identify the main national actors in your field (usually associations and federations) again because these will usually be the main driving forces behind a government position.
   4. Use the Permanent Representation to assist you in the tasks of identification of national officials; failing that, the GSC might be able to help.
   5. Build a national network if you are working on an issue in which a (or more than one) Member State is pivotal and use intermediaries based in the capital to assist you in this.
   6. National associations are usually powerful national players and as part of a European association/federation good contacts can be established.
   7. Use any subsidiaries, partners, and embassies/missions that you have in the Member State in question to access and engage with national decision-makers.
   8. Meet/inform the national civil servants/experts about the issue(s) you are following. Take a long-term perspective. You can try to meet national officials on their Brussels visits but bear in mind many fly in and out for meetings making it difficult to catch them outside of their official duties. If it is really important you need to work with them in the national capital.
   9. Remember that national civil servants are likely to be experts on the dossier in question: be prepared for this and explain your position in a technical manner.
   10. Remember also that the official might be acting on instructions 'from above' and not have any room for negotiation - making identification of the decision-making structures in the Member State even more important.
   11. Working with national officials can be difficult due to cultural and linguistic reasons which is why working through/with national actors can be very useful.
   12. Finally it is worth remembering that a Directive goes back to the national level for transposition, and your national contacts could be very useful for this later stage.

2. Presidency

The importance of the Presidency in driving the agenda and work of the Council for a six-month period makes it a key actor to work with. Having noted that all Presidencies are extremely busy during their term of office, some are more open than others to engage with stakeholders running up to and during their time in the hot seat. The Presidency is especially useful to know the timelines, the direction of discussions on a file and the compromises that are likely to result. You should therefore aim to:

1. Establish contact with Member States holding forthcoming Presidencies well in advance so as to diminish the 'cold call' effect that you will have by simply appearing during the Presidency.
2. Understand the role and limitations of what a Presidency can (and cannot) do: for example, their influence is in the compromises and in driving the agenda not in making strong factual declarations and arguments.
3. Stay up-to-date with Presidency compromises and react to compromises through national Permanent Representation contacts. You can follow these through the Presidency itself, the GSC, Permanent Representations, or the Commission.
4. The Presidency will be concentrated on their priority dossiers and in getting things done within their six months so bear the priorities and the timetable in mind. Follow the 18-month trio programme and the operational six-month Presidency agenda - but bear in mind their flexibility.
5. The Presidency wants to broker compromises: try to offer solutions and compromises to them in your contacts. You can assist a Presidency by helping them find the middle ground.
6. The Presidency will have the procedural, timetable and negotiating information - but this will also be known to Permanent Representations in Brussels.
7. Presidencies still have a limited margin for manoeuvre to put their pet dossiers on the table, something which you can work with and need to monitor.
8. Present your priorities to an incoming Presidency - at the level of a European association/federation is more appropriate - taking account of their stated priorities, the trio programme and the national and European politics of the moment.
9. Remember that the Presidency will be negotiating in trilogues with the Parliament so they can be a very good source of information on these discussions.

3. General Secretariat of the Council (GSC)

The GSC is an under-estimated actor on the Brussels scene, contacted significantly less than its counterparts in the Parliament and Commission. The GSC has a goldmine of information at its disposal and can be a very influential actor on the internal decision-making of the Council. Like the Presidency the GSC is more useful for information than it is for direct influencing work and substance-based discussions, but the GSC will understand the issues in their technical and political dimensions and be able to analyse what this means for stakeholders better than almost any other actor around the Council. The GSC should form part of a comprehensive key actor mapping and be engaged with at all stages of the Council decision-making to establish positions, find information, contacts and further details. In addition:

1. Meet and build a network in the GSC as early as possible; don't just leave it until you have live issues on the table.
2. The GSC has a significant amount of information at its disposal - Member State positions, procedural and timetable information, latest developments, Presidency information - as it as at the heart of all the action.
3. The GSC does not need technical information and positions to the same extent that its counterparts in the Commission do, but does appreciate being kept up-to-date with developments.

4. Permanent Representations

The role of Permanent Representations was summarised in Table 2.4. While the temptation is to only work extensively with your 'own' Permanent Representation this would be a mistake. It is true that you are likely to have more support from your national representation, though this could of course depend very much on their position on your issue. Irrespective of this, however, you should always seek to establish good contacts in a number of other Permanent Representations which could then be useful for verifying information, getting additional information and which ultimately as actors you will try to influence and work with. If you have any links with other European countries these should be leveraged to build relations with other Permanent Representations. For this the following recommendations are useful:

1. Remember that Permanent Representations are informed about the positions of all other Member States so it can be useful to speak to more than one to get information. Whilst nationality is an important factor Permanent Representations do work with stakeholders of all nationalities.
2. Clearly identify, and establish contact with, the person in charge of your dossier at all levels within a Permanent Representation (and if possible across Representations). Having identified the key people try to proactively meet with them to establish contact. These contacts will help you understand the dynamics in Council meetings and where the information, compromises, positions are coming from.
3. Meet the Antici and Mertens attachés - the advisers of PRs and DPRs. They will have detailed insight on dossiers in COREPER 1 and 2 of a political, technical, procedural and timetabling nature. They are in the thick of the negotiating action, so they will have up-to-date information (remember that COREPER meets on a Wednesday (and Friday) so coordinate your meeting requests around this).
4. Permanent Representations are, like Cabinets in the Commission, more likely to meet associations and federations, in this case more likely national than European. While they have an obvious tendency to favour meeting national stakeholders, they are open to meeting all stakeholders depending on the issue and their needs/objectives.
5. Whilst the key mandates and decisions come from national capitals (this can vary across Member States and also within Member States, across files), the Brussels antenna is always a vital place to engage with. They will themselves influence the mandates and positions, adding the Brussels angle to it. Many PRs and DPRs will, on occasion, have some margin for negotiation and manoeuvre.

6. Permanent Representations will themselves be trying to influence the dossier in Brussels, so try to think how you could help them do this. Some Member States are more active (and open about their influencing work) in their Brussels activities than others. You can often be of great assistance in passing messages and making arguments on behalf of Permanent Representations that they themselves would not be able to do or make: always think of what value you can bring to their interests.
7. When working with PRs or DPRs you will need to have a good horizontal dossier overview as they will be working on, between and within several key dossiers at once.
8. COREPER is usually where dossier linkage can take place - where a deal can be suggested across dossiers - which can then be ratified by the Council. It is therefore essential to keep an eye on this process because it can change quickly and suddenly.
9. COREPER is both technical and political, with a focus on the latter, so political argument and communication is better suited.
10. COREPER will often validate trilogue negotiation mandates, so this must be taken into account when interacting on a dossier; appreciation of ongoing or upcoming negotiations with the Parliament is important.
11. The PR and DPR are interested in key elements only: the main blocking points (and why to keep them, or how to remove them), compromises and solutions.
12. Always remember that COREPER, and then the Council, can become mouthpieces for national interests. This can become very national and competitive and difficult to engage with.

8.3.4 Communication

Communication with the Council is very different to that with the Commission and Parliament given the differing nature and needs of the institutions. It is clear that for effective communication with the Council, the right balance of political, technical and national elements will come to the fore. For the Council:

1. Always maintain a double communication with Brussels Permanent Representations and national capitals. This is essential to make sure the messages are flowing between the two (national coordination issues), but the key point is to always keep in touch with the Permanent Representations as they will know the latest state of affairs.

2. National arguments and case-studies will prevail in discussions with certain Member States on certain issues, so when working with Member States on an issue it is useful to tailor information/ evidence/facts to national interests.

3. English is the lingua franca in Brussels and communication with the Permanent Representations in Brussels is usually conducted in English. This becomes much more difficult if engaging with national experts in Brussels or back in the national capitals. You need to determine your ultimate audience if submitting position papers to the Permanent Representations because if it is a national audience it should be translated and if possible delivered directly.

4. National capitals are more about providing facts and evidence but you always need a national angle/link. National case-studies will always be sought after as they will help the Member State justify a position in Brussels.

5. Brussels in contrast is more about contacts, information, visibility and European political information that can be used in negotiations - and also because the PR and DPR will be influencing the national position.

6. Communicating with Permanent Representations beyond your own Member State is essential.

7. Communicating with national officials beyond your own national capital is essential.

8. The best way to communicate is via meetings and with written briefings and position papers.

From the preceding sections it is possible to resume the key points of working with the Council in Table 8.4 below.

Table 8.4: Working with the Council – Key points

1. The Council is about Brussels and national capitals - double communication.
2. National issues will be key: indicate national angles/links; case studies will help support this.
3. Use any national networks, subsidiaries, embassies/missions, partners or other members of a European association/federation to assist you.
4. Your 'own' Permanent Representation will likely be more receptive to giving you information - but **DO NOT** neglect other Member States and the GSC.
5. For the Presidency you need to know the domestic political situation and structures, the Presidency programme and the trio programme.
6. At national capital and Working Group level it is mostly technical experts who are receptive to national technical information, case-studies, etc.
7. At COREPER and Council levels it is mostly political negotiations that take place so communication needs to change level and content.
8. Council level is a difficult to access last-chance saloon to make changes.
9. Always keep an eye out for bilateral political deals that could link your dossier to another dossier to find a solution.
10. The Council has certain standing coalitions and many ad hoc coalitions - try to stay up-to-date with these.
11. Build your contacts and relations for the long-term at all levels in Brussels and the national capitals.

8.4 Working with the European Parliament

8.4.1 General strategic

The Parliament is the most open, transparent and accessible of the EU institutions - but this does not mean that it is the easiest or most fruitful to work with. The Parliament is by definition the political body of the EU and things can move very quickly in a variety of unexpected directions; it is the institution that demands the greatest vigilance and monitoring in this respect. A day is a long time in politics and change is the only constant in the Parliament. For this reason it is important to keep updated with developments in the Parliament; the box to the right lists a set of useful ways to try and keep on top of the dossiers you are following.

Generally speaking, the Parliament lacks the human and technical resources to be on equal terms with the Council and Commission in terms of its information sources and expertise. As a result the Parliament needs and will appreciate good quality, timely, and reliable information.

A number of general strategic issues are important to address first:

> **Follow the Parliament**
>
> 1. Use **the Parliament website** - it is a goldmine of information.
>   - live Committee meetings
>   - Committee websites (newsletters etc)
>   - live Plenary Sessions
>   - individual MEP information
>   - MEP questions and answers
> 2. Use Political Group websites and news feeds
> 3. Use national party MEP websites, and regional MEP websites
> 4. Use individual **MEP websites**
> 5. Follow MEPs on **Facebook** and **Twitter**
> 6. Use **Votewatch.eu**
> 7. Try to be **present in the Parliament** for the key moments of your issues
> 8. Follow the Committees and Plenary live on your computer
> 9. Follow www.EuroparlTV.europa.eu

1. Get an annual pass to facilitate access to the building (otherwise you will need to identify friendly MEPs or Parliament staff who are happy to have their assistants sign you in on a regular basis). This goes hand in hand with being part of the Transparency Register.

2. The Parliament works according to a strict calendar. Plan your work and your interventions carefully and in accordance with this. Get yourself a pocket size Parliament Calendar - you never know when you might need it.

3. Your window of opportunity can be very short in the Parliament. While a dossier can be prepared over a number of months, decisions can be taken suddenly and without prior warning, so it is essential to monitor developments carefully.

4. Brussels is very good for more substantive meetings and for ongoing legislative files and issues.

5. Strasbourg is very good for networking and short pre-vote meetings. Note also that trilogues often take place in Strasbourg as do exceptional Committee meetings and Political Group meetings to organise Plenary positions.

6. You need to understand the MEPs you are working with - things such as their personal beliefs, national ties, National Delegations, European Group affiliations, national political affiliations and positions. You can find much of this on Votewatch.eu, their own websites and Facebook pages, press releases and by watching them in Committees and Plenary session.

7. MEPs are usually not experts in the particular field that concerns you and they will have numerous open files under consideration at any given time. They need understandable and easy to use information - and most of all real life examples that spell out the implications for business, jobs, living standards, etc.

8. In the Parliament, like the Council, a national approach to your issue is likely to be easier in terms of access but significantly limiting. You need to work across groups and nationalities for the most success in the Parliament.

9. You need to know the positions and structures of the Political Groups. They are key actors in the Parliament decision-making process (and they vote coherently) and to work successfully with the Parliament, you need to work with the groups.

10. Secretariat staff and Political Group staff in the Parliament are extremely useful contacts, sources of information and interlocutors on your dossiers. You can find their details on the Parliament and Political Group websites.

11. When working with the Parliament you should ideally not be working with more than 30 key MEPs. Focus your attention on the key influencers and drivers in the Parliament (usually rapporteurs, shadow rapporteurs, Group coordinators and key issue MEPs in Committees).

> 'Information must be concise, yet thorough; personal without being invasive; and applicable to local, national and EU-wide constituents - no easy task.'
>
> **Emma McClarkin MEP**
> Public Affairs News January 2011 page 15

12. It is usually not necessary (except perhaps as a last resort), to contact all MEPs. Most e-mails that start with 'Dear MEP' will end up in the spam folder.

13. Approaching all national MEPs can be very useful for an important national issue, but remember that voting along national lines is very rare in the Parliament.

14. Working with the Parliament is always about the numbers game, be it in Committee or in Plenary. You always need to monitor and work with the voting numbers.

15. MEPs like to have local/regional constituency links and angles, so if possible try to research such a position when working with an MEP.

When trying to work with an MEP, two things are frequently mentioned as being important: **national links and constituency links**. When an MEP is working in the Parliament both of these will inevitably come into play, but they will vary in importance according to the role of the MEP and the circumstances. Nationality and national party power over MEPs is something that, as was noted in Chapter 3, is a waning force in the Parliament in terms of voting patterns. MEPs often have stronger allegiance to their European Political Group, and the Political Groups in the Parliament vote with very high levels of coherence. MEPs also have much more in common (politically) with the MEPs in their own Group, irrespective of nationality, than they will with other same-nationality MEPs in other Political Groups. National MEPs can become united around a national issue, one of the rare occasions when nationality-based work in the Parliament can be successful, but otherwise nationality is more an issue for accessing an MEP than for influencing their position. One aspect of nationality is, however, important: the question of how an MEP gets onto (and stays on) a national party list for the next elections. This was mentioned in Chapter 3 and is an important point because despite an MEP's adhesion to their European Political Group, they need to be on a national party list (and as high as possible on the list) to get re-elected. This fact is always important to bear in mind because it can have an influence on how an MEP interacts with their national party, especially in the run up to elections.

> **MEPs and Constituency**
>
> MEPs will have close links to their constituency and they will likely:
> - Visit their constituency
> - Monitor local press for stories of interest
> - Deal with constituency requests
>
> To work with an MEP understanding their constituency will help you situate your arguments.

The second issue is that of constituency links. This is very much a spill-over from national politics because it is less important in Brussels than in a national capital, but it is nonetheless not something to be ignored. For a start, many Member States do not have small defined local constituencies for MEPs (remember there are not that many MEPs per country), therefore most MEPs have to cover large areas. The fact that MEPs are elected from national party lists, and also that MEPs have reduced visibility in the national and local media, tends to result in MEPs being more distant from their voters than national-level politicians. But while allowing for the fact that the constituency link is weaker than in national politics, it is still the case that most MEPs are receptive to good constituency evidence and links as they still must keep their eye on their electorate. Many MEPs monitor the local press in their constituency to follow any European issues or developments that might help them in their work in Brussels.

The most important time to work with an MEP is usually in the Committee stage because this is where the Parliament does the bulk of its work. Here the key for stakeholders is to convey their arguments to a number of MEPs in a tailored way that respects the diversity of the MEPs they are trying to work with. Giving MEPs information that they can use in Committee to persuade their fellow MEPs is very important - the best being case-studies and real life examples that bring an issue to life in Parliamentary discussions and debates. Also important to note is that when you are working with the Parliament the best people to know how things stand and how best to proceed are usually the MEPs themselves, so never hesitate to ask how they see things; this information can be very useful to help you develop your positions and refine your arguments and strategy. You will always need to advance your positions according to the changing context of the Committee discussions, both in terms of substance and politics.

8.4.2 Decision-making

Chapter 3 highlighted the different stages of the Parliament decision-making process, culminating in Table 3.6. This will serve as the basis for how to work with the different stages of work in the Parliament decision-making procedure, as follows:

1. Choice of Political Group and rapporteur

1. Try to anticipate who the key MEPs related to your dossier will be and get to know them (and about them) before the Commission proposal arrives in the Parliament - the better your existing contacts, the easier your access once the issue is live and MEPs are being flooded with requests for meetings.
2. Always check to see if the rapporteur has been named in advance of the file arriving in the Parliament, which can happen for major dossiers, rotation deals and if the Political Groups have reached some compromise in the past.
3. There is a tacit rule in the Parliament that if an MEP has drafted an own-initiative report on an issue that they will automatically get the legislative proposal if one is drafted by the Commission. This makes it very important to follow the nomination of rapporteurs for own-initiative reports because the long-term consequences can be very important.
4. It is very useful to try and keep informed, through the Political Groups and/or Committee Secretariat, of likely Group and rapporteur nominations; this can give you a head start in your work.
5. At this stage it is also important (at times particularly important) to follow the nomination of shadow rapporteurs. Shadows can play an extremely important role and trying to ensure a Political Group nominates a specific shadow, one with whom you can work, is something not to neglect.

2. Committee work

1. The Committee is the key stage of work to follow in the Parliament – as was highlighted in Chapter 5.4 on the Ordinary Legislative Procedure - because often positions found in Committee can pass through Political Groups to Plenary largely unchanged.
2. The key element in working with MEPs in Committee is to provide them with the right information: real life cases and evidence that they can use to convince their colleagues. MEPs need information that they can use, so bite-size information and sound bites work very well.

3. Follow the debates and stay informed of the state of play: you can do this by following Committee meetings, hearings, etc. and through your contacts. You can follow Committee meetings live on the Internet.
4. When following debates in the Committee, be alert for Group co-coordinator positions, any opposition and for timetable information; these are all key and will need to be acted upon.
5. Identify all the key players in the Committee you are working with and do your homework on their political backgrounds. Look through past MEP questions to identify the key issues that these MEPs are interested in (available on Votewatch.eu).
6. Suggest amendments to MEPs that you have identified as being favorable to your position. Long-standing, well-respected MEPs, coordinators, shadows and rapporteurs with good cross-party contacts are more likely to bring support to your amendment.
7. Amendments can be tabled by any MEP but the standing of the MEP in the Committee will be crucial to the amendment's chances of success. Great care should be taken about which MEPs you work with to table your amendments because it could also impact your reputation in the Parliament.
8. If you are presenting amendments then follow the strict amendment guidelines presented below. Present your amendments in the right format at the right time.

Get your amendments right

There are three major types of amendment and if you intend to submit a suggestion to an MEP you will need to get it right:
1. **Deleting** a provision in the Commission proposal
   - *Bold italic* on the left, 'removed' on the right
2. **Modifying** a provision in the Commission proposal
   - *Bold italic* on the right
3. **Adding** a provision in the Commission proposal
   - *Bold italic* on the right and 'new' in the title

You only need one amendment per modification - be aware of how this impacts the rest of the text. In addition to the amendment you wish to propose, you should add a **justification** (legislative only), which is also required. This should explain the rationale for the proposed change in a clear and concise manner (max. 500 characters). Look through a few Committee reports to understand these rules.

---

9. If you want to work effectively with an MEP at this stage of the process working within their constraints is essential. For explanatory statements and preparatory working documents the page restrictions are as follows: seven pages for a non-legislative report, six pages for a legislative report and three pages for an opinion. Motions for Resolutions should be no more than four pages and conclusions to non-legislative opinions one page. When there is an amendment the justification should be no more than 500 characters (a page being 1,500 characters).

10. In the Committee stage any MEP can table an amendment, but having it tabled by the rapporteur or a Political Group coordinator or a leading MEP will obviously add weight to your case because the MEP will have to justify, explain and find support for it - and these MEPs will be better placed to do this. It also frequently happens that you get co-signed amendments by different Groups and nationalities, an initiative that brings broader support and weight.
11. Work with assistants, Secretariat staff and Political Group staff - all will be involved in the dossier at the Committee stage.
12. Through these contacts the aim is to follow the politics; try to track the compromises that are forming within and between the Political Groups and to indirectly influence the key MEPs around the dossier.
13. A key document to get hold of is the voting list. These can be obtained from the Committee Secretariat, and also from Political Group staff.
14. Check who tables which amendments as this is useful information for the dossier as it develops and also for future work. It is also possible to go back to past Committee work and analyse the amendments tabled; this will give you a very good source of information on MEP and Group positions.
15. Follow the voting numbers in Committee and try to help the MEP as much as you can in the numbers game; this will be appreciated.
16. Remember that the Committee could also be preparing for a trilogue negotiation with the Council. Your position needs to be in the Parliament negotiating position to have any chance of being in a final compromise; and the Parliament's position is often established before the Committee vote.
17. If a text voted by Committee has been agreed in trilogues for a first reading agreement then the Groups and Plenary have very limited room to change anything (for fear of undoing the compromise), so working with the Committee is vital.
18. Committee work is all about compromise between and within Political Groups (much more than nationalities) so you need to show awareness of compromise solutions.

3. Plenary stage

1. Follow the agenda and your item very carefully. Keep in contact with key people close to the dossier to see if it remains on the agenda: things change.
2. In preparation for the Plenary you need to keep in contact with the Political Groups to see what deals are being made or amendments prepared. This should be done during the Group week that proceeds the Plenary week and then also during the Plenary week itself.
3. The Plenary week is an active week for negotiating between Groups and things change very quickly - it is best to be physically present or in contact with someone close to the dossier to keep updated.
4. Proposing amendments at Plenary is by Political Groups, a Committee, or a Group of at least 40 MEPs.
5. As at Committee stage, try to get hold of a voting list.
6. Again the numbers game is important - at the level of the individual MEPs but more importantly at the level of the Political Groups. Track voting history on similar issues on Votewatch.eu to try and understand the dynamics at play.

7. At the Plenary stage the rapporteur, Committee coordinators and shadows remain key figures as they try to steer their Committee compromise deal through Plenary. They will try to keep their own Group in line with what they agreed, on the Group's behalf, in the Committee stage. Whilst a number of amendments will be tabled at this stage, the majority are merely political posturing and not substantive amendments. It is however always interesting to assess who is tabling what amendments (also at Committee stage) as these are key indications of their positions and the interests to which they are playing - all of which could come in useful in future work with the Parliament.

> **Check individual MEP voting records:**
> www.votewatch.eu/cx_search_results.php?tip_cautare=search_meps&search_pressed=1
>
> **Check Political Group voting records:**
> www.votewatch.eu/cx_epg_votes.php

An example of Votewatch.eu data is below with the screenshot taken from their website - in this case simply the first MEP in alphabetical order. This screenshot gives you an excellent indication of the wealth of information you have at your fingertips when it comes to working with individual MEPs, National Delegations, the Political Groups and through all of this with the Parliament as a whole.

Figure 8.2: Example MEP profile on Votewatch.eu

MEP » Lars ADAKTUSSON		Sweden	Parliamentary activities		Disclaimer
	Start of mandate:	01.07.2014	Participation in roll-call votes: **85.03%**	460 out of 541 votes in the plenary. Ranking: 574th	
	Last name:	ADAKTUSSON			
	First name:	Lars	Loyalty to political group: **83.04%**	382 out of 460 votes Ranking: 632nd	
	Born:	06.08.1955, Jönköping	Loyalty to national party: **100.00%**	460 out of 460 votes Ranking: 1st	
	Group:	Group of the European People's Party (Christian Democrats)			
			Last updated: 27.03.2015		Info
	Party:	Kristdemokraterna			
	Committees:	⧉ Foreign Affairs (Member) ⧉ Human Rights (Member) ⧉ Transport and Tourism (Substitute)	Reports as a Rapporteur:	0	
			Reports as a Shadow Rapporteur:	0	
	Delegations:	⧉ Delegation for relations with Afghanistan (Member) ⧉ Delegation for relations with Bosnia and Herzegovina, and Kosovo (Substitute)	Opinions as a Rapporteur:	0	
			Opinions as a Shadow Rapporteur:	0	
			Reports amended:	3	
ALL VOTES KEY VOTES		All policy areas ▼ Choose date	Parliamentary questions (PQs):	1	
Found 548 entries					

Source: www.votewatch.eu

From the screenshot in Figure 8.2 there are a number of important elements if you are working with the Parliament. The MEP's loyalty to their Political Group and their national party is very important information. You can even break this data down into policy areas and individual Plenary voting patterns, providing solid empirical evidence to base your work on. This individual homepage provides a goldmine of information that you can use to really understand each and every MEP you seek to work with.

One further piece of information that can be seen on Votewatch.eu relates to the issue of **voting cohesion** within the Political Groups - because the more cohesive the Groups, the more important it is to work with them (as opposed to individual MEPs), and the Delegations that compose them. The Votewatch.eu report, *Voting in the 2009-2014 European Parliament*, shows that there is very high cohesion within the Political Group voting habits in the Parliament. Votewatch.eu finds that transnational political voting is higher than it has ever been - and significantly more important than national voting. There is only one policy area that does not fit this pattern, i.e. where national voting predominates: agriculture. This shows that working with the Political Groups, and their key Delegations and MEPs in Committees, is vitally important: the Political Groups vote along Group lines and not along national lines.

A second key aspect of this analysis of Plenary voting is the coalitions that form in the Parliament - something to be very aware of when trying to work with the different Political Groups. Figure 8.3 shows that the ALDE Group, despite being the third largest group in the Parliament, has been on the 'winning' side more than any other Group. This has led Votewatch.eu to name it the 'Kingmaker' Group in the EP.

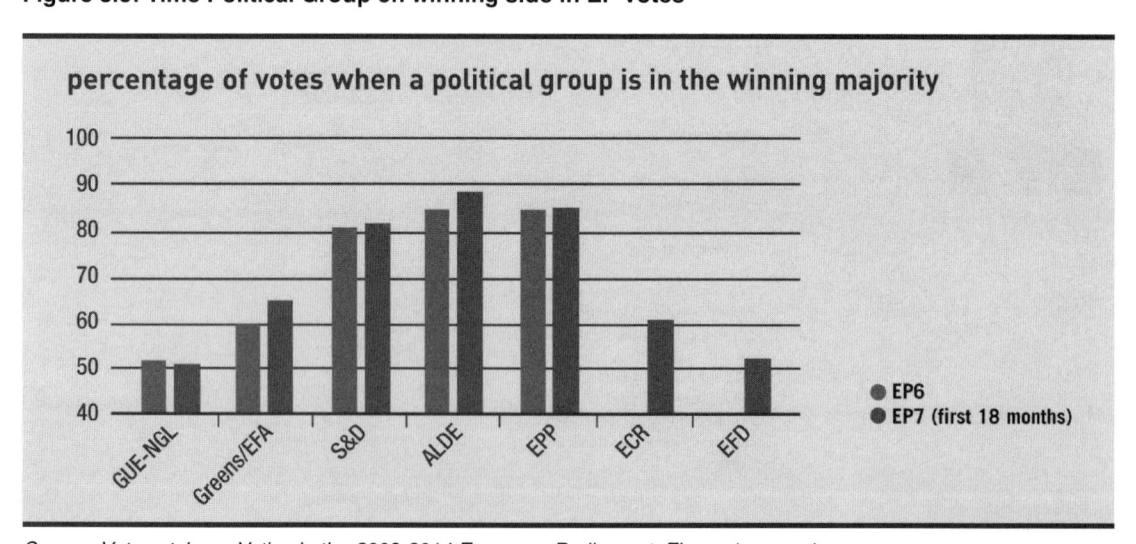

Figure 8.3: Time Political Group on winning side in EP votes

Source: Votewatch.eu, Voting in the 2009-2014 European Parliament, Figure 1, page 4

This is taken one step further with their analysis of coalitions in the EP, which can be seen in Table 8.5 below.

Table 8.5: Voting coalitions in the EP

the extent to which political groups vote with one another

Voting coalitions in the 2004-2009 European Parliament (full term)
All roll-call votes (6,149 votes)

	GUE/NGL	G/EFA	SOC	ALDE	EPP-ED	UEN
G/EFA	74%					
SOC	62%	70%				
ALDE	52%	62%	75%			
EPP-ED	41%	50%	70%	77%		
UEN	45%	49%	63%	71%	81%	
IND/DEM	41%	39%	40%	45%	51%	54%

Voting coalitions in the 2009-2014 European Parliament (first 18 months)
All roll call votes July 2009 – December 2010 (1,351 votes)

	GUE/NGL	G/EFA	S&D	ALDE	EPP	ECR
G/EFA	74%					
S&D	61%	77%				
ALDE	52%	69%	78%			
EPP	38%	53%	69%	77%		
ECR	35%	40%	47%	59%	65%	
EFD	34%	37%	44%	50%	57%	58%

Source: Votewatch.eu, Voting in the 2009-2014 European Parliament, Figure 2, page 5

The data from Votewatch.eu are essential reading for any serious engagement with the Parliament as they provide a fundamental level of understanding of the likely politics that will occur on any given dossier.

1. With this in mind, try to help the MEPs that support you to build coalitions and alliances – the support of one Political Group is never sufficient to get a majority in Plenary.

2. Always remember that an MEP will be interested in media stories at the Plenary stage of the process (more so than at the Committee stage), so any opportunities you can develop will be warmly welcomed.

8.4.3 People

At the level of people in the Parliament it is important to make a series of specific comments and recommendations about the different actors involved. As with the other two institutions, it is again very useful to try and map out all your potential contacts in the Parliament. To take things one step further, you can then use Votewatch.eu to ensure that your interaction with any MEP is based on a solid picture of who they are and how they work.

1. MEPs

1. Understand how MEPs work - this will help you work with them.
2. Develop long-term relationships with MEPs to foster mutual trust. Things can change quickly in the Parliament and long-term trusted contacts are the only way to mitigate this and keep updated.

3. Group politics: identify the MEPs who 'call the shots' in a European, or national, Political Group. This will entail understanding the National Delegation dynamics. Take a look at Votewatch.eu where they present the convergence/loyalty of each national party to the European Political Group it belongs to. The data can be broken down by Political Group, country, policy area and time interval, thus helping you easily identify the national parties who would be most/least likely to defect in a vote on a particular issue and, consequently, whom to approach.
4. National Delegations are important actors and need to be engaged with and understood; this is especially the case for specific policy areas in which they can play a big role. They might not have the numbers to carry a vote but they have influence in the Political Group - and they also have inside information on all the deals being done there.
5. Identify opinion leaders and 'builders' of compromises within and between the Political Groups.
6. Meet the major players before, when and after you need to work with them.
7. Be aware that there will likely be turf wars between various factions trying to influence and guide the rapporteur (and other key actors), as much from the outside world as from inside the Parliament itself.
8. Check whether an MEP is from a national governing party or the opposition as this could have an influence on their activity in the Parliament.
9. MEPs are elected by being placed on national party lists in their Member States; therefore (especially in the run up to elections), the National Delegations and their links to national capitals are very important.
10. The constituency link is less strong at the EU level - as most MEPs will have large shared areas that they cover (and some are national lists) - but MEPs still like the local links if possible.
11. Know what else is on the table of the MEP at the moment you meet them; likewise know the political context of the moment.
12. You will likely only have a short time to convince an MEP, so you need to be concise and to the point. Knowing what they need, and when they need it, is essential.
13. Try to present suggested amendments to an MEP as this could help them in their task - along with justifications to help them sell and support your suggestion.

2. MEPs' Assistants

1. Develop long-term relationships with MEPs' assistants as they are vital gatekeepers to the MEPs themselves.
2. You need to identify the role the assistant plays within an MEP's office - are they keeping the agenda, providing policy expertise, etc? This can be very important.
3. You can find MEPs' assistants on the Parliament website - and you can search by assistant or by MEP: www.europarl.europa.eu/members/expert/assistantAlphaOrder.do?language=EN. Or you can find the name of the assistants on Votewatch.eu, on the profile page of each MEP.

3. **Committee Secretariat**

    1. Developing a long-term relationship with Committee Secretariat staff is an excellent investment.
    2. Committee Secretariat staff have a very good understanding of the state of a dossier, timetable information, voting lists, information on technical details and sticking points, and in some cases they have a strong influence over the content and direction of a file.
    3. Committee officials often have a good institutional memory of how things work in the Committee - they will be able to tell you about the dynamics, inter-personal relations and key drivers in the Committee as they follow it every day.

4. **Political Group staff**

    1. Political Group staff are often somewhat overlooked in contacts with the Parliament, which is a lost opportunity to network and get information.
    2. Political Group staff work very closely with the MEPs in their Committee - so they have a privileged position for information and influence.
    3. Political Group staff have detailed information about the workings of the Committee and of the politics surrounding all files on the table.
    4. Political Group staff have privileged access to voting lists and other internal information and documents.
    5. You should work with all Groups - you never know when you will need them.
    6. Political Group staff are often senior experts with competence in the subjects of their Committee.

8.4.4 Communication

1. The Parliament is very unwieldy from a news perspective. There can be multiple press releases on the same day from the Parliament and MEPs on the same subject. It is important to know what to respond to, and how.

2. Strasbourg is very useful as you have access to a lot of people in a short period of time within the same buildings. MEPs are interested in the dossiers under discussion that week, so communicate on these.

3. Brussels is for communicating on dossiers under discussion in Committee, as well as other issues you may have that are of interest to the MEP.

4. Your communication will have to strike a balance between the technical and political and also between the European, national and local dimensions.

5. Provide short, concise and detailed information that has strong emotional/political/media content.

6. If possible provide real life cases and easy to use information for MEPs in their Committee and Political Group work.

7. MEPs will need different angles to the information from the other institutions.

8. Facts and figures should have relevant practical illustrations of their meaning, with very clear explanations and an identification of what this means for the MEP.

9. Positions presented to MEPs need to be well-argued and be something that an MEP could use in their interactions with other MEPs and stakeholders.

10. Do not use too much technical jargon: the argument needs to be crystal clear. Remember that Parliament reports are not usually technical or jargon-filled.

11. Try to link your information to the institutional/constituency interests of the MEP.

12. Generally you will not have much time to convince an MEP as meetings can be very short. You need to get your message across in a clear and concise manner, whilst being able to elaborate if required.

13. A relationship built on trust is more important than what you are trying to sell. If you can consistently back up your information over a period of time you will be able to create a relationship of confidence in which you are a trusted source of information.

14. MEPs, like other officials identified in this chapter, are most susceptible to face to face meetings and good written material - but MEPs also engage in dinners and lunches (in Strasbourg and Brussels), so more events can be planned.

15. You can also raise awareness of your issues with MEPs through exhibitions (e.g. photographic), events (e.g. report launches) and informal lunches at the Parliament or in and around Brussels/ Strasbourg.

16. Do not mass mail MEPs - this does not work very well.

17. Share reports and interesting information with them by e-mail: much like the Commission, you never know what might be of use/interest to them. MEPs and officials in the Parliament are the most open to informal meetings and coffees.

18. Written briefings should keep to the one-page rule to be most effective.

19. Never try to impose your views/ideas or positions on an MEP: you are there to provide information and justifications.

As this section attests, working with the Parliament requires much more work, but this is a function of the greater opportunities and the more dynamic nature of decision-making in the Parliament. Something worth bearing in mind when working with the Parliament is that most MEPs are very heavily solicited by external stakeholders, and as a result of this you need to be able to differentiate yourself by the quality of your information, knowledge and timing - to make yourself a long-term contact who an MEP contacts themselves when they want/need information. The key elements to draw from this are listed below in Table 8.6.

Table 8.6: Working with the Parliament: Key points

1. Know the MEPs you are working with - do your homework (use Votewatch.eu).
2. Create a good network of contacts around your dossier, including the MEPs, assistants, Committee staff and Group staff.
3. Always remember the numbers game: this means you will have to work across Groups and nationalities.
4. You need to provide technical information but package it for political use. You need to balance European, national and local arguments.
5. You should only try to work with the key MEPs on any given dossier - which should be 20-30. Mass contacts and mailings are only actions of last resort.
6. You will always need to try and work with: rapporteur, Political Group coordinators and shadows, so try to build up long-term contacts in your key Committees.
7. Work with the Parliament Calendar; get a copy to take around with you.
8. Never forget the media and how you can get them involved (national and European).
9. Understand the structures, dynamics and politics of the Groups in the Parliament.
10. Know the Delegations within the Groups and within the Parliament as they are very influential players both in Brussels and in national capitals.
11. When you have a 'live' issue, be very attentive to any changes - things move quickly towards the trilogue negotiations and/or Plenary votes.
12. Be clear, accurate, concise and direct with MEPs.
13. Always build for the long-term in all your contacts in the Parliament.

9. Practical Guide to Working with EU Decision-Making

By Alan Hardacre

Section 2 of this book detailed how the two main levels of EU decision-making work, outlining all the key stages and key actors within the Ordinary Legislative Procedure (OLP) (summarised in Table 5.4) and then Delegated and Implementing Acts (D&I Acts) (summarised in Table 6.5). Those chapters are fundamental building blocks to understanding how to work with EU decision-making, as are the chapters on the individual institutions in Section 1.

One of the most frequent poor lobbying practices by stakeholders is failing to understand the decision-making processes and procedures. There is no excuse for not getting this right. Section 2, by describing how the decision-making procedures work goes a long way to addressing this issue, and this chapter will complement it with further recommendations and guidance. This chapter will necessarily build on the individual institutional sections of Chapter 8, because working with EU decision-making is about working with the EU institutions within defined contexts and circumstances. As with the last chapter there are a number of fundamental rules that are applicable, to both OLP and D&I Acts, so the chapter starts with these.

> There is no one size fits all solution for how to work with EU decision-making: no two dossiers are the same, politics change, people change and you will need to change with them.
>
> One thing, however, is fundamental: **you must know the procedures inside out if you want to work effectively with EU decision-making.**

9.1 Working with EU Decision-Making: The fundamentals

EU decision-making, as Section 2 highlighted, is a complex interaction of the three core institutions and other EU bodies and agencies around rules and procedures and informal practices. There are usually a number of interests at play, and all working, on any given dossier at the same time, each with their own objectives and motivations. The first place to start when considering working with the two levels of EU decision-making is a series of **Working with EU Decision-Making Guidelines**. The overarching guidelines for working with EU decision-making are as shown in Table 9.1.

Table 9.1: Fundamentals for Working with EU Decision-Making

1. Know the decision-making procedure you are working with inside-out. Know the procedural/informal aspects, timelines, possibilities, roles of different actors.
2. Know, and work to, the procedural timetables: be as early as possible. Time your interventions according to the institutional timelines.
3. Know who can do what for you in the decision-making procedure: know the key people on the dossier for information, influence and guidance.
4. You need to monitor developments closely and establish a good network of contacts. You need timely information to be able to act.
5. Stay alert to new developments - always think through what they mean for you, for the key actors in the process and for other key stakeholders: be prepared.
6. Be clear about your objectives and what you want to achieve. Know that you will be unlikely to get 100% of what you want in EU decision-making.
7. Evidence-based work is essential: make sure you do your homework on every aspect of your work in decision-making and bring the evidence with you.
8. Be prepared and flexible: pre-empt counter-arguments and positions and prepare yourself - you are never working alone.
9. Revisit your ideas, strategy, approach and communication on a constant basis: things change and you need to change with them.
10. Working with EU decision-making is in fact a series of back-to-back mini-campaigns - and these can take time (sometimes years), so be patient.
11. Follow the politics very carefully: this is where issues can change, compromises emerge and decisions get taken.
12. Tailor your message to each actor in the procedure but keep a core consistent message that identifies you.
13. Determine where and when to best use your resources: a strategy may be good but resources are still needed to implement it, so choose carefully.
14. You should always be working with the three institutions as they will all be involved in some way.
15. Always think about the potential aftermath of your lobbying: remember, decision-making is also for the long-term.
16. Always be open and transparent in your dealings with the institutions.

The Guidelines in Table 9.1 are fundamental to any work with EU decision-making and will obviously need to be used and respected in line with the rules devised in the previous chapter on how to deal with each EU institution. Three core elements from Table 9.1 require a little more explanation;

1. Guideline No. 9 in the table. One of the most important aspects of working with EU decision-making is that you must never hesitate to revisit your ideas, your position papers, your research, your communication, your target audiences – in short every aspect of your approach and objectives – and make changes if necessary, which will often be the case. Working with EU decision-making is a very fluid and dynamic environment in which you will have to work with

the three core institutions and a number of other engaged stakeholders all at the same time over a long period of time. This can generate beneficial synergies and momentum just as much as it can create divisions and brick walls. Hence the need to constantly evaluate what is being done and whether it needs to be changed.

2. The best way to work with EU decision-making is to be flexible and adaptable enough to see when a change is needed, and then organised and knowledgeable enough to implement the change at the right time. In this respect it is vitally important to watch out for new issues that might impact your position, become connected to your position or even be traded-off against your position - all of which is usually in the politics of a dossier. Whilst this flexibility is crucial in working with the OLP, or D&I Acts, it is also essential to maintain a consistent core message that does not change across all your audiences and stakeholders. If you are seen to be changing your main position every time the wind changes direction in Brussels, you will very quickly lose credibility and not be taken seriously - and the wind often does change direction several times during the lifespan of any OLP or D&I Acts dossier.

3. There is one final aspect of working with EU decision-making that is important to highlight. It relates to the availability of information and how and when 'decisions' or 'agreements' are taken or made. There are many transparent aspects of EU decision-making, such as European Commission Green Papers, European Parliament Committee meetings, and Council meetings streamed live on the Internet - but these are rarely the places where decisions and negotiations take place. For this reason it is important to stay close to your dossier at all times by knowing good contact people connected to the file. When you work on a specific dossier you will soon discover the Brussels 'village' effect, because you will likely find that institutionally (and in terms of major stakeholders) there are rarely more than 30-40 key people working on a single file. Within this circle, information will flow with fluidity and you need to be connected.

9.2 Working with OLP: First reading

Working successfully with OLP will, in reality, be a number of back-to-back campaigns (Table 9.1, Guideline 10) that all try to build on previous successes, or learn from previous setbacks. This used to be much more the case when Codecision dossiers went through two and three readings, but even with over 85% of files now being agreed in first reading you will still have to run a number of back-to-back campaigns to be successful. Working with OLP can be a drawn out process, and things can happen at short notice, meaning that patience and vigilance are always required in equal measure. In addition, working with OLP is largely based on the delivery of information and expertise in order to modify proposals, as opposed to trying to kill them - the notion of consensus that was detailed in all the institutional chapters (Chapters 1-3). And, finally, working with OLP will entail having to find out information from negotiations that take place behind closed doors, because for all the transparency that exists, OLP relies on informal meetings and negotiations to find agreement. These are just some of the challenges of working with OLP that will be addressed in this section.

In the following pages we will look at how to work with the three different stages of the OLP: first reading (Chapter 9.2), second reading (9.3) and third reading (9.4). All three phases require different approaches, information, communication and engagement. The most attention will obviously be devoted to the first reading stage given the fact that you should always engage with a file at the earliest possible moment and also because so many files are concluded in first reading.

Key documents

1. **Commission proposal** - basis for all discussions.
2. **Commission Impact Assessment** - evidence base for discussions.
3. **Parliament draft Committee report** - usually basis for trilogue negotiations.
4. **Council WP texts** - usually the basis for trilogue negotiations.

The principle of 'the earlier the better' is especially valid because you need to establish yourself as a key stakeholder at the very beginning of the first reading. Firstly, this is because there is a high chance of the dossier being agreed in first reading, and secondly, because should the dossier go any further, you will need to have established contacts to work with. Overall in the OLP procedure the first reading is the key opportunity to get your views across to MEPs, the Commission and the Member States. It is here where changes can be made and where points of principle need to be won. After first reading the debate narrows and closes down, and your room for action and influence also shrinks accordingly. First reading is not your only chance to work with a dossier but it will always be your main chance. The institutions, through the OLP procedure, are aiming to conclude the best possible outcome at the earliest possible stage - this is always the starting logic on a dossier - so it makes sense to bring your arguments and evidence to the table as soon as possible.

Following OLP

Phone - map your contacts and call them.
E-mail - can be less invasive and used for less urgent/sensitive issues.
Meetings - using meetings is useful for passing on information.

Trade association/federations

Legislative trackers:
Legislative Observatory
www.europarl.europa.eu/oeil

Pre-Lex
http://ec.europa.eu/prelex/apcnet.cfm?CL=en

RSS Feeds/Press/Alerts
Monitoring service
Events/Networking/Contacts

Following OLP in detail will mean trying to follow all the formal and informal developments - notably the latter. The box on the left highlights the best ways to try and follow the OLP. The legislative trackers are good for background information and an overview of the file but they can be slightly out of date and they do not cover any informal aspects, such as trilogues for example. Likewise all RSS Feeds, Google Alerts and the press are only likely to inform you of when something happened - not when it is going to happen - and obviously if you want to influence the process you need to know things in advance. The single best way to do this is, having identified and mapped all the key actors on the dossier, to try to call around and find out the information you want from your established contacts around the file.

A very good source of information will always be the European associations/federations. They should be closely plugged into their key dossiers, and they have extremely good contacts and networks of information that usually enable them to have the informal information at the right times.

It is clear that working with OLP is often about getting the latest information as soon as possible. This is something that frequently happens via Chinese whispers because much EU decision-making takes place in informal settings - and the information slowly but surely leaks outwards until it is common knowledge. Having the right information at the right time is, however, only useful if you are able to understand it, its context and implications, enabling you to then act on the information in the right way.

A further important point is that an OLP file, through the negotiations that take place within the institutions and then between the institutions, is often an **accumulated compromise**. This is another reason why working from the earliest possible moment, and with all three and not just one institution, is essential. Once these compromises take shape, they get harder and harder to change as the process advances without unravelling prior agreements. This point is particularly valid when it comes to the informal trilogue negotiations in first reading, particularly with regard to the stage in the Parliament's internal decision-making when they take place. As identified in Chapter 5.4, these informal agreements can be made before Committee votes take place, which can make changing things from there on very difficult. These negotiations are therefore vitally important to follow for all first reading dossiers. Firstly it is in these meetings that the two legislators, along with the Commission, try to find a compromise position for a final text - possibly trading things off against each other to reach their final compromise. It is for this reason that working with both legislators is essential otherwise your positions risk being negotiated away as concessions.

> **Informal trilogues**
>
> Possibly the most important moment in first reading is the informal trilogue negotiations, when the institutions try to negotiate a final agreement.
> It is important to find out:
>
> 1. when they will take place
> 2. what the issues in the negotiations are
> 3. what the outcome is
>
> You can follow this by:
> 1. Having good contacts in the three institutions
> 2. Looking at COREPER agendas to see when reports are made on trilogues

Secondly, it is important that your position, and evidence, has been presented to the legislators before they start their trilogue negotiations, because when you step in to the decision-making process after the start of such an accumulated compromise, your position may no longer be possible to negotiate. For the Parliament this is very important because it can mean that, through informal trilogue agreements, certain issues can no longer be discussed in the Committee, by the Groups or in the Plenary. If a rapporteur strikes a deal with the Council and the Commission on a first reading agreement during the Committee stage then that text needs to stay unchanged (except for minor points) during the Committee vote, the Group week for tabling compromises in Plenary and then through the Plenary vote.

A successful OLP file needs consensus and compromise within each institution and also between the institutions which means that coalition-formation is important between Member States, within the Parliament and by, and between, stakeholders. As the previous chapter outlined, coalitions are important to understand, monitor and work with. Although they will not be explicitly discussed in their own right in this chapter, it is always worth remembering that representatives from national parliaments, the Committee of the Regions (CoR), the European Economic and Social Committee (EESC) and the staff of the EU Agencies can all play a meaningful role in the OLP, and should not simply be forgotten.

> **First reading**
>
> - no time limit
> - open debate
> - principles need to be won
> - all issues on table
> - wide range of actors engaged
> - any amendments possible
> - strategy to cover three institutions, key stakeholders and media
> - simple majority in Parliament
> - QMV in Council

For an average OLP file you will have to identify about 30-40 key people across the Parliament, Commission and Council. In this sense working with first reading can be a very small world - and you soon discover that Brussels is a village. This is why the previous chapters have stressed that maintaining trust, credibility, confidentiality, integrity and honesty is important at all times. It is also why the Transparency Register is now fundamental to a stakeholder's activities in Brussels. Within these key institutional contacts, notably from the three core institutions, you need to be aware that they will work very closely together and share information on a frequent basis.

As an OLP dossier proceeds, you will discern a clear context and structure to the debate and negotiation and this is something you will have to take into account in your actions. Bearing in mind that you will not be able to influence everything in an OLP file, you will also need to prioritise and act accordingly, and be ready to revisit these priorities regularly as the context changes. This will also entail understanding the broader OLP environment and all the stakeholders that are engaged on the dossier on which you are working; and you will also need to know the positions of the key external stakeholders, notably European associations and federations.

These general strategic points are outlined on the next page in Table 9.2 on the general guidance for working with OLP first reading.

In a general strategic sense first reading is a good opportunity to work with the EU institutions and to put your points across to them, from a variety of different angles and through a variety of different mediums. Knowing the procedures and timelines will allow you to get to the right person at the right time.

Table 9.2: Ordinary Legislative Procedure first reading: General guidance

1. Act as early as possible - it is essential to be as early as possible in first reading to influence ideas before they hit paper; create networks and become identified with the subject.
2. You should work with the Commission first during the IA phase, but be aware that the Parliament and Council can influence the Commission heavily in its thinking stages (Parliament Own Initiative Report or Council Conclusions for example).
3. Work with all three institutions at once: by keeping them all informed you keep in touch and find out more information, and they will always influence each other.
4. Remember that first reading agreements involve inter-institutional negotiations - so make sure your position does not get used as a negotiating chip; you need to ensure the support of both legislators (and Commission).
5. Follow trilogues very carefully - it is essential to understand the negotiations as they unfold. This means knowing the politics.
6. Know the procedure/timelines: you need to know when things will happen in each institution as windows of opportunity can easily be missed.
7. Know each institutional procedure: you need to know all the possibilities and margin for manoeuvre as this will give you more opportunities.
8. Know the political/institutional context - you need to show an awareness of the context and situation of the dossier you are working on.
9. Be involved whatever your position as things can change very quickly.
10. First reading is vital to set up your engagement campaign and establish contacts.
11. Set your objectives for the campaign; be realistic and clear about what you want.
12. Create your supporting material so it is ready for when you need to use (tailor) it.
13. Map all the stakeholders you could need - you never know when you will need them.

9.2.1 Actors: First reading

When it comes to the key actors at first reading it is a question of combining the people analysis in the previous chapter on the individual institutions. The core people can be summarised as shown in Figure 9.1 on the next page.

Figure 9.1 shows the key actors who will take part in the trilogues. Working with any OLP file, it will be essential to try and find at least one good contact within that inner circle of decision-making to be able to get the latest informal information. Figure 9.1 also nicely illustrates the need to engage simultaneously with these three institutional levels when your file is active - as all three will be working on it at the same time with varying levels of influence on each other. Aside from this in terms of people:

Figure 9.1: Ordinary Legislative Procedure first reading: Key actors

Council	Parliament	Commission
Presidency Rep. WP or COREPER General-Secretariat	Rapporteur Shadow rapporteurs **Trilogues**	HoU on dossier Lead official on dossier Secretariat-General
Big MS Key MS on dossier National capitals Brussels-based national associations in key MS Other key national stakeholders National media	Chair of responsible Committee Coordinators Key MEPs in Committee Political Groups National Delegations Political Groups staff MEP assistants National/European media	Other DGs & Services Cabinet of lead DG Other Cabinets

1. One or two close contacts on a dossier can be sufficient to keep you updated.
2. The key actors on the dossier will work very closely together across institutions.
3. Use a multiple-pronged approach as there are different people who can assist in OLP. You will need to establish on a case-by-case basis who to work with and when to work with them.
4. Never neglect the role of the Commission in first reading. OLP is formally about the co-legislators but the Commission sits in all trilogue meetings, in all Council meetings and all Parliament meetings. It is hugely influential in its role of mediator and facilitator. Keep the Commission informed of your position throughout the process, and remember that it will always usually have the most up-to-date information.
5. The fact that the number of core people working on a dossier is so small means that transparency, honesty and integrity are essential - your information will flow quickly between institutions.
6. Always keep the long-term in mind; this small circle will likely follow these issues for some years to come, so you will need to work with them again.
7. You will likely need to establish two distinct networks: one network, or set of contacts, for information, and another for influencing.
8. Always try to canvass the key people you are in contact with for their opinions. They know the dossier and the people involved in it better than anyone else, so they usually have very good ideas on how to proceed/approach things.

9.2.2 Communication: First reading

Communication was dealt with in the last chapter in relation to each institution. There are however a few rules that are useful to consider specifically for OLP:

1. You need to tailor your messages for each meeting, even within the institutions. This does not necessarily mean having a new briefing paper/position paper or amendment, but it does mean having an appreciation of the different people you interact with and what they need/want in relation to the OLP file under discussion.
2. While you need to tailor your messages, you need to have a consistent core message and communication across, and between, the three institutions and all key stakeholders.
3. Prepare for all meetings thoroughly: background, evidence, political messages, context, procedure, timelines, etc.
4. Adapt your messages to the evolving public policy objectives and priorities. The debate will move and you need to move with it.
5. Always be short, concise and to the point. Make sure you employ user friendly language in your communication.
6. Use reasonable arguments that strive towards consensus and compromise with each institution and also between the institutions.
7. Do not try to defend (or promote) entrenched positions as this will only harm your credibility and damage your long-term work.
8. Have alternative positions/options/messages: i.e. if you see that plan A is not going to work, have a plan B.

9.3 Working with OLP: Second reading

If your file moves to second reading then the way you work with OLP will have to change in light of the new procedural situation and the fact that negotiations in first reading broke down. Whilst the key people will probably remain the same (only the Presidency is likely to change since it lasts just for six months), the way these key persons interact and the issues on which they interact will change significantly. The fact that a file has come into second reading means that it was not possible to find agreement in first reading, so the very first thing to find out is what the reasons were - why did the Parliament and the Council not agree at the first reading stage? You need to know:

1. What were the technical sticking points from first reading?
2. What were the political sticking points from first reading?
3. What were the interpersonal dynamics in first reading?
4. Who were the sources of resistance/support?
5. What were the compromises suggested that failed - and what was the last suggested compromise?

Answers to these five questions will be essential to understanding the inter-institutional dynamics and the issues on the table in second reading. At second reading, larger majorities are required in the Parliament for support, and the debate becomes more inter-institutional and based on principles.

It is much harder to make large or important changes at this stage, but it can be very important to work with the institutions on their second reading - especially if your issue is particularly contentious or one that could still be traded to find a final compromise.

Working with second reading also, almost by definition, requires that you have already worked with first reading. Only in this way will you have access to the right people and will you know the exact context and dynamics of the issue and the negotiations. The key points for working with second reading are in Table 9.3 below.

Table 9.3: Ordinary Legislative Procedure second reading: General guidance

1. The debate closes down, making it much harder to work at second reading.
2. Strict time limits are applicable: 3+1 months for each legislator. Your window of opportunity is very limited.
3. Amendments are under strict conditions and need absolute majority support to pass in the Parliament, making it more difficult to get positions supported.
4. The negotiation is about first reading issues, not new issues. Admissibility rules mean new issues are not allowed.
5. Because only previous amendments, and new ones relating to modifications by the Council, are admissible this makes your engagement in first reading even more important. If you did not make your point then, it is too late now.
6. The debate in Parliament tends to be less about content and more about inter-institutional issues - so knowing the history and having been proactive at first reading will help.
7. Re-establish links with all the key stakeholders from first reading, and reiterate positions and arguments.
8. Second reading agreements will need new elements of compromise to find a consensus: follow the informal discussions very closely to see what possible compromises could be.
9. Revise your objectives, strategy, communications and material from first reading - the game has changed and you need to change with it.

Table 9.3 makes it quite clear that working with second reading can be very limited and also very difficult, and even more so if you were not engaged with first reading. This highlights the importance of why you need to be engaged for the long-term with the EU institutions. Your work at second reading will largely depend on what you already did and worked on, for, against, with, etc. at first reading - and how you decided strategically to pursue this. Clearly you are now limited in time and also in terms of room for manoeuvre, so your objectives might need to be modified along with your approach and communication. Second reading is an entirely different procedure to first reading, so you need to adapt to the new situation as fast as possible.

9.3.1 Actors: Second reading

If you worked with first reading, second reading will be a question of continuing your working relationship with the contacts you have already established. MEPs, the Presidency, Member States and the Commission are very reluctant to work with anyone who was not active in the first reading. The key aspects in terms of people are:

1. Re-ignite first reading contacts.
2. Understand the new political context of your interactions.
3. Ask your contacts for their opinion on possible compromises and solutions and take all of these on board.
4. Keep a multi-pronged approach, but be aware that the room for manoeuvre is now limited.

9.3.2 Communication: Second reading

Much like the issue of people, the majority of communication will be based on what you did at first reading, and will build from there in second reading. There should, however, be a few changes:

1. You need to review your communication and materials for second reading in order to take account of the inter-institutional and political focus that has likely taken prominence.
2. You will need to be more political at second reading; you will need to show awareness of the wider context or your lack of understanding will dent your credibility.
3. Tailor your materials and messages to the new political and inter-institutional context.
4. The key is now inter-institutional compromise.

In essence it is unlikely that you will need to do the same level of convincing in second reading because the positions will already be defined and will have been defended. Your job is more to stay tuned into the negotiations and continue to support those actors who you worked with in first reading.

9.4 Working with OLP: Third reading

If the file you are working on fails to find an agreement at second reading, the first thing is again to understand why this happened - something that will be much more transparent and obvious than in first reading. To start with, the divisive issues were already known at first reading and simply could not be resolved. As with second reading it is therefore essential to understand:

1. Why was a compromise not possible?
2. Who/what was blocking the compromise - where was the resistance/support?
3. What were the proposed compromise texts that failed?

These three questions will help you situate third reading. The very first thing to note about working with third reading is that only last ditch attempts for successful changes should be attempted, and any expectations should be watered down. If you have not won over support for your views before third reading, your chances of winning support now are very slim. Third reading is all about inter-institutional dynamics and compromise - the arguments have been around since first reading and the positions are usually very clear. The key, as for second reading, is to find the inter-institutional compromise that has proven impossible to reach during the two previous readings. The main elements of working with third reading are in Table 9.4 below.

Table 9.4: Ordinary Legislative Procedure third reading: General Guidance

1. It is not easy to influence or obtain information at this stage of OLP; it is therefore very difficult to work with third reading.
2. The debate has been reduced to inter-institutional negotiation.
3. The issues and positions are usually common knowledge now; the key is an inter-institutional agreement/compromise position.
4. At this stage it is unlikely that the Council or Parliament will need, or be interested in, external views as the issues will be well known.
5. It is essential to try and get information through the participants in the trilogues, which reduces contact down to a small number of people.

Once a file gets to third reading it will probably have been worked on for at least three years, with the majority of the same people still in the negotiating room. For this reason the contact networks, channels of influence, coalitions, positions, arguments, blocking positions, etc. are all known. The discussion is no longer a technical issue-based one: it is all about the legislators trying to find a compromise that means no one is seen to lose face and that is amenable to all. It is for this reason that working with third reading can be very difficult - you can only really re-iterate your previous positions. If your key issue is still on the table you will obviously need to work with your key contacts again, but more from the perspective of getting information than from giving them anything new (if they supported you in first and second reading it is quite likely they will continue to support you). The key, for most stakeholders at this stage of the OLP procedure is to get information out of the informal procedures that make up third reading.

Time is also limited in the third reading stage, to six (+ two) weeks to form the Conciliation Committee and six (+ two) weeks for the Committee to find an agreement (or not). In essence, the majority of these 12 weeks will be spent negotiating in trilogues in order to try and find a compromise amendable to both legislators.

9.4.1 Actors: Third reading

Much like second reading the key actors and the networks remain very much as they were - and will simply need to be reactivated - but as the dossier is a political hot subject, a number of high-level political figures enter into the discussions. When a proposal gets into third reading, the Presidency will have changed several times. If there have been elections for the European Parliament during the negotiations on the file, the main contact persons within this institution might be different.

9.4.2 Communication: Third reading

When it comes to communication at third reading, the options are very limited because, as highlighted before, the positions are well-known and the debate is inter-institutional. Communication is now very much about personal contacts and getting information from the negotiations. If you are still actively involved on a live issue in third reading, then the key is to make sure you communicate with your contacts to increase the chances that they continue to support your issue - again whilst trying to always understand what possible compromises are on the table and how your issue could get linked.

9.5 Working with Delegated and Implementing Acts: New Comitology

Part of the long-term nature of working with EU decision-making relates to the fact that once you have finished working with OLP it is quite likely that there will be tasks delegated to the Commission that will require D&I Acts - so your work needs to start again (or continue). Given that the devil is often in the detail, and the impacts of D&I are much more localised, it is just as (if not more) important to work with D&I Acts. Chapter 6 outlined the procedures of these two different types of acts. The world of D&I Acts is a challenging one to work with, requiring solid procedural and technical knowledge, but it can also be very rewarding because here small changes can have important impacts. Despite the reputation of D&I Acts as being difficult to work with, on a general level one can say that:

1. The process is increasingly transparent and accessible, notably for Delegated Acts. Finding information and following the process is becoming more straightforward.
2. It offers more and more opportunities for stakeholders because of the shared powers of the legislators, especially the Parliament, though the volume of acts that have to be assessed is challenging.
3. One has more time than before, notably for Delegated Acts, because the extra control of the legislators takes longer.

Having outlined, in Chapter 6, the main actors and processes for D&I Acts, it is first possible to draw up some generic suggestions for how to approach and engage with both of these processes. Many of the comments in the previous part of this chapter, on OLP, remain valid for D&I Acts and should be read again with D&I Acts in mind (notably Table 9.1).

On the next page Table 9.5 outlines the basics of working with D&I Acts.

Table 9.5: Fundamentals for Working with Delegated & Implementing Acts

1. D&I Acts do not start in the implementation phase; they should be monitored and engaged with as of the legislative thinking phase.
2. Work with D&I Acts through OLP: small changes there can make an important difference later.
3. A good knowledge of the procedures for D&I Acts is essential - more so than for OLP because it is generally less well understood (by the Institutions as well).
4. You need to understand how D&I Acts work within the three main institutions and the exact roles that each can play.
5. Timing is essential for D&I Acts - the windows of opportunity are much smaller than those for OLP.
6. D&I Acts are inherently technical dossiers so you will need to have solid technical expertise to deliver, but packaged the right way for your different audiences.
7. D&I Acts (especially Delegated Acts) can also be political so do not neglect the importance of the politics that surrounds each dossier.
8. The circle of key actors is much reduced, so having long-standing contacts and networks can be invaluable.

The basics of working with D&I Acts build on all the work from the OLP procedure, especially in relation to contacts and networks, because invariably it is the same people within the institutions, especially the Commission, who will be working on D&I Acts after OLP. This is a clear illustration of how important engagement in OLP can be: if you have already established yourself as a transparent, honest and essential provider of information in OLP your task will be much easier with D&I Acts - but if you did not take the long-term view and made mistakes in OLP, working with D&I Acts can be very difficult.

One further horizontal element that is very useful in the context of working with D&I Acts is to understand the differences between the two types of acts. On the next page Table 9.6 outlines the differences that were described in Chapter 6, with a focus on the key elements we need to retain if working with D&I Acts.

Table 9.6 sets out a useful summary of the key elements of D&I Acts including the procedural information essential for working with both of them. Having outlined the key differences between and the fundamentals for working with D&I Acts, it is now possible to look at how we identify D&I Acts in legislative texts - an essential exercise before starting to work with them.

Table 9.6: Difference between Delegated and Implementing Acts

Implementing Acts (Article 291 TFEU)	Delegated Acts (Article 290 TFEU)
1. Routine implementation of EU legislation 2. Can only implement clearly defined tasks 3. Can be issues of general or individual scope	1. Sensitive implementation matters for the legislators 2. Can supplement, amend or delete non-essential elements of legislative act 3. Always issues of general scope
1. A binding framework - Implementing Acts Regulation 2. Horizontal framework - selection from two procedures (advisory and examination)	1. No binding framework - Common Understanding 2. No horizontal framework - objectives, content, scope and duration are decided on a case by case basis in each legislative act
1. Obligatory consultation of Comitology Committee 2. Committee = 1 representative of each MS (possible Observers like EU Agencies, EFTA Countries, etc.) 3. Chaired by Commission	1. No consultation of Comitology Committee 2. Probable use of Expert Groups, EU Agencies and other sources of information
Control by (Comitology Committee or Appeal Committee): 1. Advisory: Simple majority vote - non-binding opinion 2. Examination: Qualified majority vote (QMV) to approve Commission proposal 3. Appeal Committee: referrals from Committee dealt with by representatives at 'appropriate level'	Control by (EP and/or Council): 1. Veto - object to an individual Delegated Act on any grounds within the deadline set by the legislative act (usually 2+2 months) 2. Revocation - revoke the delegation of powers to the Commission altogether
Observations: 1. Special cases for Common Commercial Policy 2. Flexibility for the Commission, which MAY adopt the draft measures where there is no qualified majority against 3. Right of Scrutiny for EP and Council - at any time	Observations: 1. Parliament and Council on perfect equal footing 2. Both legislatures define the modalities of Delegated Acts, but can revoke the delegation afterwards without the other's consent

9.6 Identifying Delegated and Implementing Acts

The first place to start working with D&I Acts is in the final legislative text itself, which you will have been working with in OLP. For this there are a series of steps that need to be followed. When you have a legislative act in front of you, you need to address the following:

1. **The recitals**
   The recitals come at the front of the legislative text. They define the scope of the legislative act and its respective articles, and therefore form a sort of guidance note to national administrators (and anyone else who is interested) who will have to work with the legislation at the national level. There will always be at least one recital concerning Delegated Acts and one concerning Implementing Acts if they are part of the legislation. This can sometimes be useful to help understand what has been delegated, and why. This short read can give you some useful context.

2. **The Delegated or Implementing Acts article(s)**
   The next things to look for are the articles that outline the procedures under which either a Delegated or Implementing Act can be decided - these are usually three to four articles from the end of the legislative text. There will usually be one Implementing Act article that will describe the procedures that are to be used (Examination or Advisory). There will usually be three Delegated Act articles describing, firstly, the exercise of the delegation (duration, scope, etc.), secondly, revocation and, finally, one on objections to Delegated Acts. For example Article 40 of a text could be entitled 'Implementing Act', 40.1 will name the Committee to be used, 40.2 will identify the Advisory procedure and 40.3 will identify the Examination procedure. After that, Article 41 could be entitled 'Exercise of the delegation', Article 42 'Revocation of the delegation' and Article 43 'Objections to Delegated Acts'.

3. **The tasks that have been delegated**
   Once you know the Articles for Delegated and/or Implementing Acts you need to find references to these articles in the text because this is where the exact tasks delegated to the Commission are identified. For example you could find, in Article 5, a requirement for the Commission to draft a Delegated Act to modify some specific criteria (by amending or modifying) and this (in the example given above) will have an explicit reference to Article 41 - hence you know that it is a Delegated Act, and within Article 41 all the conditions will be explained.

If you follow these three steps you will have identified all the key elements of D&I Acts in the legislative text and be ready to work with them. To highlight the three stages above let's take the example of Regulation No. 995/2010: A Regulation laying down the obligations of operators who place timber and timber products on the market. Here we can see the three stages as follows:

Example recital

(28) The Commission should be empowered to adopt delegated acts in accordance with Article 290 of the Treaty on the Functioning of the European Union (TFEU) concerning the procedures for the recognition and withdrawal of recognition of monitoring organisations, concerning further relevant Risk Assessment criteria that may be necessary to supplement those already provided for in this Regulation and concerning the list of timber and timber products to which this Regulation applies. It is of particular importance that the Commission carry out appropriate consultations during its preparatory work, including at expert level.

> *Article 15*
> **Exercise of the delegation**
>
> 1. The power to adopt the delegated acts referred to in Articles 6(3), 8(7) and 14 shall be conferred on the Commission for a period of seven years from 2 December 2010. The Commission shall make a report in respect of the delegated powers not later than three months before the end of a three-year period after the date of application of this Regulation. The delegation of powers shall be automatically extended for periods of an identical duration, unless the European Parliament or the Council revokes it in accordance with Article 16.
> 2. As soon as it adopts a delegated act, the Commission shall notify it simultaneously to the European Parliament and to the Council.
> 3. The power to adopt delegated acts is conferred on the Commission subject to the conditions laid down in Articles 16 and 17.

> *Article 16*
> **Revocation of the delegation**
>
> 1. The delegation of powers referred to in Articles 6(3), 8(7) and 14 may be revoked at any time by the European Parliament or by the Council.
> 2. The institution which has commenced an internal procedure for deciding whether to revoke the delegation of powers shall endeavour to inform the other institution and the Commission within a reasonable time before the final decision is taken, indicating the delegated powers which could be subject to revocation and possible reasons for a revocation.
> 3. The decision of revocation shall put an end to the delegation of the powers specified in that decision. It shall take effect immediately or at a later date specified therein. It shall not affect the validity of the delegated acts already in force. It shall be published in the *Official Journal of the European Union*.

The recital clearly indicates the tasks that have been delegated to the Commission, and also how the Commission will go about preparing these, with the assistance of an Expert Group. We also find the articles dealing with the D&I Acts and the procedural information we need to know.

These four boxes for articles 15-18 (see also next page), three of them outlining Delegated Acts and one of them Implementing Acts, outline all the details of how the two types of acts can be formulated and what procedures apply. It is essential to know this information in advance - for example to see if there is an Expert Group mentioned in the recital, or to find the name of the Committee that will be used: all information that will be needed later in the work with D&I Acts.

Instead of presenting general guidance on both categories, this section will present guidance on how to work with D&I Acts separately, because it can be much more tailored and specific.

> *Article 17*
> **Objections to delegated acts**
>
> 1. The European Parliament or the Council may object to a delegated act within a period of two months from the date of notification. At the initiative of the European Parliament or the Council this period shall be extended by two months.
> 2. If, on expiry of that period, neither the European Parliament nor the Council has objected to the delegated act, it shall be published in the *Official Journal of the European Union* and shall enter into force on the date stated therein. The delegated act may be published in the *Official Journal of the European Union* and enter into force before the expiry of that period if the European Parliament and the Council have both informed the Commission of their intention not to raise objections.
> 3. If the European Parliament or the Council objects to a delegated act, the act shall not enter into force. The institution which objects shall state the reasons for objecting to the delegated act.

> *Article 18*
> **Committee**
>
> 1. The Commission shall be assisted by the Forest Law Enforcement Governance and Trade (FLEGT) Committee established under Article 11 of Regulation (EC) No. 2173/2005.
> 2. Where reference is made to this paragraph, Articles 5 and 7 of Decision 1999/468/EC shall apply, having regard to the provisions of Article 8 thereof.
> The period laid down in Article 5(6) of Decision 1999/468/EC shall be set at three months.

9.7 Working with Implementing Acts

Working with Implementing Acts is the first category we need to assess. It is also the category where there is the most accumulated experience, given that it is the realm of 'old Comitology' and the Committees that assist the Commission. Whilst Implementing Acts are acts of routine implementation of EU legislation, the devil can be in the detail so if you are following an issue into Implementing Acts the stakes can be very high.

The first thing to consider is the operation of the Committees themselves, and the key actors that are in them, as they will be the focal point of your work with Implementing Acts. They are as follows:

Implementing Acts: Committees

1. **Representatives of 28 Member States.**
2. MS representatives normally have mandates from their home Ministry.
3. Possible observers from third countries, EU Agencies, International Organisations Industry, Non-governmental Organisations (or others depending on the needs of the Committee).
4. Committees can invite experts of concerned parties to address the meetings.
5. **Chaired by Commission**
6. Objective = consensus.
7. Very consensual and collaborative with good exchanges of information/views.
8. Member States can suggest and make changes to the Implementing Act under discussion.

A few points about the Committee need to be highlighted at this stage. The first is that although the key actors are always going to be the Commission and the Member State representatives, it is still worth trying to find out if any observers will be in the Committee meeting. The Commission will always be in the driving seat but any Member State can propose changes (and have them accepted), and if there is a majority opinion away from a Commission position it will usually prevail.

From outlining the people in the Committee, it is useful next to look at how a Committee operates because these rules are procedurally very important. These are the standard rules of procedure of a Committee, and they are an invaluable source of information. **Every Committee has its own Rules of Procedure** - so always ask (the Commission) to get the ones for the Committee you are working with. The main aspects of the standard RoP are as follows:

1. **Convening a meeting:** initiative of the chairman (Commission) or at the request of a simple majority of members.

2. **Agenda:** drawn up by the chairman (Commission) with two parts:
   - proposed Implementing Act(s) submitted to the vote;
   - other issues regarding information.

3. **Documentation to be sent to the members:** to be sent by the chairman to the Committee members no later than 14 days in advance (the chairman may shorten this period on his/her own initiative or at the request of a member).

4. **Informing the Parliament:** under OLP, transmission at the same time as to the Member States (see box later for more detail on what is transmitted).

5. **Opinion of the Committee:** Voting rules: simple majority in Advisory procedure (15 Member States) and qualified majority voting in the Examination procedure. The chairman may postpone the vote until the end of the meeting or a later meeting if a substantive change is made to the proposal during a meeting, the text for voting has been submitted during the meeting, a new point has been added to the agenda because of extreme urgency or documents have not been sent within the deadline.

6. **Quorum:** Majority required for a successful vote (15 Member States).

7. **Representation:** One person per delegation is reimbursed (Member State experts can be present with the chairman's agreement).

8. **Working Groups:** the Committee may create Working Groups of experts. These can be standard Expert Groups, hence also chaired by the Commission.

9. **Admission of third parties:** participation of third countries or third organisations in accordance with a Council act. With the status of observer they do not vote and should leave the room when a vote takes place.

10. **Written procedure:** Response period for the Committee's opinion may not be less than 14 days. In cases of urgency the deadline may be shorter. If a member requests that the measure(s) be discussed at a meeting, the Written procedure will be terminated.

11. **Minutes and summary report:** Minutes are drafted by the chairman for the Committee members and a summary report which does not mention the individual position of Member States for the Parliament and the general public.

12. **Attendance list:** The Commission shall draw up an attendance list specifying the authorities or bodies to which the persons appointed by the Member States to represent them belong - but there should be no individual names.

13. **Correspondence:** always to be addressed to the Permanent Representations by e-mail and to the Commission (service responsible).

14. **Transparency:** the Committee's discussions are confidential. Application of transparency rules through application of Regulation 1049/2001 (see Chapters 7 & 8 for more information).

These RoP are very important to understand if working with Implementing Acts, and they also give a feel for how Committees work in practice. In general the Commission circulates the documents in advance, including the draft Implementing Acts, so that experts in the Member States can evaluate their national positions. The Committee then meets with a clear agenda that separates items for vote (and under which procedure) and items for information and discussion. The Commission uses these meetings to improve and finalise its draft Implementing Acts and tries to obtain a consensus in the Committee. The Commission will then call a vote once it has a consensus, or if positions are unlikely to change irrespective of any modification to the Implementing Act that the Commission could make. For the most part, deciding on Implementing Acts has been a consensual practice with consistently few problems (the exception being GMOs), but knowing the rules of the Committees can be very useful when working on more problematic dossiers.

The best way to understand many of the points listed above is to take a look at the Commission Comitology website which can be found at: http://ec.europa.eu/transparency/regcomitology/index.cfm?CLX=en. The **Commission Comitology Register** is home to a significant number of documents related to Implementing Acts, and all of the documents mentioned above can be found here. The documents in the register also correspond to the documents that are sent to the Parliament to exercise its various powers under the Implementing Acts Regulation. This means that before the meeting of the Committee (and at the same time as the Member States) the Parliament gets:

1. Draft agenda of the meeting.
2. Draft initial Implementing Act(s) submitted to the Committee.

After the meeting the Parliament will then get:

1. List of participants (not individual names).
2. A summary record (not Member State positions).
3. Voting results (not individualised).
4. The draft final Implementing Act(s) following the Committee opinion.

If a measure relates to a Special Legislative Procedure (SLP), then the documents are the same except for the drafts of the Implementing Act itself, which are not transmitted to the Parliament. The register is thus a must for following the work of Committees, with one obvious limitation - it is rarely updated in time for you to work on live issues. If you want to work effectively with (not simply monitor) Implementing Acts you cannot rely on the register for your information: you will need to be in close cooperation with the key actors in the process. It is therefore essential to know exactly where else you can find the information. The most important source of information on Implementing Acts will always be the Unit responsible for drafting the Implementing Act in the Commission - which is why it is worth looking at the flow of an Implementing Act through the Commission, described below in Figure 9.2.

Figure 9.2: The Commission and Implementing Acts

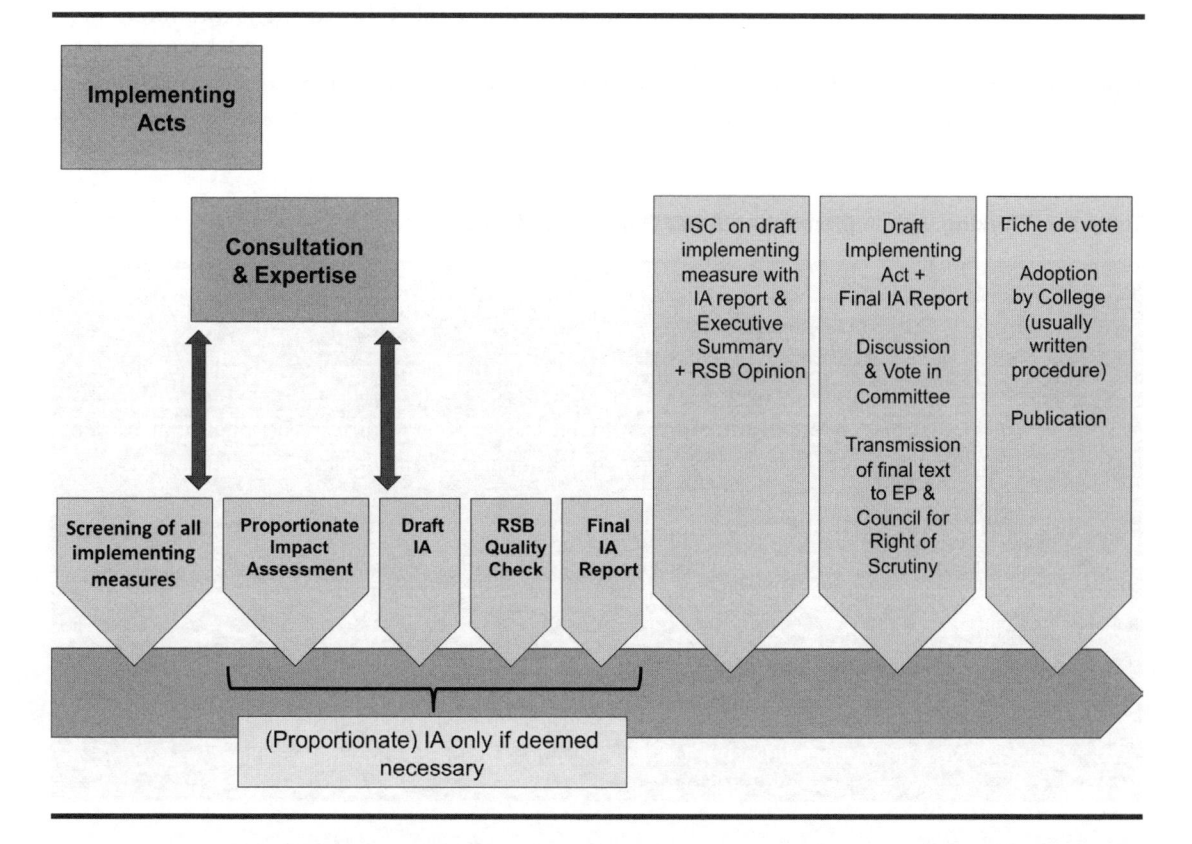

The key institution for Implementing Acts is without doubt the Commission because, through the powers conferred on it, it drafts the actual texts of the acts. The process in the Commission does not differ greatly from that of a legislative file, as outlined in Chapter 1. The Secretariat-General, in conjunction with the Directorates-General (DGs) and Services screens all forthcoming Implementing Acts to see if they require an Impact Assessment (IA). IAs for Implementing Acts remain quite unusual (though not exceptional) and it is more likely that Delegated Acts will be subject to IA. However, it should not be ruled out that in the future more Implementing Acts will be subject to proportionate IAs.

The key moment in the process is when the Unit in the lead DG drafts its Implementing Act, using input from Expert Groups, informal consultations, EU Agencies, Committee members and its own resources. This draft text might be circulated formally, or informally, to the Committee to gather opinions before the lead DG submits the text into Inter-Service Consultation (ISC) for other DGs to give their views. Once the Commission has an agreed text from ISC, it will submit it to discussion and a vote in the Committee itself. Assuming a positive vote (over 99% of cases), the **voting sheet** (*fiche de vote*) will then be needed by the lead DG to launch an adoption procedure by the Commission. Before the lead DG submits its file for final College approval it will forward the document to the Parliament and Council for them to exercise their right of scrutiny - which is seldom exercised. When the file goes for final approval in the Commission this will usually be a Written procedure, so all Cabinets will have a last look before the Implementing Act is adopted by the Commission, after which it is published in the Official Journal (OJ) and enters into force.

From the preceding sections it is possible to draw a series of conclusions about working with Implementing Acts.

Table 9.7: Working with Implementing Acts: General guidance

1. Follow the legislative drafting of the Commission for the insertion of the Advisory and Examination procedures. This could also involve an Expert Group.
2. Work with the three institutions during the OLP phase on how Implementing Acts will work in the legislative act; the more clarity at this stage the better.
3. Read the final legislative act to understand exactly what has been delegated to the Commission.
4. Identify the Expert Group, or Agency, assisting the Commission in drafting the Implementing Act and work with them, with technical evidence.
5. Work with the Commission services drafting the Implementing Act.
6. Identify the Inter-Service Consultation on the Implementing Act.
7. Identify the relevant Comitology Committee and the members of the Committee - and start to work with them.
8. Follow the work of the Comitology Committee and work with the Commission and Member States to suggest modifications in Committee.
9. Once the Implementing Act has been voted on in Committee the European Parliament and Council have a right of scrutiny - but it is very difficult to motivate them to use this.

> 10. If there has been a negative vote or 'no opinion' in the Examination procedure and the Implementing Act is referred to the Appeal Committee, work with members of the Committee to try and make modifications.

Table 9.7 highlights the general guidance for working with Implementing Acts. It is essential to emphasise that this work should always start at the very earliest opportunity, i.e. working with the Commission when it is drafting the legislative proposal. It is important to ensure that the tasks delegated to the Commission are in accordance with your interests. Once you get to the actual drafting of Implementing Acts your room for manoeuvre is limited, because the Commission is working within a well-defined legislative context to implement the legislation. Again you will have to work with all three institutions, as per the guidance in the previous section of this chapter on OLP, with the explicit objective of modifying or supporting aspects of the draft Implementing Act.

Once the text has been voted by the Committee, the Commission will move to adopt and bring into force the Implementing Act - leaving only one last resort avenue for work, the **Council and Parliament's right of scrutiny**. Here you need to bear in mind the limitations of this power and the difficulty of generating sufficient momentum to deliver a forceful enough opinion to get the Commission to change its mind. Nonetheless keep the Parliament and Council informed of your issues for future reference, as you never know what could come around again. The majority of this work will be of a technical nature and you will need to make sure you are well-versed in the technicalities of your file because your interlocutors will likely be experts in the field. Your communication should therefore be evidence, fact and case-study based.

9.8 Working with Delegated Acts: The Commission

Working with Delegated Acts is very important because, as highlighted in Chapter 6 and in Table 9.6, the Commission is granted the power to amend, supplement and/or delete non-essential elements of the legislative act. Here it is important to stress that this can mean very important and far-reaching changes with significant consequences. With Delegated Acts the impacts of changes are much more localised and hence much more important for specific sectors and stakeholders than the impact of the OLP file. This section will be structured in the same way as the previous one on Implementing Acts, although given the need to work more extensively with all three institutions, and understand their internal decision-making procedures for Delegated Acts, there will be three sections to detail the nature of each of these processes.

Before looking at the process of Delegated Acts within the three EU institutions, one aspect of interest concerns the negotiation of Delegated Acts in the legislative phase. While conceding that a grey zone will continue to exist in some cases as to whether a Delegated Act or an Implementing Act should or could be used, the practice of RPS showed that these differences were simply absorbed into a part of the OLP negotiation process. This pattern will doubtless continue but the Parliament will have much more incentive to negotiate Delegated Acts into a text because they will benefit from significantly more powers. In addition, in the future, the negotiation of Delegated Act provisions will be more difficult because the conditions need to be agreed on a case-by-case basis. So in OLP, Delegated Acts will become a more important focus of negotiation than the RPS was due both to their inclusion and the conditions laid out in each case.

The way the Commission prepares and adopts a Delegated Act is shown in Figure 9.3.

Figure 9.3: The Commission and Delegated Acts

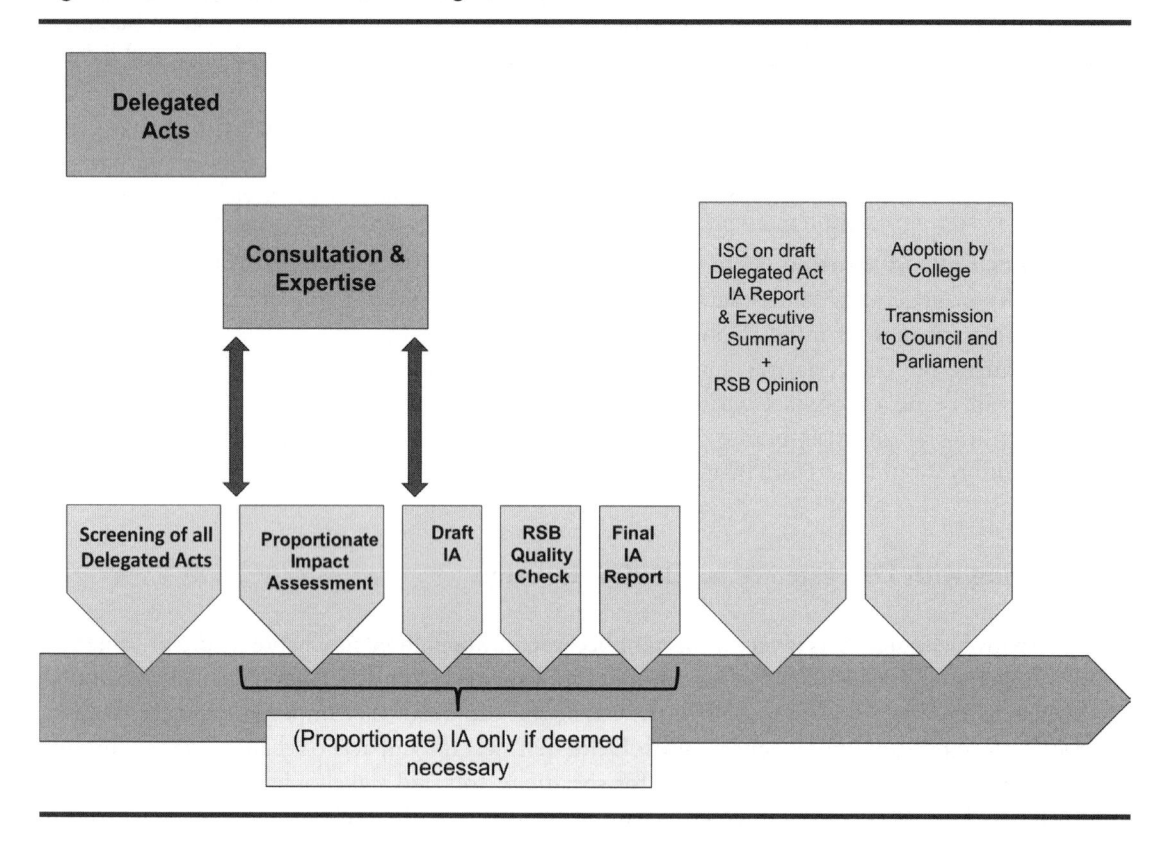

Figure 9.3 shows a very similar process to that for Implementing Acts, with the major difference that there is no longer a Committee stage and the Commission adopts the Delegated Act before sending it to the legislators. The phase of screening for an IA is more important for Delegated Acts as a number of Delegated Acts have already been given proportionate IAs - a trend that is likely to continue in the future. If this is the case, it is important to work with the Commission as it drafts the IA. Such a proportionate IA will be carried out and submitted to the RSB exactly as explained in Chapter 1.

A second key difference here relates to the consultation phase in the drafting of a Delegated Act, as the Commission now uses Expert Groups, EU Agencies and other sources of expertise to improve its Delegated Acts. From this perspective the Commission is likely to be more open to working with engaged stakeholders on Delegated Acts.

Like an Implementing Act, a Delegated Act will also go through ISC and then Cabinet approval. There is only one potential difference in this process, which is that the Cabinet has more room for manoeuvre for making changes with Delegated Acts (because when a Cabinet sees an Implementing Act it has already been adopted by the Committee). Once the Commission has adopted the Delegated Act (again usually by Written procedure) it will be forwarded to the Parliament and Council for them to exercise their control. The Commission will remain very active through this period as it tries to steer its proposal through the two legislators without any problems - so the Commission will still be very engaged. Experience with RPS showed that when either legislator was considering opposing an RPS measure the Commission mounted serious campaigns of its own to keep its measures as they were. This is something that needs to be understood if you are working with the legislators against a Delegated Act: you will be working against the Commission.

9.9 Working with Delegated Acts: Parliament

Once the Delegated Act is forwarded to the Parliament it follows the same route as a legislative proposal, as identified in Chapter 3. Hence the Committee responsible will be sent the Delegated Act and they will have to decide whether to object to the individual act or revoke the delegation - or do nothing during their period of control.

When it comes to how the Parliament deals with the volume of Delegated Acts and their technical nature it is a rather complicated, and evolving, picture. The Parliament outlines its internal procedures in Article 105 of its RoP. There are a number of issues with how the Parliament deals with Delegated Acts which need to be understood if working with them. Firstly, it is clear from both a capacity and a technical perspective, that further efforts are needed by the Parliament to deal with the influx of Delegated Acts. In 2015 nearly all parliamentary Committees are still striving to find their own best practice for dealing with them, and some Committees, due to the increased number of Delegated Acts they have to deal with, are more advanced than others. There are important horizontal efforts to streamline best practice and deal with Delegated Acts in a more uniform way. The real key in this regard is that it is vital to make sure that MEPs are fully briefed on the developments in the importance and use of Delegated Acts, so that they understand what they are and how they can use their powers. This is especially important just after elections when many MEPs will be new to the Delegated Acts and their implications. From a procedural perspective we are likely to see a continuation of the trend of a few key MEPs driving the scrutiny of Delegated Acts within Committees: the coordinators, OLP rapporteurs, Committee chairs, Secretariat and Political Group staff.

From this it is clear that Delegated Acts offer an opportunity for stakeholders to work with MEPs:

1. To bring the Delegated Act to their attention: it is unlikely to be top of their priority list so you might need to alert them to it.
2. To explain what it is and why it is important; this is why you have to understand Delegated Acts and the procedures so well.
3. To outline your position clearly - this is not easy if you have a 300-page technical Delegated Act, so you need to make it user-friendly and understandable
4. To explain how the MEP can support you: which means you need to know the procedure and timelines.

A key aspect of this engagement with MEPs will be the level of understanding and interest of MEPs in engaging with Delegated Acts. The Parliament is first and foremost a legislative body and MEPs are mainly concerned with this aspect of their work. Whilst it is not difficult for an MEP to get to grips with the procedure of Delegated Acts, it is a different story for them to grasp all the implications of the substance of individual acts, especially within such short deadlines. In addition there is the element of an MEP's interest in these detailed Delegated Acts, which is usually quite low given that an MEP has limited time and resources. Delegated Acts give the Parliament much greater powers than it has had in the past, and there is a trend towards increased visibility and interest in using these powers within the Parliament - but this continues to depend on stakeholders 'selling' this to MEPs.

The procedure in the Parliament is now taken up in the next three figures.

Figure 9.4: The European Parliament and Delegated Acts (1)

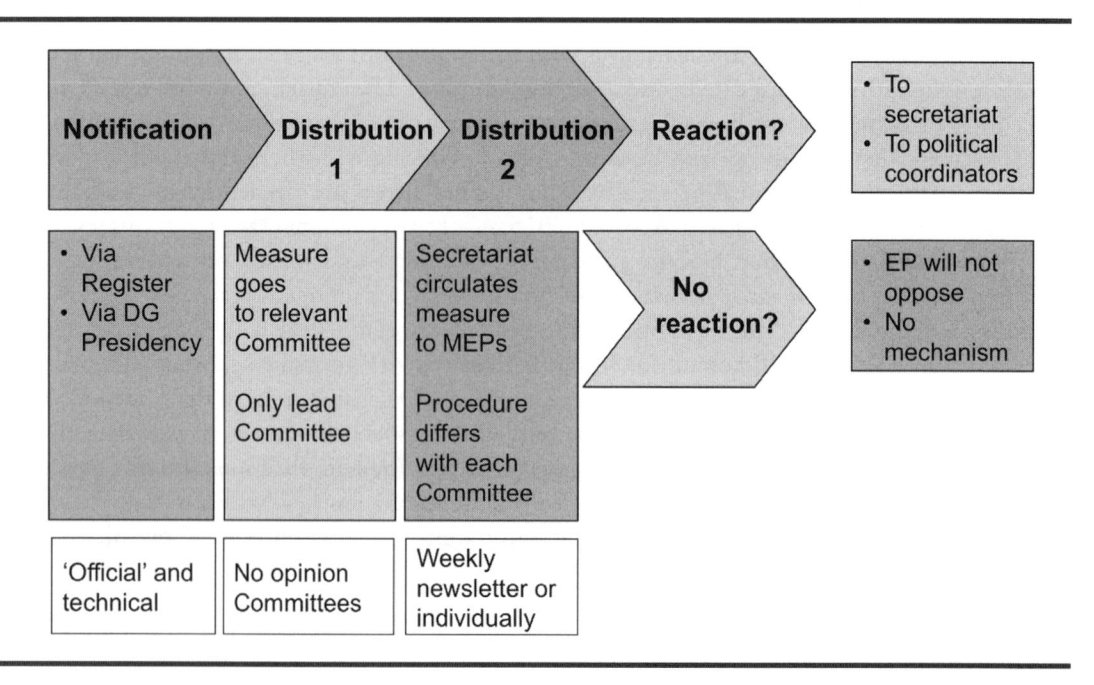

Notification → Distribution 1 → Distribution 2 → Reaction?

- To secretariat
- To political coordinators

Notification:
- Via Register
- Via DG Presidency
- 'Official' and technical

Distribution 1:
- Measure goes to relevant Committee
- Only lead Committee
- No opinion Committees

Distribution 2:
- Secretariat circulates measure to MEPs
- Procedure differs with each Committee
- Weekly newsletter or individually

No reaction?
- EP will not oppose
- No mechanism

Figure 9.4 shows the beginning of the Delegated Acts process in the Parliament. A Delegated Act is received via DG Presidency in the Parliament and is attributed to the appropriate Committee. Like in OLP second reading, the act only goes to the **Committee responsible**, as there is limited time to incorporate opinion-giving Committees. The next stage is a vital one in the Parliament - how does a Committee notify its members of the Delegated Acts that have come in, and with what level of analysis and comment? Some Committees circulate every act individually as they come in, and others combine them into fortnightly newsletters. This is important because it is through this distribution that an MEP in the Committee, at this stage, needs to assess whether or not to proceed with an objection to the Delegated Act, or to revoke the delegation. There are three likely sources of information as to whether or not to proceed with an objection or revocation: an individual MEP with a close interest in the issue, such as the rapporteur of the basic act; Secretariat or Political Group staff with technical expertise or whose job it is to look at Delegated Acts; or from an outside stakeholder. Past practice, with RPS, has shown that in the majority of cases the Parliament has not attempted to object to measures, but whether this was due to the measures themselves or a lack of knowledge and interest is not clear.

If the Parliament decides to proceed with an objection or a revocation then it follows the process outlined in Figure 9.5.

Figure 9.5: The European Parliament and Delegated Acts (2)

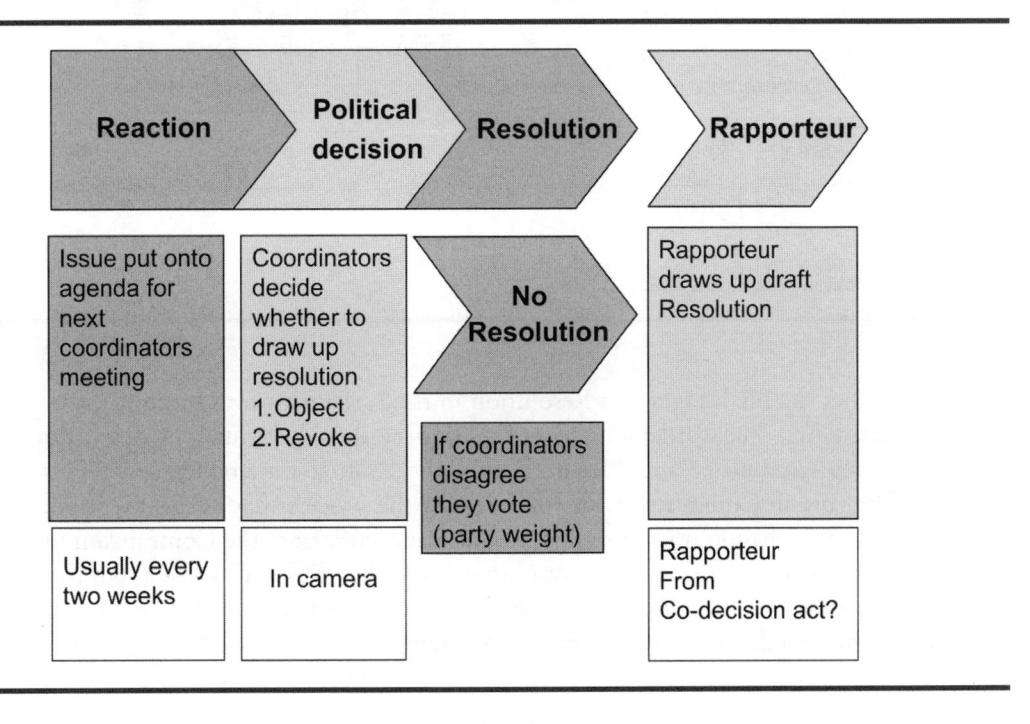

Figure 9.5 shows the stage in the Parliament where the decision to draft a **Resolution to object, or revoke**, is taken. If an MEP, or a number of MEPs, have indicated problems with the Delegated Act it will be placed on the next coordinators agenda, and the decision to take an objection or revocation further is taken by the coordinators at their 'in camera' meeting. If they decide to continue with opposition, or revocation, the next step is to appoint a rapporteur. This is usually the same MEP who drafted the legislative text, if they are still in the Parliament and in the same Committee, although in 2015 this is unlikely given the high turnover in the last elections in 2014 and the nature of rapporteurship assignment (see Chapter 3 for more details). The rapporteur is tasked with drawing up a Resolution for opposition to the Delegated Act, or for revocation of the delegation, which only needs to outline what the Parliament objects to. Remember that the Parliament cannot modify the Delegated Act - it can only object - but that if its objection is successful then the Commission will most likely incorporate its modification in a new Delegated Act - so modification is possible through this form of '**soft amendment**' (albeit difficult). The Resolution will thus be a short document specifying the exact objections of the Parliament, which will then need to be voted through the Committee and Plenary, as shown in Figure 9.6.

Figure 9.6: The European Parliament and Delegated Acts (3)

Committee vote → Plenary vote ⇒ Act rejected / Delegation revoked

- One member one vote
- Absolute majority (376)

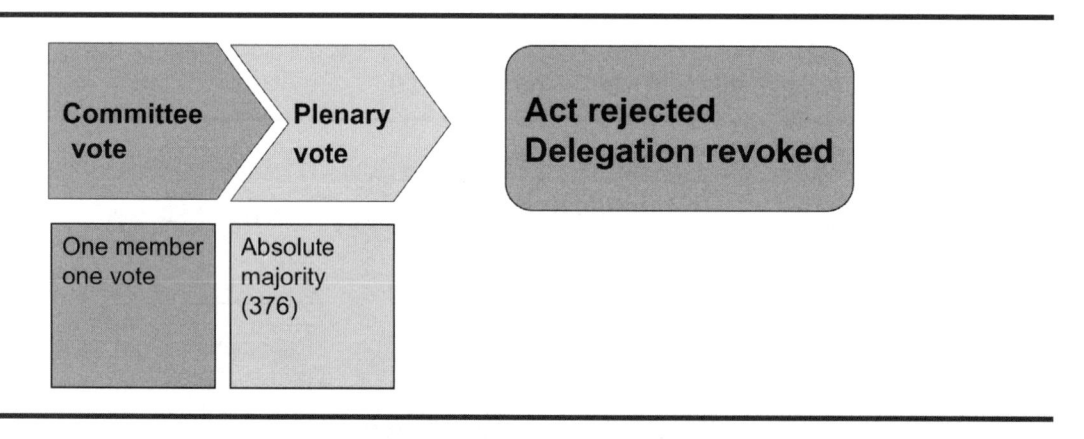

Figure 9.6 shows the final stages of a Resolution in the Parliament for objection to, or revocation of, a Delegated Act. The Parliament has to work very quickly to draft a Resolution and vote it through both Committee and Plenary within the allotted timeframes (usually two to three months). The vote in Committee is the first part of the process that needs attention, because as noted earlier in this chapter it will usually involve heavy work from the Commission to support its Delegated Act. A simple majority in a Committee is not that difficult to attain, but the discussions will take place in a very short period of time. The absolute majority in Plenary, if a Resolution to object or revoke gets this far, is very difficult to obtain.

9.10 Working with Delegated Acts: Council

The final institutional process is that of the Council, which is somewhat more straightforward as Figure 9.7 highlights.

Figure 9.7: The Council and Delegated Acts

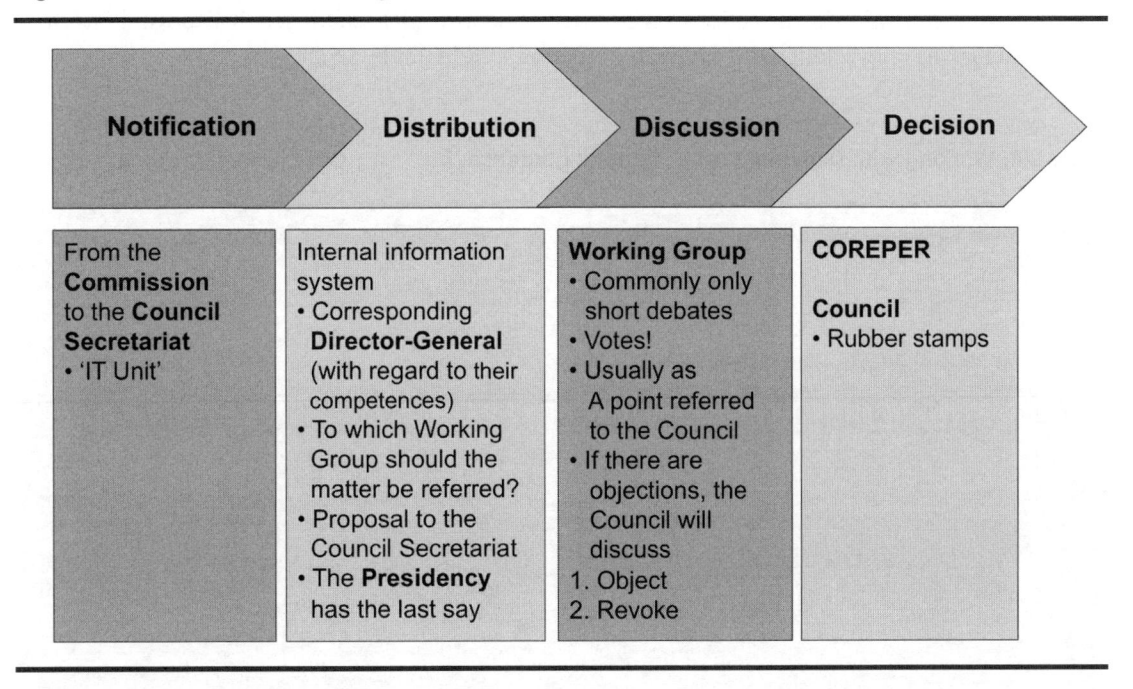

Notification	Distribution	Discussion	Decision
From the **Commission** to the **Council Secretariat** • 'IT Unit'	Internal information system • Corresponding **Director-General** (with regard to their competences) • To which Working Group should the matter be referred? • Proposal to the Council Secretariat • The **Presidency** has the last say	**Working Group** • Commonly only short debates • Votes! • Usually as A point referred to the Council • If there are objections, the Council will discuss 1. Object 2. Revoke	**COREPER** **Council** • Rubber stamps

Figure 9.7 illustrates the process of dealing with Delegated Acts in the Council. Actually both Delegated and Implementing Acts are treated in the same way, simply because the Council has the expertise and architecture to deal with both categories of acts in the same way. In essence if there is strong national coordination, then the Member States in Council should already be aware of the acts because their experts will have assisted the Commission either via an Expert Group, or in the Comitology Committees.

For Delegated Acts, each act is sent to the relevant Working Group in the Council where there are short debates. If there are problems identified in the Working Group, or if nothing comes of the discussion, the acts are then sent up the hierarchy to COREPER. At this level there will be a final, more political, check of the Delegated Act to see whether the Council will object or revoke. In the past Working Parties rarely had any problems with Delegated Acts or RPS measures, but COREPER has picked up a number of issues that led to several Council objections. Some of these objections arose from the Commission having included correlation tables (obligations on Member States to report to the Commission demonstrating how EU legislation has been transposed into national law) in RPS measures. This was something that experts in Working Groups did not see a problem with but that COREPER took exception to. COREPER is thus an important actor when it comes to the scrutiny of Delegated Acts in the Council architecture. The decision of COREPER to object, to revoke or to do nothing will then be forwarded for final sign-off by the next available Council meeting - a mechanism that sees the Council effectively agree to D&I Acts, which it is not formally required to do.

From these three institutional sections on how to work with Delegated Acts it is possible to draw some conclusions on working with Delegated Acts, as seen in Table 9.8.

Table 9.8: Working with Delegated Acts: General guidance

1. Follow the legislative drafting of the Commission for the objectives, scope, duration and the conditions to which the delegation is subject. This could also involve an Expert Group.
2. Work with the three institutions during the OLP phase on how Delegated Acts will work in the legislative act to get as much clarity as possible.
3. Read the final legislative act: understand exactly what has been delegated and to what conditions it is subject: remember they could be different in each case.
4. Identify the Expert Group, or Agency, assisting the Commission in drafting the Delegated Act and work with them.
5. Work with the Commission service drafting the Delegated Act.
6. Identify the Inter-Service Consultation on the Delegated Act - it is the last real chance to modify the text.
7. Once the Delegated Act has been transmitted to the Council and Parliament you have to identify what your objectives are: support or reject the act, or revoke the delegation.
8. It will usually be easier to work with the Parliament to support or reject a Delegated Act, so identify the competent Committee, the coordinators, the Secretariat staff, the interested MEPs, the OLP rapporteur.
9. Working to reject a Delegated Act will require an absolute majority so political work as well as technical arguments are needed.
10. Remember that working against a Delegated Act means working against the Commission, so consider the long-term consequences that this could have.
11. Also work with Council experts and COREPER: they too will be working with the Commission and Parliament.

Table 9.8 shows that working with Delegated Acts is very much focused in time, in context and in terms of the small group of interested actors. Working with the insertion of Delegated Acts into legislative files is very important, because it will define how you work with individual Delegated Acts at a later stage. And remember all the conditions can change in each legislative act, so you need to be vigilant.

The main thing is to keep in touch with the Commission to know when Delegated Acts are being prepared, at which stage you need to identify the Expert Group the Commission is using to assist it in drafting the act. You will have the time the Delegated Act is being prepared to work with the Commission and the Expert Group and/or Agency that is advising them (which can be a number of months). The Commission needs good quality technical input to draft its Delegated Acts, so they are more open to constructive and engaged stakeholders (especially ones they know from the Impact Assessment and OLP phases). At this stage you should also contact the Parliament to keep them informed of your position vis-à-vis the Delegated Act that will be coming their way in the not too distant future. This will help you once the Parliament is considering the Delegated Act in question.

When the Delegated Act has been forwarded to the legislators you need to engage with both at the same time, both to communicate your position and also to find out what the legislators are thinking or doing. The timelines are very short so things can change on a day-to-day basis, making close monitoring and contacts important. Your job at this stage is to work with the Member State experts, COREPER and MEPs to object to an individual act, to revoke the delegation or to support the act as it is. It is not possible to modify the text of a Delegated Act once it has been adopted by the Commission, so changes will only happen if the Delegated Act is rejected or the delegation itself revoked. This explains the importance of working with the Commission in the drafting phase - because objecting to a Delegated Act to get a change introduced is really a last ditch strategy with limited chances of success. During the scrutiny phase you will need to keep an eye on the timelines and the temperature in both legislators and always remember that if you are trying to generate support for objection you will almost certainly be working against the Commission - which is a delicate political manoeuvre only to be attempted when absolutely necessary.

10. Conclusion: Designing a Successful EU Lobbying Campaign

By Natacha Clarac and Stéphane Desselas

The objective of this chapter is to provide a complete methodological toolkit to build and execute a successful **lobbying strategy**. The structure will be detailed step-by-step. It will draw together the key elements of the previous chapters, and combine the information on how to work with the EU institutions with the knowledge on how they function internally. This chapter will set out a clear and practical methodology using the following process: identification of major issues, monitoring of EU developments, assessing the EU arena leading to the development and implementation of a lobbying strategy based on concrete actions. The chapter will provide practical guidance, examples and **lobbying tools** to bolster the methodology.

> Working with the EU institutions and EU decision-making requires a well-structured and thought out strategy taking into account the available resources. It also relies on a clear methodology. The best lobbying strategy will deliver nothing without adequate resources to implement it. Even with limited resources, it is vital (and possible) to create a good (and implementable) lobbying strategy.

In an ideal world, a stakeholder who holds all the information well in advance, who is known as a legitimate counterpart and who has a solid network of contacts has the capacity to conduct **proactive lobbying** - i.e. lobby for future actions and changes. This is ideal-type lobbying because the focus is on structuring the future debate around your own priorities. This type of proactive approach requires new ideas and suggestions to be brought to the table very early. It also requires solid thought leadership to bring them to the top of the European political agenda. It is, however, very much an ideal-type form of lobbying because in most cases stakeholders are unable to devote the required resources to future looking actions; they are simply too busy reacting to current initiatives and circumstances. They are mainly engaged in **reactive lobbying**. This chapter will outline a lobbying approach that lies between the two main forms of lobbying: proactive and reactive. Obviously, this chapter will take into account the more likely need to engage in reactive lobbying.

In a real life lobbying strategy, the sequential steps identified below are rarely carried out in the way presented here. Often many steps are, or have to be, taken in parallel under severe time pressure and with only a few resources, making the task even more challenging than it already is. Nonetheless, presenting the methodology sequentially is useful to see how a more ideal-type lobbying should be undertaken. It should be noted that when it comes to the sequencing and timing of actions one of the key messages from previous chapters will again be highlighted in this chapter: the earlier the better. Once the institutions have defined a position, it is very difficult to find alternative solutions and compromises. Moreover, even a well-developed, sequenced, and planned lobbying campaign will only bear fruit if it is conceived in a strategic way.

The preceding chapters highlighted the main challenges that need to be met by a good lobbying strategy:
- the complexity of the European multi-level decision-making process;
- a very intense flow of information that has to be processed in order to capture what really impacts us;
- the time constraints dictated by the EU decision-making procedures, into which stakeholders have to fit their actions;
- and finally the need to conduct at the same time a large number of actions, often with limited resources - especially human resources.

These challenges make the setting-up of a solid lobbying system and methodology, with mechanisms to cope with these issues, essential. That is what this chapter is about.

The key phases in a lobbying strategy are outlined below in Figure 10.1, all of which take place within a given schedule driven by the European institutions. The four phases that are outlined in the framework below will be detailed in this chapter.

Figure 10.1: Four key phases in a lobbying strategy

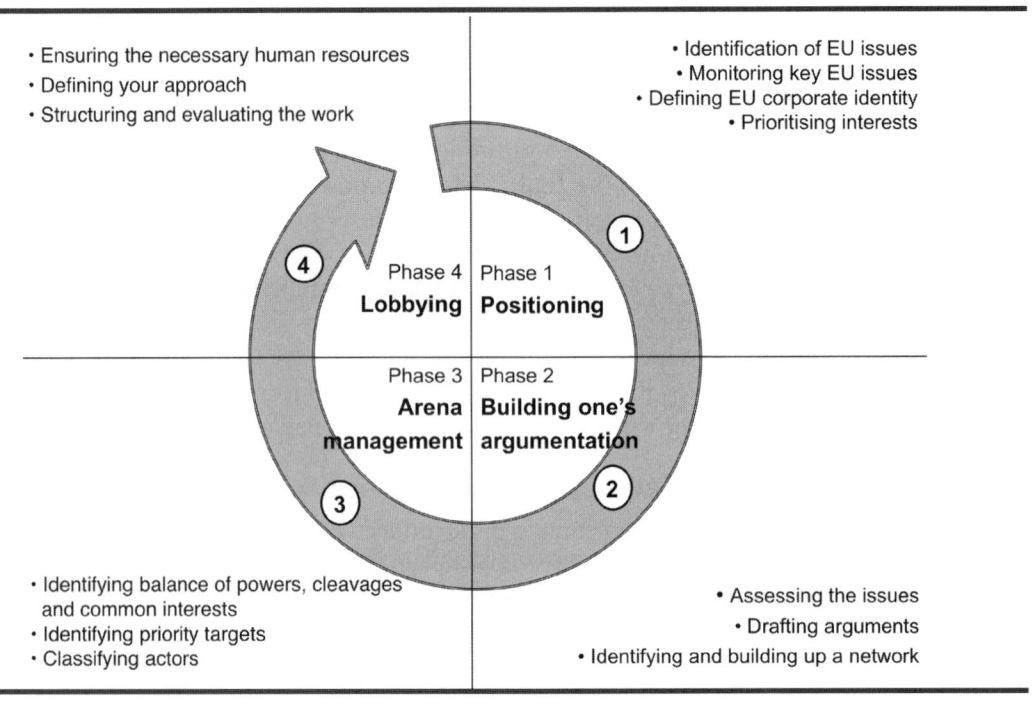

Phase 1 – Positioning
- Identification of EU issues
- Monitoring key EU issues
- Defining EU corporate identity
- Prioritising interests

Phase 2 – Building one's argumentation
- Assessing the issues
- Drafting arguments
- Identifying and building up a network

Phase 3 – Arena management
- Identifying balance of powers, cleavages and common interests
- Identifying priority targets
- Classifying actors

Phase 4 – Lobbying
- Ensuring the necessary human resources
- Defining your approach
- Structuring and evaluating the work

Source: Athenora Consulting

We will now go through the phases outlined in Figure 10.1 one by one to outline each key aspect. As the figure shows, a lobbying strategy begins internally, with upstream actions such as the selection and approval of the issues to concentrate on. This exercise must carefully take into account the interests and goals pursued by the organisation. The strategy then expands outwards, through the development of key messages and lobbying material that will be deployed across the EU institutions and interested stakeholders to influence the decision-making process. We will now take these phases in order.

10.1 Phase 1: Selecting and monitoring your interests

The identification and approval phase, an essential part of any successful strategy, refers to three successive steps: the monitoring of European issues, the defining of an EU image, and then evaluating your own interests. Stakeholders can be impacted by several pieces of EU legislation at the same time and/or forthcoming proposals. This makes it virtually impossible to follow every single initiative. Therefore it is crucial to identify those that will likely have the greatest impact, pose the greatest threat or offer the most opportunity. This priority identification exercise needs to be done as early as possible and as carefully as possible to ensure focus on the key issues.

The identification process starts with the gathering of information through the setting up of a monitoring system in order to map all current and forthcoming European initiatives. Then it goes on to the evaluation of the likely impacts that the various proposals will have, and an evaluation of the importance and resonance of the issues with your identity as stakeholder. After this comprehensive analysis, you will be able to build a more solid EU lobbying strategy based on clear business priorities. This phase is inherently inward looking because it is all about what interests a stakeholder wants to actively pursue in the EU arena and how it wants to do so. This exercise requires effective internal coordination and communication to ensure consistency and coherence in the actions carried out in Brussels.

10.2 Step 1.1: Identifying European issues

When it comes to strategy in the EU, information is power. That is why the work begins with the identification of the most pertinent, and important, European issues for your organisation and an evaluation of their potential impacts.

Key European issues must be prioritised. Those with the greatest impact should be selected first, while always seeking to be as exhaustive as possible taking into account the available resources.

Priorities and realism

It is imperative to conduct the priority selection realistically. Identified priorities should be selected in view of the subsequent capacity to follow up and engage. If too many priorities are selected, resources will not be allocated in the best possible ways.

You need to know what you want otherwise others will not know either.

For each issue identified, a question must be asked about its consistency with your interests, knowing that such interests may be numerous (image, financial, etc.). The identification of each issue should take into account its impacts as well as its adequacy with your image and goals.

> **Example of key issues for a mutual insurance company in 2015**
>
> - Solvency II and linked delegated acts
> - Follow-up of the Social Business Initiative
> - Directive on intermediation
> - Regulation on data protection
> - Planned initiative on the capital markets union
> - Follow-up of the economic study on the impact of differences in insurance contract law on cross-border trade in the insurance sector
> - Implementation of the guidelines for unisex pricing (Test achats ruling)
> - Planned initiatives on e-health, patient safety, and more resilient and sustainable national health systems ...

Source: Athenora Consulting

10.3 Step 1.2: Monitoring key EU issues

Implementing a high-performance monitoring system
Once the key issues have been identified, it is important to determine the human and material resources that will be needed to follow the relevant developments.

While the determination of the European priority issues should always be a team effort involving all internal departments and the governing board, implementation of the monitoring may be entrusted to one person. However, frequent contacts should be maintained with others in the organisation to ensure continued attention to its evolving needs. The objective is to ensure that the person who undertakes the monitoring on behalf of others, properly understands their needs and expectations. This is even more important when the monitoring is outsourced - again coming back to the issue of knowing very clearly what you want. In all cases, it is essential to develop a contact management system to organise the flow of information from both sides; the receiver of the monitoring and its author. The notion of contact management systems is extremely important, hence we will see it again later when it comes to the organisation of key contacts who give added value information to enrich the monitoring report.

The person in charge of the monitoring must naturally have a solid understanding about the EU institutions and EU decision-making. He or she should also master the European institutions' websites and know the key stakeholders. Obviously, the person needs to be able to build up a good network of contacts so as to obtain useful information at the most relevant times. An analytical mind is essential in order to retain only the key elements of information amidst the wealth of information available. Ideally, the person should know how to present the monitoring so as to encourage readers to decide about a position based on the provided information. Monitoring is about presenting the right balance of the most accurate information to the right person at the earliest possible time.

Identifying monitoring recipients
European policy has multifaceted impacts and these can differ according to the stakeholders, and change with time. All the people within an organisation who could, at some stage, be mobilised to obtain, or present, information from the field, should be identified and contacted during the monitoring phase. Indeed, it is important to mobilise all internal departments in the monitoring phase, in order to raise their awareness and understanding of European issues. In essence it is about making sure that each stakeholder gets the right internal buy-in and is able to count on its own resources as and when it needs them. This can be a difficult 'sell' when many colleagues are somewhat removed from EU work, but it is the job of those responsible for EU work to engage their colleagues properly in this process. The lobbying strategy will also be even more effective when senior management is involved from the beginning, understands the stakes, gives political guidance and defines the messages to carry this out. Then the stakeholder will just have to translate the political angle into a **position paper** and **amendments**. This involvement of the senior management will also facilitate the participation of all levels within the organisation, especially when under time pressure (which is quite often), to get concrete facts and figures from the field that are expected by EU decision-makers.

An effective solution is often the establishment of a 'European working group' that brings together representatives of the different internal departments and main monitoring recipients. This group can meet physically or virtually depending on needs but some form of dynamism and 'club effect' is helpful. In practical terms, a clearly identified and discussed distribution list will ensure that no recipient is overlooked. Once a year, a **monitoring evaluation questionnaire** can be sent out to improve the service performed and ensure that the monitoring is meeting the needs and expectations of the internal recipients.

Identifying information sources available on the Internet
Many information sources are available online and it may be difficult to process all of this information in a meaningful way. Undeniably, the European institutions' websites are essential, but they alone are insufficient. The work of all key stakeholders (competitors, the European industry federations (Eurofeds), Expert Groups, NGOs, think-tanks, etc.) must also be followed - no stakeholder works in isolation. In addition, specialised media on European issues are important sources of information. This raises more a problem of information processing than one of collection. The main sources of information in Brussels will be identified later in the mapping section.

> **Save time in gathering information**
>
> Easy-to-use tools allow precious time to be saved while searching for information, leaving more time to process the data collected.

> **Standard RSS** represents a way to stay informed about new content on a website, without having to view it regularly. RSS feeds allow frequent readers of a website to detect updates to the site using an aggregation module or an RSS reader. It is then possible to see in one place the latest news from dozens, or even hundreds, of websites without having to visit them.
>
> Most European institutions' sites offer RSS and, for those which do not, there is often the possibility to create one. The same applies to think-tanks and Eurofeds.
>
> The time saved is invaluable for the person in charge of monitoring, who can then make more effective use of the time and apply the information for the purposes of influencing.
>
> Another widely used tip is **Google alerts** which allows you to save time by monitoring the web and keep you alerted of new interesting content. By using Google alerts you are notified by email when new articles matching your search terms are published. You can track the evolution of a topic, institutional activities and even personalities.
>
> In recent years we have also witnessed the emergence of **tweets**, the text-based posts of up to 140 characters. In order to keep track of them, feeds have been created allowing you to display on your profile page the tweets you want to follow. More and more parliamentary assistants, famous bloggers and Commissioners are using this form of communication, where sometimes useful nuggets of information can be found.

Source: Athenora Consulting

Building up a network of contacts

A network of contacts is an essential tool in the monitoring phase. In fact, the most useful information is usually that obtained informally, through someone's close contacts and network. A network is something that needs to be created, maintained and constantly updated, which is not an easy task. It can seem like a thankless task but in many cases you simply do not know when and where you will need to use your network, so it is always worth the investment.

Building up a network tends to be done on an issue-oriented basis and requires constant care to be effective. But, over time, it is essential to build up as wide a network as possible. Building such a network will always be a two-way exercise, as you will be an important element of someone else's network: to obtain useful information one must be in a position to reciprocate in some way. Attending meetings, seminars or even cocktail parties are great ways of expanding your network.

Identifying a monitoring format

Too often monitoring becomes confused with news reports and simply results in a copy-paste type of forwarding of information. If the information has an obvious direct interest then this is fine. Generally speaking, however, effective monitoring needs to be more qualitative and action-oriented, with a focus on a limited number of topics. Thus, effective monitoring should be designed as a tool for internal decision-making - not simply as the passing on of information in its basic form. Many formats are possible to do this effectively, from newsletters and e-mail alerts to more detailed individual analysis. The key is to choose an easy-to-use tool which allows you to maximise the information you want/need which will in turn help you save time by staying well-informed. Whatever its format, the document must be relevant in terms of the lobbying strategy and it should display the key information listed in the box below.

> **Essential elements of monitoring reports**
>
> Conceived as a lobbying preparatory tool, a monitoring report should be carefully written. Writing a report on monitoring is a stylistic exercise that should adhere to certain rules:
>
> 1. The title should identify the issue as clearly as possible.
> 2. The first line is a short summary. Just like a newspaper article, it must briefly highlight the key elements.
> 3. The body of the text aims to answer the following questions: Who? What it is about? When? What will the next steps be? How? Why?
> 4. Where appropriate, the report may conclude with a proposal for action.
> 5. Links to the documents mentioned must always be included.

Source: Athenora Consulting

Monitoring documents

Monitoring requires a subtle balance between comprehensiveness and brevity. It must be focused on key issues, be sufficiently specialised and draw attention to the challenges and opportunities that exist.

Regularity is a major issue as it is important to maintain the interest of monitoring recipients. A quarterly debriefing meeting on key issues is a good idea to strengthen buy-in and mobilise recipients around the issues. As we already mentioned, the organisation of the information flows within a structure is crucial in order to ensure that the monitoring can be effective. Regular feedback between the author and the recipients of the monitoring is necessary.

Too often, the monitoring is done but its internal processing lacks coherence or regularity, which leads to a situation which impedes a lobbying strategy's effectiveness. A monitoring document should not be confused with other types of documents such as an in-depth analysis, which is a more comprehensive document on a specific issue which aims to decipher a proposal and identify its stakes and impacts. The monitoring document should act as a prompt for action and identification of any suggested/required follow-up should be made clear.

There are three main types of documents for a monitoring system: first what we call '**information/ general monitoring**', second '**legislative trackers**' and third '**briefing notes**'. We will refer to them in the following paragraphs. Every organisation has to choose the one(s) that suits its own needs.

1. **General monitoring**

   General monitoring seeks to provide relevant information on previously identified major issues. It consists of short reports, tables, information notes etc. that can be quickly reviewed. The ideal frequency for this type of intelligence is a weekly mailing with real-time information sent by e-mail when the issue is of great importance. The goal is not to follow a subject in too much depth but to put an emphasis on the key procedural stages and to foresee important upcoming developments.

   To be effective, this type of monitoring must necessarily go beyond merely reading the press. It means following legislative debates or stakeholder events, reading specialised publications and most importantly, maintaining regular contacts with decision-makers and other interested stakeholders. Monitoring covers proposals that are currently being discussed and follows-up on emerging issues to enable action as far upstream as possible. To be complete, it should not only focus on the work of European institutions but also on that of other key stakeholders working on the same issues.

   Key information to monitor

   A good monitoring system relies on the following information to be as comprehensive as possible:
   1. Speeches from key decision-makers (Commissioners, MEPs, EU Presidencies etc.)
   2. Positions displayed by the main stakeholders
   3. 'What's new' pages of relevant DG websites within the European Commission
   4. Minutes of the parliamentary Committees and Political Groups meetings
   5. Events/hearings organised by the European institutions, think-tanks and stakeholders
   6. State of play within the Council and its various Working Groups
   7. Documents from the Secretariat-General to others institutions
   8. Press releases from EU institutions and key stakeholders
   9. Direct contacts through your network

   Source: Athenora Consulting

2. **Legislative trackers**

   Targeting a particular issue or set of issues, legislative trackers aim to compile, into a single visual document, key information about current legislative issues. To be useful, this tracker must be updated regularly, whenever an event occurs (presentation of a draft report by a rapporteur, meeting of a Council Working Group or a parliamentary Committee). A good legislative tracker will include the elements in Table 10.1.

Table 10.1: Example of a Legislative tracker

Name of the proposal + Type of proposal (legislative/non-legislative/delegated acts…)
EU objectives and main stakes
Previous steps (consultation, own initiative report, high level group…)
Next steps (need to be regularly updated) – Discussions, votes, trilogues, amendments deadline
Main elements of the proposal
Impacts on the organization (which is linked to the desired changes)
Contacts: Commissioner's member of cabinet, Lead DG, Unit Name (Position + contact), other DGs Rapporteur + Shadow + opinion leaders on the topic: name, nationality, political party, background + contact details Adviser in charge of the issue in the key Permanent Representations + in the MS holding the Presidency
List of key meetings and actions carried out taking into account the decision-making process
Hyperlinks to document and references

Source: Athenora Consulting

3. Briefing notes

Briefing notes, another very useful monitoring format, are designed to provide a summary of the proposed legislation under consideration. It is not a summary of the proposal but an analysis of the problematic issues as identified by the stakeholder. This 3-4 page document provides information on key elements of the proposal text for which action is considered necessary. Focusing on the problems identified, this note can serve as the first basis for the development of a future position. It is written in the form of a document with an introduction outlining the main background elements, an issue analysis and concludes with a recommended plan of action.

Benefits of successful monitoring

In lobbying, the goal of monitoring is to anticipate changes in EU legislation. It is not enough to conduct monitoring for its own sake. The objective is to translate the information collected into actions. It is vital to have the right information at the right time to be able to act in the most appropriate way. In fact, successful monitoring should not be characterised merely as a race to obtain information. The added value lies in the ways the collected information is processed and dealt with. Obtaining a European Commission draft proposal very early is pointless if no action is taken to evaluate the text in terms of the stakes involved and, where necessary, to present alternative proposals. Finally, to be effective, monitoring should be limited only to issues with the greatest impacts, and on which the stakeholder can promote a position.

> We saw in this section the various types of documents that are part of an effective monitoring system. Whatever its format, in order to be relevant in terms of lobbying, the monitoring document should display key information listed on the next page.

1. The background of the proposal (where do we come from?) and its references
2. The main objectives pursued by the legislator and its solutions
3. The impact on the organisation
4. The short-term action plan with the schedule
5. The type of procedure
6. The procedural steps within each institution (where are we?)
7. The upcoming events
8. The key decision-makers in each institution and the more influential stakeholders
9. The link to the various relevant documents and background information

Source: Athenora Consulting

10.4 Step 1.3: Defining your EU identity

A stakeholder's EU identity expresses an overall position on the EU and its ongoing legislative concerns in Brussels. It represents its distinctive EU identity in relation to other actors and legitimises its own actions. One thing should clearly be kept in mind: as a stakeholder, you are not automatically known in Brussels or you may want to take a position on a new issue, where decision-makers do not know you. Therefore, the first action is to raise awareness of your organisation and your objectives in order to establish your credentials and, to an important extent, your legitimacy. The notion of your EU identity summarises the major themes tied to your identity and core activity. It is directly linked to your values and actions.

The purpose of an EU identity is to:
1. structure outsiders' views on your identity;
2. ensure consistency between positions adopted and public statements made;
3. ensure that you have a distinctive identity in relation to other stakeholders;
4. focus on priority issues related to your interests;
5. bring out new subjects in compliance with your interests.

Defining an EU identity requires strategic work to be conducted at the highest levels of the organisation. It is vital that senior management is fully supportive and gives political guidance about the key messages to deliver through lobbying actions. Although topics of interest may change, a strong EU identity implies consistency. This is what will determine the values while developing the lobbying messages. Often, an EU identity emerges from brainstorming, which in itself usually reflects the overall European strategy and will provide a good understanding of the

Key elements of EU identity

1. **Your role in the EU**
   Key interests of your organisation
2. **Vision for the EU and the future**
   Not just a focus on active issues
3. **View of society and strong brand**
   Not just about profits
4. **Long-term thinking and engagement**
   Constructive commitment to the EU
5. **Involved senior management**
   Seeking dialogue and exchange

impacts Europe can have. The starting point for the brainstorming should be the socio-economic role your organisation plays in the EU. This role can often be split in several aspects. For example, an NGO could be a thought leader on issues such as workers' rights or environmental protection while a company could base its identity on the products it sells, the jobs it creates and where these are created, corporate social responsibility (CSR) policies and on its tax contribution.

The goal of this exercise is to ensure the adequacy of the investments in terms of lobbying on a topic detected based on the monitoring activities. It is often useful to use a **matrix** to define interests. The matrix is an easy-to-use tool, transferable and adaptable for any stakeholder, which can quantify the potential benefits before investing in lobbying on a given issue. Each relevant issue identified through the monitoring should be examined from several angles to determine the level of importance and the level of investments needed. Thus, for each issue it can be determined whether the stakes are low, medium, high or critical (on a scale of 1 to 4 for example).

In order to be useful, this process must be conducted in groups during a brainstorming meeting. Obviously, the idea is to link issues identified through the monitoring with the EU identity in order to assess how this identity might be threatened or promoted by new EU initiatives. This exercise will help to focus more on the EU initiatives with the greatest impacts. The different types of interests can be put into perspective using a matrix such as the one depicted in Figure 10.2 below.

Figure 10.2: An interest matrix

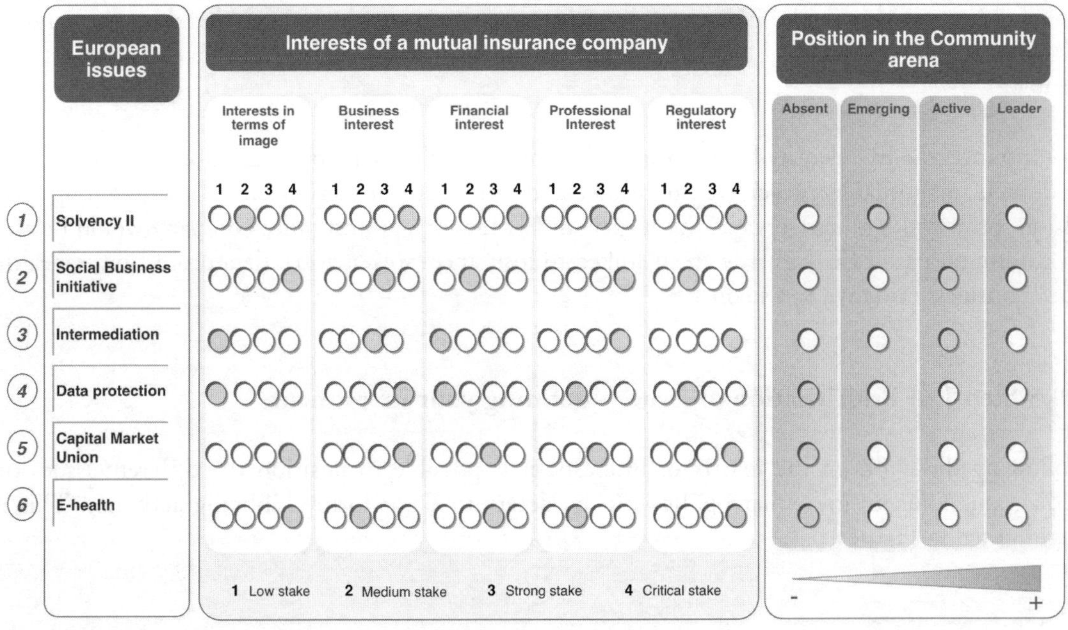

Source: Athenora Consulting

In this example, the completed matrix could show that the issues where the stakeholder is most active and engaged are not always those with the greatest impact on their activities and/or finances. When working with such a matrix a number of key elements need to be identified:

> The definition of a stakeholder's EU corporate identity and the consideration of their interests and position in the EU arena are two essential phases that ensure the legitimacy and credibility of the positions taken by a stakeholder.
>
> The more thought out the position of a stakeholder the easier it is to communicate.

1. The importance of image, including its relevance with regard to the EU identity promoted.
2. Commercial interest, or the impact on the way activities are deployed.
3. Financial interest, that is to say an assessment of potential costs resulting from the new initiative or the absence of a proposal.
4. Professional interests, concerning possible changes in how the stakeholder works.
5. Regulatory interest, that is to say whether or not the initiative is feasible and workable.

Thus, any given EU issue may have a strong impact in terms of image, such as sustainable development, but may be of little business or financial interest. On the other hand, an issue may have a strong regulatory interest and a real impact on the stakeholder's activities and their way of working.

The use of a matrix to clearly define interests ensures that any investment in lobbying is well-aligned with the true potential impact on the stakeholder. This matrix also enables one to identify the stakeholder's position in the EU arena for each issue, namely, is the stakeholder absent, emerging, active or a leader? This dual analysis enables one to take sound decisions about investment and strategy.

For instance, the EU identity for an insurance company could relate to being a non-profit enterprise dedicated to affordable, preventive, innovative and safe healthcare services for all, with a long-term vision for providing these services. With such an EU identity, an insurance company would be able to communicate on EU legislative texts linked to insurance (solvency II), data protection, e-health, social business initiative and so on.

10.5 Step 1.4: Prioritisation of issues - defining your investment

Following the work on the matrix of interests, it is possible to position the different issues on a diagram. Thus an investment policy can be determined for future lobbying activities. This is highlighted in Figure 10.3.

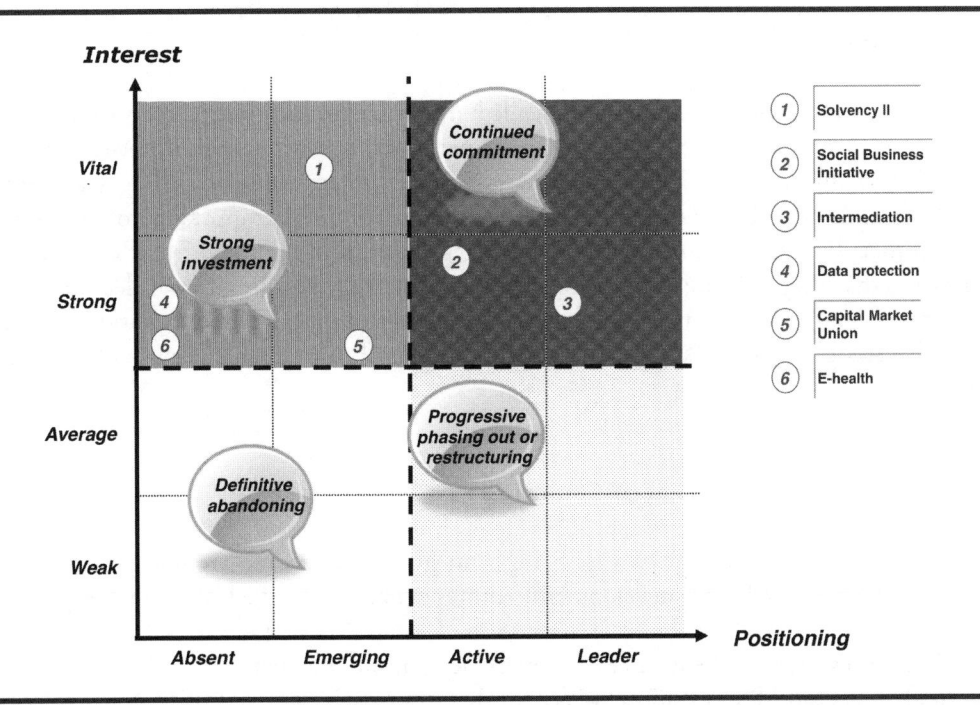

Figure 10.3: An interest matrix & positioning for action

[Figure showing a 2D matrix with Interest (Weak, Average, Strong, Vital) on the Y-axis and Positioning (Absent, Emerging, Active, Leader) on the X-axis. Labels in quadrants: "Strong investment" (upper-left), "Continued commitment" (upper-right), "Definitive abandoning" (lower-left), "Progressive phasing out or restructuring" (lower-right). Numbered items plotted: 1-Solvency II, 2-Social Business initiative, 3-Intermediation, 4-Data protection, 5-Capital Market Union, 6-E-health]

Source: Athenora Consulting

Issues in which the stakeholder has a low or medium interest could be abandoned or gradually withdrawn from according to a stakeholder's positioning and the development of topics. Conversely, if the interest is strong, or vital, and the stakeholder is absent or emerging, then it will be necessary to implement a policy of strong investment to reach the desired position. Figure 10.3 helps to visually develop the portfolio of issues for priority investment.

The first section of this chapter has detailed, step-by-step, the **preparatory actions** that are of the utmost importance to ensure a successful lobbying strategy. Indeed, without a reliable monitoring system, you cannot identify the issues that impact your activities. You would also miss opportunities to become a key player identified by the EU institutions for the expertise you might provide. The work on the EU identity allows you to operate in the EU with consistent messages. The objective of this internal process is to match European issues with your identity and objectives. Throughout the process, the methodology helps to identify the issues on which it is crucial to invest in terms of lobbying. This investment ultimately requires dedicating resources in order to reach clearly prescribed objectives. The latter should be set out at the very beginning of the lobbying strategy to ensure coherence.

After this first phase, you have the ability to identify the priority issues in which you must invest. You can then knowingly decide how to approach the EU arena by deploying a lobbying strategy. This is the next key phase in a lobbying strategy.

The deployment of a lobbying strategy, also called '**downstream lobbying**', refers to several stages: the development of messages, the building up of networks, the evaluation of power relations and the actual lobbying itself. This process depends on the development of messages and lobbying material that will be used. Stakeholders often underestimate the importance of this stage and jump into their lobbying actions, without having given adequate thought and consideration to the messages that they will use. Deploying a lobbying strategy requires a very clear and coherent assessment of the messages so that they highlight the objectives. Yet, the elaboration of a message is not such a straightforward exercise; therefore a number of recommendations will be made in the next part of this chapter.

10.6 Phase 2: Building your argumentation

The first step in the deployment of a lobbying strategy is to build the argumentation, also called 'message development'. Message development requires a preliminary dual-phase process:

- firstly, an assessment of the issues raised by EU legislation or activity
- secondly, a decision about realistic objectives that can be achieved

Only once these two processes have taken place can the drafting of arguments, positions and supporting material proceed. These documents and supporting materials can take various forms, from a formal position paper, a proposed amendment, infographics, and short videos to media adverts and stories. These different forms will be discussed later in the section on lobbying vehicles.

10.7 Step 2.1: Assessment of the issues

A useful way to start thinking about message development is to consider the possible different aspects of the message you want to concentrate on. Some different message ideas are brought together in Table 10.2.

Table 10.2: Message matrix

Political issues Impacts of international relations	Economic constraints Technological constraints
Community / Consumer protection Environmental issues	Legal issues Procedural aspects (competencies)

Source: Athenora Consulting

Legislative files are inherently multifaceted: political issues (balance between the institutions, ideology, general principles, coherence between EU policies or objectives, etc.); international relations (relations between the EU and a third state, participation in international organisations such as the WTO, ICAO, etc.); economic issues (financial, trade, revenues, jobs and other impacts on a sector); technology issues (availability of new technology, standardisation); social issues (impact on consumers, viewpoints of NGOs, public opinion, etc.); environmental issues (impacts on climate, air, waste, etc.); legal issues (competence of the EU, legal basis, etc.); and lastly, procedural issues (voting rules, institutions' internal positions, conflicts within and between the institutions, etc.). An example of how this works in practice can be seen in the box below.

Analysis of issues in the draft Directive on cross-border healthcare: key issues

EU issues: Does the proposal guarantee the freedom to receive and provide healthcare services throughout Europe by effectively removing barriers to the provision of cross-border healthcare? Does the proposal reflect the values held by European citizens since it does not at any time mention the link between EU issues and health? Indeed, the concept of health as relevant to the general interest is absent from the text. By allowing better-informed patients to pay in advance the costs of seeking treatment abroad, is Europe at risk of developing medical tourism and expanding a two-tier healthcare system?

Economic issues: Who will pay for the costs of treatment abroad? Who will pay for setting up the central contact points to which patients should go?

Political issues: While the proposal pushes for increased mobility of patients and health professionals, at no point does it mention the usefulness of a European statute for mutual societies that could provide greater European protection on matters of health.

Legal issues: The legal basis used is the internal market. Does this prism risk assimilating health to a mere commodity? Does the proposal recognise the competence of the Member States, which are responsible for the definition of social security benefits and for the stakeholder and delivery of healthcare, medical care and social security benefits?

Procedural issues: Does the proposal offer an adequate legal response to the numerous judgements of the Court of Justice? It seems that it raises more questions than it solves. For example, it cites quality standards without defining them and the definitions provided are very vague, especially regarding hospital care.

Technical issues: How to build up an effective database to ensure that patients have - in their own language - access to all relevant information to enable them to make informed decisions, particularly with regard to availability, price and the results of healthcare provided? How to ensure the interoperability of medical records, while ensuring confidentiality of data?

Source: Athenora Consulting

A comprehensive analysis of issues, such as the one suggested on the previous page, allows all aspects of a Regulation, Directive or text, to be understood. It also supports the development of a variety of different arguments and lobbying tools.

Analysis of legislative impact

Assessing the issues raised in a draft text allows one to clearly determine the impacts. Logical steps should be followed when analysing a draft text to understand its different aspects. This exercise will help you prepare your own arguments, and also understand the arguments of others.

Having performed this exercise, the relevant interests that will require action should be relatively clear. You should be as clear as possible about the impacts that the draft text

> The EU arena is governed by reason. In order to convince decision-makers about the validity of your position, you will need to bring evidence and facts to the table and to put aside opinions and beliefs. This highlights the importance of defining precisely the impact that an EU initiative will have - in order to extract the relevant facts supported by evidence. Obviously it is important to structure the facts and evidence to the needs of the audience in order to convince them. Therefore it is necessary to have a **'drawer strategy'** with various arguments, evidence and case-studies to present to different audiences as and when needed. Only then will you be able to communicate effectively and persuasively.
>
> Always think about the following question: what does the decision maker need to know to take a sound decision and be able to defend it?

will have on your activities in terms of image, business and finance (quantification of the impact is always very useful) and on your professional practices (which may also be extended to the technological impact, for example). It is possible to carry out this work by relying on the expertise available internally, possibly supplemented by the participation of external consultants if required. It can then be summarised into a report that will serve as the foundation for the construction of arguments.

Table 10.3: Questions to ask during the issue evaluation

> 1. What is the nature of the problem addressed by the Commission's proposal, what is its extent and its evolution?
> 2. What are the objectives of the Commission's proposal? Are they compatible with the objectives of the stakeholder? If not, what might be the alternative objectives? Are they shared by other stakeholders?
> 3. What are the risks and uncertainties for the stakeholder of the political choices presented in the Commission's proposal? What are the possible alternatives?
> 4. What are the environmental, economic and social (direct and indirect) impacts of the proposal and how do they impact the stakeholder?
> 5. What is the impact of these issues in qualitative, quantitative and monetary terms?
>
> The questions above are pretty much in line with the European Commission's own Impact Assessment; to a certain extent, your evaluation could be used to raise issues regarding the EC's political choices.

Source: Athenora Consulting

Defining desired changes - setting objectives and priorities

Following the evaluation of the different impacts, it is possible to set a number of objectives and priorities in terms of changes desired in the text being adopted. Practice shows that a limited number of objectives will ultimately be reached and that pursuing too many decreases one's ability to influence. Moreover, without clear objectives, it is impossible to determine the extent to which lobbying has produced the desired results.

It is important to start from the assumption that you will not obtain 100% of what you want. Therefore it is important to rank your priorities in order to be able to adapt your lobbying strategy as you carry it out. **Realism** in your priorities is important to set expectations and allow for a fair evaluation of the actions taken later on. Moreover, with a too extreme or inflexible position, you will risk being sidelined when it comes to the institutional negotiations, which is a key component of the decision-making process in Brussels.

Any lobbying strategy must therefore have clear objectives, directly related to the proposed action and the resolution of the problems identified. The definition of objectives is often an iterative process, to be refined throughout the lobbying campaign.

To be more effective, goals should be expressed through the **'SMART' model**:

Specific (precise and concrete)
Measurable
Accepted (by the stakeholder - notably senior management)
Realistic and
Time-constrained

It is necessary to list a few goals and, above all, to rank them according to the triptych of non-negotiable, negotiable and secondary, meaning that they can be dropped easily to create a favourable climate for negotiating.

Another complementary method is the **'SWOT' model** which consists of assessing both from an internal and external point of view the strengths and opportunities as well as the weaknesses and threats linked with a specific draft text.

> **Sample objectives**
>
> - Translate into reality the principle of diversity of forms of entrepreneurship in obtaining a European statute for mutual insurance companies.
> - Recognise in the Directive on cross-border healthcare the connection between social services and health services and limit medical tourism in Europe.
> - Take health services out of the Directive on services in the internal market.

The SWOT exercise will allow the stakeholder to highlight its strengths and to communicate them. On the other hand, the stakeholder can identify where it should emphasise its lobbying efforts in order to address the weaknesses, or at least to minimise them. This will help later to define arguments.

This classification determines the negotiating margin of the lobbying actions to be implemented. Only non-negotiable objectives should be preserved (and pursued) to the end. These will obviously justify greater investment and energy. The secondary objectives allow you to start the negotiating game with a margin of flexibility in the positions you propose. Negotiable objectives allow for compensation to be obtained in exchange for their withdrawal, i.e. simple negotiating chips because, as already stated above, you will never get 100% of what you are trying to achieve.

Failing to have clear objectives is one of the main explanatory factors behind many lobbying failures (too many objectives, lack of prioritisation, overly rigid or too flexible positions). Once the objectives have been clearly defined, it is possible to go on to the next stage in the process: drafting the **arguments for lobbying**.

10.8 Step 2.2: Drafting arguments

Types of arguments and their presentation
The analysis of issues and the assessment of the impact of draft EU measures are essential preliminary steps in the development of lobbying arguments. The latter should not examine all of the issues in the legislation, but be limited to explaining and pursuing pre-determined objectives. This will make it possible to establish a clear table that links the desired objectives to the regulatory issues and the arguments to advocate in favour of your position.

For example, the goal of trying to reduce the scope of a legislative proposal in order to avoid a product being banned from sale can be linked to a legal issue (EU competence), an economic issue (cost), or a technological issue (new product) and can mean being able to have arguments in three different areas: legal (EU non-competence), economic (disproportionate cost) and technology (new product not a suitable substitute for the one banned). Once the argument table is complete, it is much easier to produce a lobbying document, be that a letter, position paper or case-study - the different types will be discussed later. Both written and oral material can follow this outline:

1. Presentation of the context (a particular proposal, amendment).
2. Position taken (exemption, new threshold, deadlines, objectives etc.).
3. Arguments in defence of the position (three or four arguments using the matrix: political, economic, EU, etc.).
4. A clear request (revision of an article, new preamble, etc.) without hesitating to make a draft proposal.

At this stage it seems relevant to raise the following comment. In order to communicate effectively and persuasively, a stakeholder should understand the limits to the arguments they are working with. This requires an understanding of the ideological constraints. Not just any kind of argument is admissible and well-received in a given institutional context. Each institution tends naturally to produce its own ideology, a core of ideas and more or less intangible values - and these need to be respected at all times.

Thus, at the European level, it is very difficult, or impossible, to argue against the principle of free trade in favour of oligopolies or long-term contracts, without clashing with the 'free trade and open competition' ideology of the EU. Only a principle of at least the same value, such as protecting the environment, for example, could be used to obtain exceptions to the principle of free and undistorted trade. It is always possible to play one principle against another and create a favourable balance of power. This is shown below in Figure 10.4.

Figure 10.4: Square of European arguments

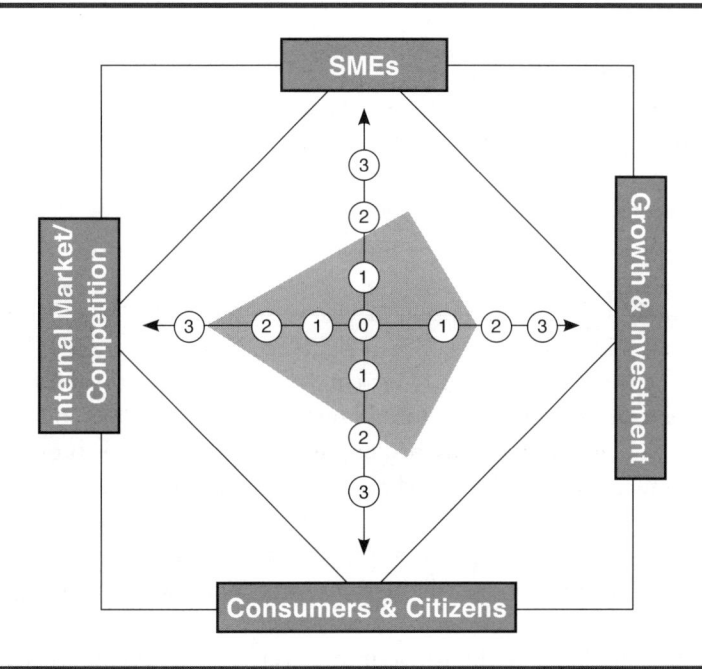

Source: Athenora Consulting

The magic square of European arguments, shown in Figure 10.4, is a reminder of the weight and strength of some principles at the European level. The more the arguments are consistent with these principles, the more likely they are to be heard in Brussels. Returning to our example, the economic argument of cost may be strengthened by highlighting the additional costs for SMEs and consumers. The competition aspect may also be highlighted in the economic sphere in relation to the disappearance of a subsidiary and the formation of a de facto quasi-monopoly.

Drafting amendments, providing evidence, writing position papers
Lobbying means acting in order to create a desired change. Thus lobbying is much more successful if a text amendment is proposed. It is the logical extension to arguing for a change to be made - and provides you with an answer to one of the most often heard questions in Brussels lobbying: 'So what

exactly do you want?' This is the legal and operational translation of the arguments that have been developed. It is essential to translate these arguments into amendments, otherwise they remain merely rhetorical. Thus, for instance, an argument which highlights unfair international competition should be translated into amendments seeking to ensure reciprocity with third countries. Amendments are an essential part of lobbying work in Brussels and knowing what to propose, to whom, how, and when is vitally important.

An argument that has no translation into an amendment can be more easily dismissed by the institutions, or other stakeholders, as *a priori* irrelevant since it does not have any operational relevance.

1. **Submitting concrete amendments**

    Translating positions, arguments, as well as objectives, into concrete amendments is a genuinely useful exercise that will help deliver clarity in your messages. The drafting of amendments is, however, not always easy. Indeed, they must scrupulously respect the drafting constraints of the European institutions. They should also be expressed in very specific legal styles. To assist the drafter with this task, the main types of amendments are listed below:

    1. Change an obligation into an option or vice versa (example: 'Member States shall/may set up call centres to inform citizens of their rights regarding cross-border health services').
    2. Reduce the scope (example: 'This Directive shall not apply to the following activities: social services of general interest such as social housing, aid for children and assistance to families and persons who are permanently or temporarily in need that is provided by the State, by providers mandated by the State or charities recognised as such by the State.').
    3. Extending the deadlines for implementation is a classical type of amendment that involves changing the dates. For example, if the Commission wishes for implementation by 2019, the purpose of the amendment will be to propose 2022, while justifying the time required for the actors to be able to prepare.
    4. The technique of changing an article into a recital is less common. For example, it may consist of highlighting values that will be included in the preambles rather than in an article.
    5. Adding new provisions to highlight specific needs. Those amendments are the most difficult to write because there is no basis. The creativity needs to strictly follow legal writing.

At this stage, the preparation of lobbying actions is complete and the stakeholder now has the tools to effectively start their engagement in the EU arena.

2. **Writing accurate position papers**

    The first, and most common, method of communicating with the EU institutions is done with a position paper - perhaps the single most important part of a lobbying strategy. A position paper is a written vehicle to communicate your position to decision-makers and other stakeholders.

Obviously, your position paper should always clearly present the interest behind the words. In a manner as illustrative as possible, you should provide key figures that show your legitimacy and your socio-economic relevance on the one hand, and your expertise on the other hand. Infographics are very useful when you want to present yourself in a user-friendly and easy to understand way. A link to an online video is also a stimulating way to keep your interests in your audience's mind.

Having evidence and good arguments is in itself not enough to communicate efficiently and to catch your audience's interest. In a nutshell, writing a good position paper requires style and clarity from the writer - it is very much an acquired skill. Evidence and arguments are only the rough material of a 'position paper'. It presents your side of what is probably a multi-faceted issue. The goal of writing a position paper should be to convince the specific audience (tailored messages are key) that your position is well-founded and sound. The main 'do's' and 'don'ts' of a position paper are to be found in Table 10.4.

Table 10.4: The content of a good position paper

The do's	The don'ts
• Translate your position into language that your audience understands.	• Your position paper has an internal focus and does not take into account the audience.
• Draft short and clear positions.	• It is confusing (acronyms, technical jargon) or too long.
• Adopt a 'facts and figures' and/or legal approach.	• There is no clear hierarchy in the messages.
• Pay attention to the presentation.	• It lacks concrete examples and evidence to support your claims.
• Be constructive and positive.	• It is too general.
• Personalise the messages to the audience.	• It does not mention the author clearly - you are not identified.
• Present open options.	• The spokesperson lacks charisma and the position does not come to life.
• Follow up your position paper with meetings.	
• Be clear about what you want.	
• Make your paper visually appealing.	

Source: Athenora Consulting

The organisation and structure of the position paper should be carefully thought out in order to make sure your audience follows your line of argument and logic. Moreover, it is important to develop your ideas in a manner that is easy for your audience to understand.

It is important to create clear paragraphs with a core idea in each and to organise them for the purpose of your overall argumentation. Particular attention should be devoted to the transitions between your ideas, making sure you provide your reader with a feeling of logic and coherence throughout the document.

A key point to raise here is about complexity. Although the content of your document is important, it will not mean much if the reader can't understand your point. This requires not being too technical. It also requires a well-structured position. You may have some great ideas in your paper but if you cannot effectively communicate them, you will not convince your audience.

Finally, it is also of the utmost importance to consider your audience when you are selecting your arguments and evidence to try and match with their specific interests. If you write a position paper for a Desk Officer in the Commission who is an expert on the topic, your analysis would be different from what you would say if you were writing to a Member of the European Parliament (MEP) who has a more general view. You need to make sure that you adjust the structure and presentation of your message to the specific needs of the decision-maker that you are addressing. Do not alter the message but, for example, summarise your message for MEPs, present data in a way that is easy to understand and place the focus on the issues they should act upon.

In order to adapt to your audience, you will have to be selective about the words you use, the background information you supply and the degree of detail you provide. Table 10.5 below highlights the key elements for a good position paper.

Table 10.5: The structure of a good position paper

Organisation of a good position paper
Limit yourself to two/three pages - pay attention to the visual presentation

Introduction - Identification
Introduce the issue (context)
Outline your position with a one-sentence statement
Be positive and provide solutions to any issues raised
Indicate clearly your request and expectations

Body: explain your view
For each point give an informed opinion and provide evidence with concrete examples
Number your points for clarity - try to limit yourself to a reasonable number (5-7)
Avoid using emotional terms
Use uncontroversial well-known references, speeches or data
Briefly, but objectively, itemise counterclaims and provide information to refute them (the SWOT analysis is often very useful)

Conclusion
Restate your key arguments
Be clear about your request
Put your contact details
Give details about your organisation to establish your identity

> Look at the closed consultations of the Commission to get more ideas on position papers - this is a wealth of information on how to (and not to) draft position papers:
> http://ec.europa.eu/yourvoice/consultations/2014/index_en.htm

Source: Athenora Consulting

10.9 Step 2.3: Identifying and building up a network

Having a broad and diverse network is a key factor in terms of influence. A network begins upstream of an issue and is built on a detailed identification of institutional actors and stakeholders who are active in your fields of interest. Networks should cover all of the European institutions (Commission, Parliament and Council) at their political levels (Commissioners, Cabinets, MEPs, Ministers, Permanent Representatives and Deputy Permanent Representatives) as well as technical levels (Desk Officers, Secretariat-General officials, public relations advisers, MEP assistants). Networks should also cover the various stakeholders that are active on your issues: the Eurofeds, journalists, think-tanks, NGOs or competitors. Moreover, university networks should not be underestimated (College of Europe and École Nationale d'Administration (ENA) for example).

Stakeholders need to devote time in order to build a comprehensive network as they serve several functions at the same time. Some networks are useful in order to get inside information. Others might be used to test ideas before putting them into a position paper or to get advice. Others might be useful for their knowledge on specific issues, such as detailed institutional knowledge that you will always need. Some ideas on how to build a good network are outlined in Table 10.6.

Table 10.6: How to build an effective network

> **The formation of an effective and lasting network takes place by following several golden rules:**
>
> 1. Closely identifying the relevant stakeholders on any given subject, and contacting those of interest.
> 2. Participating in seminars, conferences and cocktail parties in order to meet people on the basis of shared interests.
> 3. Participating in panels at conferences allows one to be identified as an expert.
> 4. Following up on contacts made. Too often, business cards collected at meetings are not followed up on.
> 5. Embracing the principle of 'give and take', since the more you bring to your network, the more useful information it will offer you. Sharing knowledge is key to strengthening one's network.
> 6. Third-party recommendations are a great way to expand one's network.

Source: Athenora Consulting

324 Conclusion: Designing a Successful EU Lobbying Campaign

The key actors were presented in the chapters on the European institutions and decision-making. It is very important to build a network beyond these institutions to include stakeholders who, by their actions, are also involved in the development of EU policies. Some stakeholders are actually themselves natural networks such as national or European professional associations and federations. All pan-European umbrella organisations offer excellent networking opportunities. Also do not forget the associations representing customers, suppliers, consumers, Non-governmental Organisations (NGOs), local communities, unions and think-tanks.

10.10 Phase 3: Arena management - stakeholder mapping

No stakeholder is isolated in defending and promoting their interests. So it is important to identify all actors present and active on a given dossier, their respective importance and any existing or potential coalitions. This exercise, stakeholder mapping, is also essential to define one's primary targets and from there develop the types of communication needed to work most effectively with them. Stakeholders must analyse whether the positions they are promoting are on the agenda of decision-makers or other key actors and whether they receive wide support or not. This mapping exercise will help in placing your own organisation in relation to the other actors, and is highlighted in Figure 10.5.

Figure 10.5: Mapping the lobbying arena

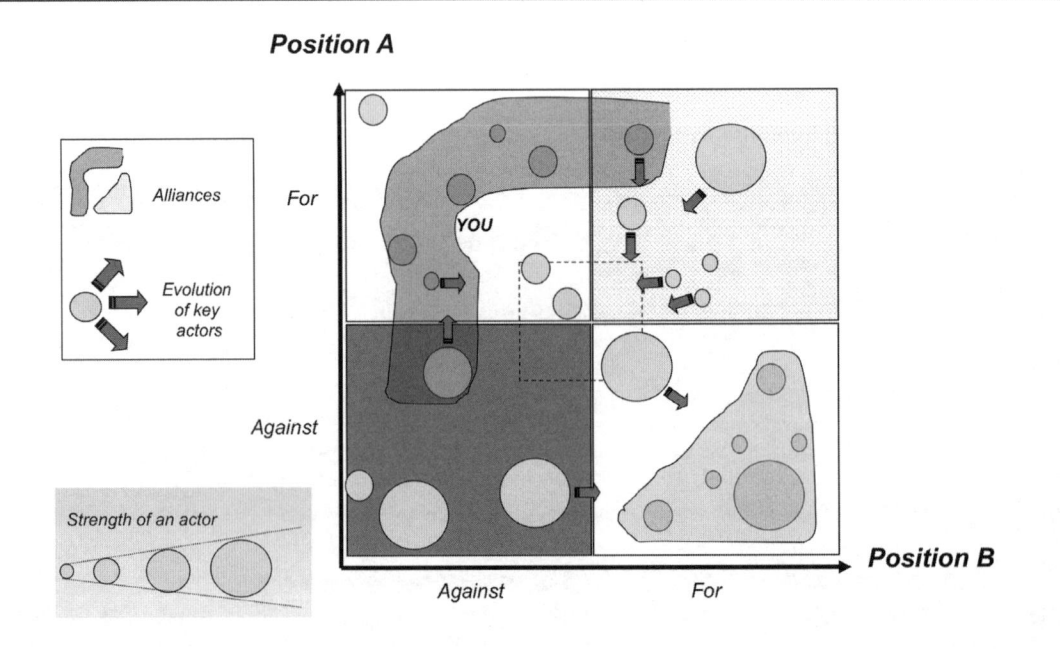

Source: Athenora Consulting

10.11 Step 3.1: Identifying balance of powers, cleavages and common interests

First of all this mapping exercise serves to identify the major divisions on a given issue which structure debates at the European level. The objective is to ensure that, in studying an issue, one has, or will have, the ability to rally the largest possible support. The idea is also to ensure that your position will be in line with a majority of actors. Basically, issues can be addressed through two opposing views: competitiveness versus social protection; free market versus regulation, etc.

There are often two ways to address a single issue, as the two sides of a coin. For instance, either you are in favour of more competitiveness because you believe that it brings growth, or you are in favour of social protection to promote workers' status.

This dual approach can be illustrated for many topics. If we take health services as an example, there might be a split on the treatment of health services in the internal market. Proponents of treating health services like other service sectors could be in opposition to those believing that health services cannot be reduced to a mere commodity, but are something to which access must be guaranteed for all. In such a case the mapping exercise is useful for identifying all the actors and where they stand on the different key elements.

The most important part of mapping involves identifying the actors working on the issue. Even if it is possible to separate out institutional actors and other stakeholders, it is more efficient to combine the two. This will give a more complete picture and reduce the chance of surprises later. The important thing is to maintain the readability of the map, by selecting a small but significant number of key actors to visualise the situation. The importance of the actor depends on their power and influence in the arena (economic, political, social or cultural). This work involves highlighting formal and informal coalitions and determining where the balance of power lies on an issue in order to acquire information for building a strategy. If the actors' positions change during the procedure, this is important to recognise in the mapping because it is often a sign of the crystallisation of a majority position.

Lastly, you must place your own organisation on the arena map. You can then identify both the strengths and weaknesses of your position and also your distance from, or proximity to, other actors, especially the influential ones. An example stakeholder map is shown on the next page in Figure 10.6.

In the example shown in Figure 10.6, the matrix compares actors favourable to the European statute for a mutual insurance company to the unfavourable ones by studying several types of actors (Member States, influential individuals, European institutions, European associations and companies). The mapping also evaluates the actors' levels of interest in order to target only those who are most interested in this issue.

There are other possible ways to visualise the balance of power on a specific issue. You may for instance simply use a Microsoft Word or Excel document with a list of the main stakeholders with a colour code system according to their position (red = against, green = ok, and orange = to be convinced).

Figure 10.6: Example stakeholder mapping

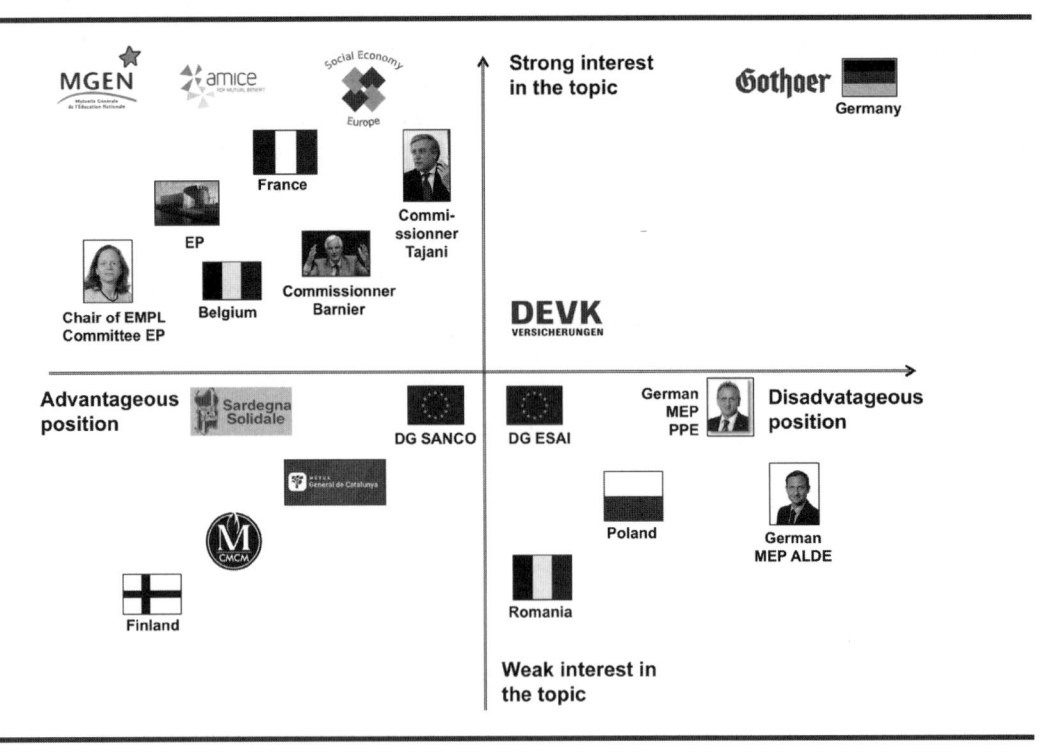

Source: Athenora Consulting

10.12 Step 3.2: Identifying priority targets

The main question is how to identify who should be included in the mapping. Usually, 50 contacts are sufficient to get a good picture of the balance of power. The contacts which are usually the ones identified are listed in Table 10.7.

The next question is where to find the information. Of course when it comes to the European institutions the online organisational charts (organigrammes) are a good first source for contact details. And when there are some doubts about who is in charge, some phone calls will help to decipher who does what.

For the other stakeholders, this is slightly more difficult. But there are easy means to get the information such as reading consultation responses or

> **How to map stakeholders**
>
> - Read consultation responses on Your Voice in Europe
> - Check websites of stakeholders for information
> - Use your network
> - Go to events and hearing
> - Social media monitoring (blogs, twitters, Facebook and LinkedIn)

Table 10.7: Priority targets

	Commission	Parliament	Council	Stakeholders
Political level	Members in charge of the issue in all relevant Commissioners' Cabinets	MEPs (rapporteur, shadow rapporteur, opinion leaders on the topic, Chairs and Vice-Chairs of the relevant Committees, heads of key National Delegations, Group coordinator)	National Experts from the key Members States	Users or consumers organisations Professional federations at European and national levels Business representatives
Technical level	DG Civil Servants and Desk Officer	Civil Servants from Committees and Political Groups	General Secretariat Civil Servants Members of the Permanent Representations	Think-tanks, NGO, Media Regions Trade Unions

Source: Athenora Consulting

checking media releases or speeches. The monitoring of key stakeholders' websites is also useful as many publish press releases or their position papers. Once again your network can help and by participating regularly in events on a specific dossier, you will be able to clearly identify the opinion leaders and the key contacts.

Ultimately, this work helps you to understand the position of other stakeholders and the prevailing consensus on a dossier. This is vital to assess whether the climate is favourable, unfavourable or neutral to your objectives. The mapping is an essential phase for the implementation of various tactical actions that may then be mobilised in response to what you have found. We shall return to the typology of actions to take in the section on lobbying measures. At this stage it is important to understand how the early identification of relative strengths, and the nature of the arena, underpins the rest of a good lobbying strategy.

Building up a network and establishing a comprehensive mapping of the actors can lead to a proliferation of potential targets that you may wish to work with - carrying the risk of spreading limited resources too thinly, without necessarily achieving any results in terms of influence. To counter this, a matrix of priority targets should be developed. It allows the identification of key contacts on the basis of objective criteria.

Figure 10.7: Matrix of priority targets

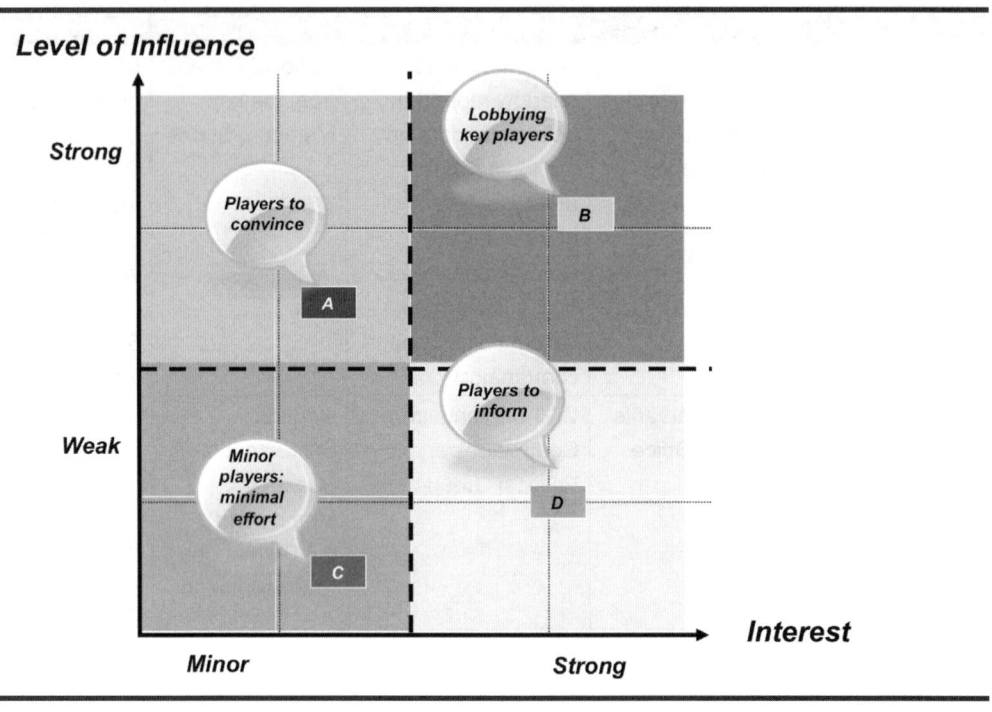

```
Level of Influence
        │
 Strong │    Players to      │  Lobbying
        │    convince        │  key players
        │         A          │       B
        │ - - - - - - - - - -│- - - - - - -
        │                    │  Players to
        │  Minor players:    │  inform
  Weak  │  minimal effort    │
        │         C          │       D
        └────────────────────┴──────────────→ Interest
              Minor                Strong
```

Source: Athenora Consulting

From this it is possible to target those who, within all the identified contacts, are the most relevant at any given moment in time. This will ensure an optimum use of resources. This matrix is constructed along two axes: the target's level of influence and their interest in the issue. These two criteria are crucial for transforming every encounter into an opportunity for positive influence. By definition, the key lobbying actors are the most influential and those most interested in the issue. Logically and in light of often-limited resources, very little effort should be directed to actors with low influence.

If interest in an issue can be easily identified (speeches, questions, participation in conferences, etc.), the **degree of influence** is a more subjective concept. It may, however, be objectified by defining certain criteria. Thus, an MEP's level of influence may be measured by his or her membership in a Political Group and their role within it (e.g. coordinator), their role on the parliamentary Committees on which they sit (Chair, Vice-Chair) nationality and place in the National Delegation, their career in Parliament (number of reports, Resolutions), and so on.

10.13 Step 3.3: Classifying actors

Once a list of targets has been identified, it is possible to define approach tactics depending on whether the target can be classified as an ally, neutral or an adversary. An 'ally' target is an actor who shares the same position as that promoted by a stakeholder. A 'neutral' target is an actor who has not defined their position vis-à-vis the subject at hand, and thus constitutes a target to be convinced in order to ensure a favourable **balance of power**. It may be a competitor or an institutional actor or even a European or national federation. A target described as an 'adversary' is an actor who does not share the viewpoint promoted by a stakeholder, and sometimes one who does not even share the same values. This is an actor who, in most situations, cannot be rallied to a position, but whose actions should be watched carefully to be able to respond and counter, and not let an opposing balance of power take over.

It is important to make this **classification of actors** as allies, neutrals or adversaries because it will help define actions and strategies moving forward - it will help you understand how to select your interlocutors and also understand developments on your issue much better. In fact, for each category a different lobbying strategy should be applied. Of course, the priority targets are the neutral actors; the influential actors; and those concerned by, and engaged in, the issue.

10.14 Phase 4: Lobbying actions

Table 10.8 indicates appropriate actions to be taken in each of these situations. The key is of course to find support and secure allies, for which several actions can be undertaken.

Table 10.8: Lobbying targets - Tactics

Actions / Position	Allies	Neutral parties	Adversaries
Objective	Secure	Convince	Divide
Offensive actions	Work together / Mobilise	Commit	Attack/destabilise vulnerable/weak members
Defensive actions	Avoid disagreements	Inform	Counter arguments / Counter attacks

Source: Athenora Consulting

Coalitions and joint actions

The legitimacy of a position promoted by stakeholders at the European level is largely related to the representativeness that they have. It is therefore important to work together, with greater representativeness, with the European decision-makers. This may, for example, result in the creation of an **ad hoc coalition** or an issue-oriented working group with an original message. These coalitions might be either vertical, from consumers to producers, or horizontal, gathering different competitors from the same field. The Commission has recently recognised the importance of these coalitions by requesting that they register on the Transparency Register.

Other joint actions are possible, such as organising an event together, a common response to a Commission consultation or a position paper (and amendments) co-signed by several groups. The key is to avoid the splintering of the group, especially during long campaigns, and prevent divisions that may occur by sticking to unified issues. Having the leadership of the group, or coalition, may help in facilitating the adoption of one's own views. This indirect lobbying is not dissimilar to the strategy of working with the relevant European or national associations and federations to put forward your position.

Convincing neutral actors is the core of influencing work, which aims not only to win them over for a specific position, but also to turn them into active relays for promoting one's positions. The ways to do this can be diverse in nature, but it is always based on an argument illustrated by facts and figures. Furthermore, such convincing can only be done on the basis of shared values.

The old saying of 'divide and conquer' is also something to be aware of because it is a tactic that is frequently employed in Brussels. Staying informed of the arguments and actions of adversaries allows one to judge one's own lobbying actions (counter-arguments, press releases, expert reports, etc.) in order to reverse the balance of power, or at least introduce doubt among decision-makers about the merits of the arguments raised by opponents. As stated before, you will never be lobbying alone and you will not get 100% of what you want, so you need to be aware of what is going on around you.

Having outlined the various stages of preparation and mapping, the next stage in lobbying is that of actually communicating your messages and positions, which can be done in a variety of different ways depending on your objectives, networks and strategy. However, before looking at these actions, it is first important to address the development of a lobbying team - or the requisite skills within an individual who has to exhibit all of these abilities.

10.15 Step 4.1: Key skills for lobbying

Lobbying is inherently a group activity, although very often, as mentioned above, it is undertaken by a small group of people or indeed a single person. A stakeholder should not act in isolation vis-à-vis his or her organisation, and a good relationship between them often determines the success of lobbying actions. Traditionally, lobbying requires the skill set identified in Table 10.9.

Table 10.9: Skills of a lobbyist

Profiles	Missions	Timing
Legal expert	Overview of the legal arguments	Upstream and when lodging amendments
Economist	Drafting of the arguments	Upstream: facts & figures
Lobbyist	Receive the right message from the right person at the right time Mapping/monitoring	During the procedure
Media/PR	Creation of a favourable arena to disseminate messages/improve the company's image	Upstream in order to evaluate the image, during the proceedings
Spokesperson	Meet with decision-makers and present arguments	Upstream (prior to any statement of position) and during meetings

Source: Athenora Consulting

In the skills outlined in Table 10.9 you find the following key roles:

1. **Legal:** the primary role is to understand the likely impacts of a proposal and provide the legal translation of the organisation's positions into amendments and objectives. This is required during the phase of objective definition, in order to validate the coherence of objectives, and during the amendment proposal and lobbying material development phases.

2. **Economic:** the main role is to quantify as early as possible the impact of the proposal on the organisation and identify facts and figures that will then support the arguments. This role is increasingly important since European decision-makers are constantly seeking concrete evidence - something that has grown since the introduction of the 'Smart Regulation' agenda and the systematic use of Impact Assessments by the European Commission.

3. **Press and public relations:** the main role is to work early on during the construction phase of the organisation's image in Brussels, and throughout the proceedings in connection with the organisation of events to support the lobbying strategy (symposiums, press conferences, etc.).

4. **Spokesperson:** this position may be held by several people within the group depending on the hierarchical and technical level of the decision-makers. Thus, for the Cabinets of Commissioners, the spokesperson should be the chairman or Director-General; while, at the level of Desk Officer, the spokesperson may be a technical expert. The key is to ensure that the spokesperson is, on the one hand, representative of the organisation and, on the other hand, charismatic enough to hook their audience. Language skills are also a factor to keep in mind at the European level.

5. **Lobbyist:** is responsible for coordinating the work of the team, planning projects and coming up with a strategy. They step in at each phase, from the monitoring to lodging of an amendment, via the mapping and development of arguments.

Having outlined the various roles and skills that lobbying requires, be it through a team of people or by one person, we can now turn our attention to the types of lobbying actions that can be used.

10.16 Step 4.2: Defining your lobbying approach

Working on the edge of the issue environment

Lobbying requires many tactical actions depending on the type of situation where the lobbying strategy is to be carried out. To be effective, a lobbying strategy must take into account the overall situation and not merely pursue a strategy defined by its own goals, without taking into account trade-offs and external influences. Therefore, it is critical to establish in advance the mapping of all relevant actors before defining the strategy to be followed. The work to be undertaken depends on the situation (favourable, unfavourable or neutral).

Typology of lobbying actions

One must further categorise the situation according to the following criteria:

1. Identify and secure allies (those actors with whom a coalition is possible) to ensure the mobilisation of actors open to the ideas promoted, sometimes taking on a leadership role or position.

2. Divide or respond to adversaries (the actors who hold opposing positions) in order to reverse a negative balance of power, particularly by winning over new actors and those not yet mobilised due to lack of awareness, or to create doubt as to how well-founded their position is.

3. Obtain support from neutral actors (those who have not yet taken a position) through influence, a reasoned approach and the use of negotiation techniques.

The work of the lobbyist is to identify all of the issues related to a specific dossier and to prioritise their objectives in order of importance, attempting where possible to assess the likely political receptiveness to determine as early as possible which ones could gain acceptance. This step leaves behind technical issues and returns to the political arena through the values and objectives promoted. For example, it would not be enough to talk narrowly about the Directive on cross-border healthcare in Europe: it is necessary to discuss health in Europe in general, the quality of care, the fight against the commoditisation of health, etc.

This step also helps in learning the positions of actors on various aspects of the same issue, and in identifying those with whom it is possible to work together. Obviously the timetable of these actions is mainly driven by the European institutions, so this will always be one of the most important elements to monitor and react to. The timetables between, and within, the institutions are never linear and they are never known in advance - they need to be attentively followed. Any mistake with the timelines can mean that well developed strategies can go to waste.

If the situation is positive, the lobbyist must ensure that the issue is kept high on the agenda and accelerate the timetable so that this positive trend does not lose momentum over time. However, the opposite is true in a negative environment where the lobbyist may use their influence to delay the adoption of an initiative, in particular in the Council, where a blocking minority can slow down the process.

Mastery of the calendar is essential for any successful strategy of influence. In general, intervention as early as possible is the key to success, meaning that the Commission is always the first institution to work with. Knowing the internal procedure that a dossier will follow in the Commission is the first place to start (see Chapter 1). If you are active at the very beginning there are however two possible disadvantages; firstly, that it makes you visible from the outset and secondly, your activity might alert other stakeholders to an issue they had not been working on. This risk needs to be assessed on a case-by-case basis.

Working on the edge of the issue environment refers to the delicate balance of any influencing strategy, whereby an external event has the capacity to strengthen or weaken the position you have taken. If the situation is favourable, the lobbyist must ensure that new related issues do not take over the debate by bringing in new and powerful stakeholders. However, if the situation is negative, changing these boundaries may be a good strategy, by expanding the pool of stakeholders who could be interested in the issue. Lastly, if the situation is neutral, expanding the list of stakeholders whose awareness is to be raised is a good way of creating a favourable balance of power.

Defining the degree of visibility of your lobbying actions
The degree of visibility that the stakeholder wants to give to their lobbying can fluctuate between two strategic extremes, that of the iceberg and the buoy.

1. The buoy strategy aims to enhance the visibility of the stakeholder and their positioning and focus attention on their actions and influence. It is often a feature of NGO strategies for example, and it is usually accompanied by a strategy of direct lobbying - which we will come to later in the chapter.

2. The iceberg strategy, on the other hand, seeks to exert influence in a more discreet and non-direct manner, using relays and more general vehicles. This type of strategy usually results in the establishment of more indirect lobbying actions.

Figure 10.8: Degree of visibility

> Discreet or visible:
>
> How intense?   Which combination?

Iceberg strategy

Part played by visible actions

Part played by hidden actions

Buoy strategy

Source: Athenora Consulting

In most cases, a lobbying strategy integrates and combines both discreet and visible actions. It is important to point out that a very discreet strategy is more and more difficult to conduct in the EU. Firstly, Brussels is a village and it is quite easy to identify the interests behind a position. Secondly, the recent moves towards greater transparency (see Chapter 7) reflect a strong desire on the part of decision-makers to know exactly who they are talking to.

How to communicate your message

1. **Direct or indirect lobbying**

   The next element is the consideration of **direct** or **indirect lobbying**. This is highlighted in Figure 10.9 on how to approach a rapporteur in the Parliament. This is just one example used for the purpose of demonstration and it can easily be duplicated for other targets. The key principle to understand is that to reach a given target, there are many channels that can be used, either direct or indirect. The key aspect of this is to identify which channels have the greatest influence on the audience in question.

Figure 10.9: Example - Direct and indirect approaches to a rapporteur in the Parliament

How to influence a rapporteur?

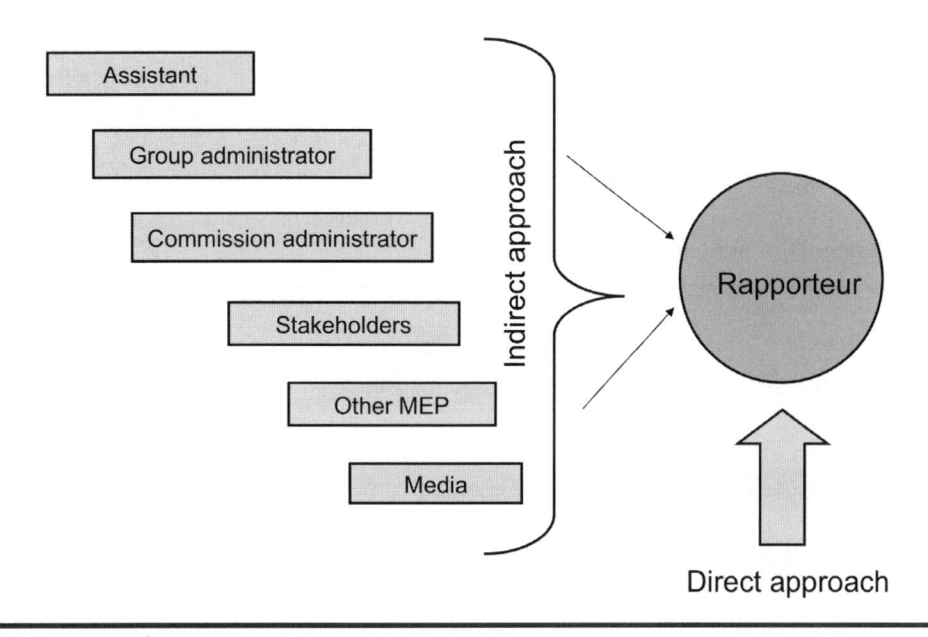

- Assistant
- Group administrator
- Commission administrator
- Stakeholders
- Other MEP
- Media

} Indirect approach → Rapporteur

↑ Direct approach

Source: Athenora Consulting

Sometimes lobbying may do more harm than good, depending on the reception given to the person who transmits the message. A direct lobbying strategy involves direct contact with the decision-makers and other key stakeholders of the institutions. This means meeting with them to spread your message verbally and through the distribution of lobbying material. These direct contacts may be formal or informal. This is a useful strategy if the organisation has a specific message to convey and its own expertise to advance. The goal is not just to meet anybody for the sake of meeting people but, on the basis of having identified key people in the stakeholder mapping exercise, to organise meetings to present arguments to the key people at the right time. Indirect lobbying, on the other hand, separates the sender from the message, and it offers a number of advantages in certain circumstances:

1. The first is that the sender remains somewhat dissociated from the message, as for example when a European federation presents their position - the position of individual members is aggregated and not put on display.
2. The second is that the receiver gets the message from a new source, other than the sender, who is perhaps more convincing, representative, or influential because they are closer to the dossier and/or decision-makers being contacted.
3. Lastly, if opposition appears, it does not directly harm the sender.

The risk of indirect lobbying is obviously that the message becomes distorted, associated too closely with another sender, or is indeed picked up by others who you would prefer not to have notified at that time. The main relays for an indirect lobbying strategy are the national and European associations, technical experts, scientists, think-tanks, the media and ad hoc groups created specifically to promote a position. They are often referred to as 'third parties'. They may also be European decision-makers, an MEP speaking to their Political Group, a Commission civil servant educating their colleagues, a Permanent Representation convincing other National Delegations, and so on. Indirect lobbying more broadly refers to the concept of 'agent of influence' which can be seen below in Figure 10.10.

Figure 10.10: Agents of influence - Multipliers

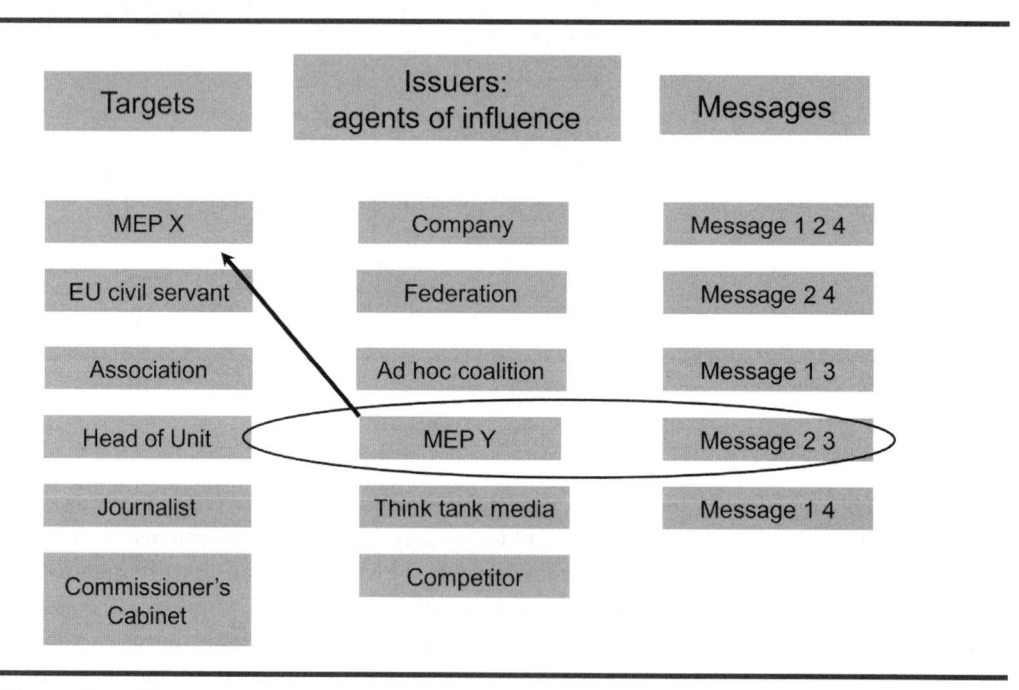

Targets	Issuers: agents of influence	Messages
MEP X	Company	Message 1 2 4
EU civil servant	Federation	Message 2 4
Association	Ad hoc coalition	Message 1 3
Head of Unit	MEP Y	Message 2 3
Journalist	Think tank media	Message 1 4
Commissioner's Cabinet	Competitor	

Source: Athenora Consulting

Influence can be defined as the ability to change the position, or behaviour, of another individual or group of individuals. The term '**agent of influence**' refers to people whose social position, status and political actions are deemed to give them greater powers of persuasion than could be mobilised by a third party. The idea behind this concept is based on '**the medium is the message**'. Sometimes, what matters most in terms of influence is not so much the content of the message (which is very important of course) but the channel of transmission itself. The message carrier acts as an agent of influence that can affect the targets much more than multiple lobbying actions. The influence is primarily based on mutual trust and reciprocity. Often an agent of influence will be able to tell you what tactics and strategies are best used in different circumstances.

The objective of using an agent of influence is three-fold:
1. To separate the messenger from the message.
2. To provide the necessary repetition of messages without exhausting the target by too visible a presence.
3. To take advantage of the natural authority of a person to promote their own ideas.

A person may be approached in various ways, directly as part of a direct lobbying strategy or indirectly through the use of all those who have an influence on the final target. The example we used of a rapporteur in the Parliament illustrates the many agents of influence that exist, from the closest (their parliamentary assistant or national State), to the institutional (the other shadow rapporteurs or the coordinator of the Political Group), to the furthest (members of the press and lobbyists). The goal is to make the chosen contacts aware of your position and interests in order for them to convince the MEP thereafter.

2. **Inside or outside lobbying**

   The aim of lobbying is to spread the right message, in the most appropriate form and with the required content, to the right person at the right time. Thus, influence requires a carrier, a vehicle that can be defined as a set of channels that can be mobilised to send a message. We distinguish between **inside lobbying**, which uses vehicles of influence directed at targeted individuals, and **outside lobbying**, which seeks to reach a wider audience (see also Figure 10.11 on the next page).

The first category is essentially based on the expertise of the bearer of the message and can be formatted in different ways: for example, writing a letter or e-mail to a decision-maker or taking a well-argued position when participating in a hearing organised by the European institutions. Inside lobbying relies heavily on the shaping of expertise from the field. It is particularly important in the Brussels arena given the 'facts and figures' approach of European decision-makers in relation to actors seeking to influence decision-making. It allows control to be kept over the content of the message - as long as it is direct lobbying.

Outside lobbying is based on a set of tools that can change the content of the message since the sender is not directly associated with the target. The most striking example of this is when journalists distribute stories and information, because the content is never 100% controllable. The advantage of outside lobbying is that these channels can reach a wider audience to raise awareness and to establish the stakeholder as an interested and credible actor. The Commission itself employs these tools, for example when presenting its **Eurobarometers** in support of its positions and underlining the expectations of European citizens on a specific issue. While it is still relatively infrequent, in the future the use of civil society could develop through the European Citizens' Initiative.

The main Brussels media

Financial Times; EUobserver; Reuters; Europolitique; Euractiv; BBC Online; Google news; Agence France Press; Politico (formerly European Voice); The Economist; International Herald Tribune; EU blogs; Euronews Associated Press; Agence Europe; Le Monde; Le Bulletin Quotidien.

Figure 10.11: Inside and outside lobbying

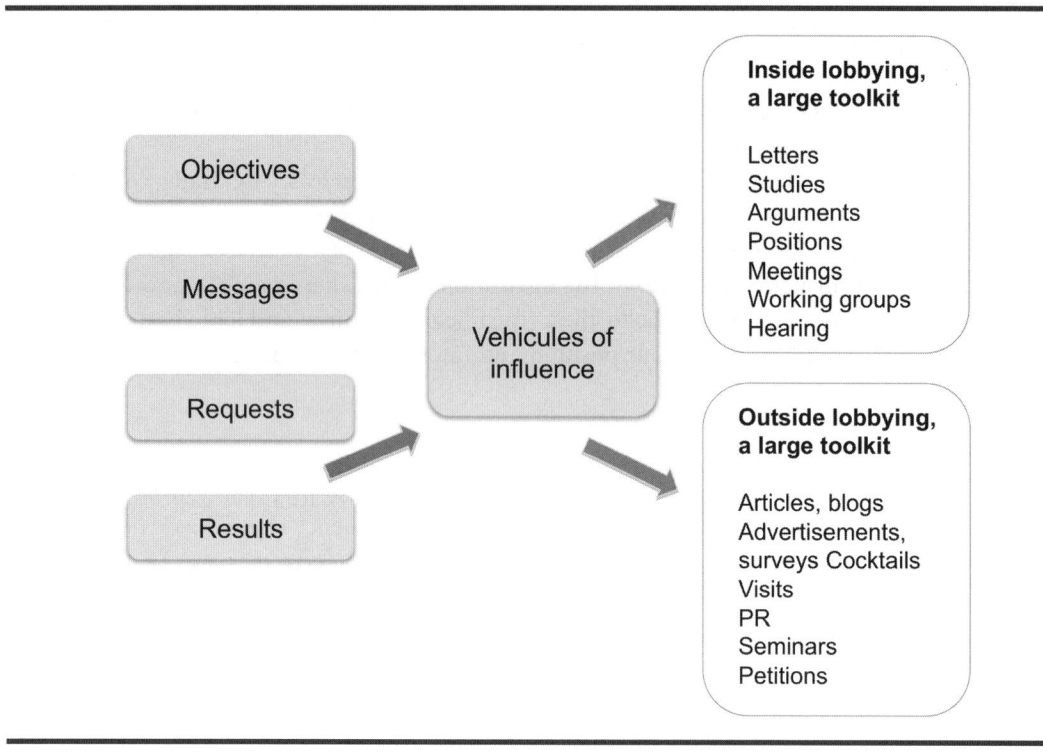

Inside lobbying, a large toolkit

Letters
Studies
Arguments
Positions
Meetings
Working groups
Hearing

Outside lobbying, a large toolkit

Articles, blogs
Advertisements,
surveys Cocktails
Visits
PR
Seminars
Petitions

Objectives, Messages, Requests, Results → Vehicles of influence

Source: Athenora Consulting

Organising seminars can reach a wider audience and spread expertise as well as setting the terms of the debate in order to present your own specific views on an issue. Field visits (factories, clinics, businesses) enable decision-makers to meet with European businesses and for the latter to better represent their daily challenges in order to ensure that the EU legislation being adopted provides an effective response to their needs.

Either vehicle, inside or outside, must be used wisely and most often a lobbying strategy will involve both types of measures. What matters most is to adapt the message and to assign clear objectives in order to measure the results of the approach.

10.17 Step 4.3: The lobbying plan - How to structure and evaluate the work

A lobbying strategy is divided into a series of actions to be carried out both internally (defining objectives, establishing a project team, preparing documents, stakeholder mapping) and externally (organising meetings, participating in events, disseminating press releases, etc.).

Thus, each step of lobbying should be defined with great care with regard to its objective, the target contacts, the methods of approach (direct/indirect lobbying), the vehicles (inside/outside), the scheduling and the outcome.

Table 10.10 provides a complete overview of all of the steps in this process.

Table 10.10: Summary of all lobbying actions

Action	Deadline	Person responsible	Vehicle chosen	Expected result
Gathering together and handling key elements of a file	Within 5 days of the identification of an issue by monitoring	Lobbyist working with the organisation's internal departments impacted by the subject	Creating a file on issues for the organisation with a matrix of interests	Total control of the file, its issues and the institutional schedule
Defining the organisation's issues and objectives in its lobbying campaign	Within 10 days of receipt of the file on the issues	Lobbyist with internal departments including a political authority within the structure	Summary of the objectives pursued through lobbying	Able to assess the results of the action
The mapping of key players	About 10/15 days	Lobbyist	Visual document with all contact details (address, e-mail, phone number) and subjects' main points of interest, pathway as well as their position in relation to issues pursued	Able to contact the right people and know the arguments likely to interest them

Able to identify allies, neutral parties and adversaries |
| Developing a position with arguments and proposed amendments to the original text | About a month | Lobbyist with internal departments including a political authority within the structure | A visual document (e.g. PowerPoint) of about 4 pages with figures, examples and specific requests | Having a document consistent with the editorial policy that will allow the organisation to make its position known |

Action	Deadline	Person responsible	Vehicle chosen	Expected result
Organising targeted meetings with decision-makers	Within two months of identifying the issue	Lobbyist with an organisational spokesman consistent with the level of contacts (political or specialised)	Direct lobbying: meetings	Raise awareness and convince the decision-makers
Dissemination of the organisation's position through multiple channels	Continuously throughout the campaign	Lobbyist with the person in charge of communications/media	Depending on the arena: press release, conference, attendance at meetings	Create a positive balance of power

Source: Athenora Consulting

The second element of the **full lobbying plan** is a schedule for action. The lobbying plan is completed by this schedule in order to reinforce the visibility and awareness of important deadlines (e.g. deadline for introducing amendments). By definition, a lobbying campaign is thought out and carried out over time. Time is marked by the agendas of European institutions (the date of publication of the text by the Commission, appointment of rapporteurs in European Parliament, discussions, Council of the EU meetings, the date for submission of amendments and votes, etc.). Timings are very important because things can move and change very quickly, or very slowly, from one dossier to another - and the element of acting at the right time has been consistently stressed as important in this book.

The timings are dictated to the lobbyist because they are beholden to institutional developments, and the challenge is to consistently make their own individual actions count at each stage of the process. An average campaign can last in the region of 18 to 24 months for legislative files - although a truly proactive campaign that started with thought leadership goals could last upwards of ten years. It must also be mentioned that lobbying around an issue should never really end because there will perhaps be Delegated and Implementing Acts and there will always be a legislative review. Hence, the need to stay on course and be ready to adapt the strategy defined in advance in order to avoid becoming too rigid and obtaining nothing in the end, having failed to take new timing elements into account. An example of this can be seen in Figure 10.12.

Figure 10.12: An example lobbying schedule

Actions timetable

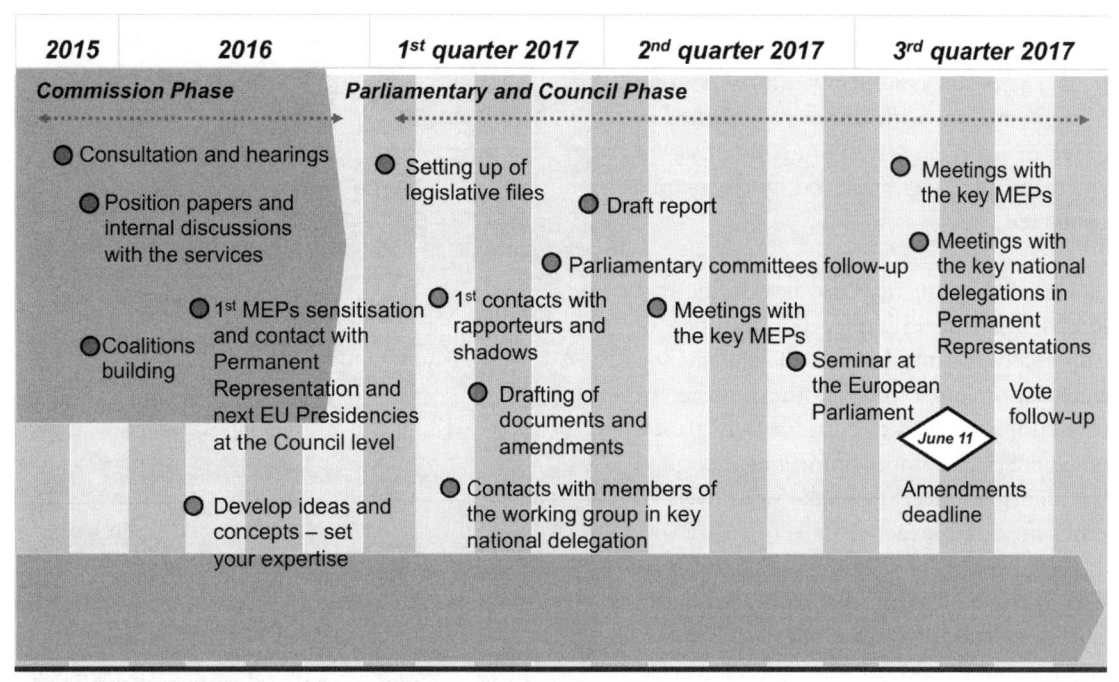

2015	2016	1st quarter 2017	2nd quarter 2017	3rd quarter 2017
Commission Phase		**Parliamentary and Council Phase**		

- Consultation and hearings
- Position papers and internal discussions with the services
- Coalitions building
- 1st MEPs sensitisation and contact with Permanent Representation and next EU Presidencies at the Council level
- Develop ideas and concepts – set your expertise
- Setting up of legislative files
- 1st contacts with rapporteurs and shadows
- Drafting of documents and amendments
- Contacts with members of the working group in key national delegation
- Draft report
- Parliamentary committees follow-up
- Meetings with the key MEPs
- Seminar at the European Parliament — June 11
- Meetings with the key MEPs
- Meetings with the key national delegations in Permanent Representations
- Vote follow-up
- Amendments deadline

Source: Athenora Consulting

The very last stage of a lobbying strategy, perhaps too often neglected, and certainly one of the most difficult, is to **evaluate the strategy** and learn for the future. Lobbying is an activity whose results are very difficult to quantify, but it is possible to evaluate successes and failures against specific Key Performance Indicators (KPIs), provided the stakeholder has clearly defined their objectives from the start.

The goal of evaluation is not to impose penalties, but to assess what worked and what did not work and to try to identify the reasons. These reasons may be internal to the organisation (poor organisation, taking a position too late, unclear messages, lack of senior management engagement, etc.) or external (unfavourable balance of power, trade-offs on other issues, etc.). This method allows continuous improvement of one's lobbying practices. Several concrete elements may be analysed. One key aspect of this is to ensure that lobbying objectives focus on outcomes/actions and do not simply read like a wish-list of legislative changes.

First of all there is the perception of political decision-makers in relation to the organisation and the position taken. Questions to ask during this evaluation revolve around the following: Did we clearly identify ourselves? Who did we mobilise for an amendment? Did we have more allies than at the beginning? Which influence relays did we call upon within each decision-making structure and among stakeholders?

It is useful to conduct a survey among decision-makers with whom you worked in order to learn how well your organisation and your ideas were received by the people contacted.

Concrete elements may also help refine that knowledge: for example, the number of calls received from decision-makers seeking clarification on a subject, the number of invitations received to participate in panels of experts, the number of meetings accepted by identified decision-makers, as well as other measurable facts.

The second element that this evaluation can demonstrate is the relevance of the arguments developed in the lobbying campaign. Several questions also deserve to be asked: 'Were my arguments credible? If they have been challenged, by whom and on what basis? Were my arguments understood by my contacts? Which ones were taken up and why?' This assessment allows the consistency of the positions taken in the chosen situations to be validated and ensures that the organisation is mobilising arguments that will be heard in Brussels.

> **Evaluation questions**
>
> 1. **Evaluate the decision-makers' perception**
>   - Have we been well identified? By whom?
>   - Who can we mobilise on an amendment?
>   - Do I have a network of contacts to be informed?
>   - Do we have more allies than at the beginning?
>
> 2. **Evaluate your arguments' relevance**
>   - Were your arguments credible? Concrete? Understood? Adopted? Used by others?
>   - Which arguments failed and why?
>
> 3. **Evaluate the success with respect to the final text**
>   - How many amendments were adopted?
>   - Which ones and why?
>   - Why did the other amendments failed?
>
> **Improve your future lobbying based on this assessment**

The final element involves evaluating the results obtained in terms of changing the original text, as well as its success in terms of not making any changes. Several questions may be asked: 'How many amendments were included? Which ones? Why have the others failed?' The final step, therefore, is to learn the lessons and improve one's lobbying skills before the next campaign.

This chapter has outlined a methodology for how to structure engagement with the EU institutions, and other stakeholders - a full lobbying methodology. One of the most important aspects of a lobbying strategy is that you must never hesitate to revisit your ideas, your position papers, your evidence and facts – in short, every aspect of your approach, objectives and strategy - and make changes and modifications if necessary. The lobbying environment can be very fluid, especially when the politics move, and as a lobbyist you need to make sure you are flexible and adaptable enough to move in the right directions at the right times because you will have to anticipate and move accordingly. It is also important to stay alert to new issues that might impact your position, become linked to your position or even be traded off against your position. Whilst this is vitally important to give you the best chances of success, you must have a consistent core message that does not change across all your audiences and stakeholders. If you are seen as changing with the direction of the wind you will not be taken seriously for too long, because the wind can change direction a number times during an EU legislative process.

While all of the four phases identified in this chapter are important, it is necessary to re-emphasise the importance of the preparatory phase for working with the EU institutions and decision-making, because this underpins the creation of a solid and coherent lobbying campaign. An analysis of the issues in a draft text, the definition of arguments and amendments, the mapping of stakeholders and the establishment of networks are the keys to successful lobbying. All of this, coupled with the ability to develop a detailed action plan and timetable, enables one to conduct a truly professional lobbying campaign that will benefit not just you but the decision-makers you interact with.

Figure 10.13: Overview of a structured lobbying campaign

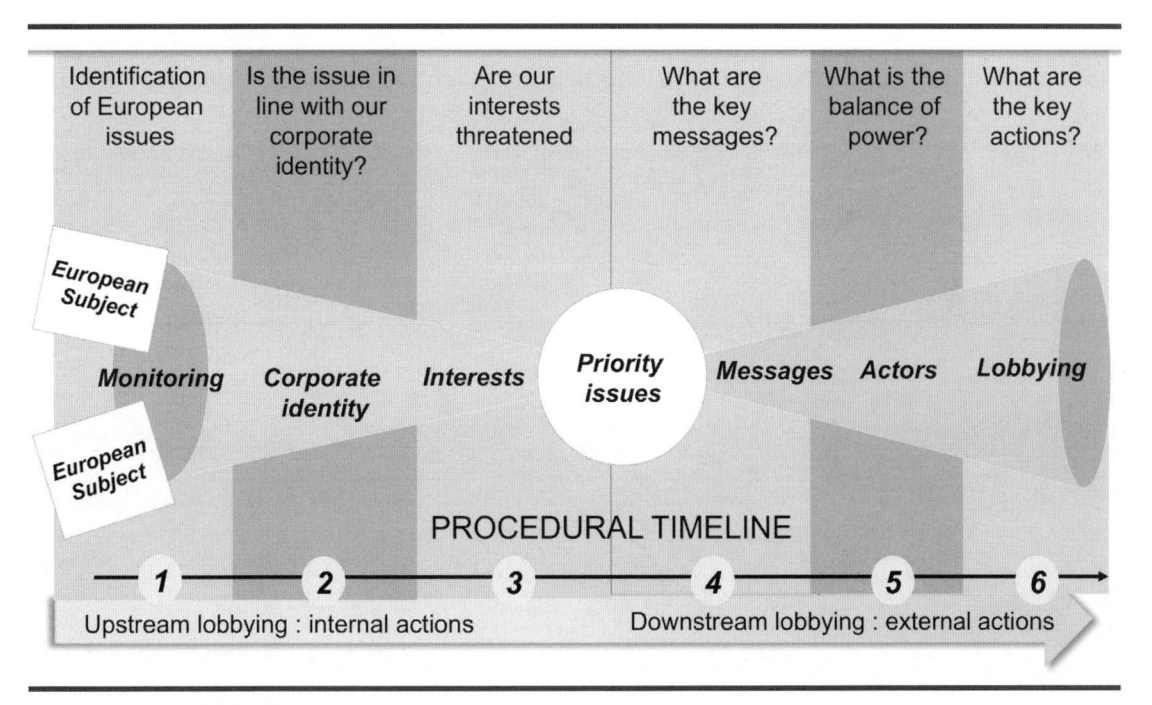

Source: Athenora Consulting

Appendix: Suggested Reading and Social Media

Chapter 1: The European Commission

Akse, E. (2013) *Influencing the Preparation of EU Legislation: A Practical Guide to Working with Impact Assessments*, London: John Harper Publishing.

Curtin, D. (2009) *Executive Power of the European Union*, Oxford: Oxford University Press.

Egeberg, M. (2006) 'Executive politics as usual: role behaviour and conflict dimensions in the College of European Commissioners', *Journal of European Public Policy* 13(1): 1-15.

Eppink, D-J. (2007) *Life of a European Mandarin: Inside the Commission*, Tielt: Lannoo Publishers.

Hooghe, L. (2001) *The European Commission and the integration of Europe: images of governance*, Cambridge: Cambridge University Press.

Hooghe, L. & Nugent, N. (2006) 'The Commission's Services', in Peterson, J. and Shackleton, M. eds., *The institutions of the European Union*, 2nd ed., Oxford: Oxford University Press.

Nugent, N. (2001) *The European Commission*, Basingstoke: Palgrave.

Nugent, N. (2006) *The Government and Politics of the European Union*, Basingstoke: Palgrave Macmillan.

Sabathil, G. & Joos, K. (eds.) (2011) *The European Commission: An Essential Guide to the Institution, the Procedures and the Policies*, London: Kogan Page.

Schmidt, S. (2000) 'Only an Agenda Setter? The European Commission's Power over the Council of Ministers', *European Union Politics* 1(1): 37-61.

Schön-Quinlivan, E. (2011) *Reforming the European Commission*, Basingstoke: Palgrave Macmillan.

Spence, D. (ed.) (2006) *The European Commission*, London: John Harper Publishing.

Suvarierol, S. (2007) *Beyond the Myth of nationality: a study of the networks of European Commission Officials*, Delft: Eburon.

Szapiro, M. (2013) *The European Commission: A Practical Guide*, London: John Harper Publishing.

Trondal, J., van den Berg C. & Suvarierol, S. (2008) 'The Compound Machinery of Government: The Case of Seconded Officials in the European Commission', *Governance* 21(2): 253-274.

Wonka, A. (2008) 'Decision-making dynamics in the European Commission: partisan, national or sectoral', *Journal of European Public Policy* 15(8): 1145-63.

> **The European Commission on Social Media**
> You can follow the Commission on: Facebook, Google +, Instagram, LinkedIn, Pinterest, Storify, Twitter, Vine, YouTube.
>
> Individual members of the Commission, such as the Commission President, Commissioners, Spokespersons and even Commission Representations are present on Twitter, Facebook or both.
>
> The link to the overview of the Social Media presence of the European Commission:
> http://ec.europa.eu/dgs/communication/services/journalist/social-media_en.htm

Chapter 2: The Council of the EU and the European Council

Bocquillon, P. (2015) 'The European Council and European Governance: The Commanding Heights of the EU', *West European Politics* 38(1): 255-257.

Bostock, D. (2002) 'Coreper revisited', *Journal of Common Market Studies* 40(2): 215-234.

Dinan, D. (2013) 'The Post-Lisbon European Council Presidency: An Interim Assessment', *West European Politics* 36(6): 1256-1273.

Eggermont, F. (2012) *The changing role of the European Council in the institutional framework of the European Union: consequences for the European integration process*, Cambridge: Intersentia.

Häge, F. (2008) 'Who Decides in the Council of the European Union?', *Journal of Common Market Studies* 46(3): 533-38.

Hayes-Renshaw, F. & Wallace, H. (2006) *The Council of Ministers*, 2nd ed., Basingstoke: Palgrave Macmillan.

Naurin, D. & Wallace, H. (eds.) (2010) *Unveiling the Council of the European Union: Games Governments Play in Brussels*, Basingstoke: Palgrave Macmillan.

Puetter, U. (2014) *The European Council and the Council: new intergovernmentalism and institutional change*, Oxford: Oxford University Press.

Sullivan, J. & Selck, T. (2008) 'Bargaining Power in the European Council', *Journal of Common Market Studies* 46(3): 687-708.

Tallberg, J. (2006), *Leadership and Negotiation in the European Union*, Cambridge: Cambridge University Press.

Thomson, R. (2013) 'Double versus Triple Majorities: Will the New Voting Rules in the Council of the European Union Make a Difference?', *West European Politics* 36(6): 1221-1238.

Werts, J. (2008) *The European Council*, London: John Harper Publishing.

Westlake, M., Galloway, D. & Digneffe, T. (2006) *The Council of the European Union*, London: John Harper Publishing.

The Council of the European Union Register

The Register lists references to documents produced in the General Secretariat of the Council of the EU since 1/1/1999 in the official languages. The database includes agendas of meetings, draft conclusions of Council meetings and a wide range of other documents. Though a large proportion of the documents in the register are not available in full text due to classification rules, the register is the first step in your search, providing you with, at the very least, information on the existence of the document. In addition, the register also contains documents from other institutions, relevant for decision-making in the Council.

The Council and the European Council on Social Media

You can follow the Council and the European Council on: Facebook, Flickr, Google +, Instagram, Storify, Twitter, YouTube.

The link to the overview of the Social Media presence of the Council and the European Council: http://www.consilium.europa.eu/en/contact/social-media/

Chapter 3: The European Parliament

Corbett, R., Jacobs F. & Shackleton, M. (2011) *The European Parliament*, 8th ed., London: John Harper Publishing.

Costello, R. & Thomson, R. (2010) 'The policy impact of leadership in Committees: rapporteurs' influence on the European Parliament's opinions', *European Union Politics* 11(2): 219-240.

Gabel, M. (2003) 'Public Support for the European Parliament', *Journal of Common Market Studies* 41(2): 149-70.

Hix, S., Noury, A. & Roland G. (2007) *Democratic Politics in the European Parliament*, Cambridge: Cambridge University Press.

Hix, S., Kreppel, A. & Noury, A. (2003) 'The Party System in the European Parliament: collusive or competitive?' *Journal of Common Market Studies* 41(2): 309-331.

Judge, D. & Earnshaw, D. (2008) *The European Parliament*, 2nd ed., London: Palgrave Macmillan.

Kaeding, M. (2004) 'Rapporteurship Allocation in the European Parliament: Information or Distribution', *European Union Politics* 5(3): 353-371.

Kreppel, A. (2002) *The European Parliament and Supranational Party System*, Cambridge: Cambridge University Press.

Lodge, J. (2010) *The 2009 Elections to the European Parliament*, Basingstoke: Palgrave Macmillan.

McElroy, G. (2006) 'Committee representation in the European Parliament', *European Union Politics* 7(1): 5-29.

McElroy, G. & Benoit, K. (2010) 'Party policy and Group Affiliation in the European Parliament', *British Journal of Political Science* 40(2): 377- 398.

Priestley, J. (2008) *Six Battles That Shaped Europe's Parliament*, London: John Harper Publishing.

Ringe, N. (2009) *Who decides, and how? Preferences, uncertainty, and policy choice in the European Parliament*, Oxford: Oxford University Press.

Rittberger, B. (2005) *Building Europe's Parliament: Democratic Representation Beyond The National State*, Oxford: Oxford University Press.

Selck. T. & Steunenberg, B. (2004) 'Between Power and Luck: The European Parliament in the EU Legislative Process', *European Union Politics* 5(1): 25-46.

Settembri, P. & Neuhold, C. (2009) 'Achieving consensus through Committees: Does the European Parliament manage?' *Journal of Common Market Studies* 47(1): 127-151.

Slapin, J. & Proksch, S. (2010) 'Look who's talking: Parliamentary debate in the European Union', *European Union Politics* 11 (3): 333-357.

Whitaker, R. (2005) 'National Parties in the European Parliament: An Influence in the Committee System?' *European Union Politics* 6(1): 5-28.

Whitaker, R. (2011) *The European Parliament's Committees: National Party Influence and Legislative Empowerment*, London: Routledge.

OEIL - Legislative Observatory Database

http://www.europarl.europa.eu/oeil/home/home.do?lang=en

The Legislative Observatory (OEIL) gives an excellent overview on decision-making files in which the Parliament is involved. Its focus is on the Parliament's role and contributions to legislative files, as well as housing all the documents and noting all the key events relating to a given procedure. The database provides direct links to relevant documents (COM, SEC, EP documents, EP reports, debates and opinions, etc), together with summaries of every stage of the decision-making procedure in which the European Parliament is involved.

Since 2006 the database provides a direct link to IPEX (Interparliamentary EU Information Exchange - www.ipex.eu) where one can find documents and information relating to the scrutiny of National Parliaments as well as on issues related to subsidiary and proportionality.

There are two different ways to search the OEIL database, namely, either via the procedures page or through the topical subject page. Under the section 'Procedures' one can search the database using multiple criteria such as: words in title or full-text document, document reference (author, legislative act type, OJ), agent in procedure (rapporteur, EP committee, Political Group, Council, Commission DG) etc. In addition the 'topical subject' section allows one to browse the content of the database by topic (enlargement, the budget, environment, employment, area of freedom security and justice, police, judicial and customs cooperation, consumer protection). This is a very convenient way of following all developments in the legislative process relevant to certain broad subject areas.

The website offers the possibility to subscribe for the Observatory Tracker which allows users to sign up for an automatic notification of new legislative developments.

The European Parliament on Social Media
You can follow the EP on: Facebook, Flickr, Foursquare, Google +, Instagram, LinkedIn, Newshub, Pinterest, Spotify, Twitter, Vine, YouTube.

Almost all individual members of the Parliament are present on Twitter, Facebook or both - and increasingly use them to share information and exchange views with stakeholders.

The link to the overview of the Social Media presence of the European Parliament:
http://www.europarl.europa.eu/atyourservice/en/20150201PVL00030/Social-media

Chapter 4: Other EU institutions and bodies

Court of Justice of the European Union:

Alter, K. (1998) 'Who are the "Masters of the Treaty"? European Governments and the European Court of Justice', *International Organization* 52: 121-147.

Beck, G. (2013) *The Legal Reasoning of the Court of Justice of the EU*, Oxford: Hart Publishing.

Broberg, M. & Fenger, N. (2010) *Preliminary References to the European Court of Justice*, Oxford: Oxford University Press.

Carrubba, C. (2003) 'The European Court of Justice, Democracy and Enlargement', *European Union Politics* 4(1): 75-100.

Garrett, G., Kelemen, R. & Schulz, H. (1998) 'The European Court of Justice, National Governments, and Legal Integration in the European Union', *International Organization* 52: 149-176.

Panke, D. (2010) *The Effectiveness of the European Court of Justice: Why Reluctant Member States Comply*, Manchester: Manchester University Press.

Moorhead, T. (2014) *The Legal Order of the European Union: The Institutional Role of the Court of Justice*, London: Routledge.

Moser, P. & Sawyer, K. (2008) *Making European Community Law: The Legacy of Advocate-General Jacobs at the European Court of Justice*, London: Edward Elgar Publishing.

Rosas, A., Levits, E. & Bot, Y. (2012) *The Court of Justice and the Construction of Europe: Analyses and Perspectives on Sixty Years of Case-law*, The Hague: T.M.C. Asser Press.

Stone Sweet, A. (2001) *Governing with Judges*, Oxford: Oxford University Press.

Waegenbaur, B. (2012) *Court of Justice of the European Union: Commentary on Statute and Rules of Procedure*, Oxford: Hart Publishing.

Committee of the Regions and European Economic Social Committee:

Christiansen. T., & Lintner, P. (2005) 'The Committee of the Regions after 10 Years: Lessons from the Past and Challenges for the Future', *Eipascope* 1: 7-13.

European Economic and Social Committee (2010) *The EESC: A Bridge between Europe and Organised Civil Society*, Sarrebruck: Dictus Publishing.

European Economic and Social Committee (2011) *The New Shape of Enlargement: The Particular Role of the EESC*, Sarrebruck: Dictus Publishing.

Goergen, P. (2006) *Lobbying in Brussels. A practical guide to the European Union for cities, regions, networks and enterprises*, Brussels: Goergen.

Goergen P. (2004) *Le lobbying des villes et des régions auprès de l'Union européenne*, Brussels: Goergen.

Gollub, J., Hönnige, C. & Panke, D. (2012) 'Voice without Vote - Comparing the Impact of CoR and EESC on National and Supranational Positions in the EU's Multi-level Governance', Madrid: World Congress, IPSA.

Huysseune, M. & Jans, T. (2008) 'Brussels as the capital of a Europe of the Regions? Regional offices as European policy actors', *Brussels Studies*, Issue 16.

Kaniok, P. & Dadova, L. (2013) 'Committee of the Regions: from advisory body to the second chamber of the European Parliament?', *Transylvanian Review of Administrative Sciences* 40E: 114-136.

Mendoza Jiménez, J. (2013) 'The Committee of the Regions: A Springboard for the Citizens', *Baltic Journal of European Studies* 3(2): 38-49.

Moore, C. (2008) 'A Europe of the Regions vs. the Regions in Europe: Reflections on Regional Engagement in Brussels', *Regional & Federal Studies* 18(5): 517-535.

Hönnige, C. & Panke, D. (2013), 'The Committee of the Regions and the European Economic and Social Committee: How Influential are Consultative Committees in the European Union?' *Journal of Common Market Studies* 51(3): 452-471.

Panara, C. & De Becker, A. (eds.) (2011) *The Role of the Regions in EU Governance*, Heidelberg: Springer.

Pucher, J. & Radzyner, A. (2014) *The European groupings of territorial cooperation and the single market*, Luxembourg: Publications Office of the European Union.

EU Agencies:

Busuioc, M. (2013) *European Agencies: Law and Practices of Accountability*, Oxford: Oxford University Press.

Busuioc, M., Groenleer, M. & Trondal, J. (eds.) (2012) *The Agency Phenomenon in the European Union: Emergence, Institutionalisation and Everyday decision-making*, Manchester: Manchester University Press.

Busuioc, M., Curtin D., & Groenleer, M. (2011) 'Agency Growth Between Autonomy and Accountability: the European Police Office as a "Living Institution"', *Journal of European Public Policy* 18(6): 848-867.

Busuioc, M. (2009) 'Accountability, Control and Independence: The Case of European Agencies', *European Law Journal* 15 (5): 599-615.

Everson, M., Monda, C. & Vos, E. (eds.) (2014) *European Agencies in between Institutions and Member States*, Alphen aan den Rijn: Kluwer Law Publishing, European Monographs 85.

Groenleer, M. (2009) *The Autonomy of European Union Agencies: A Comparative Study of institutional Development*, Delft: Eburon.

Groenleer, M., Kaeding, M. & Versluis, E. (2010) 'Regulatory governance through Agencies of the European Union? The role of the European Agencies for maritime and aviation safety in the implementation of European transport legislation', *Journal of European Public Policy* 17(8): 1210-1228.

Rittberger, B. & Wonka, A. (2011) 'Agency Governance in the European Union', *Journal of European Public Policy* 18(6), special issue.

Suvarierol, S., Busuioc, M., & Groenleer, M. (2013) 'Working for Europe? Socialization in the European Commission and Agencies of the European Union', *Public Administration* 91(4): 908-927.

Chapter 5: Ordinary Legislative Procedure

Best, E. (2014) *EU Law-making in Principle and Practice*, London: Routledge.

Burns, C., Rasmussen, A. & Reh, C. (2013) 'Legislative codecision and its impact on the political system of the European Union', *Journal of European Public Policy* 20(7): 941-952

Costa, O. & Brack, N. (2014) *How the EU Really Works*, Farnham: Ashgate.

Costello, R. & Thomson, R. (2013) 'The distribution of power among EU institutions: who wins under codecision and why?' *Journal of European Public Policy*, 20(7): 1025-1039

De Ruiter, R. & Neuhold, C. (2012) 'Why is fast track the way to go? Justifications for early agreement in the co-decision procedure and their effects', *European Law Journal* 18(4): 539-554.

European Parliament Guide to the Ordinary Legislative Procedure, available at: http://www.europarl.europa.eu/aboutparliament/en/0081 f4b3c7/Law-making-procedures-in-detail.html

General Secretariat of the Council (2011) Guide to the Ordinary Legislative Procedure, available at: http://www.consilium.europa.eu/uedocs/cms_data/ librairie/PDF/QC3212175ENrevGPO2012.pdf

Häge, F. M. & Naurin, D. (2013) 'The effect of codecision on Council decision-making: informalization, politicization and power', *Journal of European Public Policy* 20 (7): 953-971.

Héritier, A. (2013) 'Twenty years of legislative codecision in the European Union: experience and implications', *Journal of European Public Policy* 20 (7): 1074-1082.

Huber, K. & Shackleton, M. (2013) 'Codecision: a practitioner's view from inside the Parliament', *Journal of European Public Policy* 20 (7): 1040-1055.

Lord, C. (2013) 'The democratic legitimacy of codecision', *Journal of European Public Policy* 20 (7): 1056-1073.

Radmussen, A. & Reh, C. (2013) 'The consequences of concluding codecision early: trilogues and intra-institutional bargaining success', *Journal of European Public Policy* 20 (7): 1006-1024.

Reh, C., Héritier, H., Bressanelli, E. & Koop, C. (2011) 'The Informal Politics of Legislation: Explaining Secluded Decision Making in the European Union', *Comparative Political Studies* 46(9): 1112-1142.

Schoutheete, P. & Micossi, S. (2013) 'On Political Union in Europe: The changing landscape of decision-making and political accountability', *Politics and Institutions*, CEPS Essays 4.

Siemssen, M. & Kreuzeder, M. (2012) *Negotiations and Decision-Making in the European Union: Teaching and Learning through Role-Play Simulation Games*, Saarbrücken: AV Akademikerverlag.

Strohmeier, R. W. & Habets, I. (eds.) (2013) *EU Policies: an Overview - From Decision-Making to Implementation*, Köln: Druckhaus Süd.

Wallace, H., Pollack, M. & Young, A. (2014) *Policy-Making in the European Union*, Oxford: Oxford University Press.

Chapter 6: Delegated and Implementing Acts: New Comitology

Best, E. (2014) *EU Law-Making in Principle and Practice*, London: Routledge.

Blom-Hansen, J. (2008) 'The Origins of the EU Comitology System: A Case of Informal Agenda-Setting by the Commission', *Journal of European Public Policy* 15: 208-26.

Brandsma, G. J. & Blom-Hansen, J. (2012) 'Negotiating the Post-Lisbon Comitology System: Institutional Battles over Delegated Decision-Making', *Journal of Common Market Studies* 50(6): 939-57.

Burson-Marsteller 'Comitology the New EU Political Battleground', available at: http://burson-marsteller.eu/innovation-insights/eu-insights

Christiansen, T., Oettel, J. & Vaccari, B. (2009) *21st Century Comitology. Implementing Committees in the Enlarged European Union*, Maastricht: European Institute of Public Administration (EIPA).

Christiansen, T. & Dobbels, M. (2013) 'Delegated Powers and Inter-Institutional Relations in the EU after Lisbon: A Normative Assessment', *West European Politics* 36(6): 1159-77.

Hardacre, A. & Damen, M. (2009) 'The European Parliament and Comitology: PRAC in practise', *Eipascope* 1: 13-18.

Hardacre, A. & Kaeding, M. (2010) 'Delegated and Implementing Acts: The New Comitology' EIPA Essential Guide. Available at: www.eipa.eu/files/publications/Comitology_Brochure_web.pdf

Héritier, A., Moury, C., Bischoff, C.S. & Bergström, C.F. (2013) *Changing Rules of Delegation. A Contest for Power in Comitology*, Oxford: Oxford University Press.

Kaeding, M. & Hardacre, A. (2013) 'The European Parliament and the Future of Comitology after Lisbon', *European Law Journal* 19(3): 382-403.

Szapiro, M. (2013) *The European Commission. A Practical Guide*, London: John Harper Publishing (chapter IV.3 on Commission's executive powers to adopt non-legislative acts).

Voermans, W.J.M., Hartmann J.M.R. & Kaeding, M. (2014) 'The Quest for Legitimacy in EU Secondary Legislation', *Theory and Practice of Legislation* (2)1: 5-33.

Chapter 7: Ethics and transparency in the EU

Ainsworth, S. (1993) 'Regulating Lobbyists and Interest Group Influence', *Journal of Politics* 55(1): 41-56.

Bertók, J. (2008) *Lobbyists, Governments and Public Trust: Building a Legislative Framework for Enhancing Transparency and Accountability in Lobbying*, Paris: OECD.

Chari, R., Hogan, J. & Murphy, G. (2010) *Regulating Lobbying: A Global Comparison*, Manchester: Manchester University Press.

Greenwood, J. (1998) 'Regulating Lobbying in the European Union', *Parliamentary Affairs*, 51(4): 587-599.

McGrath, C. (2008) 'The development and regulation of lobbying in the New Member States of the European Union', *Journal of Public Affairs*, 8(1-2):15-32.

McGrath, C. (2009) *Interest Groups and Lobbying: Volume 1 - The United States and Comparative Studies*, Lewiston: Edwin Mellen Press.

Chapter 8: Practical guide to working with the institutions

Akse, E. (2013) *Influencing the Preparation of EU Legislation: A Practical Guide to Working with Impact Assessments*, London: John Harper Publishing.

Beyers, J. (2004) 'Voice and Access. Political Practices of European Interest Associations', *European Union Politics* 5(2): 211-240.

Bouwen, P. (2004) 'The Logic of Access to the European Parliament: Business Lobbying in the Committee on Economic and Monetary Affairs', *Journal of Common Market Studies* 42(3): 473-495.

Burson-Marsteller (2009) 'A Guide to Effective Lobbying of the European Parliament', available at: http://burson-marsteller.eu/innovation-insights/eu-insights/

Burson-Marsteller (2005) 'The Definitive Guide to Lobbying the European Institutions', available at: http://burson-marsteller.eu/2006/10/burson-marsteller-report-the-definitive-guide-to-lobbying-the-european-institutions/

Coen, D. (2007) 'Empirical and Theoretical Studies of EU Lobbying', *Journal of European Public Policy* 14(3), special issue.

Craig, M. 'Lobbying at the European Parliament - Two legislative cases: F-gases and REACH' Commissioned by the Greens European Free Alliance, 2008.

Curtin, D. (2003) 'Private Interest Representation or Civil Society Deliberation? A Contemporary Dilemma for European Union Governance', *Social and Legal Studies* 12(1): 55-75.

Derschewsky, K. (2008) What Next for Brussels' Lobbyists?: *The Impact of the European Parliament's Increasing Legislative Competences on Future Lobbying Practice in the European Union*, Saarbrücken: VDM Verlag.

Greenwood, J. (2011) *Interest Representation in the European Union*, 3rd ed., Basingstoke: Palgrave Macmillan.

Lorenzo, A. (2003) 'The Role of Interest Groups in the European Union Decision Making Process', *European Journal of Law and Economics* 15(3): 251-61.

Knill, C. (2001) 'Private Governance Across Multiple Arenas', *Journal of European Public Policy* 8(2): 227-46.

Pollack, M. (1997) 'Representing Diffuse Interests in EC Policy-Making', *Journal of European Public Policy* 4(4): 572-90.

Szapiro, M. (2013) *The European Commission: A Practical Guide*, London: John Harper Publishing.

Chapter 10: Designing a successful EU lobbying campaign

Akse, E. (2013) *Influencing the Preparation of EU Legislation: A Practical Guide to Working with Impact Assessments*, London: John Harper Publishing.

Aumont, L., Lavadoux, F. & Desselas, S. (2005) 'Systèmes politiques et exercice de l'influence au niveau communautaire: une comparaison France-Allemagne', *Eipascope*.

Biliouri, D. (1999) 'Environmental NGOs in Brussels: How powerful are their lobbying activities?' *Environmental Politics* 8: 173-182.

Carlier, J-V., Desselas, S. & Pertek, J. (2003) 'Vers des autorités de régulation communautaires indépendantes?', *Journal des Tribunaux*, Droit européen.

De Cock, C. (2010) *ilobby.eu: Survival Guide to EU Lobbying*, Delft: Eburon Academic Publishers.

Desselas, S. (2007) *Un lobbying professionnel à visage découvert, enquête sur l'influence des Français à Bruxelles*, Paris: Editions du Palio.

Eising, R. (2007) 'Institutional Context, Organisational Resources and Strategic Choices: Explaining Interest Group Access in the European Union', *European Union Politics* 8(3): 329-362.

Gelak, D. (2008) *Lobbying and Advocacy: Winning Strategies, Resources, Recommendations, Ethics and Ongoing Compliance for Lobbyists and Washington Advocates*, Washington: TheCapitol.Net.

Greenwood, J. (2011) *Interest Representation in the European Union*, 3rd ed., Basingstoke: Palgrave Macmillan.

Guéguen, D. (2008) *European Lobbying*, 3rd ed., Brussels: Europolitics.

Gullberg, A-T. (2009) 'Strategy Counts, Resources Decide: Lobbying EU Climate Change Policy' (PhD, University of Oslo).

Mahoney, C. (2008) *Brussels versus the Beltway: Advocacy in the United States and the European Union*, Georgetown: Georgetown University Press.

McGrath, C. (2005) *Lobbying in Washington, London and Brussels*, New York: Edwin, Mullen, Drew.

Miller, C. (2000) *Guide to Political Lobbying*, London: Politicos.

Nownes, A. (2006) *Total Lobbying: What Lobbyists Want (and how they try to get it)*, Cambridge: Cambridge University Press.

Pedler, R. (ed.) (2002) *EU Lobbying - Changes in the Arena*, Basingstoke: Palgrave Macmillan.

Rodrigues, S. & Desselas, S. (1998) 'Marché unique et services publics : la Cour de justice poursuit sa quête d'équilibre', Commentaire sous CJCE, 23 octobre 1997, n° C-159/94, *Les Petites Affiches*, n° 20, 16 février 1998, pp. 9-16.

Rodrigues, S. & Nicolas, M. (eds.) (1998) *Dictionnaire économique et juridique des services publics en Europe, ouvrage collectif,* ASPE Europe.

Schendelen van, R. (2010) *More Machiavelli in Brussels: The Art of Lobbying the EU*, Amsterdam: Amsterdam University Press.

Thomson, S. & John, S. (2007) *Public Affairs in Practice: A Practical Guide to Lobbying*, London: Chartered Institute of Public Relations.

Zetter, L. (2008) *Lobbying: The Art of Political Persuasion*, London: Harriman House.

Index

Page references against a heading with subheadings indicate major coverage of a topic. The following abbreviations are used in the index: EP = European Parliament; D&I Acts = Delegated and Implementing Acts; OLP = Ordinary Legislative Procedure

I items 78
II items 78

A

A items 42, 43, 45, 79, 81
access passes, for EP 213, 219, 255
access to documents 220-22, 227
Advisory procedure, Implementing Acts 187-8
Agencies 135-41
    historical development 135-6
    importance of engaging with 141
    key facts 135
    listing 137-9
    reading list 350-51
    reasons for expansion 136
agents of influence 336
Agriculture and Fisheries Council 69
air safety 186
ALDE (Alliance of Liberals and Democrats) Group 262
ALTER-EU (Alliance for Lobbying Transparency and Ethics Regulation) 226
Antici group 68-9, 77, 78, 247-8
Appeal Committee, Implementing Acts 190, 197
Area of Freedom, Security and Justice (AFSJ) 80, 125
Article 36 Committee (CATS) 69
assistants, MEPs 89-90, 225, 264

B

B items 42, 43, 79, 81
Barroso, President 23
Better Regulation package 33, 35, 198
'biocide case' 198
blocking minorities, in Council 55, 82, 246
blogging 234
blue-card questions 115
briefing notes 309
Brussels 1-2, 232, 255
budget 14, 24, 58, 87
buoy strategy 333

C

C items 42
Cabinets
    Chefs de Cabinet 20, 41-2, 45, 46, 239
    Commissioners' 20-21, 239, 240
    Special Chefs meetings 41-2, 45, 46, 239
case law 125
Casini, Carlo 213
CATS (Article 36 Committee) 70
CFSP (Common Foreign and Security Policy) 56, 69

CIS (Inter-Service Consultation, ISC/CIS) 28, 36-8, 46, 199
CIS-Net 36-7
Civil Service Tribunal 124, 125
coalitions
   Council 245-6
   EP Political Groups 263
   for lobbying purposes 214-15, 244, 245-6, 330
   of member states 245-6
Codecision procedure 146, 149-52
   see also Ordinary Legislative Procedure (OLP)
codes of conduct
   Commission (for lobbyists) 206, 209-210
   Commissioners and staff 222-4
   EPACA 209
   European Parliament (for lobbyists) 210-211
   for Joint Transparency Register 215-16, 218
   OLP negotiation for EP 161
College of Commissioners 17-19
   censure motions 18
   collegiate responsibility 22, 45
   Delegation (DL) decisions 36, 38
   Empowerment Procedure (PH) 36, 38
   Finalisation Written Procedure 42, 45
   meetings 42-3, 47, 239
   minutes (Procès-Verbal (PV)) 43
   Oral (PO) and Written (PE) procedures 36, 38-9, 40-41, 239
   Ordre du Jour (OJ) 42
   Vice-Presidents 20
   see also Commissioners
Comitology
   changing nature of 176-7
   Comitology Register 288-9
   definition 175
   measures by policy sector 182
   numbers of (2007-13) 181
   rise and spread of 182-5
   see also Delegated Acts; Delegated and Implementing (D&I) Acts; Implementing Acts
Commission see European Commission

Commission Work Programme (CWP) 23-5, 26, 29, 45
Commissioners
   accountability 19
   appointment procedures 18
   codes of conduct 223
   numbers 18-19
   oath 17
   see also Cabinets
Committee for Civilian Aspects of Crisis Management 70
Committee on Internal Security (COSI) 70
Committee of Permanent Representatives see COREPER
Committee of the Regions (CoR) 130-34
   reading list 349-50
Committees, European Parliament
   hearings 106
   key players 120, 121
   list of 98
   meetings and membership 92, 99
   opinion-giving Committees 103, 104, 107, 108
   political group coordinators 97-8, 112, 119-20, 261
   political groups in 104
   rapporteurs see rapporteurs
   report preparation 105-110, 258-60
   Secretariats 99, 107, 110, 119, 265
   shadow rapporteurs 104, 108, 119-20, 258
   vote in Committee 108-110
   voting lists 110, 113-14, 260
   websites 99, 106
Common Agricultural Policy (CAP), and Comitology 182
Common Foreign and Security Policy (CFSP) 56, 69
Common Security and Defence Policy (CSDP) 56
communication
   Commission 241
   Council 253-4
   OLP 241, 277, 279, 281

Parliament 265-7
Compte Rendu (CR) 42
Conciliation Committee, OLP third reading 169-72
Conclusions
   Council 58, 246
   European Council 52
Conference of Community and European Affairs Committees of Parliaments of the EU (COSAC) 153
consensus
   College of Commissioners 43
   Council of the EU 56, 81-2, 84
   Council Working Parties 70-71, 77
Consent (legislative procedure) 87, 147
consultancies 208
   see also lobbying
Consultation (legislative procedure) 87, 147
consultations, of stakeholders 29-31, 106, 119, 204, 224, 237-8
contact management systems 304
contact networks 306, 323-4
COPS ambassadors 69
CoR (Committee of the Regions) 130-34, 349-50
COREPER 66-9
   agenda/dossier preparation 77-80, 78-80, 83, 84, 162
   Antici/Mertens attachés 68-9, 77, 78, 247-8
   composition 66-7
   and D&I Acts 200
   and Delegated Acts 297-8
   roles and functioning 61, 67-9
   third OLP reading 170, 172
   and trilogues 159-60, 163
   websites 243, 249-50
   working with 243-4, 246-8, 252-3
COSAC (Conference of Community and European Affairs Committees of Parliaments of the EU) 153
COSI (Committee on Internal Security) 70
Council of Europe 48

Council of the European Union 49-84, 81-2, 242-54
   agenda/dossier preparation 64-5, 80
   attaché-only WP meetings 77
   budgetary role 58
   coalitions 245-6
   communication methods 253-4
   Conclusions 58, 246
   configurations 61, 62
      Agriculture and Fisheries Council 69
      Economic and Financial Council (ECOFIN) 69
      Foreign Affairs Council (FAC) 64
      General Affairs Council (GAC) 61-2
   consensual culture 56, 77, 81-2, 84
   Council of Ministers 61-3
   and D&I Acts 192, 200, 297-8
   decision-making 73-4, 80-82, 84
   decision-making stages 245-6
   difficult files 83-4
   executive powers 59
   Friends of the Presidency group 77
   General Secretariat (GSC) 53, 54, 65, 66, 72-3, 251-2
   informal meetings 63
   internal structure 59-60
   key facts 53
   key stages and actors 82-4, 254
   languages 53, 253
   lobbying strategy 242-4
   location 53
   lunch discussions 82
   meetings 62-3, 79-82, 246
   Ministerial attendance at 60, 62
   OLP stages
      agenda preparation 80
      COREPER consideration 77-80
      and EP amendments 156
      first reading 173, 174
      negotiating constraints 162
      second reading 165-9, 174
      third reading 169-72, 174
      trilogue discussions 157-60, 162-4
      Working Party consideration 75-7

Council of the European Union *cont.*
   Presidency programmes 63-6, 83, 84
   reading list 346
   Register 347
   roles 54-9
   rotating Presidency 53
   Rules of Procedure 61-2, 65, 76
   shared right of initiative 13
   Trio-Presidencies 57, 64, 73-4, 84
   voting 55-6, 81-2, 84
   voting calculator 245
   websites 243, 244, 245
   webstreamed meetings 62
   Working Parties/Groups (WP/WG) 53, 59, 69-71, 75-7, 83, 84, 248-9
   see also Member States
Council of Ministers
   see Council of the European Union
Court of Auditors (CoA) 123
Court of Justice of the European Union (CJEU) 124-6
   and D&I Acts 198
   infringement proceedings 131
   reading list 349
CR (Compte Rendu) 42
CSDP (Common Security and Defence Policy) 56
cultural differences, of officials 232-3
CURIA website 125

D

D&I Acts
   see Delegated and Implementing (D&I) Acts
decision-making
   Commission 237-40
   Council 73-4, 80-82, 84
   EP 154-5, 258-63
   fundamental guidelines 269-71
   long-term nature of 232, 235, 240, 281
   Treaty of Lisbon procedures 145-6
   types of legislation 27, 145-6
degressive proportionality 89

Delegated Acts 194-7, 291-9
   Commission stage 292-3
   compared to RPS 194, 196-7
   Council stage 297-8
   Expert Groups 196
   identification in legislation 283-5
   Impact Assessment 292
   key facts 176-7, 283
   key stages and actors 198-9, 298-9
   legal basis 175, 194
   objections to 286
   Parliament stage 293-6
   procedure 194-7
Delegated and Implementing (D&I) Acts
   Better Regulation package 33, 35, 198
   case law 198
   Delegated vs Implementing Acts 282-3
   evolution 178
   fundamental guidelines 269-71, 282-3
   identification in legislation 283-5
   introduction of 175-6
   key facts 176-7
   key stages and actors 198-9
   measures by policy sector 182
   part of policy-making cycle 179-80
   reading list 352-3
   reasons for delegation 178-9, 180-81
   technical or political decision-taking 184-6
   see also Comitology; Delegated Acts; Implementing Acts
Delegation (DL) decisions 36, 38
Delegations (overseas)
   Commission 15
   EP 100
Deputy Permanent Representatives (DPR) 66, 246-7
direct lobbying 334-7
directives, definition 27
Directorates-General and Services (DGs)
   Annual Activity Reports (AAR) 26
   Management Plans (MP) 25, 237
   open hearings 29
   Roadmap documents 25

Secretariat-General (SG) 19, 44
structure 17, 21, 241
DL (Delegation) decisions 36, 38
documents, access 220-22, 227
downstream lobbying 314
DPR (Deputy Permanent Representatives) 66, 246-7
Durant, Isabelle 213

E

E-Greffe 39
'earlier the better' approach 231, 235
Economic and Financial Committee (EFC) 69, 70
Economic and Financial Council (ECOFIN) 69
Economic Policy Committee (EPC) 69, 70
Economic and Social Committee (EESC) *see* European Economic and Social Committee
reading list 349-50
EEAS (European External Action Service) 15, 64
EESC (European Economic and Social Committee) 126-30, 133-4, 349-50
EFC (Economic and Financial Committee) 69, 70
electoral system, EP 88-9
electronic vote (EV) 112, 115, 116
Employment Committee, Council 70
Empowerment Procedure (PH) 36, 38
entertainment, Commission rules 223-4
EPACA (European Public Affairs Consultancies' Association) 209
ethics
for Commission officials 222-4
future prospects 225-6
key points 227
reading list 353
see also lobbying
EuroparlTV 106
Europe 2020 24, 58

European associations/federations 232, 273, 324
European Central Bank (ECB) 123
European Citizens' Initiative (ECI) 14
European Commission 11-47, 235-42
censure motions 18
Code of Conduct (lobbying) 206, 209-210
Commissioners *see* College of Commissioners; Commissioners
D&I Acts *see* Delegated and Implementing (D&I) Acts
decision-making stages 237-40
DGs *see* Directorates-General and Services (DGs)
effective communication methods 241
European Transparency Initiative (ETI) 204-5
external relations function 15
key facts 11
key lobbying points 242
key stages and actors 45-7
languages 11
lobbying guidelines 235-42
lobbying strategy 235-6
officials *see* staff (below)
OLP stages
approval by College 38-9, 40-41
dossier preparation 27-34
and EP amendments 155
Expert Groups 31-2, 238
external consultation 29-31, 46, 224, 238
impact assessment
see Impact Assessment (IA)
Inter-institutional Relations Group (GRI) 155
Inter-Service consultation 28, 36-8, 46, 239
opinion in Plenary 115
Regulatory Scrutiny Board (RSB) 28, 34-5
second reading 168
third reading 170
transmission of draft proposals 43-4, 152
trilogues 159, 160
Working Party consideration 75, 76

European Commission *cont.*
  publications
    Commission Work Programme (CWP) 23-5, 26, 29, 237
    Political Guidelines for the Next Commission 23, 237
    Rules of Procedure 16
    State of the Union address 23, 45, 237
    Synthesis Reports (SR) 26
    Working Methods of the Commission 2014-2019 16
  reading list 345
  Register of Interest Representatives 205-8, 211-12
  right of initiative 13-15, 115
  roles 12-15
  staff
    contact details 240
    ethics 222-4
    gifts 223-4
    meals 223-4
    numbers 12, 16
    rotation 21
    Staff Regulations 222, 225
    travel rules 223
  structure 16-22
European Council 49, 50-53
  Conclusions 52
  meetings 51-2
  passerelle clauses 56
  reading list 346
European Economic and Social Committee (EESC) 126-30, 133-4
  reading list 349-50
European External Action Service (EEAS) 15, 64
European Investment Bank (EIB) 124
European Parliament 85-121, 255-67
  access passes 213, 219, 255
  Bureau 91
  calendar 92, 255
  code of conduct (for lobbyists) 210-211
  and Comitology 183-4
  Commission appointments 18
  Commission censure motions 18
  committees
    see Committees, European Parliament
  communication methods 265-7
  Conference of Committee Chairmen 91
  Conference of Presidents 91
  and D&I Acts 189, 192, 200, 293-6
  decision-making stages 258-63
  Delegations 100
  EuroparlTV 106
  Intergroups 100-101
  key facts 85-6
  key stages and actors 119-21, 267
  legislative terms 102
  lobbying strategy 255-8
  and the media 88
  membership by Member State 89
  MEPs *see* MEPs
  OEIL database 348
  OLP stages
    amendment guidelines 259-60
    Committee allocation 102-3
    Committee amendments and vote 108-110, 258-60
    Committee stage 108-110
    decision-making summary 154-5
    desire for right of initiative 87
    draft report preparation 105-110
    first reading 173, 174
    key players 120, 121
    opinion-giving Committees 103, 107, 108
    Plenary rejection 155
    Plenary stage 260-63
    Plenary voting 111, 112, 115-18, 260-63
    possible outcomes after vote 118
    powers 86-7
    proposal received 102-3
    rapporteur nomination 103-5, 258
    second reading 165-9, 174
    shadow rapporteurs 104, 108, 119-20, 258
    third reading 169-72, 174
    trilogue discussions 157-65

own-initiative reports 101, 106, 258
Plenary sessions *see* Plenary sessions
Political Groups *see* Political Groups
   powers 86-7
   President 90-91
   Quaestors 91
   questions 115, 118-19
   reading list 347-8
   roles 86-8
   Rules of Procedure 86, 157, 160-62, 210, 225
   Secretariat-General 91-2
   staff 224
   structure 90-91
   websites 99, 106, 348
      Votewatch.eu 117-18, 261-2, 263, 264
   webstreamed meetings 106, 114
   written declarations 103
European Police College 152
European Protection Order 152
European Public Affairs Consultancies' Association (EPACA) 209
Examination procedure, Implementing Acts 188-90
exclusive competences 14
Executive Agencies 140-41
experts
   Commission Expert Groups 31-2, 238
   Council Working Parties/Groups (WP/WG) 53, 59, 69-71, 75-7, 83, 84, 248-9
   Delegated Acts 196
external affairs 64

F

Facebook 255, 256
false B items 42, 81
Finalisation Written Procedure 42, 45
financial disclosure
   lobbyists 211-12
   MEPs 225
financial framework, multiannual (MFF) 25, 58
five minute 'catch-the-eye' debates 115

Foreign Affairs Council (FAC) 64
Friends of the Presidency group 77

G

General Affairs Council (GAC), role 61-2
General Secretariat (Council, GSC) 53, 54, 65, 66, 72-3, 251-2
gifts
   Commission officials 223-4
   MEPs 225
Google alerts 272, 306
green papers 29-30
GRI (Inter-institutional Relations Group) 156
GSC (General Secretariat of the Council) 53, 54, 65, 66, 72-3, 251-2

H

Heads of State *see* European Council
healthcare 315
hearings 29, 106
Hebdo meetings 42, 46, 239
High Representative for Foreign Affairs and Security Policy 50, 64
Hughes procedure 103

I

IA *see* Impact Assessment (IA)
iceberg strategy 333
identity, EU 310-311
Impact Assessment (IA)
   Better Regulation Guidelines 33, 35
   D&I Acts 290, 292
   IA/Interservice Steering Group 29
   Impact Assessment Board reform 34
   legislative proposals 25, 32-5, 39, 46
   Regulatory Scrutiny Board (RSB) 28, 34-5
   stakeholder consultation 29-31, 237-8
Implementing Acts 187-93, 197, 286-91
   Advisory procedure 187-8
   Appeal Committee 190, 197

Implementing Acts cont.
  Comitology Register 288-9
  Commission stage 289-91
  Committees 286-8
  Examination procedure 188-90, 193
  Exceptional Cases 192-3
  identification in legislation 293-5
  Immediately Applicable Acts 192-3
  and Impact Assessment 290, 292
  key facts 176-7, 283
  key stages and actors 198-9, 290-91
  legal basis 175, 187
  Regulatory Procedure with Scrutiny (RPS) 177, 184, 191-3
  Rules of Procedure 287-8
  summary 197
Inception Impact Assessments (Roadmaps) 25, 29
indirect lobbying 334-7
infringement proceedings, EU law 13, 131
institutions 6, 123
insurance companies, lobbying example 304, 312, 325-6
Inter-institutional Relations Group (GRI) 156
Inter-Service Consultation (ISC/CIS) 28, 36-8, 46, 199
Inter-Service Coordination Group (ISCG) 28, 46
interest matrix 311-13
interest representatives see lobbying; Registers, Interest Representatives
Intergroups 100-101
internet
  alerting systems 272
  live meetings coverage 62, 106, 114
  see also social media; websites
IPEX (Interparliamentary EU Information Exchange) 348
iPhone app 234
ISC (Inter-Service Consultation) 28, 36-8, 46, 199
ISCG (Inter-Service Coordination Group) 28, 46

J

Juncker Commission 18
Juncker, Jean-Claude, President 19-20, 23, 226
jurisprudence, access to documents 221

K

key stages and actors
  Agencies 135
  Commission 45-7
  Council 53, 82-4, 254
  D&I Acts 176-7, 198-9
  Delegated Acts 298-9
  EP 119-21, 267
  Implementing Acts 290-91
  OLP 148, 172-4, 275-6

L

languages
  Commission 11
  Council 53, 253
law firms 212, 214
legal norms 145-6
legislation
  Better Regulation package 33, 35, 198
  identification of D&I Acts 283-5
  infringement proceedings 13, 131
  legislative tracker websites 272, 308-9, 348
  national parliaments 43, 44, 153, 348
  types of 27, 145-6
Legislative Observatory (OEIL) 348
legislative procedures
  'evaluate first' principle 35
  Special Legislative Procedures (SLP) 57-8, 87, 146-7, 151, 289
  see also Ordinary Legislative Procedure (OLP)
Leinen, Jo 213
Lisbon Treaty see Treaty of Lisbon
Liste des Points Prévus (LPP) 42
lobbying
  Brussels a key location 1-2, 232, 255

categories of 207, 214, 217
complaints procedure 217-18
definition 3, 205-6, 211
'earlier the better' approach 231, 235, 272
European approach 231, 232, 236
financial disclosure 207-8, 219
financial disclosure requirements 211-12
fundamental guidelines 230-35
future prospects 225-6
key dimensions 4-5
long-term nature of 232, 235, 240, 281
proactive/reactive 301
professional approach 231
proposal for mandatory register 226
quality of registration details 208
reading list 355-6
Register of Interest Representatives 205-8, 211-12
skills required 330-32
strategy *see* lobbying strategy
submissions, public access to 227
transparency 231, 236
working with the Commission 235-42
see also codes of conduct; communication; Transparency Register

lobbying examples
healthcare 315
insurance companies 304, 312, 325-6
Plant Reproductive Material 155
Port Services Directive 155, 172
REACH 33
Right2Water 14
SWIFT data transfer agreement 87, 147

lobbying strategy 231, 235, 301-343
argument presentation 318-23
classification of actors 329
contact management systems 304
contact networks 306, 323-4
direct/indirect lobbying 334-7
downstream lobbying 314
EU identity 310-311
evaluation of campaign 341-2
evaluation of issue 316-18
identification of issues 303-4
influence, agents of 336
inside/outside lobbying 337-8
interest matrix 311-13
key phases 302, 338-41
message development 314-24
monitoring see monitoring
nationality and culture 232-3
objective setting 317-18
position papers 321-3
reading list 353-5
and senior management 305, 310
stakeholder mapping 324-9
target audience 231
target prioritisation 326-8
timing 231, 235, 272, 333, 340-41
visibility of action 333-4
working on the edge of the issue 332-3
local authorities, and lobbying 217

M

Maastricht Treaty 149, 183-4
meals, Commission rules 223-4
media
Brussels press 337
and Parliament 88, 115
rules for working with 233-4
see also Facebook; social media; Twitter
Member States
CoR members 129, 132
D&I Acts 181, 190
European Economic and Social Committee members 129
legislative initiative rights 152
MEPs 89
MEPs' national links 257
Ministerial representation 60
national delegations (EP) 95-6, 118, 264
national officials 250
right of initiative 152
small Member States' influence 56, 245
subsidiarity 14, 44, 131, 153-4
see also COREPER; Council of the European Union; experts; national parliaments

MEPs
   assistants 89-90, 225, 264
   by Member State 89
   committee memberships 99
   communication methods 265-7
   constituencies 257
   electoral system 88-9
   financial disclosure 225
   national party lists 257
   votewatch.eu profiles 117-18, 261-2, 263, 264
   voting behaviour 117-18
   working with 256-8, 263-4

Meroni doctrine 135-6
Mertens group 68-9, 77, 78, 247-8
Military Committee 70
mobile phone app 234
monitoring 304-310
   briefing notes 309
   identification of issues 304-5
   information sources 305-6, 308
   legislative trackers 272, 308-9, 348
   person responsible for 304-5
   recipients of 305
   report types 307-8

multiannual financial framework (MFF) 25, 58
mutual insurance companies,
   lobbying example 304, 325-6

N

National Delegations, Political Groups 95-6, 118, 264
national parliaments
   IPEX (Interparliamentary EU Information Exchange) 348
   scrutiny of legislative proposals 43, 44, 153, 348
   yellow/orange card 43, 44
nationality, cultural differences 232-3
networking 304, 306, 323-4
NGOs 208, 212, 217, 226
Nice Treaty 149
Nicolaidis group 69
Non-governmental Organisation (NGOs) 208, 212, 217, 226

O

oath, Commissioners' 17
OEIL Legislative Observatory 348
Ombudsman, access to documents 220
opinion-giving Committees 104, 107, 108
Oral Procedure (PO) decisions 36, 38-9, 40-41, 239
oral questions 118-19
orange card 153
Ordinary Legislative Procedure (OLP) 146, 148-74, 269-81
   acts adopted (1993-2014) 151
   agreements (2009-2014) 150
   average completion times 156, 167, 170
   Commission consideration
      see European Commission, OLP stages
   Commission proposal drafted 27-47
   communication methods 277, 279, 281
   consultations with other actors 152-4
   Council consideration *see* Council of the European Union, OLP stages
   early second reading 165-6
   EP consideration *see* European Parliament, OLP stages
   first reading 152-65, 173, 271-7
      average completion time 152
      in Council 75-7
      key to understanding whole process 152
      in Parliament 102-121
      flow charts 75, 102, 153, 157, 159, 166, 171
      fundamental guidelines 269-71
   inter-institutional stages
      fast-tracking 158
      first reading importance 57
      four-column document 164
      Joint Declaration on practical arrangements (2007) 158, 160
      trilogue location 163
      trilogues 173
      trilogues, first reading trilogues 106-7, 113, 157-65, 273
      trilogues, second reading 165-6, 167, 169
      trilogues, third reading 171, 172, 174

key documents 272
key facts 148
key stages and actors 172-4, 275-6
methods of engagement 272-3
policy areas subject to OLP 150-51
reading list 351-2
right of initiative 13-15, 87, 115, 152
rise and spread of use 149-52
second reading 165-9, 174, 277-9
third reading 169-72, 174, 279-81
Treaty modifications 149-52
Ordinary Written procedure, Council 82

P

Part-sessions *see* Plenary sessions
participatory democracy 2
passerelle clauses 56
Permanent Representatives (PR) 67-9, 246-7, 253-4
see also COREPER
PH (Empowerment Procedure) 36, 38
Plenary sessions 111-19
agendas 114
blue-card question 115
calendar 92
Commission opinion on amendments 115
Conciliation text rejection 172
five minute 'catch-the-eye' debates 115
inter-institutional preparation 111
live internet coverage 106, 114
press conferences 115
question time 118
'rainbow' verbatim report 114
rejection of proposal 155
State of the Union address 23, 45, 237
tabling of amendments 111-14
voting 111, 112, 113-18, 261-3
PO (Oral Procedure) decisions 36, 38-9, 40-41, 239
policies
areas subject to OLP 150-51
areas subject to SLP 151

evaluation 26
exclusive competences 14
policy cycle 6
public consultations 29-31, 106, 119, 204, 224, 237-8
see also lobbying examples
political advisers (EP) 97
Political Groups (CoR), Committee of the Regions 132-3
Political Groups (EP)
coalitions 263
Committee coordinators 97-8, 112, 119-20, 261
cross-Group compromises 94
formation of 94
group weeks 92, 95, 97, 112
influence in Committees 104, 107, 108, 110
key actors 119-21
list (2014-19) 92-3
national delegations 95-6, 118, 264
organisation 95-6
political advisers 97
staff 97, 265
tabling Plenary session amendments 112
voting behaviour 117-18, 262-3
websites 93
whip sanction system 96
Working Groups 97
Political Guidelines for the Next Commission 23, 45
Political Parties 94
Political and Security Committee (PSC/COPS) 69
Port Services Directive 155, 172
position papers 321-3
PR (Permanent Representatives) 67-9, 246-7, 253-4
see also COREPER
Pre-Lex 272
presidencies
Council 53, 63-6, 244
Friends of the Presidency group 77
rotating 53

presidencies *cont.*
    styles 65
    and trilogues 163
    Trio-Presidencies 57, 64, 73-4, 84
    working with 244, 251
President
    Commission 19, 23
    European Council 50, 52
    Parliament 90-91
press *see* media
Procès-Verbal (PV) 43
Prodi Commission 22
professional associations 232, 273, 324
proportionality principle 14
PSC (Political and Security Committee) 69

Q

Quaestors 91
qualified majority voting (QMV) 55-6, 81
questions, EP 118-19

R

rainbow verbatim reports 114
rapporteurs
    key actors 119-20
    lobbying approaches 335-6
    report drafting 105-110, 106-8
    selection of 103-5
    see also shadow rapporteurs
REACH (Registration, Evaluation, Authorisation & Restriction of CHemicals) 33
reactive lobbying 301
reasoned opinions, national parliaments 43, 153
recommendations, Commission 27
Registers
    Council Register 347
    Expert Groups 238
    future prospects 225-6
    Interest Representatives 205-8, 211-12
    Transparency Register 203, 212-19, 236

regulations, definition 27
Regulatory Agencies 140-41
Regulatory Procedure with Scrutiny (RPS) 177, 184, 191-3, 293
Regulatory Scrutiny Board (RSB) 28, 34-5
religious communities 207, 214
right of initiative
    Commission's 13-15, 115
    Council of the European Union 13
    EP's desire for 87
    Member States' 152
Roadmap documents 25, 29
roll-call votes (RCV) 112, 115, 116-17
rotating Presidencies 53
RPS (Regulatory Procedure with Scrutiny) 177, 184, 191-3, 293
RSB (Regulatory Scrutiny Board) 28, 34-5
RSS feeds 272, 306
Rules of Procedure
    Council 61-2, 65, 76
    European Commission 16
    Implementing Acts Committees 287-8
    Parliament 86, 157, 160-62, 210, 225

S

Santer Commission 22
Schengen border case 198
Secretariat-General (SG) 19, 44
Security Committee, Council 70
Šefčovič, Maroš 212-13
shadow rapporteurs 104, 108, 119-20, 258
show of hands (EP voting) 116
Silence procedure, Council 82
silo effect 22
Single European Act 149, 183
Small and Medium-sized Enterprises Test (SME Test) 30
small Member States 56, 72, 245
SMART objectives 317
social media 233, 346, 347, 349
Social Protection Committee, Council 70
Special Chefs meetings 41-2, 45, 46, 239

Special Committee on Agriculture (SCA) 69
Special Legislative Procedures (SLP) 57-8, 87, 146-7, 151, 289
SPP (Strategic Planning and Programming) cycle 22-6
square of European arguments 319
Staff Regulations 222, 225
stakeholders
    and EP consultation 106, 119
    public consultations 29-31, 204, 224, 237-8
    stakeholder mapping 324-9
    see also lobbying; lobbying strategy
State of the Union address 23, 45, 237
Strasbourg 256
Strategic Committee for Immigration, Frontiers and Asylum 70
Strategic Planning and Programming (SPP) cycle 22-6
subsidiarity 14, 44, 131, 153-4
SWIFT data transfer agreement 87, 147
SWOT analysis 317
Synthesis Reports (SR) 26

T

TEU (Treaty on European Union) 2
TFEU (Treaty on the Functioning on the European Union) 15, 175, 186
think-tanks 212, 232
timing, lobbying strategy 231, 235, 272, 333, 340-41
trade agreements 15, 147
trade associations/federations 232, 273, 324
Trade Policy Committee (TPC) 70
transparency
    Conciliation Procedure lacking 172
    and decision-making 271
    future prospects 225-6
    importance for a lobbyist 231, 236
    Inter-Institutional Agreement (2014) 216-17
    key points 227
    reading list 353
    summary 203
    see also lobbying

Transparency Register 212-19
    alerts system 225
    categories 217
    Code of Conduct 215-16, 218
    complaints procedure 217-18
    criticisms 226
    financial disclosure 219
    Joint Transparency Register Secretariat (JTRS) 216
    website 219
Treaties, Commission's guardianship role 12-13
Treaty on European Union (TEU) 2
Treaty on the Functioning on the European Union (TFEU) 15, 175, 186
Treaty of Lisbon 2*note*
    areas subject to OLP 150-51
    D&I Acts 175, 179, 186-7
    decision-making procedures 145-6
    stakeholder dialogue 204
Treaty of Maastricht 149, 183-4
Treaty of Nice 149
trilogues *see* Ordinary Legislative Procedure (OLP), inter-institutional stages
Trio-Presidencies 57, 64, 73-4, 84
Tusk, Donald 50, 51
Twitter 255, 306

U

United States 13, 87, 147
Units, DGs 21, 241

V

van Rompuy, Herman 50, 51
Vice-Presidents, Commission 20
Votewatch.eu
    and Council 244
    and EP 117-18, 261-2, 263, 264
voting
    Council 55-6, 81-2, 84
        blocking minorities 55, 82, 246
        qualified majority (QMV) 55-6, 81

voting *cont.*
    EP 111, 112, 115-18, 260-63
        absolute majority 116
        electronic vote (EV) 112, 115, 116
        MEPs and faulty machines 118
        roll-call votes (RCV) 112, 115, 116-17
        show of hands 116
        simple majority 116
    EP Committees 108-110
        see also consensus
voting lists
    EP Committees 110, 260
    Implementing Acts 290
    Plenary sessions 113-14

W

Wallis, Diana 212-13
water, Right2Water 14
websites
    COREPER 243, 249-50
    Council 243, 244
    CURIA 125
    EP 106, 117, 261
    EP Committees 99, 106
    EP Political Groups 93
    EU Whoiswho 249-50
    legislative trackers 272, 308-9, 348
    time-saving tools 306-7
    Transparency Register 219
    Votewatch.eu 117-18, 244, 261-2, 263, 264
    Your Voice in Europe 30, 224
webstreamed meetings 62, 106, 114
whip sanction system, Political Groups 96
white papers 30
Working Methods of the Commission 2014-2019 16
Working Parties/Groups (WP/WG), Council 53, 59, 69-71, 75-7, 83, 84, 248-9
Written declarations, EP 103
Written Procedure (PE) decisions 36, 38, 41, 42, 45, 239
written questions 118-19

Y

yellow card 153
Your Voice in Europe 30, 224